Language, Literacy and Learning
in Educational Practice

Language and Literacy in Social Context

This Reader is part of an Open University Course (E825) forming one module in the MA in Education Programme. The selection is related to other material available to students. Opinions expressed in individual articles are not necessarily those of the course team or of the University.

Other volumes published as part of this course by Multilingual Matters Ltd in association with The Open University:

Language and Literacy in Social Practice
 JANET MAYBIN (ed.)
Media Texts: Authors and Readers
 DAVID GRADDOL and OLIVER BOYD-BARRETT (eds)
Researching Language and Literacy in Social Context
 DAVID GRADDOL, JANET MAYBIN and BARRY STIERER (eds)

Other books of related interest, published by Multilingual Matters Ltd:

Critical Theory and Classroom Talk
 ROBERT YOUNG
Language Policy Across the Curriculum
 DAVID CORSON
Language, Minority Education and Gender
 DAVID CORSON
School to Work Transition in Japan
 KAORI OKANO
Reading Acquisition Processes
 G. B. THOMPSON, W. E. TUNMER and T. NICHOLSON (eds)
Worlds of Literacy
 D. BARTON, M. HAMILTON and R. IVANIC (eds)

Please contact us for the latest book information:
Multilingual Matters Ltd,
Frankfurt Lodge, Clevedon Hall, Victoria Road,
Clevedon, Avon BS21 7SJ, England.

Language and Literacy in Social Context

Language, Literacy and Learning in Educational Practice

A Reader edited by

Barry Stierer and Janet Maybin

at The Open University

MULTILINGUAL MATTERS LTD
Clevedon • Philadelphia • Adelaide
in association with
THE OPEN UNIVERSITY

Library of Congress Cataloging in Publication Data

Language, Literacy and Learning in Educational Practice: A Reader/Edited by
Barry Stierer and Janet Maybin
p. cm.
Includes bibliographical references and index.
1.Language arts. 2. Reading. 3. Oral communication.
4. English language–Composition and exercises–Study and teaching.
I. Stierer, Barry. II. Maybin, Janet, 1950- .
LB1576.L315 1993 93-29911
428'0071–dc20 CIP

British Library Cataloguing in Publication Data

A CIP catalogue record for this book is available from the British Library.

ISBN 1-85359-218-8 (hbk)
ISBN 1-85359-217-X (pbk)

Multilingual Matters Ltd

UK: Frankfurt Lodge, Clevedon Hall, Victoria Road, Clevedon, Avon BS21 7SJ.
USA: 1900 Frost Road, Suite 101, Bristol, PA 19007, USA.
Australia: P.O. Box 6025, 83 Gilles Street, Adelaide, SA 5000, Australia.

Cover design by Bob Jones Associates.
Index compiled by Meg Davies (Society of Indexers).
Printed and bound in Great Britain by WBC Ltd, Bridgend.

Contents

Preface

This is one of four volumes of readings compiled as a part of an Open University MA course called *Language and Literacy in Social Context* (E825). The course draws on a variety of work in sociolinguistics, grammar, semiotics, media studies, anthropology, psychology and education and the interdisciplinary nature of the course is reflected in the articles collected together in this series. Each volume contains a mix of classic and newly published material which will be of interest to a wide audience.

Anyone who studies these papers will inevitably be drawn in to some of the most exciting intellectual debates of the closing years of the 20th century. The authors deal with many of the 'big issues' relating to life in the postmodern world — identity, social relations, social control, ideology, freedom, democracy, power, aesthetics, pleasure — but always with a concern for the way these very abstract notions manifest themselves in individual lives.

I would like to take the opportunity of thanking all those who, in various ways, supported, encouraged (and sometimes cautioned), the course team during the production process. In particular, I should mention Myra Barrs, Rebecca Bunting, Jane Cooper, Norman Fairclough, Gordon Gibson, Gunther Kress, Gemma Moss, Brian Street, Terry Threadgold, Gill Watson, many students and tutors of a predecessor course on language and literacy (E815), and colleagues in the School of Education at The Open University.

David Graddol
Course Chair

Sources

We would like to thank the authors and publishers concerned for kindly granting permission to reproduce copyright material in this reader. Every effort has been made to trace the correct copyright owners, both authors and publishers, as listed in the Contents and by chapter below.

1. Edited from Chapter 1 of *The New Literacy*. London: Routledge, 1990.
2. Edited version of Chapters 1 and 2 of *The Emergence of Literacy*. by Nigel Hall. Sevenoaks: Edward Arnold, 1987.
3. Edited version of article in *Journal of Curriculum Studies* 24 (4), 297-313. London: Taylor and Francis, 1992.
4. Edited chapter from *Thought and Language*. Cambridge, MA: MIT Press, 1968; and also edited version of 'Interaction between Learning and Development' in *Mind and Society: The Development of Higher Psychological Processes*. Cambridge, MA: Harvard University Press, both by L.S Vygotsky. © 1978 by the President and Fellows of Harvard College.
5. Edited extracts from *Child's Talk: Learning to Use Language* by Jerome Bruner. Oxford: Oxford University Press, 1983.
6. Substantially revised version of article in *Language and Literacy from an Educational Perspective: Volume 1, Language Studies* by Neil Mercer (ed.). Milton Keynes: Open University Press, 1988.
7. Commissioned chapter.
8. Edited extracts from *Sponsored Reading Failure: An Object Lesson*. Warlingham: IPSET Education Unit, 1990.
9. Edited version of article in *Language Matters* 3, 2-8. London: Centre for Language in Primary Education, 1990/91.
10. Commissioned article.
11. From *Language and Education* 7 (2), 97-114. Clevedon: Multilingual Matters, 1993.
12. From *Language and Education* 6, 247-258. Clevedon: Multilingual Matters, 1992.
13. Edited version of Chapter 7 of *Common Knowledge: The Development of Understanding in the Classroom* by D. Edwards and N. Mercer. London: Methuen & Co. (Routledge), 1987.
14. From *Harvard Educational Review* 57 (4), 396-420. Cambridge, MA: Harvard Educational Review. © 1987 by the President and Fellows of Harvard College. All rights reserved.
15. From Open University Study Pack *Talk and Learning 5-16* (P535). Milton Keynes: The Open University.
16. Edited version of paper in *The Place of Genre in Learning: Current Debates* by I. Reid (ed.). Geelong, Victoria: Centre for Studies in Literary Education.
17. From *Language Matters* 1, 9-16. London: Centre for Language in Primary Education, 1991/92.
18. Edited version of paper in *Literacy for a Changing World* by F. Christie (ed.). Victoria, Australia: Australian Council for Educational Research, 1990.
19. Edited version of a paper in *Knowledge about Language and the Curriculum. The LINC Reader* by R. Carter (ed.). Sevenoaks: Hodder and Stoughton, 1990.
20. Edited version of Chapter 15 from *Literacy, Language and Learning* by David R. Olson (ed.). Cambridge: Cambridge University Press, 1985.

Introduction

This volume brings together specially-commissioned and previously-published articles which examine the implications for educational practice of research and scholarship in the field of language, literacy and learning. It is one of four Readers compiled as part of the course *Language and Literacy in Social Context* (course code E825), which is one module of the (UK) Open University's MA in Education programme.

Classroom practice in the area of language and literacy has in recent times been the focus of a number of conflicting pressures. In Britain particularly, though not exclusively, this area of education has seen a succession of policy initiatives and political interventions. There has been intense media attention on such issues as the initial teaching of reading, the place of standard English, suitable texts for literature teaching, standards of spoken and written language, and methods of assessment. Changes to the processes for funding public education, and in the share of the public purse available to the education service, has resulted in reductions in staffing and resources. Such developments have demonstrated that language and literacy are highly contested areas of the curriculum, and that questions of what should be taught, how it should be taught and who should control such decisions may be subjected to public scrutiny, debate and challenge in a manner which is often more a reflection of competing social and political values than of theory and research evidence. In such an atmosphere of controversy and contention, it is hardly surprising that there is no compelling consensus, and that many education practitioners — regardless of their approach in the classroom — feel dissatisfied with the level on which much public debate occurs. Each of the articles in this volume, in its own way, points to ways in which education practitioners in the language and literacy area may attempt to reconcile this range of conflicting pressures.

During the same period there has been a rapid development of new conceptual frameworks for understanding language, literacy and learning. From anthropology and cultural studies a perspective has emerged which casts these processes as social practices, embedded in the cultural fabric of everyday communication and dependent for their meanings on the negotiation of identity. From psychology, the social constructivist paradigm has contributed a view of learning as an essentially social process of negotiating meaning. And from the field of critical language study, a more politically aware approach to the study of language use has developed, which examines the discourses used within and between social groups as a site of dynamic tension between the forces for stability and those for change.

Whilst it is possible to identify significant continuities between these developing frameworks, and indeed to suggest a certain complementarity, their implications and applications for educational practitioners have not yet been comprehensively addressed. For example, critical questions have been raised by this new work about the initial teaching of reading, about teachers' interventions in children's talk, and about how schools can foster a more critical awareness of language functions and at the same time promote technical competences in language and literacy. The papers in this collection have been chosen because they will help readers to consider ways in which these new developments in theory and research may be applied to the everyday practice of those working the field.

Part 1: Conceptualising Changing Perspectives

Part 1 consists of three articles which, in different ways, chart changing perspectives on language and literacy teaching by attempting to analyse the conceptual significance of new approaches to curriculum and pedagogy.

1. John Willinsky

Willinsky draws together a range of disparate innovations in the teaching of language and literacy, mainly in the English-speaking world, and traces their common features, values and intellectual origins. He argues that 'New Literacy' practices pose an implicit (and sometimes explicit) challenge to traditional models of language and literacy, and to traditional notions of teaching and learning.

2. Nigel Hall

Hall reviews some of the more prominent research studies which have contributed to the development of the 'emergent literacy' perspective on early literacy learning. Literacy, according to this perspective, emerges from the (often very young) child's observation of, and participation in, purposeful literacy practices in the home and elsewhere. Such a view represents a challenge to more conventional notions of 'readiness', with their emphasis upon visual and perceptual aspects of print processing, and upon a threshold before which the teaching of reading or writing would not be fruitful.

3. David Buckingham

Buckingham uses the specific area of media education to raise a number of fundamental questions about curriculum and pedagogy in the language and literacy field. In terms of media education, Buckingham critically analyses the competing traditions and models underlying approaches to this area of the curriculum, and in particular the specialised concepts which have emerged as the distinctive subject knowledge in media education. The article can also be read as a case study example of a critical analysis of a particular set of reading and writing activities in the classroom.

Part 2: Language and Learning in Culture and Practice

The four articles in Part 2 examine a range of socially-orientated perspectives on language and learning, which have important implications both within and outside the classroom.

4. L. S. Vygotsky

One of the most powerful theoretical influences on the recent development of new conceptual frameworks for understanding language, literacy and learning has been the work of the Russian psychologist Lev Vygotsky. Working in Russia in the 1920s and 30s, his ideas were suppressed during the Stalinist period but have become increasingly popular in the West since the first translation of his book *Thought and Language* into English in 1962. In Vygotsky's view language performs a crucial role in mediating between the cognitive development of an individual and their cultural and historical environment. In the extracts from his book reprinted here, he explains how the development of language and thought originates within social interactions, how language plays a vital continuing role in concept development, and how the process of bringing the outer social world inwards through language to thought interlocks with the impetus in the opposite direction, from motives through thoughts and meanings into words.

The second section of the article comes from the collection of essays *Mind and Society*. Here Vygotsky examines the interaction between development and learning and introduces the idea of the 'zone of proximal development', which has become an important concept in neo-Vygotskian research.

5. Jerome S. Bruner

Bruner has been an important interpreter of Vygotsky's work in the West, and has been influential in moving psychological theories of child development on from their dominance by Piagetian ideas towards a greater recognition of the role of language, communication and instruction in the development of knowledge and understanding. In the article here Bruner traces the links between cognitive development, language acquisition and culture, suggesting that infants are inherently communicative, but that the development of language can only occur in the context of social interaction, where adults support this development in crucial ways.

6. Barbara Mayor

The complexity of the relationship between language development and the social and cultural environment is revealed particularly vividly in the multilingual context. Mayor's article unpacks some of the complexities involved in bilingualism, and looks at the range of social, political and religious factors which influence bilingual people's use of language in different contexts. She discusses language development in the bilingual child, and considers various arguments concerning the advantages and disadvantages of bilingualism within the educational context.

7. Neil Mercer

Mercer discusses three aspects of Vygotskian theory and their potential to help researchers and practitioners understand and develop practices of teaching and learning in the classroom. He looks at the notion of 'scaffolding' as a specific kind of help offered by teachers to children, the idea of the 'zone of proximal development' and its potential to shift conceptions of the teaching and learning process, and the concept of 'appropriation' as applied to the pedagogic functions of teacher–pupil discourse.

Part 3: The Discourse of Reading Pedagogy

The two articles in Part 3 contribute to a view of the teaching of reading as an area of educational practice characterised by competing *discourses* as described, for example, by Fairclough (1989). These discourses are shaped by factors such as the history of the different academic disciplines which have contributed to the development of initial reading pedagogies, the status and power commanded by different discourses in their appeal to 'common-sense', their ability to attract resources and so on. The way in which competing positions within this debate function as discourses is further demonstrated by the way in which they become associated with wider *political* positions with respect to the place of schools in society and the roles of teachers and pupils.

8. Martin Turner

This is an edited version of a monograph by the same name which was widely covered in the British media when it appeared in 1990, and made a dramatic impact upon public opinion and on the policy agenda at the time. In the article, Turner asserts that standards of reading among seven-year-olds in England fell significantly during the 1980s, and that the only compelling explanation for this marked decline was what the author describes as a widespread adoption by teachers of a 'real books' approach to initial reading. The article includes Turner's recommendations for changes to the way in which schools are funded and managed in order to reverse the professional and political conditions which, in his view, made such a decline possible.

9. Barry Stierer

Stierer offers a critique of Martin Turner's position. He raises questions about the methods, assumptions and motives underlying Turner's claims, and suggests some future directions for reading research which might help to reduce the degree of polarisation in this area of educational debate.

Part 4: The Practice of Talk in the Classroom

Part 4 includes six articles which address the topic of talk in classrooms. Educational policy and funding in the 1980s reflected a consensus (in Britain at least) that spoken language is not only central to children's learning but also an area of competence ('oracy') in its own right, to be fostered (and, of course, *assessed*) along with other areas of the curriculum. However, this unprecedented degree of official recognition should not lead us to lose sight of the fact that talk has not always been so valued, and that even in these more talk-tolerant times there are many problematical issues surrounding the place of talk in the classroom which remain contested.

10. Margaret MacLure

MacLure provides a 'map' of the issues and of the various 'discourses' which have been called into service to represent different positions with respect to talk. She terms these four rationales 'oracy for functional communication', 'oracy for personal growth', 'oracy for learning', and 'oracy for cultural transformation'. MacLure traces the professional, political and intellectual roots of each of these rationales, and discusses the ways in which each of them might manifest themselves in everyday teaching and learning.

11. Eunice Fisher

Fisher develops a tentative framework for understanding and analysing children's peer-group talk, through an examination of small groups working at the computer. Her framework is grounded in a socio-cultural perspective on language and learning, and her research questions focus upon the relative contribution to children's learning made by 'cumulative', 'exploratory' and 'disputational' talk.

12. Joan Swann

Swann describes the main features of what she observes as three broad approaches to the study of, and provision for, equality of opportunity in classroom talk as it relates to gender: the 'anti-sexist' perspective, the 'liberal' perspective and the 'pro-female' perspective. Several aspects of spoken language are included in her framework, such as the relative amount of time girls and boys are 'given the floor', the number of times girls and boys are called upon, the relative value accorded to the spoken language characteristically used by boys and girls, and so on.

13. Harry Torrance

Torrance reviews the main debates and dilemmas surrounding the assessment of spoken language in schools. He distinguishes between two dimensions here: 'oral assessment' and 'assessment of oral communication'. The first dimension invokes theories of learning which place importance upon dialogue as a learning tool, while the latter casts talk as a worthwhile competence in its own right and relates to sociolinguistic concepts such as 'communicative competence'. However, as Harry Torrance points out, it is exceedingly difficult (if not impossible) to separate the two elements within any particular instance of talk.

14. Derek Edwards and Neil Mercer

Developing Vygotsky's proposal that children internalise dialogue and that their thought processes are radically reorganised as a consequence, Edwards and Mercer place teacher–pupil discourse at the centre of the educational process. Using the notions of 'scaffolding' and the 'zone of proximal development', they investigate how far teachers and pupils construct a shared understanding through dialogue about what they are learning in the classroom, and how far that knowledge is 'handed over' to the pupils.

15. Anne Dyson

Dyson examines the role played by informal and apparently off-task talk in the development of young children's competence in writing. She suggests that children's comments on each other's work and their use of each other as audience helps to shape individual story development. In addition, their ongoing relationships and dialogues are written in as part of the content. Using case studies she offers evidence that children's cognitive functions develop first in a social, interpersonal context and are then internalised at an individual level.

Part 5: The Practice of Writing in Classrooms

Part 5 contains articles which examine new approaches to the study of writing in schools.

16. J. R. Martin, Frances Christie and Joan Rothery

Martin, Christie and Rothery have been closely associated with the development of the 'genre' approach to teaching writing in Australia. Building on Michael Halliday's functional linguistics, their article argues that the fundamental differences between written and spoken language cannot be absorbed by children in the course of reading and writing activities unless the specific features of written genres are explicitly taught. They argue that children who are not given the opportunity to develop a confident command of written genres, and an awareness of their functions and variation, are disadvantaged and disempowered.

17. Myra Barrs

Barrs offers a critique of the genre approach. In particular, she argues that genre theory fails to take into account (a) the significant similarities between children's acquisition of spoken language and their acquisition of written language, (b) the way in which children increase their sensitivity to the forms of different written language registers through their reading, and (c) the ways in which certain dominant written language genres have come to occupy such privileged positions.

18. Pam Gilbert

Gilbert attempts to uncover some of the values and assumptions underlying the metaphors of 'creativity' and 'authoring' as they feature in much of the 'progressive' discourse for the teaching of writing in schools. For Gilbert, the notion of 'creativity' (whether applied to 'creative writing' or to a reader's 'creative response') is an artefact of a romantic and individualistic ideology which assumes that a 'text' can reflect the authentic voice of the writer. She argues that such an assumption sets up a complex 'double bind' for pupils in school, in that it privileges particular notions of originality but fails to provide the practical knowledge to achieve it, and perpetuates some pupils' disadvantage by pretending that all children naturally possess the cultural and linguistic resources required in order to become 'authors', when in fact these resources are unequally distributed in society.

19. John Richmond

Richmond provides some useful background to the political and professional debates in the area of language awareness and knowledge about language (KAL), and also looks in detail at some examples of teaching and learning in classrooms in order to indicate principles of good practice. Richmond adopts a broad definition of 'language awareness' which encompasses knowledge of how spoken and written language functions in social contexts. The examples he chooses focus on children's developing (and *implicit*) understanding of syntactic and semantic features of language as evidenced through their writing.

20. Marlene Scardamalia and Carl Bereiter

This chapter, written by two cognitive psychologists, draws together findings from their research into composing processes in writing. It focuses on the question of whether writing can develop thought. The authors suggest that a conflict is generated between the nature of the content a writer wants to communicate and the textual structures through which that content has to be expressed. Achieving this dialectical process, which involves changes to both the writer's beliefs and to the text, is a necessary part of the development of expert writing and also generates knowledge and understanding. Inexperienced writers often find ways of avoiding this conflict but can be helped to develop the appropriate strategies.

Acknowledgement

The editors gratefully acknowledge the advice they received from Myra Barrs, Director of the Centre for Language in Primary Education, London, in the compilation of this Reader.

Reference

Fairclough, N. (1989) *Language and Power*. Harlow: Longman.

1 Introducing the New Literacy

JOHN WILLINSKY

Three Scenes from the New Literacy

> *Not ideas about the thing but the thing itself*
> Wallace Stevens

Scene 1: In a Nova Scotia classroom, Kathleen Hefferman has her students keep journals for their study of kites; eight-year-old Craig begins his first entry with, 'one time i was flying a kit with my freind,' and Kathleen reflects on this process:

> The journal in our classroom is a dialogue journal between student and teacher, and therefore Craig is aware of his audience — a trusted adult. The relationship between teacher and student has been built up over several months of communicating in the journal. Craig knows that the journal is his place for recounting events, sharing feelings, and asking questions. He knows that the message he has to share is more important to this particular reader than his accurate spelling and punctuation so he writes freely, says what he has to say about his kite experience and considers the piece finished. What the teacher does now in response to the writing, and in response to the child as author, has the potential either to inhibit the child's writing or to encourage, nurture, and extend it. (Hefferman, 1982: 85)

Scene 2: In an Australian high school, Garth Boomer is observing a sophomore class that has been reading a novel and is now finding a way into the work that can be the source of both personal and group response to it:

> Later in the lesson, as requested by Mrs. Bell, they negotiate themselves into friendship or 'convenience' groups and each group receives a worksheet which asks them to establish what is meant by 'self-awareness', and 'in search of inner self' in relation to the novel. It is suggested that they brainstorm personal examples and then report to the class. After this they are to prepare a reading/performance or presentation of a poem which reveals one of these themes, explaining how it relates to the novel. The instruction reads: 'Decide how the group will go about this. In what way can the group support each other? How will you present the poems and your reactions? Decide on group and individual tasks'. (Boomer, 1985: 102)

1

Scene 3: In a college in the United States, Walker and Elias are working with a writing program that guides students through scheduled conferences between the writing instructor and the writer:

Teacher: I probably might start by having you tell me a little bit about how this went for you while you were writing it and how you felt about it when it was done.

Student: Well, um, I liked my ideas . . . I started writing about something more like we talked about in class and I got off on a little bit different subject, as you can tell, which I was a lot more interested in what we were doing, so I was more excited to write about that, and I had quite a few ideas on the subject. I had trouble fitting it into categories, so I was a little concerned about coherence as a whole.

Teacher: What would you say worked out the best for you in writing the paper? What do you remember as being the best thing about it?

Student: The ideas, probably.

Teacher: Good, I think you're right. That's exactly what the strength of the paper is. What are you least satisfied with? What would you have liked to work on more?

Student: I didn't think my diction, my sentences were good, cuz I had time to work on it, but not enough . . . (Walker & Elias, 1987: 276)

Such is this educational phenomenon which I am terming the 'New Literacy', if only in three of its many guises. Although it may not seem so at first glance, these classroom programs share a common core of radical assumptions about teacher and student, and about language and literacy. Yet at this point they share these assumptions without knowing it, without being part of a concerted educational movement. There is no overarching body, such as there once was with Progressive Education Association which provided a collective identity for an equally diverse set of innovative programs earlier in this century. For want of this public sense of a common cause, for what might be gained by comparing notes on a shared approach to education, I feel justified in reaching with a free hand across the international educational community to pull together this particular array of programs under a single title. The strength of the connections among them is part of this book's argument, as is the fact that each of these innovations falls within a much larger educational phenomenon than a simple adding up of the different reading and writing strategies would suggest.

My interests in the New Literacy go beyond proposing connections. In the first instance, these programs have something to learn from each other, as they operate at different educational levels and on different aspects of literacy. By assembling the common assumptions about literacy that link them, by digging about in the roots of these assumptions in search of a greater coherence for this larger project that unites them, I hope to clarify the direction they appear to be headed in this collective sense. At its most presumptuous, this would add to these innovations by making something larger of them, by setting them within a theater of educational and intellectual developments; it would confront this New Literacy with the implications that arise from what is, in essence, a radical and subversive proposal for changing the nature of literacy in the schools, even as it begins with the seeming innocence of keeping a journal about flying a kite. But, as well, the story of the New Literacy remains a personal one for me. As I have sought to understand my own attraction to these different but linked manners of teaching, I hope to help others see what is at stake in this alternative approach to literacy in the schools.

The innovation in these programs is not so much the classroom strategies that they have introduced. Soliciting personal responses to poetry or conducting writing conferences between instructor and writer can amount to little more than a gimmick that enlivens a lesson. More interesting is the conception of literacy that underlies these experiments and explorations in the teaching of students to read and write. I am contending that beneath these teaching strategies is a desire on the part of the educator to restructure the life of the classroom through an approach to literacy which challenges conventions of classroom organization and the typical roles of teacher and student. Which is to say that this *new literacy* is about more than instructional techniques for reading and writing, just as literacy is about more than the ability to score at or above the mean on standardized tests. To begin to think about what this new literacy might be about requires, in the first instance, a different manner of thinking about literacy.

However, before getting under way I must qualify my presumptuous designation of a *New Literacy*. I am not so 'new' myself as to imagine that each of the programs described here is not without precedents in earlier, education experiments. Among the earlier claims on new-ness is John Dewey's program of 'New Education' (1900) introduced at the University of Chicago Elementary School; in Great Britain, shortly thereafter, the New Education Fellowship became well known for its 'taint of pedagogical and political radicalism' (Cremin, 1961: 248). More recently, with an assist from Marshall McLuhan, a 'new literacy' has been declared for the 'reading' of film and other media (Foster, 1979; Gordon, 1971). The point is well taken, and I would graciously acknowledge these two precedents in the use of this book's title. However, the concern among the innovations I am reporting on is with a literacy that resides in its original home with print and the concerns of reading and writing; this speaks to a change in the educational climate over the last decade, in the ways of renewal and redefinition in education. Thus, after thinking a good deal about an appropriate label for this phenomenon, I decided that I could do no better than group these reading and writing programs under the somewhat generic heading of the New Literacy, with the upper case treatment serving as an extra touch of boldness to assist me in making the case for its existence. The use of 'new' has its own ironies in our society, no less so in education than in a commercial sense. It retains about it that hopeful quality and offers no further description of what it modifies than the wish to be seen to freshen up or revitalize an older product or concept.

My claim is that a 'New Literacy' lies latent and unrealized among a host of different experiments in the teaching of reading and writing. My use of this label is meant to form an umbrella under which I can gather and examine an array of innovations in the teaching and researching of reading and writing, innovations that have made inroads in programs from the primary grades to college composition. An umbrella may be a particularly apt metaphor for the process of pulling together these programs, if only because they must weather continuing indifference, if not outright opposition, from the elements of political conservatism that continue to hold sway on the educational front. The times are not entirely conducive to the literal inclinations of the New Literacy.

In Great Britain, they were opposed repeatedly by the *Black Papers* of the 1970s which took great issue with 'this "sociological" attitude', as an early *Paper* put it, and the apparent rejection of standards: 'The progressive emphasis on either endogenous creativity (undisciplined by any inwardness with the language of greatness) or social relevance (applying the human reductiveness characteristic of much of the contemporary) has replaced an earlier concern with quality' (Bantock in Cox & Boyson, 1975). More recently, the *Kingman Report* (Kingman, 1988), which dared a moderate path in rejecting grammar lessons while setting attainment targets in standard English, was cooly received by a considerably less progressive government and press. In the United States, storms of accountability began to break in the 1980s hitting the schools in waves, amid headlines on the declining standards in the schools and a bevy of blue-ribbon committee reports of a nation at risk. In an unusual proclamation of public interest in declarations of the educational decline of the west, E. D. Hirsch's *Cultural Literacy* (1987) and Allan Bloom's *The Closing of the American Mind* (1987) spent a good deal of time on the best-seller lists during the period in which I have been writing this book. Yet in spite of having to make allowances for this turn in the weather, the New Literacy is still on its way to being a major player in the educational marketplace, to pick up on the language of the times, and one that speaks in a relatively new way to the place and standard of literacy in society.

The Work of the New Literacy

To begin to gain a sense of what is being revitalized in the case of the New Literacy, it would be helpful to imagine literacy as a way of working the world. This may strike you as an odd and not very promising beginning for literacy, but it will prove helpful in appreciating how it is to be redefined in these innovative classrooms. I use the term 'work' to stress the sense in which literacy can be understood as a social practice that takes certain materials and turns them to certain ends in a given setting, an activity that takes up a place in a life, as working on something does. In this scheme of things, as I will reiterate throughout this book, literacy is better understood *not* as an isolated skill, as something one can do on demand, but as a social process in the daily landscape; one works with someone else's writing or writes for another under a roof of one sort or another in building something that will be of use to yourself or others. Although I will go on to make much more of literacy as a psychological and political event in this book, I want to begin with this initial belabored conception of it. This regard for literacy as actively making something of the world is part of the reorientation that is necessary to appreciate the New Literacy project.

To begin with what will be a bookfull of definitional statements about this project, I would suggest that New Literacy programs are intent on altering the meaning of this classroom work. As can be seen from the three scenes cited in the opening of this chapter, the shift involves increasing the students' control over the text and its meaning. But to shift this meaning of literacy also necessarily alters the relationship between teacher and student. The teacher, as an authority on what needs to be known and done, begins to turn over more of this responsibility to the student and to the meaning that comes from somewhere within the student's work with literacy. In these terms, then, the New Literacy's proposal is to reshape the *work* of the classroom around a different form of reading and writing. The moral, psychological, and social worth of this literacy begins with the students as sources of experience and meaning.

One of the major contentions of this book is that the New Literacy is as much about the way educators work with students and texts in a classroom as it is about actually improving instruction in literacy. Although I want to bring before you instances from the research on literacy that support, temper, and undermine the case for the New Literacy, I believe that there is another story underlying the reasons that educators turn to or away from the sorts of programs that fall under my rubric of the New Literacy. Rather than basing its claims on comparative research with other programs, the New Literacy begins with a much simpler, if more profound, question for educators who have grown a little weary of waiting for the definitive research answer to effective education. The New Literacy poses the question in terms of a personal philosophy and the sense made of how people should work together in a classroom: Are these the lessons that I want students to learn about literacy? Is this how I want to spend my days, working in this way with students and with books? These are the questions that raise the doubts about the common fare and initiate the interest in what New Literacy programs have to offer.

Yet it would be misleading to suggest that questions of classroom effectiveness and accountability are spurious for advocates of the New Literacy. The New Literacy consists of programs that have students actively engaged in writing and reading, programs that produce hours of focused discussion, reams of notes and drafts, scores of performances and publications. While attention is given to process in a whole new way, these are the processes that are productive, that are effective in eliciting from the student indications that learning is going on in one form or another. Yet it is also fair to say that these indications of process — the talk, drafts, and finished pieces — have not produced a consensus within the educational community that this is a superior way of teaching literacy. The research comparing the New Literacy to other programs has not often decided in its favor, although neither has it conclusively refuted its value. This is why I return to the one point that does seem clear about the New Literacy: it constitutes a different form of thinking and practice about teaching and literacy. That is to say, the New Literacy is about new institutional goals for these schools, new professional goals for teaching, and new educational goals for literacy. In fact, I wish to make this principle of shifted goals in the work of the classroom a defining characteristic of the New Literacy: *The New Literacy consists of those strategies in the teaching of reading and writing which attempt to shift the control of literacy from the teacher to the student; literacy is promoted in such programs as a social process with language that can from the very beginning extend the students' range of meaning and connection.*

This statement stands against a literacy which is defined as the ability to perform at a certain level on a standardized test and which asks education for preparation and practice in that ability. It is to resist treating literacy simply as a competence that people have or do not have at some arbitrary level. Which is to say, the New Literacy challenges traditional conceptions of learning to read and write when it declares that purpose and intent are foremost concerns with literacy. But more than that, New Literacy programs would shift the locus of intention and purpose to the student as much as possible, rather than letting it reside in the teacher and the curriculum guidebook.

In this frame of mind, 'literacy' is nothing in itself. Literacy is understood as the working of language in its written form, in reading a novel of a favorite author or writing a resignation letter, and that work takes place in a setting which contributes to its meaning, whether in a classroom or an office; the nature of that experience of literacy in the classroom is what constitutes an education. This is an aspect of the New Literacy taken from the educational philosophy of John Dewey who held that the classroom is poorly conceived as a preparation for life; it should be treated as the thing itself, or as he put it in his *Pedagogical Creed,* 'education which does not occur through forms of life, forms that are worth living for their own sake, is always a poor substitute for the genuine reality, and tends to cramp and deaden' (1988: 169).

A second, more telling, means of introducing the New Literacy is to describe the host of new hats that teachers slip on as they enter the classroom: In the literature which has heralded this alternative, teachers are often cast as *coaches* finding new ways to maximize the children's personal best in achieving their own goals in reading and writing. Once the student is up and writing, teachers can switch into patient *editors* helping the students find their own voice; they later act as *agents* promoting the work around the school and community, and *publishers* drawing on the resources of the school to get the word out. The point is that the teacher takes on a new role, in fact, a new array of roles, in mounting these programs. It becomes a process of redefining the nature of teaching. Ira Shor in his 'critical thinking' version of the New Literacy goes so far as to speak of a 'withering away of the teacher,' recalling Marx's withering away of the state in the ideal stages of communism, when all is in harmony (1977: 98).

The students, for their part, find themselves accredited as *meaning-makers* beginning in the first grade as they are awarded advanced standing on what they already taught themselves about symbol and language, from the golden twin arches to the graphics that distinguish cereal boxes. They quickly grow into *authors* in these classes, as they soon find themselves in self-expression; and then they are also junior *scientists* as they are seen to be testing hypothesis after hypothesis about the nature of language and about their own learning processes within literacy. They, too, have the chance to play editor and publisher in the enhancement and promotion of their own and other students' work.

As I noted above, this reorganization of literacy in the classroom has taken many shapes; it is not the vision of any one educational guru. The New Literacy has come along a winding road out of the Progressive Education movement. It has gladly picked up discarded ideas along the way and used them to refashion a more engaging form of literacy and learning. Yet I realize that a starting point in recent educational history would help in initially locating this project. Certainly the best candidate for realizing the moment of conception is the often celebrated meeting of British and American educators at the Anglo-American Seminar on the Teaching of English at Dartmouth College in 1966. In London that year, teachers had begun to talk about talk in the classroom which was soon to develop into the Language Across the Curriculum movement. The British had something to share at Dartmouth and the sharing gave rise at that historic meeting to what John Dixon (1967) identified as the promise of a Growth Model. Dixon contrasted this model to the two traditional, towering giants of the English program, the Heritage and Skills Models. The Growth Model drew on the work of such figures as James Britton and Douglas Barnes in England; the Americans may have been less sanguine about the meeting, but they had their comparable and inspirational figures in James Moffett and Louise Rosenblatt who were beginning to work a similar pattern of change. To foster the growth of the child through 'language and learning', 'universes of discourse', and 'transformational reading' soon became the call of this incipient New Literacy on both sides of the Atlantic.

In Great Britain, the 1970s brought what Peter Doughty (1974) confidently called a 'progressive consensus' in the teaching of English. It had introduced the fundamentals of the New Literacy into the English classes of innovative teachers. 'Workshops' were set up; teachers became 'entrepreneurs' and 'consultants' while students were transformed into 'participants' and 'researchers' (Doughty, 1974: 14): 'The progressive in English teaching requires, therefore, the establishment of a new set of social relationships for the classroom, between teacher and pupil and between pupil and pupil' (p. 16). One of the early programs that made this new attitude readily available to English teachers in Great Britain was *Language in Use* (Doughty, Thornton & Pearce, 1971). In setting English in a new political direction, *Language in Use* deliberately turned from the guiding light of literary criticism to the stark tones of sociolinguistics which was leading an intellectual fight to broaden the democratic manadate of equal opportunity in education. This orientation meant radically new lessons for the students, lessons about language in the street and home, not just in literature lessons on language's multiple functions and students' natural competence, against traditional notions of correctness and a single standard. This new tack had emerged out of a highly charged political debate over language and dialect, social class and school success; the point was eventually established that many judgements condemning the quality of students' language carry residual class and racial prejudices.[1]

This new understanding of students and the politics of language underwrites much of the New Literacy's approach to writing although it goes unspoken now for the most part. Margaret Mathieson bluntly identifies it, in her history of English teaching, as a moral and ideological effort to 'remedy social injustice' perpetrated against working-class students (1975: 159). This concern with social injustice marks the history of the teaching of English, beginning with Matthew Arnold's nineteenth-century promise that poetry would (re)form the soul of the (working-class) pupils which he supervised for many years. Yet it is well to recall that these reformers were no less morally committed than Arnold to rectifying a troubling situation through education; teaching English in that sense has remained an ethical endeavor, making up for the failings of organized religion in Arnold's day and in this case for the shortfalls of the democratic promise to hear the voice of the many.

It remains difficult to access exactly how many inroads the New Literacy has made in the teaching of English since Dartmouth and that early progressive consensus. At best, I can offer a few rough and assorted measures to give some indication of how well these programs have taken in the schools:

(1) The National Writing Project, which began introducing teachers to the writing process model in 1973, had 172 sites operating in America and abroad in 1989 and is continuing to grow.[2]

(2) In a feature article on new directions in reading, the *New York Times* reports that 'a controversial development that has come to be known as whole language' is 'happening' in 'countless' schools around America. The article notes that New Zealand, with 'one of the highest literacy rates in the world', had been using an approach similar to whole language for 25 years (Salmans, 1988: EDUC69).

(3) The Australian government has spent over $8 million on implementing Whole Language programs over a five-year period (Luke *et al.*, 1989).

(4) In Great Britain, a research team headed by Peter Mortimore has discovered that in the 50 London primary schools in their study, 19 percent of the teachers had dropped the basal reading program in favor of children choosing their own literature to read (Mortimore *et al.*, 1988: 86). Douglas and Dorothy Barnes have found that personal writing, which might serve as a crude indicator of New Literacy influence, made up 21 to 45 percent of the topics that secondary students addressed in their English classes (1988: 80–84).

(5) The province of Nova Scotia has mandated Whole Language as the approach to be taken with literacy instruction throughout the school system (Church *et al.*, 1989).

It seems safe to suggest that the New Literacy is a presence on the educational scene. Yet the issue for me is not the rising market share of New Literacy. I remain interested in the aspects of the New Literacy which draw a teacher to these programs and in where New Literacy programs are heading with literacy and learning. The question is also whether the educators advocating and participating in these programs know where they are headed.

If for many of us, the seeds of the New Literacy were planted during the 1960s reawakening of progressive education, the program has taken shape within this climate of educational restraint and crisis. The New Literacy's transformation of the child-centered experiments of the 1960s has been based on finding a more *productive,* if alternative, structure for the classroom. In light of the crisis mentality, the New Literacy has learned a lesson about what John Goodlad (1983) has identified as the 'non-events' of curriculum innovation of that earlier and daring period. With all of its interest in process, the New Literacy is still determined *to produce* writers and readers, but to produce them in a learning environment that eschews the back-to-basics response that has dominated the educational crisis mentality. On the other hand, the New Literacy also shows signs that it has brought itself on stream in educating the young for the new corporate age.

At a buzz-word level, these programs have an executive-class edge. They would, after all, encourage independent and collaborative projects while drawing on peer support networks and conferencing with professionals to enhance the production values of the final and literate product. It can all sound and seem very marble and glass, office tower work. While editorial meetings at the classroom publishing house may not be a training ground for the leveraged buy-out artists, neither is it so removed from hustling projects and prospectuses for tomorrow's Wall Street jungle. The New Literacy seeks for both teacher and student a working environment that fosters a spirit of independence and creative excitement. It can approach at times a mythical cross between the high-pressure dynamics of advertising account work and the warm, collaborative spirit of a 1960s pottery studio. But tempering both these aspects is a domestic element that is found in the furnishings of this new classroom with carpet, floor lamps, and different centers of activity for reading, playing and making things, all laid out like a renovated home with the walls knocked out. Valerie Walkerdine, who worked in one such progressive setting in the late 1960s, has described how the teacher is moved homeward: 'the teacher is no authoritarian father figure, but a bourgeois and nurturant mother' (1986: 58). This workplace, in which students are at home among teachers who would assist their individual and collaborative projects, has been aptly characterized by David Cohen as 'a distinctively cosmopolitan and upper middle-class style of family life, in which parental discipline is self-consciously relaxed, in which children have plenty of money and free time, and need not work, and in which personal independence is highly valued' (1988: 27). In Cohen's view this has limited the implementation of progressive education programs, and I have certainly met teachers who appear to reject New Literacy programs because it just does not seem to them to resemble teaching, that is, the kind of work they see themselves doing in a classroom.

But if the New Literacy offers an upper middle-class hominess with a little corporate panache, it is going to fail an overwhelming majority of the students as any form of preparation for life outside the classroom. The escape from what appears to be a late 1980s callowness lurks in a final lesson from that legacy of the 1960s. Madeleine Grumet (1988) puts her finger on it when she describes how teachers during that period naively proposed a new education in a manner doomed to failure: 'Oblivious to the far-reaching epistemological and political implications of this approach to schooling, the teachers who had transformed their classrooms into places of active exploration and group process failed to create the political and ideological structures required to sustain and enlarge the movement' (p. 24). In her work on women and teaching, Grumet has taken the first steps in offering politically sensitive structures for reorganizing teaching; Grumet recasts teaching as a form of reproductive labor, a labor connected to the personal lives of teachers and to their collaborative association with others, colleagues and students. For Grumet, teachers have it within their grasp to realize and to some degree recreate the public sphere of the classroom in their own images of education within the democratic state. As schools have failed to make good their promise to all children of an equal education, as color, class and gender continue to exert a structural influence that insures children do not have the same range of opportunities, the New Literacy had to find ways to keep these issues in the forefront of its efforts to increase the level of literate participation and enfranchisement. These are issues that the New Literacy needs to be pressed on.

Part of the New Literacy's argument with the schools is that literacy takes its meaning and force from the circumstances in which it is used and the ends to which it is put. The New Literacy is caught up in the play of power and structure in the classroom, as well as in the society at large; it is also the mediating grace between friends sharing a paperback. This is a latent political and personal challenge to the New Literacy which its programs have found ways of addressing from within the classroom. The meeting of the personal and the political is one of those powerful calls inherited from the 1960s. The challenge remains latent because this meeting is rarely realized in discussions of what the New Literacy is up to in the classroom. New Literacy programs happily embrace that friendly aspect of literacy through a regular sharing of students' stories and other forms of collaboration in the classroom. Yet the advocates of these programs are not always ready to deal with the politics of this realignment of work in the school, as if drawn to the beat of this exiting music while hesitant about what this driving beat may really be all about. These questions of power and politics in literacy need to be faced by advocates of the New Literacy and other interested parties. They need to hear from the likes of Walkerdine and Henry Giroux as educational critics who have not shied from dancing to this beat. Out of her own teaching experience with the child-centered experiments of the 1960s, Walkerdine sounds a blunt cautionary note: 'Although some have suggested that progressivism frees working class children from harsh authoritarianism, I would suggest precisely the opposite. Progressivism makes the products of oppression, powerlessness, invisible' (1986: 59). Giroux, too, lays literacy out in bold political tones: 'To be literate is *not* to be free, it is to be present and active in the struggle for reclaiming one's voice, history, and future' (1988a: 65, original emphasis).

This radical element is not something from outside the New Literacy, but lies at its center as it begins with a critique of the way literacy is treated in the classroom. To give greater credence to the reader's response to a text is to acknowledge that the reader is a major contributor to the making of the literary experience. It would have the students invest themselves in their writing and thereby risk fostering a nation of outspoken writers. It clearly portends more than improved language arts classes. But what precisely will this restructuring of the classroom around a new form of literacy produce among people who come to possess it, we might ask? Is it to amount to little more than a flood of letters to the editor of the local newspaper? Or might it mean something more to suddenly have a greater part of the population able and willing to go public with their case and stories, demanding a greater attentiveness to their voices and additional outlets for their new-found voices in the process?

In trying to realize what is at stake in this new form of literacy, I have brought together advocates of the New Literacy with those who have spoken out for students unduly silenced through the politics of gender, color, and social class. With a certain degree of idealism, I am pressing for a New Literacy that is not totally absorbed in overcoming such malaises as writer's block in the English classroom or boredom in the face of reading an assigned novel. There is something more to be done with writing and reading. The New Literacy needs to wrestle with this promise of a new empowerment in literacy. It needs to face up to what might lie in this talk of power and come clean with its best intentions. To begin to realize this potential for addressing the larger issue of literacy in this society, New Literacy programs will have to get involved in the tensions that tear at education, that continue to frustrate the dream of an equitable society. To offer students a greater say on and over the page may be a rhetorical flourish of these new programs, but then someone has to call their bluff. It may be more political than educators sometimes feel comfortable with in thinking about the young, but the challenge raised by the New Literacy is against a tradition which goes far beyond conventional teaching methods. Consider the extent of the assault: from students entering the first grade who are regarded as bringing a degree of literacy and a feel for language that makes an entire publishing industry obsolete, to the college level where the literary canon has been cracked and opened to writers who were once considered to be marginal. The New Literacy introduces a radical program of studies along two dimensions, the one unsettling the school and the other disturbing the acquired habits of the student. This to be a literacy which plays *against* institutional authority and a literacy which works *within* the student. The first might be described as a form of 'deschooling' that reconstructs the classroom around the students' rather than the teacher's pursuit of meaning. The second is taken up with the literacy that would transform the student from supplicant to advocate in search of what has not been expressed or found before, a literacy that engages the student and which would encourage a greater engagement with the world.

Notes

1. The sociolinguists who provided the grounding for this work were M. A. K. Halliday (1973) and Basil Bernstein (1971), while the landmark words in the social class and racial elements were Harold Rosen's *Language and Class* (1972), which alerted educators to the continuing class bias of Bernstein's work, and Labov's 'The Logic of Nonstandard English' (1973) which also served as a corrective to Bernstein.
2. To give an example of what a site might represent, in the city of Calgary 130 teachers (out of approximately 6,000 in this school district) by 1988 had taken a university course in the methods of the National Writing Project and are participating in the project with their own classes and through in-service with other teachers; approximately 25 new teachers are added to the project each year through these courses. The headquarters of the National Writing Project is in the Faculty of Education, University of California at Berkeley. In a similar development, there has also recently formed a North American Confederation of Whole Language Support Groups.

References

Barnes, D. and Barnes, D. (1984) *Versions of English*. With S. Clark. London: Heinemann.

Bernstein, B. (1971) *Class, Codes and Control: Theoretical Studies Toward a Sociology of Language*. Vol. 1. New York: Schocken Books.

Bloom, A. (1987) *The Closing of the American Mind: How Higher Education has Failed Democracy and Impoverished the Soul of Today's Students*. New York: Simon & Schuster.

Boomer, G. (1985) *Fair Dinkum Teaching and Learning: Reflections on Literacy and Power*. Upper Montclair, NJ: Boynton/Cook.

Church, S., Gamberg, R., Manicom, A. and Rice, J. (1989). 'Whole language' in Nova Scotia. Part 1: Benefits, difficulties and potential. *Our Schools/Our Selves* 1 (2), 46–58.

Cohen, D. K. (1988) Teaching practice: Plus ça change . . . In P. Jackson (ed.) *Contributing to Educational Change: Perspectives on Research and Practice*. Berkeley, CA: McCutchan.

Cox, C. B. and Boyson, R. (1975) *The Fight for Education: Black Paper, 1975*. London: Dent.

Cremin, L. (1961) *The Transformation of the School: Progressivism in American Education, 1876–1957*. New York: Vintage.

Dewey, J. (1900) *The School and Society*. Chicago: University of Chicago Press.

— [1897] (1988) My pedagogic creed. *In S. I. Brown and M. E. Finn (eds) Readings from Progressive Education: A Movement and its Professional Journal* Vol. 1 (pp. 169–70). Lanham, MD: University Press of America.

Dixon, J. (1967) *Growth Through English*. London: Oxford University Press.

Doughty, P. (1974) *Language, 'English' and the Curriculum*. London: Edward Arnold.

Doughty, P., Thornton, G. and Pearce, J. (1971) *Language in Use*. London: Edward Arnold.

Foster, H. M. (1979) *The New Literacy: The Language of Film and Television*. Urbana, IL: National Council of Teachers of English.

Giroux, H. A. (1988a) Literacy and the pedagogy of voice and political empowerment. *Educational Theory* 38 (1), 61–75.

Goodlad, J. (1983) Improving schooling in the 1980s: Toward the non-replication of non-events. *Educational Leadership* 41, 4–10.

Gordon, D. R. (1971) *The New Literacy*. Toronto: University of Toronto Press.

Grumet, M. R. (1988) *Bitter Milk: Women and teaching*. Amherst, MA: University of Massachusetts.

Hefferman, K. (1982) Responding to children's writing. In J. Newman (ed.) *Whole Language: Translating Theory into Practice* (Monographs on teaching and learning). Halifax, NS: Department of Education, Dalhousie University.

Hirsch, E. D. Jr (1987) *Cultural Literacy: What Every American Needs to Know*. Boston: Houghton Mifflin.

Kingman, J. (1988) *Report of the Committee on Inquiry into the Teaching of English Language*. London: HMSO.

Labov, W. (1973) The logic of nonstandard English. In N. Keddie (ed.) *Tinker, Tailor: The Myth of Cultural Deprivation* (pp. 21–66). Harmondsworth, UK: Penguin.

Luke, A., Gilbert, P., Rowe, K., Gilbert, R., Ward, G. and Baldauf, Jr, R. (1989) *An Evaluation of Literacy Strategies in Two Australian Sites*. Canberra: Department of Employment, Education and Training.

Mathieson, M. (1975) *The Preachers of Culture: A Study of English and its Teachers*. London: Allen & Unwin.

Mortimore, P., Sammons, P., Stoll, L., Lewis, D. and Ecob, R. (1988) *School Matters*. Berkeley: University of California Press.

Rosen, H. (1972) *Language and Class: A Critical Look at the Theories of Basil Bernstein*. Bristol, UK: Falling Wall Press.

Salmans, S. (1988) Go Away, Dick and Jane. *Education Life, New York Times*. November 6, pp. EDUC67–9.

Shor, I. (1977) *Critical Teaching in Everyday Life*. Montreal: Black Rose.

Walker, C. P. and Elias, D. (1987) Writing conference talk: Factors associated with high- and low-level writing conferences. *Research in the Teaching of English* 21 (3), 266–85.

Walkerdine, V. (1986) Progressive pedagogy and political struggle. *Screen* 13, 54–60.

2 The Emergence of Literacy

NIGEL HALL

The Discovery of Emergent Literacy

In the last ten years, and particularly during the last five years, considerable effort has been put into investigating the competence of children as literacy learners, and redefining what it means for them to become literate. Researchers from a variety of disciplines have been contributing knowledge which, when put together, provides a powerful image of the child as a competent enquirer into the nature and purpose of literacy. Teachers have also played their part in this revaluation and there are many across the world who are creating classroom environments which reflect this new knowledge. Much of this knowledge is not, of course, completely new — nothing ever is — and this chapter will refer to some earlier thoughts which would be quite acceptable to most recent researchers in this area. However, there are many elements which were not known or understood before the asking of certain kinds of questions became a legitimate activity. If the question, 'When do children become literate?' is answered by the response, 'When they come to school', there is no clear incentive to look at what is happening to children before they arrive at school. Fortunately some researchers have not been restricted by such answers and it is their findings which form the basis for this book.

The Western print environment is the most complex and demanding ever experienced by the human race. All of us who live in it cannot help but be substantially involved in it. The speedy advance of information technology, far from reducing the burden, has added to the complexity. The encroachment of television into our lives has increased the need to read in order for us to see what we wish to view; it has also led to the development of an audience for books related to the programmes. Children, from birth, are witnesses to both the existence of print and the relationship between print and people. It would seem strange, given the way that children involve themselves in all aspects of their world, if anyone suggested that there was one part of that visible world about which children were totally ignorant. Yet that is precisely the assumption that underpins so much conventional instruction. There has been an almost universal assumption that either children are ignorant about the nature and purpose of literacy unless they are 'taught' it, or that what children know is of no importance whatsoever in devising teaching strategies. The overall effect of such views is that there has been a devaluation of children's competence, and an emphasis on direct instructional practices.

Conventional assumptions

For most of this century the curriculum for the teaching of literacy skills in Britain and the USA has been based on a number of apparently fundamental assumptions. These are that:

- reading and writing are primarily visual-perceptual processes involving printed unit/sound relationships;
- children are not ready to learn to read and write until they are five or six years old;
- children have to be taught to be literate;
- the teaching of literacy must be systematic and sequential in operation;
- proficiency in the 'basic' skills has to be acquired before one can act in a literate way;
- teaching the 'basic' skills of literacy is a neutral, value-free activity.

These assumptions, albeit sometimes unspoken and implicit, controlled the way most educationalists dealt with literacy. The following quotation from Walcutt (in Goddard, 1974) effectively embodies most of them:

> Reading is first of all and essentially the mechanical skill of decoding, of turning the printed symbols into the sounds which are language . . . We are intensely concerned that our children understand what they read, but the mechanical decoding skill must come first if we are to get them started properly. In the earliest stages of learning to read there is very little need for thinking and reasoning on the part of the child. What he needs is a little practice in mastering a decoding skill and the thinking will come along quite some time later.

Such assumptions did not make the teaching of reading and writing any easier, nor did they resolve the problem of how to teach literacy. They did, however, provide some security; they marked the boundaries of the teacher's task, elevated the status of the teacher, and controlled perception of some of the associated phenomena.

Some of these assumptions clearly gave value to the role of the teacher. The view that children were not ready for literacy until they were five or six years old, and that they had to be taught to be literate, clearly elevates the status of the teacher. Instruction in literacy was a task for the specialist — not the parent.

The fact that reading and writing were perceived as visual/perceptual processes, and that they had to be taught in a systematic and sequential way, enabled the creation of an elaborate set of rules governing the order in which these relationships had to be taught. Once rules were clearly expressed, the teaching of these rules became an activity akin to a science, understood by most teachers to be a neutral, value-free activity. Thus, by applying the rules in a systematic way, children were inevitably supposed to become literate.

Whether the teaching was based on phonic, alphabetic, whole word, or sentence methods of reading instruction, certain elements remained unchanged. Control of the manner and rate of learning was in the hands of the teacher. It was the teacher's task to control the child's development from a state of illiteracy to becoming someone with a mastery of the skills involved in being literate; the child's role was to follow the teacher's route from beginning to end.

As a result of more recent understanding about, and awareness of, literacy, and the ways in which children develop a comprehension of literacy, it is possible to identify a number of features that are not reflected in the above assumptions.

- There was no consideration that becoming a reader and becoming a writer were closely related processes.
- There was no consideration that becoming literate might be a social process and be influenced by a search for meaning.
- There was no consideration that most pre-school children might actually have some knowledge of literacy.
- There was no consideration that becoming literate might be a continuous developmental process that begins very early in life.
- There was no consideration of the organisation and control that children might bring to becoming literate.
- There was no consideration that in order to become literate a child might need to engage in literate acts.
- There was little consideration of how language and stories might inform, in particular ways, children's understanding about literacy and text.
- There was no consideration that the knowledge that children have about literacy might be a legitimate element of their literacy development.

Although conventional assumptions may not reflect such ideas, there are perspectives on the development of literacy which do.

An historical alternative

The rediscovery and affirmation of emergent literacy was preceded by the recognition of schoolchildren's competence in learning to read. This recognition is attributable to a small number of researchers, namely Marie Clay in New Zealand, Kenneth Goodman in America, and Frank Smith in America and Canada. The work of these researchers and writers does not support the 'rule-bound' and 'teacher-controlled' stance of much literacy education. Unlike many other attacks on the deficit model of literacy education, their views have been sustained and developed, and have, in turn, generated a substantial body of multi-disciplined research which supports their claims.

The work of Clay (collected in Clay, 1982) and Goodman (collected in Gollasch, 1982) demonstrated clearly that children were not allowing themselves to be processed into becoming readers. As Clay (1982: xii) says: 'Children supplement the programme with their own efforts'. Both Clay and Goodman worked with children's errors and discovered that the common sense notion of an error being something that was simply wrong was not indicative of the reader's true response. They both found that these errors (which Goodman prefers to call miscues) revealed the considerable efforts being made by children to make sense of the material they were reading. In other words children already had some competence in reading.

Smith (1971) and Goodman (see Gollasch, 1982) both regard reading as a natural language process involving the reader in linguistic, cognitive, and social strategies in order to process print directly for meaning. Smith has also extended these principles to writing (Smith, 1982). Smith and Goodman have redefined literacy by moving away from definitions relating simply to perceptual processes to definitions based on cognitive activity in terms of making sense of print. That 'making sense of print' inevitably involves a social perspective. This conceptualisation of literacy as a meaning-based activity is not itself novel (see Thorndike, 1917, on reading), but what is relatively new is that both Smith and Goodman have applied this belief not only to the way adults engage in literate behaviour but also to the way children approach learning to read and write. They suggest that children approach print in a manner essentially similar to that of adults; children expect print to make sense. They are: 'Seekers after meaning motivated by the need to comprehend' (Goodman & Goodman, 1979) and they claim that children bring to print strategies which assume the usefulness of the medium.

This shift in emphasis clearly has implications for the assumptions identified at the beginning of this chapter. If learning to read and write are 'natural language' processes then can it really be the case that children have to wait until the age of five before they can engage in literacy-based activities? If it is a 'natural language' process then can it be the case that children have to be taught to read and write? Smith (1979) and Goodman, Goodman & Burke (1978) deny emphatically that children have to wait; indeed the basis of their claim is that children do not wait. As Goodman & Goodman (1979) put it: 'Children are aware of the functions of print and are adaptive to the characteristics of print.' For Goodman and Smith the view that literacy acquisition was a natural process generated an important question: When does that process begin? With this apparently simple question the investigation of emergent literacy was legitimised.

There were, inevitably, other reasons why researchers began to focus on literacy before schooling. One of these reasons derived from research into metacognitive aspects of learning to read (using thought to reflect on thinking), and another derived from studies of early readers. A whole set of investigations, which appear to begin with Reid (1958) apparently demonstrated that children beginning school have little idea of the purpose and processes of reading. It is sufficient to say at this point that, whether those researchers were right or wrong, they did focus attention on the knowledge about reading that children brought to school.

Equally important were a number of investigations into 'early readers' as they raised interesting questions about the relationship between knowledge about literacy and pre-school experiences. To some extent studies of early readers are studies of competence. The number of studies and the number of children found who were competent, led Torrey, in a review of such studies (Torrey, 1979), to suggest that such competence was more common than had appeared. It was clear from those studies that the early experiences children had with print played a significant role in the emergence of literacy.

The time for an alternative approach seemed right in the light of new conceptualisations of psycholinguistics, the puzzles of the metacognitive research and the insights obtained from studies of early readers. Many researchers and teachers were feeling that terms like 'pre-reading skills' or, presumably, 'pre-writing skills', or 'pre-literacy skills' were unhelpful in describing young children's print-related behaviours. As Holdaway (1979) said: 'When we apply a term like "pre-reading skills" to such behaviour we demean their real status as early literacy skills, for they actually display all the features of mature strategies already achieving sound and satisfying outcomes' (p. 56).

A current alternative

I began this chapter by considering a number of assumptions contained in conventional literacy instructional strategies. It will be useful to compare

those assumptions with those of someone approaching the emergence of literacy from a rather different perspective; a perspective derived from the
work of the Goodmans and Frank Smith.

Yetta Goodman has for many years been studying the emergence of literacy. Her specific interest began when some children she was studying failed
reading readiness tests. 'Yet even these children were beyond beginning
reading. They were doing things and had developed concepts that were part
of the reading process of mature proficient readers' (Goodman, 1980: 2).
This is not unlike a comment made by Clark in her study of young fluent
readers (Clark, 1976: 32): 'It is possible for even young children to become
very fluent readers in spite of an average or below average ability to reproduce, or even to remember in their correct orientation, isolated designs sufficiently clearly to identify them from a range of alternatives.' It also brings
to mind the case of Larry Wilson who at the age of four 'Failed a reading readiness test but read material on the second or third grade level' (Krippner,
1963: 108).

Yetta Goodman does not accept that reading and writing are primarily
visual/perceptual skills involving mainly printed unit/sound relationships.
She would not deny that these relationships exist but sees their use as only
one, and often a very inefficient, strategy if used in isolation: 'Reading consists of optical, perceptual, syntactic and semantic cycles each melting into
the next as readers try to get to meaning as efficiently as possible using minimal time and energy' (Goodman & Goodman, 1979: 149). She would reject
the view that children cannot be literate until they are five or six years old.
She claims that: 'The beginnings of reading development often go unnoticed
in the young child . . . this lack of sensitivity occurs because the reading process is misunderstood, because learning to read print and being taught to
read it have been conceived as one-to-one correspondence, and because we
have been led to believe that the most common-sense notions about learning
to read suggest that it begins in a formalised school setting' (Goodman,
1980: 9).

She does not believe that children have to be taught to be literate: 'In
an environment rich with written language experiences which have real
purpose and function for the children, the concepts and oral language about
written language develop over a period of time . . . given time, children
work out for themselves what items belong in what categories' (Goodman,
1980: 25). She would not expect the teaching of literacy to be systematic
and sequential in operation. She argues: 'It helps educators in understanding the reading process to study what proficient readers do when
they read. But it is a serious mistake to create curricula based on artificial
skill sequences and hierarchies derived from such studies' (Goodman &
Altwerger, 1980: 84).

Yetta Goodman would not consider that the basic skills have to be acquired before one can act in a literate way: 'The children we have studied and worked with have received no formal instruction yet they have begun to read. Reading may be its own readiness' (Goodman & Altwerger, 1980: 84). She does believe that literacy is anything but a neutral, value-free activity. She claims that it is: 'Impossible to consider literacy development without understanding the significance of literacy in the culture — in both the larger society in which a particular culture grows and develops and within the specific culture in which the child is nourished' (Goodman, 1980: 4).

Most of the above responses are concerned with the reading process, but it is clear that Goodman accepts that those beliefs apply equally to writing. Her position is summed up when she says: 'My research has shown that literacy develops naturally in all children in our literate society' (Goodman, 1980: 31). There would appear to be a number of fundamental assumptions behind the above statements which are rather different from those underpinning more conventional beliefs about literacy:

- Reading and writing are cognitive and social abilities involving a whole range of meaning-gaining strategies.
- Most children begin to read and write long before they arrive at school. They do not wait until they are 'taught'.
- Literacy emerges not in a systematic, sequential manner, but as a response to the printed language, and social environment experienced by the child.
- Children control and manipulate their literacy learning in much the same way as they control and manipulate all other aspects of their learning about the world.
- Literacy is a social phenomenon and as such is influenced by cultural factors. Therefore the cultural group in which children grow up will be a significant influence on the emergence of literacy.

In essence Goodman proposes a model of literacy development where the child is a competent cognitive and social learner who can develop, on his/her own, knowledge about, and abilities with, literacy. The child is seen as having competence to learn by living in a world where phenomena can have meaning assigned to them. This is, clearly, quite different from the assumptions embedded in conventional instruction, particularly with regard to very young children (see Walker, 1975).

Goodman has, on several occasions, used the word 'natural' to describe the way children become literate. It is a term which has been used by a number of other writers (Curtis, 1984; Forester, 1977; Hoskisson, 1979; Malicky & Norman, 1985; Schmidt & Yates, 1985; Stine, 1980; Teale, 1982, 1984; and Torrey, 1979). It is, however, rather an awkward word, for what counts as 'natural' may vary between people. For many, the word 'natural' implies some kind of maturational phenomenon; something that occurs almost inevitably as a result of biological programming. However, in defining learning to read and write as natural processes, neither Smith nor the Goodmans are suggesting that there is some kind of biological mechanism operating; they are not suggesting an alternative literacy acquisition device (LAD). They are claiming that literacy is learnt in much the same way, and to some extent at the same time, as oral language. Both oral language and literacy development are dependent on an appropriate context for the 'natural' development of those skills. People use language and literacy in the pursuit of their everyday lives. In other words, within such contexts people engage in literacy and oracy in order that they may continue to experience the satisfaction of human needs.

Children would not learn to talk if deprived of access to purposeful oral language use. No child has ever learnt to talk by being locked in a room with an endless supply of tape-recorded language. Children have to experience language being used by people in appropriate ways, and appropriate ways are those which enable the creation of meanings and the sharing of meanings. In the same way, no child would ever learn to read if locked into the British Library. Children must have access to people using print in appropriate ways. Thus the 'naturalness' is a function of social experiences where literacy is a means to a variety of other ends.

Of course, within such environments all kinds of people — adults, siblings, and friends — help children in their learning. However, this seldom takes place as a result of systematic and sequential instructional practices; it is a consequence of playing and living with children. The same effects can be found in literacy development (Gundlach *et al.*, 1985). It is the literacy development within these contexts that Goodman and others are labelling 'natural'.

The Linguistic and Social Background of Emergent Literacy

The emergence of oral language in context

Linguists and psychologists in the 1960s were primarily interested in the acquisition of the phonological and grammatical features of language. This meant that language was, in a sense, being studied apart from its primary function — communication between human beings. Once one begins to look at oral language from a more functional point of view it becomes apparent that there are many real similarities between acquiring an understanding of oral language and acquiring an understanding of written language.

It is the work of the linguist Halliday which has had most impact on reassessing the way in which children learn language. He says: 'Learning one's mother tongue is learning the use of language, and the meanings, or rather the meaning potential, associated with them. The structures, the words and the sounds are the realisation of this meaning potential. Learning language is learning how to mean' (Halliday, 1973: 24).

According to Halliday, it is through learning how to mean that other aspects of language are acquired. Halliday claims that children do not attend to language as an atomistic, structural phenomenon as most children are expected to when they are taught to read; children are concerned with making sense because it is making sense that enables life to be lived. Thus to talk of language is to talk of the social situation within which meanings are generated.

Most of the language that children experience is embedded in the pursuit of other ends: demanding objects or actions; controlling people and events; mediating relationships; developing a concept of self; asking questions about the world; extending reality through imagination; and informing others. Language is not the focus of these interactions; it is a medium for fulfilling objectives and as such it is somewhat transparent. The child looks through language and sees the social function of the interaction. It is for this reason that children become users, indeed proficient users of language, without achieving what has come to be called linguistic awareness, i.e. an understanding of what language is, rather than an understanding of how it is used.

It could be inferred from Halliday's work that any child brought up in an environment where oral language is not related to social functioning will not be able to talk. It is difficult to conceive of circumstances occurring wherein children are mechanically maintained and subject to long hours of tape-recorded language. It is conceivable that they might imitate some of the sounds but those sounds would not enable them to perform as language users. What is a necessary condition of language learning is the existence of a context where children can grow surrounded by purposeful and meaningful use of language. The facilitators in such situations are other people who not only use language purposefully, but respond to the child as if he were an appropriate user of language.

Two important points must be understood. The first is that the above aspects appear to give the parent the role of instructor. Such 'instruction' bears little relationship to the instruction of schooling. Parents are most unlikely to be instructing in the sense of formulating specific teaching objectives and devising strategies to achieve these objectives. Rather, parents are respondents and participants. Tizard & Hughes (1984) wrote of their study into the home language of young children: 'Some mothers turned games and stories to educational advantage, while a few gave their children formal "lessons". But in most families these occasions were relatively rare' (p. 73). Most studies of young child–adult interaction show that it is usually the child who initiates and terminates the action rather than the parent. The mainly unconscious devices of the parents enable them to follow, extend, elaborate, participate, and create opportunities for language use.

The second point is that this encouragement, support, and facilitation is usually not focused on the mastering of linguistic skills. It is, as has previously been indicated, focused on the pursuit of other activities and the linguistic exercise is embedded within the achievement of those pursuits. Thus games are played not for instruction but because both the child and the parent get pleasure from playing them. Most conversations derive from living an everyday existence which demands cleaning, cooking, shopping, dressing, sleeping and so on. As Tizard and Hughes put it: 'One of our strongest impressions from this study was the amount children learned from simply being around with their mothers; discussing what each was doing, or had done, what they could do next, arguing with each other, and, above all, endlessly asking and answering questions' (Tizard & Hughes, 1984: 73). Even when parents do play a kind of instructional game, for example, 'point to your nose', the emphasis is, in incidents that I have observed, less on the linguistic proficiency and more on the knowledge of the body: parents are pleased because the child has learned where its nose is, rather than because the child can understand the linguistic nature of the question.

From this brief summary of some of the conditions under which oral language emerges, certain principles seem clear:

- Children play the major role in constructing their knowledge of oral language.
- Parents and caregivers greatly facilitate but seldom instruct children in oral language.
- The child is exposed to oral language which is embedded in the pursuit of non-linguistic ends.
- The drive to linguistic competence is the attempt to comprehend and create meanings.
- The conditions for becoming orate are the same as those conditions necessary for developing knowledge of the world.
- Becoming orate depends on social interaction.
- The functions of language understood by children allow them to regulate many aspects of their lives and in turn understand the regulation of their lives by others.

• The experience of language is primarily holistic and any segmented linguistic events that occur are usually the result of child initiation.

The emergence of literacy in context

The question now becomes: 'In what ways are the conditions under which children learn about literacy similar to those for learning about oral language? Are the above principles unique to oral language development or can they be shown to be major factors in the emergence of literacy?

It would seem that if the development of oral language can be seen as a process of learning how to mean, then it becomes possible to see very clear relationships between the emergence of oral language and the emergence of literacy. Literacy, like oral language, exists so that meanings can be created and so that communication can take place between human beings. Literacy events, like oral language events, are mostly explictly, or implicitly, social. Literacy events are, like oral language events, experienced as meaningful and are usually experienced as means to various ends. Most importantly, literacy, like oral language, is experienced as having many uses and functions because it enables the achievement of that variety of ends.

Literacy in the Western world is a fact of everyday existence. To awake and find all print removed from the environment would be an unnerving experience. One cannot opt out of the Western print world. Even adult illiterates have strategies for enlisting help in understanding print; although they may not be able to read it, they are acutely aware of its power and uses. Families which decline to read books do not opt out of the print world. They may still write and receive letters and notes, look at television guides, glance at comics and magazines, receive junk mail and circulars, read labels, follow instructions, buy postage stamps, have print on T-shirts, be given tickets of all kinds, have to fill in forms, collect coupons, receive wage slips, and so on. The failure of many people, both researchers and teachers, to recognise the extent of such activity in bookless homes is a tribute to the ability of print to hide itself within the pursuit of other ends. Indeed so well hidden are some of the literacy-oriented events in homes that Leichter, when commenting on a study of family homes as environments for literacy, noted that the researchers at first overlooked the print displayed on television. As she says: 'Locating literacy events in the stream of everyday family activities is a substantial task, especially if one wishes to avoid defining literacy in terms of previously held conceptions' (Leichter, 1984: 42).

Children's experience of literacy is, for the most part, experience of literacy as part of a complete event. The focus is on the complete event or on the aim of the event. Of course, situations do occur where the focus is directly on the nature of the literacy, just as in oral language the focus can be on the language. Parents do buy alphabet books or other instructional books, particularly as children approach formal schooling. Children themselves often initiate print-focused events, for instance when asking, 'What does that say?' or when they begin to recognise features of their own names. However, the overriding impression is of literacy as part of a larger more meaningful event and this is reflected in their play. 'Ponch' wrote tickets for parking violations (Kammler, 1984), the children in the Hall *et al,* study (1986) wrote to record orders in their restaurants, Paul Bissex wrote to gain his mother's attention (Bissex, 1980), and the children of Trackton read in order to buy groceries (Heath, 1983). A particularly clear example of the way in which literacy is embedded in other activities was recorded by Tizard & Hughes (1984). They reproduce a transcript of a conversation between a mother and her child. The mother had been making a shopping list and was discussing it with the child:

Mother: We've only got that little bit of shopping to get now (shows Pauline the list).

Child: Mummy? Can I have one of them drinks? Can I?

Mother: Get some more drink?

Child: Yeah. Can write it down on there (points to where she wants it written on the list). Up here.

Mother: I'll get you some when I go tomorrow.

Child: Aw! (disappointed)

Mother: All right? Cause I'm not getting it today.

Child: No . . . In the 'Vivo's?

Mother: Haven't got Daddy's money yet.

Child: I've got no money.

Mother: No, I haven't got enough to get my shopping. All of it.

Child: Not all of it?

Mother: Irene's just taken five pounds. She'll bring some change back. If she's got some, she'll bring some change back. It's not enough to get all that. Is it? (points to the shopping list)

Child: No.

Mother: See? So when daddy gets paid I'll get some more money and then I'll go and get the rest.

Child: Yeah. That's nice, isn't it, Mum?

Mother: Mm . . . I got one, two, three, four, five six, seven, eight, nine, ten, eleven, twelve (counts items on list).

Child: (Joins in counting) Nine, ten, eleven.

Mother: Fourteen, fifteen, sixteen, seventeen, eighteen bits.

Child: Mum, let's have a look! (Mother shows the child the list) Do it again.

Mother: We gotta get rice, tea, braising steak, cheese, pickle, carrots, fish, chicken, bread, eggs, bacon, beefburgers, beans . . . Oh Irene's gone to get them (crosses off beans) . . . peas, ham, corned beef.
Child: And what's that (points to word on the list)?
Mother: That's lemon drink (crosses off 'lemon drink'). She's just gone down to get that one. See? (Tizard & Hughes, 1984: 74–5).

This is a very complex episode. A whole range of factors are embedded in the creation of a shopping list. One can see that counting activities and a lot of work in 'economics' are involved. However, a number of literacy-related events also occur. The child witnesses that a written list is a useful way of organising and planning events; that one can redraft written language; that written language is composed of elements; that one can refer back to a written list for information; that there is a relationship between written and oral language. This family was classed by the researchers as working-class and they comment: 'It is often suggested that working-class children do not have much experience of their parents engaging in "literate" activities: yet a shopping list provides an extremely vivid demonstration of the way in which written language may be used within a meaningful human activity. The power of the written word lies in its ability to link up different contexts in space or time, and here it is doing precisely that — forming a link between the home, where the decisions and choices are made, and the shop, where they are carried out. The list can also cope with sudden changes of plan — a friend offering to do some of the shopping leads to some items being crossed off the list. The activity is thus not only emotionally but intellectually more powerful than the labelling of pictures, which is likely to be Pauline's introduction to writing when she starts at infant school' (p. 76).

In oral language emergence the role of parent or caregiver is extremely important, not as an instructor but as a facilitator, through discussion, play and demonstration. Within the field of emergent literacy such behaviour is most evident in book-reading episodes. Book-reading episodes have been extensively studied, mostly because they are fairly obvious and self-contained manifestations of literacy experience. However, it may well be the case that an abundance of similar facilitative behaviour could be found in all the other activities of everyday life, just as in the example already cited from Tizard and Hughes.

Snow (1983) identified three characteristics of parent language behaviour which occurred not only in book-reading but in other literacy events. She terms them 'semantic contingency', 'scaffolding' and 'accountability procedures'. When using semantic contingency, adults continue topics previously introduced by children. Snow says examples of semantic contingency would include: 'Answering questions about letter and number names, answering questions about words, reading out loud on request, answering questions about pictures in books, carrying on coherent conversations with children about the pictures and text in books, and giving help with writing when requested' (p. 168). Snow also found scaffolding of literacy events. The mother in her study extensively scaffolded, for her child, the task of spelling his name 'Nathaniel' by 'reminding him of what they were doing, rejecting false starts and guiding letter search' (p. 170). In this way she constrained the task to allow the child greater success. In 'accountability procedures' the mother makes demands that the task be completed, or that the child displays knowledge that it is known to possess. These three procedures then are not only typical of oral language interaction but also of the interactions which surround literacy events.

Young children's behaviour often shows that they are not simply imitating people around them. When collecting children's accounts of learning to read I found two children who remembered a time before they could 'read'. They told me: 'When I couldn't read I pretended I could read and so everybody thought I was grown up' and: 'I used to pick up my Dad's thick books and sit down and I would flick through the book slowly, pretending to read just looking at the pictures. I used to love doing this. It made me feel big and proud of myself.' Those two children clearly were not simply imitating even though their knowledge had come about partly as a result of observation. Those children had identified what reading looked like, had identified it as a distinct kind of activity, had identified it as an important activity and had identified being able to read as an achievement to be proud of. For them, being literate had social status and was a desirable goal. Thus the activity of 'pretending' to read was actually a more reflective response than simply a crude imitation of an act observed.

References

Bissex, G. (1980) *Gnys at Wrk: A Child Learns to Read and Write*. Cambridge, MA: Harvard University Press.

Clark, M. M. (1976) *Young Fluent Readers*. London: Heinemann Educational Books.

Clay, M. (1982) *Observing Young Readers*. London: Heinemann Educational Books.

Curtis, J. (1984) A teacher's role in Natural Language acquisition. Paper presented at Annual Conference of California Teachers of English, San Jose.

Forester, A. (1977) What teachers can learn from natural readers. *The Reading Teacher* 31, 160–6.

Goddard, N. (1974) *Literacy: Language Experience Approaches*. London: Macmillan.

Gollasch, F. V. (1982) *Language and Literacy: The Selected Writings of Kenneth S. Goodman* Vol. 1 and Vol. 2. London: Routledge and Kegan Paul.

Goodman, K. and Goodman, Y. (1979) Learning to read is natural. In L. Resnick and P. Weaver (eds) *Theory and Practice of Early Reading* Vol. 1. Hillsdale, NJ: Lawrence Erlbaum Associates.

Goodman, K., Goodman, Y. and Burke, C. (1978) Reading for life: The psycholinguistic base. In E. Hunter-Grundin and H. Grundin (eds). *Reading: Implementing the Bullock Report*. London: Ward Lock Educational.

Goodman, Y. (1980) The roots of literacy. In M. P. Douglass (ed.) *Reading: A Humanising Experience*. Claremont: Claremont Graduate School.

Goodman, Y. and Altwerger, B. (1980) Reading: How does it begin? In G. S. Pinnel (ed.) *Discovering Language With Children*. NCTE.

Gundlach, R., McLane, J., Stott, F. and McNamee, G. (1985) The social foundations of children's early writing development. In M. Farr (ed.) *Children's Early Writing Development*. Norwood, NJ: Ablex Publishing Corporation.

Hall, N., May, L., Moores, J., Shearer, J. and Williams, S. (1986) Literacy events in the 'home' corner of a nursery school. Paper given at the World Congress On Reading, London.

Halliday, M. K. (1973) *Explorations in the Function of Language*. London: Edward Arnold.

Heath, S. B. (1983) *Ways With Words: Language, Life, and Work in Communities and Classrooms*. Cambridge: Cambridge University Press.

Holdaway, D. (1979) *The Foundations of Literacy*. Gosford, NSW: Scholastic.

Hoskisson, K. (1979) Learning to read naturally. *Language Arts* 56, 5, 489–96.

Krippner, S. (1963) The boy who read at 18 months. *Exceptional Children*. October.

Leichter, H. J. (1984) Families as environments for literacy. In H. Goelman, A. Oberg and F. Smith (eds) *Awakening to Literacy*. London: Heinemann Educational Books.

Malicky, G. and Norman, C. (1985) Reading processes in natural readers. *Reading–Canada–Lecture* 3, 1, 8–20.

Reid, J. (1958) An investigation into thirteen beginners in reading. *Acta Psychologica* 14, 295–313.

Schmidt, E. and Yates, C. (1985) Benji learns to read naturally! Naturally Benji learns to read. Australian Journal of Reading 8, 3, 121–34.

Smith, F. (1971) *Understanding Reading*. New York: Holt, Rinehart and Winston.

— (1979) The language arts and the learner's mind. *Language Arts* 56, 2, 118–25.

— (1982) *Writing and the Writer*. London: Heinemann Educational Books.

Snow, C. (1983) Literacy and language: Relationships during the pre-school years. *Harvard Educational Review* 53, 2, 165–89.

Stine, S. (1980) Beginning reading naturally. In M. P. Douglass (ed.) *Reading: A Humanising Experience*. Claremont: Claremont Graduate School.

Teale, W. (1982) Towards a theory of how children learn to read and write naturally. *Language Arts* 59, 555–70.

— (1984) Reading to young children: Its significance for literacy development. In H. Goelman, A. Oberg and F. Smith (eds) *Awakening to Literacy*. London: Heinemann Educational Books.

Thorndike, E. L. (1917) Reading as reasoning. *The Journal of Educational Psychology* 8, 323–32.

Tizard, B. and Hughes, M. (1984) *Young Children Learning: Talking and Thinking at Home and School*. London: Fontana.

Torrey, J. W. (1979) Reading that comes naturally: The early reader. In T. G. Waller and G. E. MacKinnon (eds) *Reading Research: Advances in Theory and Practice*. New York: Academic Press.

Walker, C. (1975) *Teaching Prereading Skills*. London: Ward Lock Educational.

3 Media Education: The Limits of a Discourse

DAVID BUCKINGHAM

Discussions of critical pedagogy have often been characterized by an abstract rhetoric. Concepts like 'resistance' and 'empowerment' have been theorized about and debated in extremely scholarly terms, yet with little reference to the complex realities of classroom practice. We know a good deal about the general aims of a critical pedagogy, but much less about how these can be achieved.

The development of media education in British schools provides a valuable case study of many of the dilemmas and contradictions of progressive or critical pedagogy. Throughout its history, media education has been regarded by its advocates as a movement which has sought to bring about radical political changes, both in the consciousness of students and in the education system itself. Some very grand claims have been made about the ability of media teaching to subvert dominant ideologies, to empower the oppressed, and to revolutionize the school curriculum. Yet there remains very little evidence that these claims have been borne out in practice.

In the UK, media education in schools has been very much the poor relation of academic theory. In the 1970s, the establishment of film studies (and subsequently media studies) as academic disciplines in higher education was the major priority of key institutions in the field. Many advocates of media education appeared to subscribe to a 'top-down' model of educational change — a model which was arguably quite inappropriate to the British system, particularly at that time. In effect, it was assumed that academics would generate knowledge, and would then pass it on to teachers, who in turn would hand it down to students. The 'relations of production' of knowledge implied by this approach were clearly hierarchical, and inevitably entailed an authoritarian pedagogy (see Lusted, 1986).

Furthermore, the legitimacy of the new subject depended at least to some extent on its ability to manifest the conventional characteristics of academic scholarship. Academic media theory — like the avant-garde media practice it has often sought to vindicate — has frequently manifested a fundamental contradiction. While often claiming to be 'on the side of the people', it has also displayed a notorious tendency to intellectual obscurantism.

One consequence of this situation is that questions of classroom practice — not merely in schools, but also in higher education itself — have largely been neglected. Paradoxically perhaps, accounts of classroom practice have been conspicuous by their absence from the pages of media education journals. Even today, books about media education tend to take the form of potted summaries of academic research, with 'suggestions for teaching' appended (or not): there is little acknowledgement here of what actually happens when these suggestions are carried out.

For those seeking to promote media education in schools in the late 1970s and early 1980s (e.g. Masterman, 1980; Bethell, 1983), this privileging of academic theory posed considerable problems. As they recognized, working-class students were unlikely to sit passively absorbing the teacher's expositions of theories of ideology, or spontaneously to prefer the political purity of avant-garde film to the ideological delusions of dominant cinema. In practice, there remained a significant danger of media education being perceived as an attack on students' pleasure or on what they regarded as their 'own' culture.

Debates about the pedagogy of media education in the UK have thus inevitably been somewhat limited, although they have often been extremely polarized (see Alvarado, 1981; Masterman 1981/82; Buckingham, 1986; Masterman, 1986; Williamson, 1981/82, 1985). At the risk of caricature, it is possible to identify two contrasting positions here — positions which I would argue are far from unique to media education.[1]

The first of these is based on a belief in the inherent radicalism of media studies as a body of academic knowledge. Media education is seen as a process of 'demystification', which works in two main ways. First, it involves making previously 'hidden' information available to students. Thus, telling students about the ways in which media institutions operate — for example, about how patterns of ownership and control serve to marginalize or exclude oppositional perspectives — is seen as a means of 'opening their eyes' to the covert operations of capitalism.

Second, media education is seen to involve a training in critical analysis, for example using methods derived from structuralism and semiotics. Here too, this is assumed to have an inevitably radical effect. The 'objective' analysis of racist or sexist stereotypes in the media will, it is argued, liberate us from the false ideologies these representations are seen to support and promote.

Theoretically, this approach relies on a view of the media as extremely powerful agents of the 'dominant ideology', and of audiences as passive victims. It is often accompanied by an almost puritanical distrust of the pleasures afforded by popular media — the view that, in the words of one advocate of critical pedagogy, the media are 'the major addictive lure to the flesh-pots of our culture' (Sullivan, 1987).

In terms of educational theory, this approach finds its clearest expression in Entwistle's (1979) account of Gramsci. Entwistle rejects as merely patronizing the notion that the school curriculum should be based on what is immediately 'relevant' to students. Children from subordinate classes, it is argued, need to be given access to formal academic knowledge if they are to participate in and to change the dominant culture. In Entwistle's terms, this approach represents 'conservative schooling for radical politics'.

By contrast, the second position seeks to validate, even to celebrate, aspects of students' culture which are traditionally excluded from the school curriculum. Thus, it is argued that media education, with its focus on 'popular' rather than 'high' culture, is situated in a very different position in terms of the relation between school culture and the culture of the home or peer group. Primarily by virtue of its content, media education has the potential to challenge traditional notions of what counts as valid knowledge and culture. In the process, it is argued, it makes for much more egalitarian relationships between teachers and students: the students are now the 'experts', while the teacher is no longer the main source of authority.

Advocates of this position have increasingly drawn on a 'reader-oriented' approach to media studies. This approach seeks to identify and to celebrate the elements of 'resistance' in the audience's experience of popular media (e.g. Fiske, 1989). While this view provides a valuable corrective to the view of media as propagators of 'false consciousness', many critics have argued that it runs the risk of degenerating into superficiality and mere empty populism (e.g. Morris, 1990).

In terms of educational theory, this approach tends to draw on the 'progressivist' British tradition of English teaching and of creative arts subjects. The rhetoric is one of 'active learning', open-ended investigation, collaborative group-work, discussion and practical production. Far from emphasizing 'objectivity' and a received body of academic knowledge, this approach insists on the necessity of students arriving at their own answers, and exploring their own 'subjective' responses.

While both positions would claim to be politically 'progressive', both would seem to overestimate the possibilities of radical change. As I have argued elsewhere (Buckingham, 1986), the notion of media education as a form of 'demystification' assumes that students will agree that they are 'mystified' and will automatically accept the teacher's attempts to remove the veils of illusion from before their eyes. Yet in practice, working-class students are likely to resist what they regard as the efforts of middle-class teachers to impose their values and beliefs, however 'ideologically sound' these might claim to be (cf. Cohen, 1988; Dewdney & Lister, 1988). To assume that ideologies such as racism and sexism are primarily derived from the media, and that they can simply be overthrown by a good dose of critical analysis is, to say the least, wishful thinking (Richards, 1990).

On the other hand, the 'progressivist' version of media education appears to assume that the power relations of the classroom can easily be abolished, simply by virtue of changing the *content* of the curriculum. Again, this would seem to be a highly utopian view, which concrete studies of classroom practice have seriously questioned (e.g. Hudak, 1987; Buckingham, 1990a). As these studies make clear, there is no inherent reason why studying game shows should make for less hierarchical relations between teachers and students than studying the metaphysical poets.

Furthermore, if the 'demystification' position can easily end up reinforcing existing power relationships between teachers and students, the 'progressivist' version of media education runs the risk of simply leaving students where they are. In my experience, the study of popular media often produces the response 'so what?' While they may find the activity enjoyable, students often complain that they are not actually 'learning' anything from it. The desire merely to celebrate or validate students' existing knowledge can easily result in a form of institutionalized under-achievement.

My account of these two positions has been brief, and thus inevitably oversimplified. In practice, most British advocates of media education in schools have sought a negotiated position between them — although in many cases, this had led to a considerable degree of incoherence and contradiction. On the level of classroom practice, and in syllabuses and teaching materials, there are often tensions between the insistence on an 'objective' body of academic knowledge and the need to adopt more open-ended teaching strategies. We are often careful to assert that 'there are no right answers' while clearly believing that there are (Buckingham *et al.*, 1990).

Ultimately, the problem with both approaches outlined here is their failure to develop an adequate theory of learning. Either learning is something that 'just happens' through a process of osmosis, or it is something which follows inevitably as a result of teaching. If it is to be effective, a critical pedagogy will require a more complex understanding of the relationship between students' existing 'common-sense' knowledge about the media and the more formal academic knowledge made available in schools.

New Definitions — and Further Dilemmas

Despite the increasing constraints on educational innovation, media education in Britain has undergone a considerable expansion over the past decade. While it has consolidated its position in the upper years of secondary schooling, via the increasing popularity of the GCSE (General Certificate of Secondary Education) examination, and now with the advent of A levels, it has also moved into areas of the curriculum hitherto largely untouched.[2] There have been major new initiatives in media education at primary and lower secondary levels, and in the range of vocational and pre-vocational courses being offered both in schools and further education colleges. Perhaps most significantly, the National Curriculum for English contains a substantial component of media education, which provides an important basis for future developments (NCC, 1990).

While any expansion of the subject is broadly to be welcomed, there is a significant risk that the distinct identity of media education will be lost, and the fundamental critical challenge which it poses simply dissipated. For some media educators, the process has involved too many unacceptable compromises (e.g. Masterman, 1989). Yet on the other hand, there are those who would argue that the encounter with other subjects and the expansion into new curriculum spaces raises questions and possibilities which media educators have neglected for far too long.

The developing relationship with English can be seen to contribute to a broader questioning of both subjects which many would regard as long overdue. While most media teachers in British schools are trained as English teachers, and while most English teachers will cover aspects of the media in their teaching, there are many essential theoretical and pedagogic differences between the two areas. Media education poses a fundamental challenge to the élitist and asocial theory of culture on which a great deal of British English teaching is based. It questions many of the basic principles — the notion of 'literature', or the ideology of 'personal response' — which are taken for granted by many English teachers, and offers an approach to studying social production of meaning which is potentially much more rigorous and systematic.

On the other hand, progressive English teaching has developed a more effective and imaginative pedagogy, from which media education — with its frequent reliance on closed 'exercises' and mechanistic approaches to analysis — has a great deal to learn. Yet, as I have argued elsewhere (Buckingham, 1990c, d) bringing together English and media education should be more than a matter of simply combining media education theory with English pedagogy: on the contrary, it will require a thorough rethinking of the aims and methods of both subjects.

While these developments may ultimately prove to be extremely productive, there is nevertheless a risk that they may fatally destabilize media education, or blunt its critical edge. Now, more than ever before, it seems necessary to insist that media education is more than simply a training in technical 'skills', or just another element of English alongside poetry or creative writing.

In this context, the definition of an explicit conceptual framework for media education is crucially important. The development of Media Studies GCSE and the publication of curriculum statements for media education in recent years (Bazalgette, 1989; Bowker, 1991) would appear to mark a growing consensus — and indeed a new confidence — about the nature of the subject field. While there are minor differences between syllabus documents, there is widespread agreement on the 'key concepts' with which media education is concerned. All the syllabuses refer to the four main areas of *media language* (or *codes and conventions*), *representation, institution* (or *agency*) and *audience*.

This definition of media education in terms of concepts — rather than, for example, 'facts' or 'skills' — clearly has significant advantages. It does not specify a given content, thereby enabling the curriculum to remain contemporary and responsive to students' interests and enthusiasms. It makes it possible to compare and contrast different media, and to recognize the connections between them. And it renders the theoretical basis of the subject explicit, both for teachers and students.

At the same time, there are potential dangers here. There is a risk of teaching concepts in isolation from each other, and thus making it difficult for students to recognize the connections between them. Concepts cannot be meaningfully taught without reference to 'facts': any understanding of the structure and operation of media institutions, for example, will be superficial if it is not informed by a certain amount of factual knowledge. Furthermore, it is possible to reduce a set of concepts to a series of abstract definitions — in effect, to a body of 'content' — which can be transmitted and then tested.

Ultimately, the emphasis on conceptual learning raises some quite fundamental epistemological problems. How do we identify what children already know? What do we take as evidence of conceptual understanding? How does conceptual learning happen, and how can we make it happen? These questions have been addressed by the two research projects discussed in the following sections of this paper. Neither claims to be offering easy answers: on the contrary, both projects raise much more difficult questions about the value of the notion of 'conceptual understanding' itself. Nevertheless, as I shall indicate, there may be considerable potential here for moving beyond the rather unproductive opposition between 'conservative' and 'progressive' approaches to critical pedagogy.

Language and Learning

One recent GCSE examination paper in Media Studies required students to provide a definition of the term *representation,* although apparently only one candidate was awarded the full three points.[3] This is, certainly, one kind of evidence of conceptual understanding — although it is one which most teachers would probably regard as pretty inadequate. While it certainly serves as a useful measure of students' ability to regurgitate what teachers have fed them, the ability to use an academic discourse in itself clearly tells us very little about 'understanding'.

In a recent paper (Buckingham, 1990b) I have employed some ideas from Vygotsky and Bruner in an attempt to outline a more productive approach to the question of conceptual learning in media education. Vygotsky (1962) makes an important distinction between what he calls *spontaneous* and *scientific concepts.* Spontaneous concepts are those developed through the child's own mental efforts, while scientific concepts are decisively influenced by adults, and arise from the process of teaching. Scientific concepts — which include social science concepts — are distinct from spontaneous concepts in two major respects. First, they are characterized by a degree of distance from immediate experience: they involve an ability to generalize in systematic ways. Second, they involve self-reflection, or what Bruner terms 'metacognition' — that is, attention not merely to the object to which the concept refers, but also to the thought process itself.

To a certain extent, we might consider children's existing understanding of the media as a body of spontaneous concepts. While these concepts will become more systematic and generalized as they mature, media education might be seen to provide a body of scientific concepts which will enable them to think, and to use language (including 'media language'), in a much more conscious and deliberate way. The aim of media education, then, is not merely to enable children to 'read' — or make sense of — media texts, or to enable them to 'write' their own. It must also enable them to reflect systematically on the processes of reading and writing themselves, to understand and to analyse their own experience as readers and writers.

From this perspective, reflection and self-evaluation would appear to be crucial aspects of learning in media education. It is through reflection that students will be able to make their implicit spontaneous knowledge about the media explicit, and then — with the aid of the teacher and of peers — to reformulate it in terms of broader scientific concepts. Vygotsky argues against the 'direct teaching' of concepts — which he suggests will result in 'nothing but empty verbalism, a parrotlike repetition of words by the child'. Nevertheless, he does argue that children need to be introduced to the terminology of scientific concepts — in effect, to the academic discourse of the subject — and that they will only gradually take this on and come to use it as their own.

Bruner's (1986) notions of 'scaffolding' and 'handover' are both attempts to describe the way in which teachers can enable students to connect spontaneous and scientific concepts. For both writers, dialogue with teachers (along with more competent peers) plays a crucial role. Children do not 'discover' scientific concepts, but are aided in doing so by the systematic interventions of teachers. While Vygotsky certainly emphasizes the importance of 'active learning', he also stresses the importance of teachers enabling children to take on, and participate in, the dominant culture. In this respect, this approach could be seen to transcend the limitations of both 'conservative' and 'progressive' positions.

Nevertheless, there are several unresolved issues here. In particular, there is the question of the relationship between conceptual learning and discourse. From a Vygotskyan perspective, the relationship between language and thought is dialectical. Acquiring or using a particular discourse — for example, the academic discourse of media studies — is seen to serve particular cognitive functions. Thus, as I have indicated, Vygotsky argues that learning the language of scientific concepts enables one to think more systematically and self-reflexively: it serves as a tool which aids understanding.

For example, children will inevitably be making judgements about the modality of media texts — that is, the extent to which they can be seen as 'realistic' — from a very early age (Hodge & Tripp, 1986). These judgements may well depend on a variety of criteria, at least some of which may prove contradictory. The aim of media education would be to encourage children to make these criteria explicit, and enable them to acquire a discourse in which to analyse them — for example, by considering debates about representation, stereotyping, 'positive images' and so on. The end result of this process would not be a fixed 'position' on the question of representation (although unfortunately it often is!) but an understanding of the social and cultural debates which are at stake, and an ability to intervene in them, both through criticism and through practice.

However, recent work in discourse analysis (e.g. Potter & Wetherell, 1987) has taken a more sceptical view of language, which cautions against the notion that language merely 'reflects' cognitive processes such as attitudes or beliefs. From this perspective, acquiring or using a particular discourse has pre-eminently *social* functions: it serves to define the 'self' in relation to others, and is crucially determined by the social and interpersonal context in which it occurs.

Thus, in the context of the classroom, what children and teachers say will inevitably depend on the power relationships which obtain between them — although it will also serve to define and redefine those relationships. For example, as I have argued elsewhere (Buckingham, 1986), students may respond to the propagandist approach of some radical teachers in one of two ways. Either they will choose to play the game, in which case they may learn to reproduce the 'correct' right-on responses without necessarily investigating or questioning their own position. Or they will refuse to do so, in which case they will say things they may or may not believe, simply in order to annoy the teacher and thereby amuse themselves. A good deal of anti-racist and anti-sexist teaching has foundered on precisely this problem: for the majority of working-class students, it represents simply another attempt by middle-class teachers to impose their attitudes and beliefs, often backed up by the disciplinary apparatus of the school (Cohen, 1988).

Similarly, using the specialist terminology of academic discourse can serve as a means of demonstrating one's willingness to play the teacher's game, but it does not necessarily count as evidence of 'understanding'. The decision to adopt a 'critical' discourse about 'the media' — rather than simply talking about the good bits in the video you saw last night, for example — needs to be regarded as a social act, and not merely as evidence of cognitive understanding.

From this perspective, we would need to be much more cautious about the role of language in learning. We would need to question the view of language as a neutral tool for understanding, and the notion of academic discourse as purely 'scientific'. *All* discourse — including academic discourse — would need to be judged in terms of its social functions and effects, rather than merely in terms of its role in cognitive processes.

Indeed, there is a significant danger that an academic discourse — however 'radical' — will seek to replace, rather than build on, the popular discourses through which children already make sense of their experience of the media. The 'subjective' responses of students may simply be invalidated, in favour of the 'objective' analytical approach of the teacher. By defining the students' discourses as merely 'ideological' — and therefore lacking in legitimate status — the 'scientific' discourse of the teacher may come to serve as the only guarantee of critical authority.

Talk, Text and Context: The Social Functions of a Critical Discourse

This relationship between discourse and social context has emerged as one major focus of my current research on the development of 'television literacy'.[4] The research is based on the analysis of small-group discussions about television held with children aged between seven and 12. The study draws on approaches to audience research developed within 'British Cultural Studies', although it seeks to extend that tradition through a much closer and more self-reflexive approach to the role of language. What emerges very clearly from the research is that children's talk about television crucially depends on the context in which it occurs, and the ways in which they perceive that context. In talking about television — in selecting what to talk about and how — children are actively defining themselves in relation to others, both in terms of age and in terms of social factors such as class, 'race' and gender. Yet this process of self-definition is characterized by a considerable degree of diversity and flexibility.

One issue which is particularly relevant here concerns the role of a 'critical' discourse about television. Given the dominant view of children as passive victims of the media, it seems important to acknowledge the fact that children often display considerable critical sophistication in their discussion of television. The extent to which children will adopt a critical discourse depends on how they are choosing to define themselves, both in relation to each other and to the interviewer.

The research I have briefly described here is seeking to construct a rather different theory of 'television literacy', which rejects this normative approach. In common with recent research on print literacy, the emphasis here is on the plurality of literacies, and their social contexts and functions. Literacy is regarded here, not as a set of cognitive 'skills' which live in individuals' heads, but as a set of social practices (Buckingham, 1989). From this perspective, children's 'cognitive understandings' of television cannot be separated from the social contexts in which they are situated, or from their affective investments in the medium.

Demonstrating 'Understanding'

This issue of the relationship between discourse and conceptual understanding has also emerged as a central theme in recent classroom research in media education. The question of what one takes as evidence of conceptual understanding is brought into sharp focus when it comes to evaluation, particularly of students' practical media productions.[5]

While the importance of practical work in media education has increasingly been acknowledged — it forms at least half of most GCSE syllabuses, for example — there remain significant problems in terms of how it is evaluated, not merely by teachers but also by students themselves. Most media syllabuses require a written 'log' or diary to accompany practical projects, yet there is often very little guidance as to the form this should take.

The log appears to serve two main functions. On an instrumental level, it provides a way for examiners to account for the individual contributions of students to what are usually collective projects. More broadly, it should offer students an opportunity to reflect on the experience of practical work — for example, to think about why certain choices were made and the effects these may have had. The written log is intended to encourage students to evaluate their own work, and thereby to draw connections between the 'practical' and 'theoretical' aspects of the course. While conceptual under-standings may only be implicit in the practical projects themselves, they should be much more explicit in the written log.

However, as Grahame (1990) has indicated, there are several problems with this approach. Obviously, the emphasis on a written log discriminates against students who have problems with writing — yet these may be pre-cisely the students who have contributed most effectively to the success of the practical work itself. Yet even for the more 'able' students in Grahame's study, the written evaluation seemed to prove inhibiting and unrewarding. Many of the insights and understandings — and in particular those relating to the social, interpersonal aspects of the process — which Grahame observed in the course of her students' practical work were simply lost when it came to writing.

Grahame contrasts this approach to evaluation with a more open-ended follow-up activity, and with informal classroom discussion: here, students were able to set their own agenda, and to draw on their own experience both as producers and as audiences. As she (1990: 121) argues, the insistence on written evaluation may derive from a kind of insecurity about what students might be learning from practical work:

> However open-ended the project, we seem to need strategies which bring academic knowledge back to us in a safe and acceptable form. But by insisting that students must locate their individual accounts within a predetermined 'objective' framework, we may be putting sev-eral important learning outcomes at risk. It may be that only by allow-ing students to write freely and subjectively about their own personal perceptions of the production process can we begin to reconcile our notions of appropriate learning with what they perceive as important to them.

In my current research, similar questions have arisen in considering the differences between students' work in English and in media studies.[6] This research has involved the in-depth study of two year 10 classes in a working-class London secondary school. Here too, the question of evaluation (by both teachers and students) has brought many of the broader issues into focus.

In contrast to the emphasis on conceptual learning in media education, the aims of English teaching are often defined in terms of the mastery of practices — reading, writing, speaking and listening. Evaluation in English appears to be primarily comparative, and to a large extent intuitive: GCSE syllabuses, for example, require teachers to distinguish between 'vivid' and merely 'effective' pieces of writing, yet the theoretical principles on which these distinctions are based are rarely made explicit (Buckingham, 1990c). By contrast, these students' self-evaluations have been much less concerned with questions of cultural value, and often seem to be based on utilitarian notions of English as a form of vocational training — notions which would be anathema to many English teachers.

On the other hand, evaluation in media studies appears to be much more straightforward: one is assessing students' understanding of the 'key concepts' primarily on the basis of their grasp of the academic discourse of the subject. Yet in practice, the evaluation of students' work — and particularly their practical productions — is much more problematic. These students were often extremely adept at using dominant media genres and conventions for their own purposes. Yet particularly with 'less able' students, who found it much more difficult to articulate the rationale for their own work, we were often left guessing about their intentions.

However, over the longer term, at least some students who had difficulty with writing have progressively come to recognize the benefits of written reflection. While there often remains a sense that self-evaluation is simply a matter of 'stating the obvious', some students have come to acknowledge that writing can enable them to take a more distanced perspective on their own experiences of media production, and to 'discover' things they had not previously recognized. This appears to be much more possible with a more flexible approach to writing, in which theoretical concerns are embedded within more 'personal', expressive language.

Nevertheless, the problem is that what often seems to count in terms of formal assessment is the students' ability to employ an abstract academic discourse. Yet this discourse may not connect with their existing understandings, or with what they themselves regard as important. In this instance, the work which really succeeded in motivating students was that which offered practical opportunities to articulate and to intervene in their own subcultural concerns — for example, those of black music and street fashion. Yet if those concerns cannot be made explicit and 'theorized' in academic terms, they count for very little in terms of assessment. As in my research into television literacy, there is a distinct danger that privileging 'critical' discourses may lead us to neglect the social contexts in which they are acquired and situated, and to undervalue children's affective investments in the media.

Conclusion: The Limits of a Discourse

In this paper, I have raised a series of questions about the value and the consequences of students gaining access to 'critical' academic discourses about the media. Ideally, the acquisition of these discourses should make it possible for students to reflect on their own experience of using the media in a systematic and rigorous way. In Vygotsky's (1962) terms, an academic discourse provides a body of 'scientific concepts' which progressively transforms children's 'spontaneous concepts', and thereby gives them greater control over their own thought processes.

On the other hand, I have argued that 'critical' discourses about the media may also sanction a rationalistic approach to popular culture, which neglects or devalues children's subcultural experiences and their emotional engagements with the media. These discourses often embody a form of intellectual cynicism, and a sense of superiority to 'other people'. They may result merely in a superficial irony or indeed a contempt for popular pleasures which is merely complacent.

The implications of this debate in terms of developing a critical pedagogy in media education remain to be explored. As I have indicated, the Vygotskyan perspective may offer a productive alternative to the rather sterile opposition between advocates of 'progressive' and 'conservative' approaches to critical pedagogy. While acknowledging the central importance of children's existing knowledge and the need for 'active learning', it also stresses the necessity of students acquiring and participating in dominant academic discourse.

Yet the questions I have raised about the social functions and indeed about the limitations of 'critical' discourses also need to be taken on board. Ultimately, while I would agree that giving children access to privileged discourses is vital, it is equally important that they should learn to interrogate them. The claim that academic discourse is inherently 'scientific', and thus superior to the 'ideology' of popular discourse must be open to question. All discourses should be questioned in terms of their social functions and consequences; and the concepts and methods of analysis teachers introduce to students must be seen not as neutral tools for the acquisition of knowledge, but as themselves ideological.

Notes

1. There are significant parallels here with the current debate about 'genre' in English teaching — which itself appears to replay the Bernstein/Rosen debates of the 1970s. Jones (1989) offers a useful account of these general tendencies in critical pedagogy.
2. The GCSE examination is a common examination taken at age 16 (year 11): it replaces GCE (General Certificate of Education) ordinary levels and CSE (Certi-

ficate of Secondary Education). The GCE A level (advanced level) is taken at age 18 (year 13).
3. This question occurred in the London and East Anglian Group GCSE examination paper for 1988.
4. This project is funded by the Economic and Social Research Council, UK (Grant No. R000 221959). I would like to acknowledge the contribution of Valerie Hey and Gemma Moss to this research. My own account of the research will be published in Buckingham (1992). For an account of the theoretical background, see Buckingham (1989); and for a discussion of methodology, see Buckingham (1991).
5. As part of their assessed coursework for Media Studies GCSE and A level courses, students are required to submit a number of practical 'exercises' or productions — for example, short video or audio tapes, still photographs, storyboards, etc. These can count for as much as half of the total assessment.
6. This research is being conducted in collaboration with Julian Sefton-Green.

References

Alvarado, M. (1981) Television studies and pedagogy. *Screen Education* 38, 56–87.
Bazalgette, C. (ed.) (1989) *Primary Media Education: A Curriculum Statement*. London: British Film Institute.
Bethell, A. (1983) Media studies. In J. Miller (ed.) *Eccentric Propositions* (pp. 219–30). London: Routledge.
Bowker, J. (ed.) (1991) *Secondary Media Education: A Curriculum Statement*. London: British Film Institute.
Bruner, J. (1986) *Actual Minds, Possible Worlds*. Cambridge, MA: Harvard University Press.
Buckingham, D. (1986) Against demystification. *Screen* 27 (5), 80–95.
— (1989) Television literacy: A critique. *Radical Philosophy* 51 (Spring), 12–25.
— (1990a) (ed.) *Watching Media Learning: Making Sense of Media Education*. London: Falmer Press.
— (1990b) Making it explicit towards a theory of media learning. In D. Buckingham (ed.) *Watching Media Learning: Making Sense of Media Education* (pp. 215–26). London: Falmer Press.
— (1990c) English and media studies: Making the difference. *The English Magazine* 23 (Summer), 8–12.
— (1990d) English and media studies: Getting together. *The English Magazine* 24, 20–3.
— (1991) What are words worth? Interpreting children's talk about television. *Cultural Studies* 5 (2), 228–45.
— (1992) *Television Literacy: Talk, Text and Context*. London: Falmer Press.
Buckingham, D., Fraser, P. and Mayman, N. (1990) Stepping into the void: Beginning classroom research in media education. In D. Buckingham (ed.) *Watching Media Learning: Making Sense of Media Education* (pp. 19–59). London: Falmer Press.
Cohen, P. (1988) The perversions of inheritance. In P. Cohen and H. S. Bains (eds) *Multi-Racist Britain* (pp. 9–18). London: Macmillan.
Dewdney, A. and Lister, M. (1988) *Youth, Culture and Photography*. London: Macmillan.
Entwistle, H. (1979) *Antonio Gramsci: Conservative Schooling for Radical Politics*. London: Routledge and Kegan Paul.

Fiske, J. (1989) *Understanding Popular Culture*. London: Unwin Hyman.

Grahame, J. (1990) *Playtime:* Learning about media institutions through practical work. In D. Buckingham (ed.) *Watching Media Learning: Making Sense of Media Education* (pp. 101–23). London: Falmer Press.

Hodge, B. and Tripp, D. (1986) *Children and Television: A Semiotic Approach*. Cambridge: Polity Press.

Hudak, G. (1987) Student knowledge and the formation of academic discourse: A case study. In J. Smyth (ed.) *Educating Teachers: Changing the Nature of Pedagogical Knowledge* (pp. 55–69). London: Falmer Press.

Jones, K. (1989) *Right Turn: The Conservative Revolution in Education*. London: Hutchinson.

Lusted, D. (1986) Why pedagogy? *Screen* 27 (5), 2–14.

Masterman, L. (1980) *Teaching About Television*. London: Macmillan.

— (1981/2) TV pedagogy. *Screen Education* 40, 88–92.

— (1986) Reply to David Buckingham. *Screen* 27 (5), 96–100.

— (1989) Illumination. *Times Educational Supplement* 24 April.

Morris, M. (1990) Banality in cultural studies. In P. Mellencamp (ed.) *Logics of Television: Essays in Cultural Criticism* (pp. 14–43). London: BFI Publishing.

National Curriculum Council (1990) *English: Non-Statutory Guidance*. York: National Curriculum Council.

Potter, J. and Wetherell, M. (1987) *Discourse and Social Psychology*. London: Sage.

Richards, C. (1990) Intervening in popular pleasures: Media Studies and the politics of subjectivity. In D. Buckingham (ed.) *Watching Media Learning: Making Sense of Media Education* (pp. 151–68). London: Falmer Press.

Sullivan, E. V. (1987) Critical pedagogy and television. In David W. Livingstone and Contributors *Critical Pedagogy and Cultural Power* (pp. 57–76). London: Macmillan.

Vygotsky, L. (1962) *Thought and Language*. Cambridge, MA: MIT Press.

Williamson, J. (1981/2) How does girl number twenty understand ideology? *Screen Education* 40 (Autumn-Winter), 80–87.

— (1985) Is there anyone here from a classroom? *Screen* 26 (1), 90–95.

4 Extracts from
Thought and Language
and
Mind and Society

L. S. VYGOTSKY

Extracts from *Thought and Language*

The development of thinking

We now turn to those positive conclusions that can be drawn from our critique of Piaget's theory.

Limited in scope as our findings are, we believe that they help one to see in a new and broader perspective the general direction of the development of speech and thought. In Piaget's view, the two functions follow a common path, from autistic to socialized speech, from subjective fantasy to the logic of relations. In the course of this change, the influence of adults is deformed by the psychic processes of the child, but it wins out in the end. The development of thought is, to Piaget, a story of the gradual socialization of deeply intimate, personal, autistic mental states. Even social speech is represented as following, not preceding, egocentric speech.

The hypothesis we propose reverses this course. Let us look at the direction of thought development during one short interval, from the appearance of egocentric speech to its disappearance, in the framework of language development as a whole.

We consider that the total development runs as follows: The primary function of speech, in both children and adults, is communication, social contact. The earliest speech of the child is therefore essentially social. At first it is global and multifunctional; later its functions become differentiated. At a certain age the social speech of the child is quite sharply divided into egocentric speech and communicative speech. (We prefer to use the term *communicative* for the form of speech that Piaget calls *socialized,* as though it had been something else before becoming social. From our point of view, the two forms, communicative and egocentric, are both social, though their functions differ.) Egocentric speech emerges when the child transfers social, collaborative forms of behavior to the sphere of inner-personal psychic functions. The child's tendency to transfer to his inner processes the behavior patterns that formerly were social is well known to Piaget. He describes in another context how arguments between children give rise to the beginnings of logical reflection. Something similar happens, we believe, when the child starts conversing with himself as he has been doing with others. When circumstances force him to stop and think, he is likely to think aloud. Egocentric speech, splintered off from general social speech, in time leads to inner speech, which serves both autistic and logical thinking.

Egocentric speech as a separate linguistic form is the highly important genetic link in the transition from vocal to inner speech, an intermediate stage between the differentiation of the functions of vocal speech and the final transformation of one part of vocal speech into inner speech. It is this transitional role of egocentric speech that lends it such great theoretical interest. The whole conception of speech development differs profoundly in accordance with the interpretation given to the role of egocentric speech. Thus our schema of development — first social, then egocentric, then inner speech — contrasts both with the traditional behaviorist schema — vocal speech, whisper, inner speech — and with Piaget's sequence — from nonverbal autistic thought through egocentric thought and speech to socialized speech and logical thinking.

We see how different is the picture of the development of the child's speech and thought depending on what is considered to be a starting point of such development. In our conception, the true direction of the development of thinking is not from the individual to the social, but from the social to the individual.

We shall now summarize our investigation of inner speech. We came to the conclusion that inner speech develops through a slow accumulation of functional and structural changes, that it branches off from the child's external speech simultaneously with the differentiation of the social and the egocentric functions of speech, and finally that the speech structures mastered by the child become the basic structures of his thinking.

This brings us to another indisputable fact of great importance: Thought development is determined by language, i.e. by the linguistic tools of thought and by the sociocultural experience of the child. Essentially, the development of inner speech depends on outside factors; the development of logic in the child, as Piaget's studies have shown, is a direct function of his socialized speech. The child's intellectual growth is contingent on his mastering the social means of thought, that is, language.

We can now formulate the main conclusions to be drawn from our analysis. If we compare the early development of speech and intellect with the development of inner speech and verbal thought, we must conclude that the later stage is not a simple continuation of the earlier. *The nature of the development itself changes,* from biological to sociohistorical. Verbal thought is not an innate, natural form of behavior, but is determined by a historical-cultural process and has specific properties and laws that cannot be found in the natural forms of thought and speech. Once we acknowledge the historical character of verbal thought, we must consider it subject to all the premises of historical materialism, which are valid for any historical phenomenon in human society. It is only to be expected that on this level the development of behavior will be governed essentially by the general laws of the historical development of human society.

The problem of thought and language thus extends beyond the limits of natural science and becomes the focal problem of historical human psychology, i.e. of social psychology.

The development of concepts

Our experimental study proved that it is a functional use of the word, or any other sign, as means of focusing one's attention, selecting distinctive features, and analyzing and synthesizing them, that plays a central role in concept formation.

Concept formation is the result of such a complex activity, in which all basic intellectual functions take part. This process cannot, therefore, be reduced either to association, attention, imagery and judgment or determining tendencies. All these moments are indispensable, but they are insufficient without the use of a sign, or word. Words and other signs are those means that direct our mental operations, control their course, and channel them toward the solution of the problem confronting us.

None of the above mentioned functions undergoes any substantial change in adolescence. But once they became involved in the process of concept formation, they appear in it in an entirely new form. They enter it not as independent entities, with their own logic of development, but as subordinated functions whose performance is mediated by word or sign. It is in this new role that these functions contribute to the process of problem solving, simultaneously entering into such new interrelations with each other that only can reveal their true functional psychological meaning.

We may say, therefore, that neither the growth of the number of associations, nor the strengthening of attention, nor the accumulation of images

and representations, nor determining tendencies — that none of these processes, however advanced they might be, can lead to concept formation.
Real concepts are impossible without words, and thinking in concepts does
not exist beyond verbal thinking. That is why the central moment in concept
formation, and its generative cause, is a specific use of words as functional
'tools'.

Unlike the development of instincts, thinking and behavior of adolescents
are prompted not from within but from without, by the social milieu. The
tasks with which society confronts an adolescent as he enters the cultural,
professional, and civic world of adults undoubtedly become an important
factor in the emergence of conceptual thinking. If the milieu presents no
such tasks to the adolescent, makes no new demands on him, and does not
stimulate his intellect by providing a sequence of new goals, his thinking fails
to reach the highest stages, or reaches them with great delay.

The cultural task *per se*, however, does not explain the development
mechanism itself that results in concept formation. The investigator must
aim to understand the intrinsic bonds between the external tasks and the
developmental dynamics, and view concept formation as a function of the
adolescent's total social and cultural growth, which affects not only the content but also the method of his thinking. The new significative use of the
word, its use *as a means of concept formation,* is the immediate psychological
cause of the radical change in the intellectual process that occurs on the
threshold of adolescence.

No new *elementary* function, essentially different from those already present, appears at this age, but all existing functions are incorporated into a
new structure, form a new synthesis, become parts of a new complex whole;
the laws governing this whole also determine the destiny of each individual
part. Learning to direct one's own mental processes with the aid of words or
signs is an integral part of the process of concept formation.

From thought to word

We can now return to the definition of inner speech that we proposed
before presenting our analysis. Inner speech is not the interior aspect of
external speech — it is a function in itself. It still remains speech, i.e. thought
connected with words. But while in external speech thought is embodied in
words, in inner speech words die as they bring forth thought. Inner speech
is to a large extent thinking in pure meanings. It is a dynamic, shifting,
unstable thing, fluttering between word and thought, the two more or less
stable, more or less firmly delineated components of verbal thought. Its true
nature and place can be understood only after examining the next plane of
verbal thought, the one still more inward than inner speech.

That plane is thought itself. As we have said, every thought creates a connection, fulfills a function, solves a problem. The flow of thought is not accompanied by a simultaneous unfolding of speech. The two processes are not identical, and there is no rigid correspondence between the units of thought and speech. This is especially obvious when a thought process miscarries — when, as Dostoevsky put it, a thought 'will not enter words'.

Here one literary example will be appropriate. Gleb Uspensky's character, a poor peasant, who must address an official with some life-important issue, cannot put his thoughts into words. Embarrassed by his failure, he retreats and prays, asking the Lord 'to give him a concept'. This scene leaves the reader disturbed and depressed. But in its essence, the problem facing this poor and illiterate peasant is of the same kind constantly hounding thinkers and writers: How to put thoughts into words. Sometimes even the speech of Uspensky's character starts to resemble that of a poet: 'I would tell you all of this, my friend, concealing nothing . . . but, you know, folks of my kind cannot talk . . . It is as if they are all here, in my head, but cannot slip from the tongue. That is our, fools', sorrow' (Gleb Uspensky, 1949: 184).

In this fragment, the watershed between thoughts and words becomes highly visible. If thoughts were identical in structure and development with speech, the case described by Uspensky would be impossible.

Experience teaches us that thought does not express itself in words, but rather realizes itself in them. Sometimes such realization cannot be accomplished, as in the case of Uspensky's character. We must ask: Does this character know what he is going to think about? Yes, but he does it as one who wants to remember something but is unable to. Does he start thinking? Yes, but again he does it as one who is absorbed by remembering. Does he succeed in turning his thought into a process? No. The problem is that thought is mediated by signs externally, but it also is mediated internally, this time by word meanings. Direct communication between minds is impossible, not only physically but psychologically. Communication can be achieved only in a roundabout way. Thought must first pass through meanings and openly then through words.

We come now to the last step in our analysis of inner planes of verbal thought. Thought is not the superior authority in this process. Thought is not begotten by thought; it is engendered by motivation, i.e. by our desires and needs, our interests and emotions. Behind every thought there is an affective-volitional tendency, which holds the answer to the last 'why' in the analysis of thinking. A true and full understanding of another's thought is possible only when we understand its affective-volitional basis. We shall illustrate this by an example: the interpretation of parts in a play. Stanislavsky, in his instructions to actors, listed the motives behind the words of their parts for A. Griboedov's *Woe from Wit,* Act I:

Text of the Play	*Parallel Motives*
Sophya:	
O, Chatsky, but I am glad you've come	Tries to hide her confusion
Chatsky:	
You are glad, that's very nice; But gladness such as yours not easily one tells. It rather seems to me, all told, That making man and horse catch cold I've pleased myself and no one else	Tries to make her feel guilty by teasing her. Aren't you ashamed of yourself! Tries to force her to be frank.
Liza:	
There, sir, and if you'd stood on the same landing here Five minutes, no, not five ago You'd heard your name clear as clear. You say, Miss! Tell him it was so.	Tries to calm him. Tries to help Sophya in a difficult situation.
Sophya:	
And always so, no less, no more. No, as to that, I'm sure you can't reproach me.	Tries to reassure Chatsky. I am not guilty of anything!
Chatsky:	
Well, let's suppose it's so. Thrice blessed who believes. Believing warms the heart.	Let us stop this conversation; etc.

To understand another's speech, it is not sufficient to understand his words — we must understand his thought. But even that is not enough — we must also know its motivation. No psychological analysis of an utterance is complete until that plane is reached.

We have come to the end of our analysis; let us survey its results. Verbal thought appeared as a complex, dynamic entity, and the relation of thought and word within it as a movement through a series of planes. Our analysis followed the process from the outermost plane to the innermost plane. In reality, the development of verbal thought takes the opposite course: from the motive that engenders a thought to the shaping of the thought, first in inner speech then in meanings of words, and finally in words. It would be a mistake, however, to imagine that this is the only road from thought to word. The development may stop at any point in its complicated course: an infinite variety of movements to and fro, of ways still unknown to us, is possible. A study of these manifold variations lies beyond the scope of our present task.

We cannot close our study without mentioning the perspectives that our investigation opens up. This is even more momentous a problem than that of thinking; what I mean is the problem of consciousness. We studied the inward aspects of speech, which were as unknown to science as the other side of the moon. We tried to establish the connection between word and object, word and reality. We attempted to study experimentally the dialectics of transition from perception to thinking, and to show that a generalized reflection of reality is the basic characteristic of words. This aspect of the word brings us to the threshold of a wider and deeper subject, i.e. the problem of relation between word and consciousness. If perceptive consciousness and intellectual consciousness reflect reality differently, then we have two different forms of consciousness. *Thought and speech turn out to be the key to the nature of human consciousness.*

If language is as old as consciousness itself, and if language is a practical consciousness-for-others and, consequently, consciousness-for-myself, then not only one particular thought but all consciousness is connected with the development of the word. The word is a thing in our consciousness, as Ludwig Feuerbach put it, that is absolutely impossible for one person, but that becomes a reality for two. The word is a direct expression of the historical nature of human consciousness.

Consciousness is reflected in a word as the sun in a drop of water. A word relates to consciousness as a living cell relates to a whole organism, as an atom relates to the universe. A word is a microcosm of human consciousness.

References

Piaget, J. (1955) *The Language and Thought of the Child.* New York: Meridian.
Stanislavsky, K. (1961) *Creating a Role.* New York: Theater Art Books.
Uspensky, G. (1949) *Izbrannye proizuedeniia* (Collected Works). Moscow.

Interaction between Learning and Development (from *Mind and Society*)

Zone of proximal development: A new approach

That children's learning begins long before they attend school is the starting point of this discussion. Any learning a child encounters in school always has a previous history. For example, children begin to study arithmetic in school, but long beforehand they have had some experience with quantity — they have had to deal with operations of division, addition, subtraction, and determination of size. Consequently, children have their own preschool arithmetic, which only myopic psychologists could ignore.

It goes without saying that learning as it occurs in the preschool years differs markedly from school learning, which is concerned with the assimilation of the fundamentals of scientific knowledge. But even when, in the period of her first questions, a child assimilates the names of objects in her environment, she is learning. Indeed, can it be doubted that children learn speech from adults; or that, through asking questions and giving answers, children acquire a variety of information; or that, through imitating adults and through being instructed about how to act, children develop an entire repository of skills? Learning and development are interrelated from the child's very first day of life.

Koffka, attempting to clarify the laws of child learning and their relation to mental development, concentrates his attention on the simplest learning processes, those that occur in the preschool years. His error is that, while seeing a similarity between preschool and school learning, he fails to discern the difference — he does not see the specifically new elements that school learning introduces. He and others assume that the difference between preschool and school learning consists of non-systematic learning in one case and systematic learning in the other. But 'systematicness' is not the only issue; there is also the fact that school learning introduces something fundamentally new into the child's development. In order to elaborate the dimensions of school learning, we will describe a new and exceptionally important concept without which the issue cannot be resolved: the zone of proximal development.

A well known and empirically established fact is that learning should be matched in some manner with the child's developmental level. For example, it has been established that the teaching of reading, writing, and arithmetic should be initiated at a specific age level. Only recently, however, has attention been directed to the fact that we cannot limit ourselves merely to determining developmental levels if we wish to discover the actual relations of the developmental process to learning capabilities. We must determine at least two developmental levels.

The first level can be called the *actual developmental level,* that is, the level of development of a child's mental functions that has been established as a result of certain already *completed* developmental cycles. When we determine a child's mental age by using tests, we are almost always dealing with the actual developmental level. In studies of children's mental development it is generally assumed that only those things that children can do on their own are indicative of mental abilities. We give children a battery of tests or a variety of tasks of varying degrees of difficulty, and we judge the extent of their mental development on the basis of how they solve them and at what level of difficulty. On the other hand, if we offer leading questions or show how the problem is to be solved and the child then solves it, or if the teacher initiates the solution and the child completes it or solves it in collaboration with other children — in short, if the child barely misses an independent solution of the problem — the solution is not regarded as indicative of his mental development. This 'truth' was familiar and reinforced by common sense. Over a decade even the profoundest thinkers never questioned the assumption; they never entertained the notion that what children can do with the assistance of others might be in some sense even more indicative of their mental development than what they can do alone.

Let us take a simple example. Suppose I investigate two children upon entrance into school, both of whom are ten years old chronologically and eight years old in terms of mental development. Can I say that they are the same age mentally? Of course. What does this mean? It means that they can independently deal with tasks up to the degree of difficulty that has been standardized for the eight-year-old level. If I stop at this point, people would imagine that the subsequent course of mental development and of school learning for these children will be the same, because it depends on their intellect. Of course, there may be other factors, for example, if one child was sick for half a year while the other was never absent from school; but generally speaking, the fate of these children should be the same. Now imagine that I do not terminate my study at this point, but only begin it. These children seem to be capable of handling problems up to an eight-year-old's level, but not beyond that. Suppose that I show them various ways of dealing with the problem. Different experimenters might employ different modes of demonstration in different cases: some might run through an entire demonstration and ask the children to repeat it, others might initiate the solution and ask the child to finish it, or offer leading questions. In short, in some way or another I propose that the children solve the problem with my assistance. Under these circumstances it turns out that the first child can deal with problems up to a twelve-year-old's level, the second up to a nine-year-old's. Now, are these children mentally the same?

When it was first shown that the capability of children with equal levels of mental development to learn under a teacher's guidance varied to a high degree, it became apparent that those children were not mentally the same age and that the subsequent course of their learning would obviously be different. This difference between twelve and eight, or between nine and eight, is what we call *the zone of proximal development. It is the distance between the actual developmental level as determined by independent problem solving and the level of potential development as determined through problem solving under adult guidance or in collaboration with more capable peers.*

If we naïvely ask what the actual development level is, or, to put it more simply, what more independent problem solving reveals, the most common answer would be that a child's actual developmental level defines functions that have already matured, that is, the end products of development. If a child can do such-and-such independently, it means that the functions for such-and-such have matured in her. What, then, is defined by the zone of proximal development, as determined through problems that children cannot solve independently but only with assistance? The zone of proximal development defines those functions that have not yet matured but are in the process of maturation, functions that will mature tomorrow but are currently in an embryonic state. These functions could be termed the 'buds' or 'flowers' of development rather than the 'fruits' of development. The actual developmental level characterizes mental development retrospectively, while the zone of proximal development characterizes mental development prospectively.

The zone of proximal development furnishes psychologists and educators with a tool through which the internal course of development can be understood. By using this method we can take account of not only the cycles and maturation processes that have already been completed but also those processes that are currently in a state of formation, that are just beginning to mature and develop. Thus, the zone of proximal development permits us to delineate the child's immediate future and his dynamic developmental state, allowing not only for what already has been achieved developmentally but also for what is in the course of maturing. The two children in our example displayed the same mental age from the viewpoint of developmental cycles already completed, but the developmental dynamics of the two were entirely different. The state of a child's mental development can be determined only be clarifying its two levels: the actual developmental level and the zone of proximal development.

I will discuss one study of preschool children todemonstrate that what is in the zone of proximal development today will be the actual developmental level tomorrow — that is, what a child can do with assistance today she will be able to do by herself tomorrrow.

The American researcher Dorothea McCarthy showed that among children between the ages of three and five there are two groups of functions: those the children already possess, and those they can perform under guidance, in groups, and in collaboration with one another but which they have not mastered independently. McCarthy's study demonstrated that this second group of functions is at the actual developmental level of five-to-seven-year-olds. What her subjects could do only under guidance, in collaboration, and in groups at the age of three-to-five years they could do independently when they reached the age of five-to-seven years. Thus, if we were to determine only mental age — that is, only functions that have matured — we would have but a summary of completed development, while if we determine the maturing functions, we can predict what will happen to these children between five and seven, provided the same developmental conditions are maintained. The zone of proximal development can become a powerful concept in developmental research, one that can markedly enhance the effectiveness and utility of the application of diagnostics of mental development to educational problems.

A full understanding of the concept of the zone of proximal development must result in reevaluation of the role of imitation in learning. An unshakeable tenet of classical psychology is that only the independent activity of children, not their imitative activity, indicates their level of mental development. This view is expressed in all current testing systems. In evaluating mental development, consideration is given to only those solutions to test problems which the child reaches without the assistance of others, without demonstrations, and without leading questions. Imitation and learning are thought of as purely mechanical processes. But recently psychologists have shown that a person can imitate only that which is within her developmental level. For example, if a child is having difficulty with a problem in arithmetic and the teacher solves it on the blackboard, the child may grasp the solution in an instant. But if the teacher were to solve a problem in higher mathematics, the child would not be able to understand the solution no matter how many times she imitated it.

Animal psychologists, and in particular Köhler, have dealt with this question of imitation quite well. Köhler's special experiments, designed to determine what primates could imitate, reveal that primates can use imitation to solve only those problems that are of the same degree of difficulty as those they can solve alone. However, Köhler failed to take account of an important fact, namely, that primates cannot be taught (in the human sense of the word) through imitation, nor can their intellect be developed, because they have no zone of proximal development. A primate can learn a great deal through training by using its mechanical and mental skills, but it cannot be made more intelligent, that is, it cannot be taught to solve a variety of more advanced problems independently. For this reason animals are incapable of learning in the human sense of the term; *human learning presupposes a specific social nature and a process by which children grow into the intellectual life of those around them.*

Children can imitate a variety of actions that go well beyond the limits of their own capabilities. Using imitation, children are capable of doing much more in collective activity or under the guidance of adults. This fact, which seems to be of little significance in itself, is of fundamental importance in that it demands a radical alteration of the entire doctrine concerning the relation between learning and development in children. One direct consequence is a change in conclusions that may be drawn from diagnostic tests of development.

Formerly, it was believed that by using tests, we determine the mental development level with which education should reckon and whose limits it should not exceed. This procedure oriented learning toward yesterday's development, toward developmental stages already completed. The error of this view was discovered earlier in practice than in theory. It is demonstrated most clearly in the teaching of mentally retarded children. Studies have established that mentally retarded children are not very capable of abstract thinking. From this the pedagogy of the special school drew the seemingly correct conclusion that all teaching of such children should be based on the use of concrete, look-and-do methods. And yet a considerable amount of experience with this method resulted in profound disillusionment. It turned out that a teaching system based solely on concreteness — one that eliminated from teaching everything associated with abstract thinking — not only failed to help retarded children overcome their innate handicaps but also reinforced their handicaps by accustoming children exclusively to concrete thinking and thus suppressing the rudiments of any abstract thought that such children still had. Precisely because retarded children, when left to themselves, will never achieve well-elaborated forms of abstract thought, the school should make every effort to push them in that direction and to develop in them what is intrinsically lacking in their own development.

Similarly, in normal children, learning which is oriented toward developmental levels that have already been reached is ineffective from the viewpoint of a child's overall development. It does not aim for a new stage of the developmental process but rather lags behind this process. Thus, the notion of a zone of proximal development enables us to propound a new formula, namely that the only 'good learning' is that which is in advance of development.

The acquisition of language can provide a paradigm for the entire problem of the relation between learning and development. Language arises initially as a means of communication between the child and the people in his environment. Only subsequently, upon conversion to internal speech, does it come to organize the child's thought, that is, become an internal mental function. Piaget and others have shown that reasoning occurs in a children's group as an argument intended to prove one's own point of view before it occurs as an internal activity whose distinctive feature is that the child begins to perceive and check the basis of his thoughts. Such observations prompted Piaget to conclude that communication produces the need for checking and confirming thoughts, a process that is characteristic of adult thought. In the same way that internal speech and reflective thought arise from the interactions between the child and persons in her environment, these interactions provide the source of development of a child's voluntary behavior. Piaget has shown that cooperation provides the basis for the development of a child's moral judgment. Earlier research established that a child first becomes able to subordinate her behavior to rules in group play and only later does voluntary self-regulation of behavior arise as an internal function.

These individual examples illustrate a general developmental law for the higher mental functions that we feel can be applied in its entirety to children's learning processes. We propose than an essential feature of learning is that it creates the zone of proximal development; that is, learning awakens a variety of internal developmental processes that are able to operate only when the child is interacting with people in his environment and in cooperation with his peers. Once these processes are internalized, they become part of the child's independent developmental achievement.

From this point of view, learning is not development; however, properly organized learning results in mental development and sets in motion a variety of developmental processes that would be impossible apart from learning. Thus, learning is a necessary and universal aspect of the process of developing culturally organized, specifically human, psychological functions.

To summarize, the most essential feature of our hypothesis is the notion that developmental processes do not coincide with learning processes. Rather, the developmental process lags behind the learning process; this sequence then results in zones of proximal development. Our analysis alters the traditional view that at the moment a child assimilates the meaning of a word, or masters an operation such as addition or written language, her developmental processes are basically completed. In fact, they have only just begun at that moment. The major consequence of analyzing the educational process in this manner is to show that the initial mastery of, for example, the four arithmetic operations provides the basis for the subsequent development of a variety of highly complex internal processes in children's thinking.

Our hypothesis establishes the unity but not the identity of learning processes and internal developmental processes. It presupposes thatthe one is converted into the other. Therefore, it becomes an important concern of psychological research to show how external knowledge and abilities in children become internalized.

Any investigation explores some sphere of reality. An aim of the psychological analysis of development is to describe the internal relations of the intellectual processes awakened by school learning. In this respect, such analysis will be directed inward and is analogous to the use of x-rays. If successful, it should reveal to the teacher how developmental processes stimulated by the course of school learning are carried through inside the head of each individual child. The revelation of this internal, subterranean developmental network of school subjects is a task of primary importance for psychological and educational analysis.

A second essential feature of our hypothesis is the notion that, although learning is directly related to the course of child development, the two are never accomplished in equal measure or in parallel. Development in children never follows school learning the way a shadow follows the object that casts it. In actuality, there are highly complex dynamic relations between developmental and learning processes that cannot be encompassed by an unchanging hypothetical formulation.

References

Koffka, K. (1924) *The Growth of the Mind*. London: Routledge and Kegan Paul.
Kohler, W. (1925) *Mentality of Apes*. New York: Harcourt, Brace.
McCarthy, D. (1930) *The Language Development of the Pre-School Child*. Minnesota: University of Minnesota Press.
Piaget, J. (1955) *The Language and Thought of the Child*. New York: Meridian Books. Also International Library of Psychology (1925).

5 From Communicating to Talking

JEROME BRUNER, with the assistance of Rita Watson

If we are to consider the transition from prelinguistic communication to language, particularly with a concern for possible continuities, we had better begin by taking as close a look as we can at the so-called 'original endowment' of human beings. Might that endowment affect the acquisition and early use of language? I do not mean simply the prelinguistic precursors of grammar or an 'innate capacity' for language. The question must be a more general one. What predisposes a living being to use language and be changed by its use? Suppose we grant that there is some innate capacity to master language as a symbolic system, as Noam Chomsky urged, or even to be predisposed toward particular linguistic distinctions, as Derek Bickerton has recently proposed? Why is language used? After all, chimpanzees have some of the same capacities and they don't use them.

The awkward dilemma that plagues questions about the original nature and later growth of human faculties inheres in the unique nature of human competence. For human competence is both biological in origin and cultural in the means by which it finds expression. While the *capacity* for intelligent action has deep biological roots and a discernible evolutionary history, the *exercise* of that capacity depends upon man appropriating to himself modes of acting and thinking that exist not in his genes but in his culture. There is obviously something in 'mind' or in 'human nature' that mediates between the genes and the culture that makes it possible for the latter to be a prosthetic device for the realization of the former.

When we ask then about the endowment of human beings, the question we put must be twofold. We must ask not only about capacities, but also about how humans are aided in expressing them in the medium of culture. The two questions, of course, are inseparable, since human intellectual capacity necessarily evolved to fit man for using the very prosthetic devices that a culture develops and accumulates for the enablement of its members.

There is some point in studying early human capacities and their development in seemingly cultureless laboratories, as if they were simply expressions of man's biological dispositions and endowment. But we must also

59

bear in mind that the realization of this endowment depends on the tool kit of the culture, whatever we choose to do in the laboratory. The main trend of the last quarter century has been to look increasingly at the contexts that enable human beings to act as they do; increasingly, we can see the futility of considering human nature as a set of autonomous dispositions.

I can easily outline what seems to me, at least, to be 'infant endowment' in the so-called cognitive sphere. But to do so relevantly I must focus on those aspects that fit and perhaps even compel human beings to operate in the culture. For I think that it is the requirement of *using* culture as a necessary form of coping that forces man to master language. Language is the means for interpreting and regulating the culture. The interpreting and negotiating start the moment the infant enters the human scene. It is at this stage of interpretation and negotiation that language acquisition is acted out. So I shall look at 'endowment' from the point of view of how it equips the infant to come on stage in order to acquire the means for taking his place in culture.

Initial Cognitive Endowment

Let me begin with some more or less 'firm' conclusions about perception, skill, and problem solving in the prelinguistic infant and consider how they might conceivably predispose the child to acquire 'culture' through language.

The first of these conclusions is that much of the cognitive processing going on in infancy appears to operate in support of goal-directed activity. From the start, the human infant is *active* in seeking out regularities in the world about him. The child is active in a uniquely human way, converting experience into species-typical means-end structures. Let me begin with the unlikely example of nonnutritive sucking.

The human infant, like mammals generally, is equipped with a variety of biological processes that ensure initial feeding, initial attachment to a caretaker, initial sensory contact with the world — all quite well buffered to prevent the infant from overreacting. Nonnutritive sucking, an example of one of these buffering mechanisms, has the effect of relaxing large muscle groups, stilling movements of the gut, reducing the number of eye movements in response to excessively patterned visual fields, and in general assuring the maintenance of a moderate level of arousal in the face of even a demanding environment. That much is probably 'hard-wired'.

But such sucking soon comes under the child's own control. Infants as young as five to six weeks are quite capable, we found, of sucking on a pacifier nipple in order to bring a visual display from blur into focus —

increasing their rate of sucking well above baseline when the picture's focus is made contingent on speed of sucking. Sucking and looking, moreover, are coordinated to assure a good view. When babies suck to produce clarity, they suck as they look, and when they stop they soon learn to look away. The same infants, when their sucking in a later session produces blur, suck while looking away from the blurred picture their sucking is producing and desist from sucking while looking at the picture. (We should note, by the way, that infants do not like blurred pictures.)

Infants' behaviour from early on is guided by active means-end readiness and by search. To say that infants are also 'social' is to be banal. They are geared to respond to the human voice, to the human face, to human action and gesture. Their means-end readiness is easily and quickly brought into coordination with the actions of their caretakers. The pioneering work of Daniel Stern and Berry Brazelton and their colleagues underlines how early and readily activated infants are by the adults with whom they interact and how quickly their means-end structuring encompasses the actions of another. The infant's principal 'tool' for achieving his ends is another familiar human being. In this respect, human infants seem more socially interactive than any of the Great Apes, perhaps to the same degree that Great Apes are more socially interactive than Old or New World Monkeys, and this may be a function of their prolonged and uniquely dependent form of immaturity, as I have argued elsewhere (1974).

Infants are, in a word, tuned to enter the world of human action. Obvious though the point may seem, we shall see that it has enormous consequences for the matter at hand. This leads directly to the second conclusion about infant 'endowment'.

It is obvious that an enormous amount of the activity of the child during the first year and a half of life is extraordinarily social and communicative. Social interaction appears to be both self-propelled and self-rewarding. Many students of infant behaviour, like Tom Bower, have found that a social response to the infant is the most powerful reinforcer one can use in ordinary learning experiments. And withholding social response to the child's initiatives is one of the most disruptive things one can do to an infant — e.g. an unresponding face will soon produce tears. Even in the opening weeks of life the infant has the capacity to imitate facial and manual gestures (as Andrew Meltzoff has shown); they respond with distress if their mothers are masked during feeding; and, they show a sensitivity to expression in the mother by turn taking in vocalization when their level of arousal is moderate and by simultaneous expression when it is high.

While the child's attachment to the mother (or caretaker) is initially assured by a variety of innate response patterns, there very quickly develops a reciprocity that the infant comes to anticipate and count on. For example, if during play the mother assumes a sober immobile face, the infant shows fewer smiles and turns his head away from the mother more frequently than when the mother responds socially, as Edward Tronick and his colleagues have shown. The existence of such reciprocity — buttressed by the mother's increasing capacity to differentiate an infant's 'reasons' for crying as well as by the infant's capacity to anticipate these consistencies — soon creates a form of mutual attention, a harmony of 'intersubjectivity', whose importance we shall take up later.

In any case, a pattern of inborn initial social responses in the infant, elicited by a wide variety of effective signs from the mother — her heartbeat, the visual configuration of her face and particularly her eyes, her characteristic smell, the sound and rhythms of her voice — is soon converted into a very complex joint anticipatory system that converts initial biological attachment between mother and child into something more subtle and more sensitive to individual idiosyncrasies and to forms of cultural practice.

The third conclusion is that much of early infant action takes place in constrained, familiar situations and shows a surprisingly high degree of order and 'systematicity'. Children spend most of their time doing a very limited number of things. Long periods are spent in reaching and taking, banging and looking, etc. Within any one of these restricted domains, there is striking 'systematicity'. Object play provides an example. A single act (like banging) is applied successively to a wide range of objects. Everything on which the child can get his hands is banged. Or the child tries out on a single object all the motor routines of which he or she is capable — grasping the object, banging it, throwing it to the floor, putting it in his mouth, putting it on top of the head, running it through the entire repertory.

Nobody has done better than Jean Piaget in characterizing this systematicity. The older view that pictured the infant as 'random' in his actions and saw growth as consisting of becoming 'co-ordinated' can no longer stand up to the evidence. Given the limits of the child's range of action, what occurs within that range is just as orderly and systematic as in adult behaviour. There may be differences of opinion concerning the 'rules' that govern this orderly behaviour, but there can be no quarrel about its systematicity.

It is not the least surprising, in light of this conclusion, that infants enter the world of language and of culture with a readiness to find or invent systematic ways of dealing with social requirements and linguistic forms. The child reacts 'culturally' with characteristic hypotheses about what is required and enters language with a readiness for order. We shall, of course, have much more to say about this later.

There are two important implications that follow from this. The first is obvious, though I do not recall ever having encountered the point. It is that from the start, the child becomes readily attuned to 'making a lot out of a little' by combination. He typically works on varying a small set of elements to create a larger range of possibilities. Observations of early play behaviour and of the infant's communicative efforts certainly confirm this 'push' to generativeness, to combinatorial and variational efforts. Indeed, Ruth Weir's classic study of the child's spontaneous speech while alone in his crib after bedtime speaks volumes on this combinatorial readiness, as does Melissa Bowerman's on children's spontaneous speech errors.

The second implication is more social. The acquisition of prelinguistic and linguistic communication takes place, in the main, in the highly constrained settings to which we are referring. The child and his caretaker readily combine elements in these situations to extract meanings, assign interpretations, and infer intentions. A decade ago there was considerable debate among developmental linguists on whether in writing 'grammars' of child speech one should use a method of 'rich interpretation' — taking into account not only the child's actual speech but also the ongoing actions and other elements of the context in which speech was occurring. Today we take it for granted that one must do so. For it is precisely the combining of all elements in constrained situations (speech and nonspeech alike) that provides the road to communicative effectiveness. It is for this reason that I shall place such heavy emphasis on the role of 'formats' in the child's entry into language.

A fourth conclusion about the nature of infant cognitive endowment is that its systematic character is surprisingly abstract. Infants during their first year appear to have rules for dealing with space, time, and even causation. A moving object that is transformed in appearance while it is moving behind a screen produces surprise when it reappears in a new guise. Objects that seem to be propelled in ways that *we* see as unnatural (e.g. without being touched by an approaching object) also produce surprise reactions in a three-month-old as well. Objects explored by touch alone are later recognized by vision alone. The infant's perceptual world, far from being a blooming, buzzing confusion, is rather orderly and organized by what seem like highly abstract rules.

Again, it was Piaget who most compellingly brought this 'abstractness' to our attention in describing the logical structure of the child's search for invariance in his world — the search for what remains unchanged under the changing surface of appearance. And again, it is not important whether the 'logic' that he attributed to this systematic action is correct or not. What is plain is that, whether Piagetian logical rules characterize early 'operational behaviour' or whether it can be better described by some more general logical system, we know that cognitively and communicatively there is from the start a capacity to 'follow' abstract rules.

It is *not* the case that language, when it is encountered and then used, is the first instance of abstract rule following. It is not, for example, in language alone that the child makes such distinctions as those between specific and nonspecific, between states and processes, between 'punctual' acts and recurrent ones, between causative and noncausative actions. These abstract distinctions, picked up with amazing speed in language acquisition, have analogues in the child's way of ordering his world of experience. Language will serve to specify, amplify, and expand distinctions that the child has already about the world. But these abstract distinctions are already present, even without language.

These four cognitive 'endowments' — means-end readiness, transactionality, systematicity, and abstractness — provide foundation processes that aid the child's language acquisition. None of them 'generates' language, for language involves a set of phonological, syntactic, semantic, and illocutionary rules and maxims that constitute a problem space of their own. But linguistic or communicative hypotheses depend upon these capacities as enabling conditions. Language does not 'grow out of' prior protophonological, protosyntactic, protosemantic, or protopragmatic knowledge. It requires a unique sensitivity to a patterned sound system, to grammatical constraints, to referential requirements, to communicative intentions, etc. Such sensitivity grows in the process of fulfilling certain general, nonlinguistic functions — predicting the environment, interacting transactionally, getting to goals with the aid of another, and the like. These functions are first fulfilled primitively if abstractly by prelinguistic communicative means. Such primitive procedures, I will argue, must reach requisite levels of functioning before *any* Language Acquisition Device (whether innate or acquired) can begin to generate 'linguistic hypotheses'.

Entry Into Language

We now turn to the development of language *per se*. Learning a native language is an accomplishment within the grasp of any toddler, yet discovering how children do it has eluded generations of philosophers and linguists. Saint Augustine believed it was simple. Allegedly recollecting his own childhood, he said, 'When they named any thing, and as they spoke turned towards it, I saw and remembered that they called what one would point out by the name they uttered. . . . And thus by constantly hearing words, as they occurred in various sentences, I collected gradually for what they stood; and having broken in my mouth to these signs, I thereby gave utterance to my will.' But a look at children as they actually acquire language shows Saint Augustine to be far, far off target. Alas, he had a powerful effect both on his followers and on those who set out to refute him.

Developmental linguistics is now going through rough times that can be traced back to Saint Augustine as well as to the reactions against him. Let me recount a little history. Saint Augustine's view, perhaps because there was so little systematic research on language acquisition to refute it, prevailed for a long time. It was even put into modern dress. Its most recent 'new look' was in the form of behaviourist 'learning theory'. In this view's terms, nothing particularly linguistic needed to be said about language. Language, like any other behaviour, could be 'explained' as just another set of responses. Its principles and its research paradigms were not derived from the phenomena of language but from 'general behaviour'. Learning tasks, for example, were chosen to construct theories of learning so as to ensure that the learner had no predispositions toward or knowledge of the material to be learned. All was as if *ab initio,* transfer of response from one stimulus to another was assured by the similarity between stimuli. Language learning was assumed to be much like, say, nonsense syllable learning, except that it might be aided by imitation, the learner imitating the performance of the 'model' and then being reinforced for correct performance. Its emphasis was on 'words' rather than on grammar. Consequently, it missed out almost entirely in dealing with the combinatorial and generative effect of having a syntax that made possible the routine construction of sentences never before heard and that did not exist in adult speech to be imitated. A good example is the Pivot-Open class, P(0), construction of infant speech in which a common word or phrase is combined productively with other words as in *all-gone mummy, all-gone apple,* and even *all-gone bye-bye* (when mother and aunt finally end a prolonged farewell).

It is one of the mysteries of Kuhnian scientific paradigms that this empiricist approach to language acquisition persisted in psychology (if not in philosophy, where it was overturned by Frege and Wittgenstein) from its first enunciation by Saint Augustine to its most recent one in B. F. Skinner's *Verbal Behaviour.* It would be fair to say that the persistence of the mindless behaviouristic version of Augustinianism finally led to a readiness, even a reckless readiness, to be rid of it. For it was not only an inadequate account, but one that damped inquiry by its domination of 'common sense'. It set the stage for the Chomskyan revolution.

It was to Noam Chomsky's credit that he boldly proclaimed the old enterprise bankrupt. In its place he offered a challenging, if counterintuitive hypothesis based on nativism. He proposed that the acquisition of the *structure* of language depended upon a Language Acquisition Device (LAD) that had at its base a universal grammar or a 'linguistic deep structure' that humans know innately and without learning. LAD was programmed to recognize in the surface structure of any natural language encountered its deep structure or universal grammar by virtue of the kinship between innate universal grammar and the grammar of any and all natural languages. LAD abstracted the grammatical realization rules of the local language and thus enabled the aspirant speaker potentially to generate all the well-formed utterances possible in the language and none that were ill-informed. The universal grammatical categories that programmed LAD were in the innate structure of the mind. No prior nonlinguistic knowledge of the world was necessary, and no privileged communication with another speaker was required. Syntax was independent of knowledge of the world, of semantic meaning, and of communicative function. All the child needed was exposure to language, however fragmentary and uncontextualized his samples of it might be. Or more correctly, the acquisition of syntax could be conceived of as progressing with the assistance of whatever *minimum* world knowledge or privileged communication proved necessary. The only constraints on rate of linguistic development were psychological limitations on *performance*: the child's limited but growing attention and memory span, etc. Linguistic *competence* was there from the start, ready to express itself when performance constraints were extended by the growth of requisite skills.

It was an extreme view. But in a stroke it freed a generation of psycholinguists from the dogma of association-cum-imitation-cum-reinforcement. It turned attention to the problem of rule learning, even if it concentrated only on syntactic rules. By declaring learning theory dead as an explanation of language acquisition (one of the more premature obituaries of our times), it opened the way for a new account.

George Miller put it well (see Bruner, 1978). We now had *two* theories of language acquisition: one of them, empiricist associationism, was impossible; the other, nativism, was miraculous. But the void between the impossible and the miraculous was soon filled in, albeit untidily and partially.

To begin with, children in fact had and *needed* to have a working knowledge of the world before they acquired language. Such knowledge gave them semantic targets, so to speak, that 'corresponded' in some fashion to the distinctions they acquired in their language. A knowledge of the world, appropriately organized in terms of a system of concepts, might give the child hints as to where distinctions could be expected to occur in the language, might even alert him to the distinction. There were new efforts to develop a generative semantics out of which syntactical hypotheses could presumably be derived by the child. In an extreme form, generative semantics could argue that the concepts in terms of which the world was organized are the same as those that organize language. But even so, the *linguistic* distinctions still had to be mastered. These were not about the *world* but about morphology or syntax or whatever else characterized the linguistic *code*.

The issue of whether rules of *grammar* can somehow be inferred or generalized from the structure of our knowledge of the world is a very dark one. The strong form of the claim insists that syntax can be derived directly from nonlinguistic categories of knowledge in some way. Perhaps the best claim can be made for a case grammar. It is based on the reasonable claim that the concepts of action are innate and primitive. The aspiring language learner already knows the so-called arguments of action: who performed the action, on what object, toward whom, where, by what instrument, and so on. In Charles Fillmore's phrase, 'meanings are relativized to scenes', and this involves an 'assignment of perspective'. Particular phrases impose a perspective on the scene and sentence decisions are perspective decisions. If, for example, the agent of action is perspectively forefronted by some grammatical means such as being inserted as head word, the placement of the nominal that represents agency must be the 'deep subject' of the sentence. This leaves many questions unanswered about how the child gets to the point of being able to put together sentences that assign his intended action perspectives to scenes.

The evidence for the semantic account was nonetheless interesting. Roger Brown pointed out, for example, that at the two-word stage of language acquisition more than three-quarters of the child's utterances embody only a half dozen semantic relations that are, at base, case or caselike relations — Agent–Action, Action–Object, Agent–Object, Possession, etc. Do these semantic relations generate the grammar of the language? Case notions of this kind, Fillmore tells us, 'comprise a set of universal, presumably innate, concepts which identify certain types of judgments human beings are capable of making about the events that are going on around them . . . who did it, who it happened to, and what got changed'. The basic structures are alleged to be these arguments of action, and different languages go about realizing them in different ways: by function words, by inflectional morphemes as in the case endings of Latin, by syntactic devices like passivization, and so on. Grammatical forms might then be the surface structures of language, depending for their acquisition on a prior understanding of deep semantic, indeed even protosemantic, concepts about action.

Patricia Greenfield then attempted to show that the earliest *one-word* utterances, richly interpreted in context, could also be explained as realizations of caselike concepts. And more recently Katherine Nelson has enriched the argument that children acquire language already equipped with concepts related to action: 'The functional core model (FCM) essentially proposed that the child came to language with a store of familiar concepts of people and objects that were organized around the child's experience with these things. Because the child's experience was active, the dynamic aspects would be the most potent part of what the child came to know about the things experienced. It could be expected that the child would organize knowledge around what he could do with things and what they could do. In other words, knowledge of the world would be functionally organized from the child's point of view.' To this earlier view she has now added a temporal dimension — the child's mastery of 'scripts for event structures', a sequential structure of 'causally and temporarily linked acts with the actors and objects specified in the most general way'. These scripts provide the child with a set of syntagmatic formats that permit him to organize his concepts sequentially into sentence-like forms such as those reported by Roger Brown. The capacity to do this rests upon a basic form of representation that the child uses from the start and gradually elaborates. In effect, it is what guides the formation of utterances beyond the one-word stage.

The role of world knowledge in generating or supporting language acquisition in now undergoing intensive study. But still another element has now been added — the pragmatic. It is the newest incursion into the gap between 'impossible' and 'miraculous' theories of language acquisition. In this view, the central idea is communicative intent: we communicate with some end in mind, some function to be fulfilled. We request or indicate or promise or threaten. Such functionalism had earlier been a strong thread in linguistics, but had been elbowed aside by a prevailing structuralism that, after Ferdinand de Saussure's monumental work, became the dominant mode.

New developments revived functionalism. The first was in the philosophy of language spearheaded by Ludwig Wittgenstein's use-based theory of meaning, formulated in his *Philosophical Investigations,* and then by the introduction of speech acts in Austin's *How to Do Things with Words.* Austin's argument (as already noted) was that an utterance cannot be analyzed out of the context of its use and its use must include the intention of the speaker and interpretation of that intention by the addressee in the light of communication conventions. A speaker may make a request by many alternative linguistic means, so long as he honours the conventions of his linguistic community. It may take an interrogative construction ('What time is it?'), or it may take the declarative form ('I wonder what time it is').

Roger Brown notes an interesting case with respect to this issue: in the protocols of Adam, he found that Adam's mother used the interrogative in two quite different ways, one as a request for action, the other as a request for information: 'Why don't you . . . (e.g. play with your ball now)?' and 'Why are you playing with your ball?' Although Adam answered informational *why* questions with *Because,* there was no instance of his ever confusing an action and an information-seeking *why* question. He evidently recognized the differing intent of the two forms of utterance quite adequately from the start. He must have been learning speech acts rather than simply the *why* interrogative form.

This raises several questions about acquisition. It puts pragmatics into the middle of things. Is intent being decoded by the child? It would seem so. But linguistics usually defines its domain as 'going from sound to sense'. But what is 'sense'? Do we in fact go from sound to intention, as John Searle proposed? A second question has to do with shared or conventional presuppositions. If children are acquiring notions about how to interpret the intentions encoded in utterances, they must be taking into account not only the structure of the utterance, but also the nature of the conditions that prevail just at the time the utterance is made. Speech acts have at least three kinds of conditions affecting their appropriateness or 'felicity'; a preparatory condition (laying appropriate ground for the utterance); an essential condition (meeting the logical conditions for performing a speech act, like, for example, being uninformed as a condition for asking for information related to a matter); and sincerity conditions (wishing to have the information that one asks for). They must also meet affiliative conditions: honouring the affiliation or relation between speaker and hearer, as in requesting rather than demanding when the interlocutor is not under obligation.

Paradoxically, the learning of speech acts may be easier and less mysterious than the learning either of syntax or semantics. For the child's syntactic errors are rarely followed by corrective feedback, and semantic feedback is often lax. But speech acts, on the contrary, get not only immediate feedback, but also correction. Not surprising, then, that prelinguistic communicative acts precede lexico-grammatical speech in their appearance. Not surprising, then, that such primitive 'speech act' patterns may serve as a kind of matrix in which lexico-grammatical achievements can be substituted for earlier gestural or vocal procedures.

In this view, entry into language is an entry into discourse that requires both members of a dialogue pair to interpret a communication and its intent. Learning a language, then, consists of learning not only the *grammar* of a particular language but also learning how to realize one's intentions by the appropriate use of that grammar.

The pragmatician's stress on intent requires a far more active role on the part of the adult in aiding the child's language acquisition than that of just being a 'model'. It requires that the adult be a consenting partner, willing to negotiate with the child. The negotiation has to do, probably, least with syntax, somewhat more with the semantic scope of the child's lexicon, and a very great deal with helping make intentions clear and making their expression fit the conditions and requirements of the 'speech community', i.e. the culture.

And the research of the last several years — much of it summarized in Catherine Snow and Charles Ferguson's *Talking to Children* — does indeed indicate that parents play a far more active role in language acquisition than simply modeling the language and providing, so to speak, input for a Language Acquisition Device. The current phrase for it is 'fine tuning'. Parents speak at the level where their children can comprehend them and move ahead with remarkable sensitivity to their child's progress. The dilemma, as Roger Brown puts it, is how do you teach children to talk by talking baby talk with them at a level that they already understand? And the answer has got to be that the important thing is to keep communicating with them, for by so doing one allows them to learn how to extend the speech that they have into new contexts, how to meet the conditions on speech acts, how to maintain topics across turns, how to know what's worth talking about — how indeed to regulate language use.

So we can now recognize two ways of filling the gap between an impossible empiricist position and a miraculous nativist one. The child must master the conceptual structure of the world that language will map — the social world as well as the physical. He must also master the conventions for making his intentions clear by language.

Support for Language Acquisition

The development of language, then, involves two people negotiating. Language is not encountered willy-nilly by the child; it is shaped to make communciative interaction effective — fine-tuned. If there is a Language Acquisition Device, the input to it is not a shower of spoken language but a highly interactive affair shaped, as we have already noted, by some sort of an adult Language Acquisition Support System.

After all, it is well known from a generation of research on another 'innate' system, sexual behaviour, that much experiential priming is necessary before innate sexual responses can be evoked by 'appropriate' environmental events. Isolated animals are seriously retarded. By the same token, the recognition and the production of grammatical universals may similarly depend upon prior social and conceptual experience. Continuities between prelinguistic communication and later speech of the kind I alluded to earlier may, moreover, need an 'arranged' input of adult speech if the child is to use his growing grasp of conceptual distinctions and communicative functions as guides to language use. I propose that this 'arranging' of early speech interaction requires routinized and familiar settings, formats, for the child to comprehend what is going on, given his limited capacity for processing information. These routines constitute what I intend by a Language Acquisition Support System.

There are at least four ways in which such a Language Acquisition Support System helps assure continuity from prelinguistic to linguistic communication.

Because there is such concentration on familiar and routine transactional formats, it becomes feasible for the adult partner to highlight those features of the world that are already salient to the child and that have a basic or simple grammatical form. Slobin has suggested, for example, that there are certain prototypical ways in which the child experiences the world: e.g. a 'prototypical transitive event' in which 'an animate agent is seen wilfully . . . to bring about a physical and perceptible change of state or location in a patient by means of direct body contact'. Events of this kind, we shall see, are a very frequent feature of mother–child formats, and it is of no small interest that in a variety of languages, as Slobin notes, they 'are encoded in consistent grammatical form by age two'. Slobin offers the interesting hypothesis 'that [these] prototypical situations are encoded in the most basic grammatical forms available in a language'. We shall encounter formats built around games and tasks involving both these prototypical means-end structures and canonical linguistic forms that seem almost designed to aid the child in spotting the referential correspondence between such utterances and such events.

Or to take another example, Bickerton has proposed that children are 'bioprogrammed' to notice certain distinctions in real world events and to pick up (or even to invent) corresponding linguistic distinctions in order to communicate about them. His candidates are the distinctions (a) between specific and non-specific events, (b) between state and process, (c) between 'punctual' and continuous events, and (d) between causative and non-causative actions. And insofar as the 'fine tuning' of adult interaction with a child concentrates on these distinctions — both in reality and in speech — the child is aided in moving from their conceptual expression to an appreciation of their appropriate linguistic representation. Again, they will be found to be frequent in the formats of the children we shall look at in detail.

A second way in which the adult helps their child through formating is by encouraging and modeling lexical and phrasal substitutes for familiar gestural and vocal means for effecting various communicative functions. This is a feature of the child's gradual mastery of the request mode that we will be exploring in a later chapter.

H. P. Grice takes it as a hallmark of mature language that the speaker not only has an intention to communicate, but that he also has *conventionalized* or 'non-natural' means for expressing his intention. The speaker, in his view, presupposes that his interlocutor will accept his means of communication and will infer his intention from them. The interlocutor presupposes the same thing about the speaker. Grice, concerned with adults, assumes all this to be quite conscious, if implicit.

An infant cannot at the prelinguistic outset be said to be participating in a conscious Gricean cycle when signaling conventionally in his games with his mother. That much self-consciousness seems unlikely. But what we find is that the mother acts as if he did. The child in turn soon comes to operate with some junior version of the Gricean cycle, awaiting his mother's 'uptake' of his signalling.

In Katherine Nelson's terms, the young child soon acquires a small library of scripts and communicative procedures to go with them. They provide steady frameworks in which he learns effectively, by dint of interpretable feedback, how to make his communicative intentions plain. When he becomes 'conscious' enough to be said to be operating in a Gricean cycle is, I think, a silly question.

What is striking is how early the child develops means to signal his focus of attention and his requests for assistance — to signal them by conventionalized means in the limited world of familiar formats. He has obviously picked up the gist of 'non-natural' or conventionalized signaling of his intentions before ever he has mastered the formal elements of lexico-grammatical speech. It is the functional framing of communication which starts the child on his way to language proper.

Thirdly, it is characteristic of play formats particularly that they are made of stipulative or constitutive 'events' that are created by language and then recreated on demand by language. Later these formats take on the character of 'pretend' situations. They are a rich source of opportunity for language learning and language use.

Finally, once the mother and child are launched into routinized formats, various psychological and linguistic processes are brought into play that generalize from one format to another. Naming, for example, appears first in indicating formats and then transfers to requesting formats. Indeed, the very notion of finding linguistic parallels for conceptual distinctions generalizes from one format to another. So too do such 'abstract' ideas as segmentation, interchangeable roles, substitutive means — both in action and in speech.

These are the mundane procedures and events that constitute a Language Acquisition Support System, along with the elements of fine tuning that comprise 'baby talk' exchanges.

References

Austin, J. (1962) *How To Do Things With Words*. Oxford: Oxford University Press.
Bickerton, D. (1981) *Roots of Language*. Ann Arbor, MI: Karoma Publishers.
Bower, T. G. R. (1973) *Perceptual World of the Child*. Cambridge, MA: Harvard University Press.
Bowerman, M. (1978) The acquisition of word meaning: An investigation into some current conflicts. In N. Waterson and C. Snow (eds) *The Development of Communication*. New York: Wiley.

Brazelton, T. B., Kozlowski, B. and Main, M. (1974) The origins of reciprocity: The early mother–infant interaction. In M. Lewis and L. Rosenblum (eds) *The Effect of the Infant on its Caregiver.* New York: Wiley.

Brown, R. (1973) A First Language. Cambridge, MA: Harvard University Press.

— (1977) Introduction. In C. Snow and C. Ferguson (eds) *Talking to Children: Language Input and Acquisition.* Cambridge: Cambridge University Press.

Bruner, J. S. (1974) Nature and uses of immaturity. In K. J. Connolly and J. S. Bruner (eds) *The Growth of Competence.* London and New York: Academic Press.

— (1978) Acquiring the uses of language. *Canadian Journal of Psychology/Review of Canadian Psychology* 32, 204–18.

Chomsky, N. (1957) *Syntactic Structures.* The Hague: Mouton.

— (1959) Review of verbal behavior by B. F. Skinner. *Language* 35, 26–58.

— (1975) *Reflections on Language.* New York: Random House.

Fillmore, C. (1968) The case for case. In E. Bach and R. T. Harms (eds) *Universals in Linguistic Theory.* New York: Holt, Rinehart and Winston.

— (1968) The case for case reopened. In P. Cole and J. M. Seadock (eds) *Syntax and Semantics. Vol. 3. Speech Acts.* New York: Academic Press.

Greenfield, P. and Smith, J. H. (1976) *The Structure of Communication in Early Language Development.* New York: Academic Press.

Grice, H. P. (1975) Logic and conversation. In P. Cole and J. Morgan (eds) *Syntax and Semantics, Vol. 3.* London: Academic Press.

Meltzoff, A. and Moore, M. K. (1977) Imitation of facial and manual gestures by human neonates. *Science* 198, 75–8.

Nelson, K. (1974) Concept, word and sentence: Interrelations in acquisition and development. *Psychological Review* 81, 4, 267–85.

Nelson, K. and Gruendel, J. Generalized event representations: Basic building blocks of cognitive development. In A. Brown and M. Lamb (eds) *Advances in Developmental Psychology,* Vol. 1.

Piaget, J. (1937) *The Construction of Reality in the Child.* London: Routledge & Kegan Paul.

— (1971) *Structuralism.* London: Routledge & Kegan Paul.

Searle, J. (1969) *Speech Acts: An Essay in the Philosophy of Language.* Cambridge: Cambridge University Press.

Skinner, B. F. (1957) *Verbal Behavior.* New York: Appleton-Century-Crofts.

Snow, C. and Ferguson, C. (1977) *Talking to Children: Language Input and Acquisition.* Cambridge: Cambridge University Press.

St. Augustine (1961) *Confessions.* Baltimore, MD: Penguin Books.

Stern, D. (1977) *The First Relationship: Infant and Mother.* Cambridge, MA: Harvard University Press.

Tronick, E. (ed.) (1982) *Social Interchange in Infancy: Affect, Cognition and Communication.* Baltimore, MD: University Park Press.

Weir, R. (1962) *Language in the Crib.* The Hague: Mouton.

Wittgenstein, L. (1953) *Philosophical Investigations.* Oxford: Blackwell.

6 What Does It Mean To Be Bilingual?

BARBARA M. MAYOR

Introduction

Throughout the world people grow up, receive an education and live their daily lives through the medium of more than one distinct language or language variety. Even those who are exposed to a single language in the home may acquire a second on entering school. In other cases a second language is formally learned at later stages of schooling. Still others acquire or learn an additional language in later life because of occupational needs or personal interest. The resulting bilingualism of all these individuals will differ in crucial respects but they will all be developing two important skills:

(1) They will be learning to recognize their various languages as separate systems and to keep them apart when necessary.

(2) They will be learning how to choose the appropriate language for the circumstances (who is there, what they're talking about, etc.).

Such skills are not unique to bilinguals. So-called 'monolinguals' (who may in fact command several varieties of their single language) are also learning to make such distinctions and choices among the language varieties available to them. Dell Hymes has argued that 'Cases of bilingualism . . . are salient, special cases of the general phenomenon of variety in code repertoire and switching among codes' (Hymes, 1967, quoted in Sankoff, 1971: 33). Indeed the term 'code' is often used by sociolinguists in order to avoid making an artificial distinction between separate languages and varieties of languages. In the case of bilingualism, however, we are talking about language varieties which may be mutually incomprehensible to monolingual speakers of each, and where a *gradual* transition from one variety to the other is less likely. We need to remember, moreover, that bilinguals normally have access to more than one register and possibly more than one dialect within each of their languages, so that their overall repertoire is even greater than the term '*bi*lingual' might suggest. It is simply as a shorthand therefore that I use the term 'bilingual' throughout this article.

74

How Many Languages?

It is not always easy to determine how many languages a person knows, let alone which he or she knows 'best'. One reason is that the term 'language' itself has social rather than scientific reality. (When does a 'dialect' count as a separate language, and why?) Second, what is meant by 'knowing' a language is a matter of personal judgement. For example, a *passive* command of a language (understanding most of what is said, without necessarily feeling confident enough to speak the language) tends to get overlooked altogether. And yet if, like the Linguistic Minorities Project (1983), we accept the definition of bilinguals as 'regular *users* of two languages', we cannot ignore this level of skill.

Even having established that speaker X 'uses' languages Y and Z, we lack an accurate terminology to describe the role played by these two languages in the speaker's life. Most of the terms that are in common use prove difficult to apply with any precision because they tend to emphasize certain features to the exclusion of others. The term *mother tongue*, for example, can be quite misleading, since it may literally not be the same thing as 'father tongue' or 'grandmother tongue' and so on. Similar reservations apply to the term *home language*. In a multilingual household, a child may have a range of productive and receptive competencies in a variety of languages and/or dialects of languages even before starting school. *First language* seems to be a less ambiguous term but, like 'home language', it needs to be used with caution when referring to children from multilingual families, many of whom will be brought up to be bi- or trilingual in some degree. What is more useful to know is who speaks what language to whom and under what circumstances: for example, playing with siblings (sex and chronological position in the family will be crucial factors here) versus formal family gatherings versus religious ceremonies and so on. Such information, is, however, hard to come by. Survey data can be unreliable, in that speakers are often unaware of what they do in practice.

Community language and *heritage language* are rather different terms, referring to languages which serve a function in the local (or even national) minority community without necessarily being spoken as a language of the home. Thus, depending on their religious affiliation, British speakers of a language best described as a dialect of Punjabi may regard either standard Urdu (the national language of Pakistan) or standard Punjabi (an official language of the Indian Punjab) as their community language, since both have wide currency nationally and internationally. 'Heritage language' is used similarly, but with an even broader scope, to encompass languages which are no longer actively used in the home, for example Italian for many Italian-Americans. We are dealing here with issues of ethnic identity, which are essentially concerned with the speaker's attitudes and therefore particularly hard to measure in any objective way.

The term *native language* is perhaps most problematic of all, because it seems to imply a value judgement about a speaker's credentials. What level of linguistic competence does one need to reach to qualify as a native speaker? Can one be a native speaker of more than one language? There has recently been much discussion of this term in relation to the development of diverse national standard Englishes across the English-speaking world (see, for example, Kachru, 1986; Rampton, 1990; Cheshire, 1991; Phillipson, 1992; and Christophersen, 1992). Thus, even if we are speakers of standard British English, we are likely to acknowledge a monolingual, English-speaking American or Australian as a fellow native speaker of English, although of a clearly different variety. We may, however, hesitate to apply the term to a bilingual speaker of, say, Indian or Nigerian or Singaporean English, mistaking the different local norms in the use of English as a straightforward intrusion from other languages. Consideration of why we may react in this way raises fundamental questions about our sense of 'ownership' in the languages we use, the links we (more or less consciously) draw between language and territory, language and nation, language and culture, and the differences between all of these. Rampton (1990) advocates that we abandon notions of *biological* inheritance and *exclusive* membership of language communities in favour of notions of communicative *expertise* and language *loyalty*, whether by inheritance or affiliation. Helpful as this is, it still begs the question of whether particular languages carry a fixed (or even a dynamic) set of cultural baggage, or whether an international language can ever be truly culturally plural.

Perhaps the most important point to emphasise is that the balance between a bilingual's two (or more) languages is constantly shifting throughout life — a phenomenon very vividly described by the subjects interviewed for Miller's book *Many Voices* (1983), and by the contributors to Grosjean's (1982) *Life with Two Languages*. Any description of a bilingual person's language use is therefore in the nature of a snapshot in time. The so-called 'first language' may not remain the *primary* or *dominant* language throughout life and may not be the *preferred* language in a wide range of contexts. Truly 'balanced' bilingualism is probably the exception rather than the norm, as it does not reflect the way most naturally occurring bilingualism develops.

Switching Between Languages

In multilingual societies there is often quite an elaborate pattern of appropriateness, which either dictates or strongly influences the choice of a particular language in a particular context. Thus languages, or particular registers of them, may become polarized to cover different ranges of experience: one, for example, will become the language of literacy and formal education, another the language of family intimacy or fun. To take an example, a hypothetical primary-aged child of Muslim heritage in Britain may speak a dialect of Punjabi with parents in the home, speak Urdu as a lingua franca with other Muslim community members, be learning to read the Koran in Arabic at the local mosque, speak a local variety of English with friends in the school playground (possibly with some Asian features if the friends are of Asian origin) and be learning to read — and possibly speak — standard English in class. Over time, English may come to play an increasing part in the child's life, especially if there are older siblings and/or if the child comes to identify closely with British youth culture.

A bilingual speaker once likened this to putting on a different set of clothes according to the situation. (This does not, of course, rule out the possibility, as for the monolingual speaker, of choosing *against* the norm for special effect.) As a result of this, the languages of a bilingual speaker often come to symbolize different areas of human experience, different cultural values, even different stages in the child's development. This can lead, especially in adolescence, to a situation where the language of the home becomes associated solely with the culture of the home and local community and not with the possibility of success or acceptance in the wider society. This is not an inevitable state of affairs in a bilingual community, but rather the result of a particular kind of society in which one language group dominates all the formal institutions.

In the company of other bilinguals, the bilingual speaker also has the option of incorporating features of one language within the other (*code mixing*) or even of changing language completely within a single utterance (*code switching*). Bilingual code switching and mixing should in no way be seen as defective versions of monolingual language use. On the basis of extensive observation and analysis, Gumperz (1982) concluded that 'only in relatively few [cases] is code alternation motivated by speakers' inability to find words to express what they want to say in one or the other code' (pp. 64–65) but rather that 'motivation for code switching appears to be stylistic and metaphorical . . . code switching signals contextual information equivalent to what in monolingual settings is conveyed through prosody or other syntatic or lexical processes' (pp. 72, 98). Gumperz found that most code switches fell into the following broad categories:

(1) direct quotation from another speaker;

(2) addressing a point to a particular person;

(3) interjection of a point;

(4) repetition or rephrasing of a point;

(5) a sign of the speaker's involvement.

You may, especially if you are bilingual, be able to think of other reasons. I would want to add at least the following:

(6) using words/idioms from one language to plug gaps in the lexicon of the other;

(7) trying to impress people;

(8) a way of excluding someone.

This is by no means an exhaustive list of the possibilities. Nor does it imply that bilingual speakers are always conscious of the fact, or the significance, of their language switches, any more than monolingual speakers are aware of, say, shifts in pronunciation or rate of delivery. Nevertheless such features have communicative value. In other words there is normally a message implicit in the *choice* of language — although listeners may not always agree precisely as to its interpretation. This, as always, depends on how far they share cultural assumptions.

However, there is one important qualification to this argument. In some communities code switching has become so much a part of the linguistic norm that it can probably be regarded as a code in its own right. Poplack (1980), in her extensive study of an established Puerto Rican community in New York City, maintains that this type of code switching is more 'intimate', i.e. more likely to take place *within* a sentence. It is also less likely to form part of a conscious or unconscious discourse strategy, as claimed by Gumperz. Poplack argues that 'there is no need to require any social motivation for this type of code switching, given that, as a discourse mode, it may itself form part of the repertoire of a speech community. It is then the choice (or not) of this mode which is of significance to participants rather than the choice of switch points' (p. 164).

Language Development in the Bilingual Child

There have been several studies of the *simultaneous acquisition* of two languages by young children (see Saunders, 1983, for an overview). A more familiar situation, however, and that of most bilingual children in Britain, is *consecutive acquisition*, whereby one language is established to a greater or lesser degree before a second is acquired.

There are several crucial distinctions between the process of acquiring a first language as a baby and that of acquiring a second language in later life, however young. The various aspects of language develop at a differential rate throughout life — in very broad terms there is a rapid development of the sound system at an early age, overlapping with and followed by a rather slower development of grammatical sensitivity, and a development of meaning and the strategies of discourse that continues throughout life. As a result, each of these aspects will be more or less established in the first language at the time when the child encounters the second. To illustrate the point, consider the case of the monolingual baby, who is learning how to talk, in the sense of physically articulating sounds, at the same time as learning to distinguish the sounds of one particular language; learning to make sense of language *per se* at the same time as learning the rules of one particular system. In the case of the child acquiring a second language, these two processes — the general and specific — are separated. Finally, the baby is likely to be surrounded by linguistic input almost every waking hour, whereas input for the second-language learner may be more limited.

On the other hand, there are several ways in which acquiring the second language will be similar to acquiring the first. Inevitably input will need to precede output, in other words the developing bilingual child will need a language model, or models, and plenty of chance to listen before one could reasonably expect any speech in the second language. Even then the child will need to experiment a good deal in the process of working out the rules of the language. And it is unlikely that the child will speak at all unless he or she has a real need to communicate something.

Making grammatical sense

What, then, is going on when a developing bilingual is confronted by a mass of input in a second language? Edwards (1983) has argued that 'Children are essentially pattern learners whether in the acquisition of their mother tongue or a second language. But they operate their own rule systems aiming only gradually at the adult model of the target language' (p. 83). The young monolingual's use of 'mans' for 'men' or 'goed' for 'went' is clearly a valuable stage in working out a rule. The difference between the first- and the second-language learner is that the latter already has a linguistic system against which to judge the new input and will be developing a sensitivity to what the two languages have in common and where they differ. On the basis of past linguistic experience, the child may begin by expecting certain linguistic cues which are absent in the second language. But this is all part of an active strategy. As Corder (1978) says 'It is one of the strategies to learning to find out just how far down the scale it is going to be necessary to go before starting to build up again' (p. 90). Naturally, a speaker of a language such as Cantonese is going to have to go a great deal further 'down the scale' to find common linguistic rules with English — whether of pronunciation, grammar or vocabulary — than is a speaker of a more closely related language such as, say, Spanish.

As the developing bilingual speaker attempts to make sense of the new language input, a phenomenon known as 'interlanguage' often occurs, reflecting the learner's attempt to integrate the old with the new. It would be unfortunate to see this in purely negative terms. Trial and error, by definition, involve experimenting and making mistakes. As the child has access to more and more input, the provisional hypotheses will gradually be refined until the language approximates more closely to the idiomatic usage of a native speaker. However, the notion of 'interference' or 'transference' is not always helpful, since many 'errors' made by second-language learners resemble the developmental stages of first-language learning, such as simplification of syntax, overgeneralization of rules, and so on. For example, an analysis of the acquisition of English by two small groups of Norwegian and Spanish speakers (see Cancino *et al.*, 1974; Ravem, 1974) revealed expressions like the following, which were neither based on the speaker's first language nor yet authentic English:

Expression in first language	*Expression used*	*English 'target' expression*
Where go Daddy?	Where Daddy is going?	Where is Daddy going?
I no can understand.	I don't understand.	I can't understand.

The important thing is that a child should be given space to experiment and take risks with the language, on the principle that fluency is more likely to lead to accuracy than vice versa.

Making meaning

Where the learning of *meaning* is concerned, the situation is a little more complicated because the process of learning to mean is ongoing throughout life. A baby is forming concepts at the same time as acquiring one or more linguistic means of expressing those concepts. Adult second-language learners, on the other hand, have an existing set of quite sophisticated meanings against which to measure the new linguistic data, and initially their ability to express themselves in the second language is likely to be inadequate for their communicative needs. Young bilingual children fall somewhere between these two extremes in that they may, depending on their age and circumstances, be acquiring some concepts via one language, some via another, and some simultaneously via *both* languages, in those areas of their life where the two languages interact. (There is a good discussion of this process in Grosjean, 1982; see also Saunders, 1983.)

As we have seen, adult bilinguals differ in the extent to which their two languages come to represent separate areas of experience for them and the degree to which they are mixed or kept apart in daily interaction. They also differ crucially in terms of the relative status and roles of their two languages or speech varieties in the surrounding society. Such differences in circumstances have led psychologists (starting with Ervin &

Osgood, 1954) to postulate different types of underlying cerebral organization, leading to what they termed states of *compound* and *co-ordinate* bilingualism.

A state of compound bilingualism, according to Ervin and Osgood, is one in which two separate linguistic signs are associated with a *single* meaning. Unfortunately they failed to distinguish between two quite distinct situations which might contribute to this state of mind: that in which two languages are acquired simultaneously (typically in a bilingual home) and that in which meaning is acquired via a first language and then transferred uncritically to a second (typically via a grammar/translation method of second language learning). Other writers have termed the latter *subordinate* bilingualism. A co-ordinate system of bilingualism, on the other hand, is said to exist where the separate linguistic signs in each language are associated with 'somewhat different' meanings (Ervin & Osgood, 1954: 140). Kolers, in an influential article written in 1968, compared the underlying states of mind to single or double 'storage tanks' with a separate tap for each language. However, he demonstrated that terms for concrete objects were more likely to be held in a common store than abstract concepts (1968: 81–2). More recently the compound/co-ordinate distinction has been challenged (see, for example, Albert & Obler, 1978: 227–36) on the grounds that it tends to concentrate on vocabulary to the exclusion of syntax and does not satisfactorily account for the situation of those who habitually *switch* languages.

Underlying this issue is the question of how far the bilingual's two languages represent two distinct spheres of experience or two distinct cultures. Partly it may be a matter of somewhat different referents in the two languages: just as the French *brun* does not map exactly on to the English *brown*, neither does *crèche* cover precisely the same territory as *day care*. In other cases it may be rather a matter of the speaker's own experience in the language (the domains of use). Most bilinguals, for example, find it difficult to discuss mathematics other than in the language in which they were taught it. Scotton (1979, quoted in Grosjean, 1982: 151) describes how a Kikuyu university student in Nairobi, Kenya, switched constantly from Kikuyu to English to discuss geometry with his younger brother: 'Atiriri *angle* niati *has* ina *degree eighty*'. Similarly, many people find only one of their languages adequate for discussing their work. This does not imply that parallel terms do not exist in the other language; merely that the speaker in question has not experienced the contexts of their use. Maxine Hong Kingston describes vividly the difficulty which a bilingual may have in distinguishing what is specific to the language and culture from what is specific to one's personal experience via the language: 'Chinese-Americans, when you try to understand what things in you are Chinese, how do you separate what is peculiar to childhood, to poverty, insanities, one family, your mother who marked your growing with stories, from what is Chinese? What is Chinese tradition and what is the movies?' (Kingston, 1981: 13).

Biliteracy

Many of the issues affecting the acquisition of two (or more) languages apply equally to the learning of two (or more) writing systems. As with spoken language, we need to distinguish between the acquisition of literacy *per se* and learning to read a particular language. Lado (1975) describes the distinction in the following terms: 'Learning to write his first language he has to master the great abstraction involved in representing the sounds of a language by marks on paper. Learning to write a second language, he already knows that marks on paper can represent sounds' (p. 106; also quoted in Downing, 1973: 72). Again, as with spoken language, there is some evidence (e.g. Kaufmann, 1968; Modiano, 1968) of positive transfer of skills, especially where the scripts are the same, and only a little evidence of interference, mainly at the spelling level (see Grosjean, 1982: 306–7).

Some children have the opportunity of acquiring their biliteracy, like their bilingualism, naturally through exposure to written language in the home. In most cases, however, biliteracy is the result of formal teaching. The question facing educators is which language and/or script is most appropriate for the acquisition of initial literacy. Often (as with the related issue of dialect difference within a single language) the question is simply not addressed, and literacy, like oracy, is taught through the medium of the nationally prestigious language variety. However, this ignores some important psychological factors. Edelsky (1981: 90) has described literacy as 'an orchestration of multiple cueing systems', involving grapho-phonic, syntactic and semantic/pragmatic levels. The child whose language (or dialect) is different from the language of formal literacy may have to cope with a mismatch of input at all these levels, and will have to try and reconcile an unfamiliar symbol with an unfamiliar sound in an unfamiliar structure referring to an unfamiliar concept.

Let us look in a little more detail at each of these levels, beginning with the different writing systems. There is evidence that, especially in the early stages of reading, different strategies may be needed for different types of representation (e.g. logographic or alphabetic), but this does not appear to affect ease of reading once the system has been mastered. What may be more significant is the number of different symbols which a learner has to cope with and the number of distinguishing features between the symbols. In this respect some scripts have a distinct advantage over others for the teaching of initial literacy. (See Downing's *Comparative Reading* (1973), which draws on research from thirteen countries involving seven different scripts.) Still more significant, and of direct pedagogic relevance, is the sound-symbol correspondence between the script and a particular spoken language. In some languages, such as Spanish, Welsh and syllabically written Japanese, there is a close and fairly regular correspondence between the spoken and written word. In others, such as English and French, there is a far greater gulf to bridge (although there may be more *morphemic* regularity in these systems). It can be argued, in the case of children who are already bilingual, that initial literacy is best acquired via the language with the closest sound-symbol correspondence, since reading skills can subsequently be transferred to the language with less regular spelling. Thus teachers in Wales often claim an advantage of Welsh over English for the teaching of initial literacy in bilingual schools.

Turning to Edelsky's syntactic level, languages also differ in the extent to which grammatical information is coded in the spoken versus the written language. In an inflected language such as Spanish or German, grammatical information is present in the spoken language to which the child is exposed prior to formal schooling. In these cases writing (at least in the early stages) is simply a matter of recoding familiar information in written form. In other inflected languages, notably French, a great deal of grammatical information (such as verb endings and plurals) is not expressed at all in the spoken language and is encountered first in the written form. This poses an additional hurdle for the learner.

The issue is further complicated by the fact that many bilingual children of linguistic minority groups are taught literacy via their weaker language. There is a strong case for saying that initial literacy is best acquired via the child's first language or dialect, thus moving from the familiar to the unfamiliar. In some instances the competing demands of the more regular script versus the more familiar language will be irreconcilable, and in those instances the case for familiarity will probably be the stronger. Moreover, this usually has the advantage of drawing on the support of the home and community. Cowan & Sarmad (1976), in a very thorough study of the acquisition of biliteracy in Persian–English bilingual schools, found that reading progress was enhanced in the language that was reinforced in the home. It is impossible to say how far this is simply a result of the child encountering the written form of familiar *words*, or whether as Goodman (1969) has argued, that readers (and more specifically, beginning readers) 'can't comprehend materials which are based on *experience* and *concepts* outside their background' (quoted in Downing, 1973: 68; my italics).

Even oral code switching has its written equivalent. Here, for example, is an extract from a letter written in Hindi by an Indian research student resident in Britain to her brother in India:

इधर हमनें पंकज उधास की *Double Album*
खरीदी है। सच में एक से एक गाना वढ़कर
सुन्दर है। पंकज की *voice quality* कितनी
अच्छी है, है न? सुनो, अब रात के ग्यारह
बज गए और में सोना चाहती हूँ। कल
सुबह, में *Promise* करती हूँ में चिट्ठी को
ख़तम कर कर परसों यानी सोमवार को
डाक में डाल दूँगी। अभी के लिए, *good*
Night. खैर, अभी भारत में सुबह के साढ़े-
चार बज रहे होंगे। फिर भी, *good night.*

Translation:
Here, I have bought a double album by Pankaj Udhas. Honestly, each
song is better than the last one. Isn't Pankaj's voice quality excellent?
Listen, it is eleven at night and I want to go to bed. Tomorrow morning, I promise, I shall finish my letter and the day after tomorrow, that
is Monday, I shall post it. For now, good night. Well, at the moment it
must be half-past four in the morning in India. Still, good night.

Since this type of written code switching is, by definition, used between
members of the kind of code-switching community described by Poplack
(1980), it probably carries similar messages of intimacy and group solidarity —
although this is an under-researched area. Edelsky (1991) gives us an interesting insight into how a class of bilingual Hispanic American children may be
learning the principles of when and when not to code switch:

> The children in this study switched very frequently between English
> and Spanish in their speech, and they did so both between sentences
> and within sentences. However, they rarely code-switched in writing
> [. . .] If they code-switched at all in writing, it was in Spanish texts and
> it was referentially inspired (e.g. nouns, adjectives, verbs, and address
> terms). The use of a Spanish word in an English text, however, was four
> times more rare. If it occurred at all, it was more like a slip of the pen.
> [. . .] It was as though these children saw written English, the language
> that had stronger associations with powerful sociocultural domains like
> the educational establishment, commercial publishing, and the like, as
> a language that could not so easily be appropriated for their own voices
> — as a language one had to be careful of, a language that would not be
> hospitable to a 'stranger' in its midst. (Edelsky, 1991: 38–9)

Thus again it is apparent that children's developing bilingualism will reflect the social context in which they find themselves.

Bilingualism: An Advantage or a Disadvantage?

Many claims have traditionally been made for the benefits of 'foreign' language learning. Here are a few of them:

(1) Another language gives access to another people and their culture, and thus helps to broaden one's view of the world.

(2) Knowing a second language can give insights into the workings of language as a system.

(3) It is good mental discipline in itself.

(4) It is a marketable skill.

However, these arguments are rarely applied by linguistic majority communities to the languages of their linguistic minorities. The vast majority of the world's bilingualism is therefore devalued:

> Whereas learning a foreign language and even one or two dead ones as well has always been the *sine qua non* of a 'good' education, and whereas a child who picks up fluent French and Italian, say, because her father has been posted abroad, is likely to be thought fortunate, at an advantage, even 'finished', a child with two or three non-European languages, in some of which he may be literate, could be regarded as quite literally languageless when he arrives in an English school, where 'not a word of English' can often imply 'not a word'. (Miller, 1983: 5)

In this case, the bilingualism of the child, if it is recognized at all, tends to be seen as a disadvantage, on the grounds that it puts too much strain on the child's brain and hence has a detrimental effect on other learning ('cognitive overload'), or that it results in a relative lack of fluency or limited competence in both languages. But how valid are these claims?

Problems of assessment

What is the *evidence* of any benefits or disadvantages attaching to bilingualism? During the past fifty years or so there has been a great deal of research on this topic, and some conflicting results. (Good overviews of the research can be found in Hornby, 1977; Albert & Obler, 1978; Swain & Cummins, 1979; Grosjean, 1982; Cummins & Swain, 1986). The problem with much of the early research was that it failed to control for any socioeconomic factors and thus drew faulty conclusions about the relative performance of the (generally disadvantaged) bilingual group as compared to that of the (generally advantaged) monolingual group. Moreover, the tests on which these judgements were based were often culturally biased and conducted in only one — usually the bilingual subject's weaker — language, usually by a member of the dominant linguistic community. This could (and still can) lead to major injustices:

> Under the headline 'Startling Admission on IQ Tests' the *San Francisco Chronicle* of January 4th 1970 reported that 45% of the elementary children with Spanish surnames who had been in classes for the mentally retarded in one school system had been found to be of average or above average intelligence when tested in Spanish. One child's IQ rose from 67 when tested in English to 128 when tested in Spanish. The average score gained by the 35 pupils who had been labelled mentally retarded as a result of tests given in their weaker language was 17 points.

> The retesting in Spanish took place only as result of a federal judge ordering it to be done (after teachers, psychologists, parents and students had filed affidavits).

> (Quoted in Wright, 1982: 25–26)

Of course the full linguistic potential of the bilingual child can only ever be revealed when testing takes account of *both* the child's languages. Where vocabulary is concerned, for example, there is evidence that test scores obtained by bilinguals may be depressed relative to those of monolinguals in each language *measured separately,* since vocabulary will inevitably reflect the particular areas of life experienced via each language. In this case, combining scores across the two (or more) languages will result in a more realistic assessment of a bilingual child's knowledge. (For a fuller discussion of assessment issues, see Cummins, 1984b; Williams, 1984.)

The notion of semilingualism

There can be no doubt, however, that the situation where a linguistic minority child's home language is effectively 'inaudible' in school is far more widespread. Skutnabb-Kangas, a Finnish sociologist concerned with the nature of the educational response towards children from linguistic minorities, began to explore the potentially damaging effects of ignoring a child's first language in the state education system (Skutnabb-Kangas, 1984). This led her to claim that neglect of the home language would not only result in the gradual withering away of that language but would also hold the child back in general cognitive development because new concepts would be introduced via the (still weak) second language. In this claim she was supported by the writings of Cummins and Swain from Canada, who have long argued that:

. . . there may be threshold levels of linguistic competence which bilingual children must attain in their first and second languages in order to avoid cognitive disadvantages and to allow the potentially beneficial aspects of becoming bilingual to influence cognitive functioning. In other words, two thresholds are hypothesized: one below which cognitive growth would suffer without further linguistic development: and one above which cognitive growth would be enhanced.

(Cummins & Swain, 1986: 6)

This led Skutnabb-Kangas to postulate the notion of *double semilingualism*, meaning that the child's linguistic development in both languages would be retarded. This position has aroused a great deal of controversy in both academic and educational circles. For example, Martin-Jones & Romaine (1985) have argued that the notion of semilingualism represents a 'container' view of competence, which implies that there is some ideal, or 'full', standard of linguistic competence to which bilinguals should aspire. They challenge this view on the grounds that all language situations are dynamic and that all individuals and communities develop appropriate codes for their own communicative needs.

The potential benefits of bilingualism

There has always been a more positive school of thought in the literature on bilingualism. This is best exemplified by Vygotsky (1962), who argued that being able to express the same thought in different languages would enable a child to 'see his language as one particular system among many, to view its phenomena under more general categories', leading to 'awareness of his linguistic operations' (p. 110), a skill we might call *metalinguistic awareness*. During the 1960s and 1970s more evidence emerged to support this conjecture, notably in the work of Peal & Lambert (1962) with French-English children in Canada; Ben Zeev (1977) with Hebrew-English and Spanish-English bilingual children in the United States; and Ianco-Worrall (1972) with Afrikaans-English bilingual children in South Africa.

Other researchers have demonstrated more general cognitive benefits in being bilingual. Saunders (1983: 17–20), reviewing all the available research evidence, summarized the advantages of bilingual children over monolinguals, *when matched on other criteria,* as follows:

(1) Earlier and greater awareness of the arbitrariness of language (i.e. the realization that there is no intrinsic connection between, say, the word 'dog' and the animal it symbolizes).

(2) Earlier separation of meaning from sound (e.g. a tendency to group words according to their semantics rather than their phonology; thus cap-hat, rather than cap-can).

(3) Greater adeptness at evaluating non-empirical contradictory statements (i.e. elementary logic).

(4) Greater facility in concept formation.

(5) Greater adeptness at divergent thinking (e.g. 'Tell me all the things I could do with a paper clip').

(6) Greater social sensitivity (especially sensitivity to the effectiveness of communication, such as the needs of a listener who cannot see what the speaker can see).

All of these skills, especially 1–4, which might be said to constitute 'disembedded' thinking (Donaldson, 1978), are highly valued by the formal education system and might lead us to believe that bilinguals would automatically achieve greater educational success. However, this would be to ignore the pre-existing inequalities of race, ethnicity and social class, which have traditionally led to a correspondingly low status for certain types of bilingualism.

It is not the aim of this article to focus on issues in bilingual education, which have been well articulated elsewhere (see especially Skutnabb-Kangas, 1984; Wiles, 1985; Skutnabb-Kangas & Cummins, 1988; Bourne, 1991; Levine, 1993). I will restrict myself here to the observation that, if bilingual children are to fulfil their intellectual potential, it is important that their bilingualism should be recognised and, wherever possible, supported within school.

In the 1970s and early 1980s several formal projects (see Price & Dodson, 1978; Bedfordshire Education Services, 1980; MOTET, 1981; Swain & Lapkin, 1982; Cummins, 1984a) were set up to investigate the effects of educating children of primary age bilingually, with English — sometimes the children's first language, sometimes their second — as one of the two languages of education. (No such large scale projects have been undertaken since that time.) The following broad conclusions could be drawn from these studies:

(1) The children's general intellectual development did not suffer and in some respects benefitted.

(2) Second-language proficiency was promoted at no long-term cost to the development of proficiency in the first language.

(3) In addition, the children had acquired functional competence in their second language.

Thus none of the research evidence would lead us to believe that supporting a child's first language will have any detrimental effect on the acquisition of a second; indeed it is far more likely to enhance it, by building on firm foundations and leading to a greater awareness of how language works and how languages reflect our different understandings and experiences of the world.

References

Albert, M. L. and Obler, L. K. (1978) *The Bilingual Brain*. New York and London: Academic Press.

Bedfordshire Education Service (1980) *EC Mother Tongue and Culture Pilot Project* (1976–1980). Report prepared for the colloquium at Cranfield Institute of Technology, 24–27 March 1980.

Ben Zeev, S. (1977) Mechanisms by which childhood bilingualism affects understanding of language and cognitive structures. In P. A. Hornby (ed.) *Bilingualism: Psychological, Social and Educational Implications* (pp. 29–55). New York: Academic Press.

Bourne, J. (1991) Language in the school systems of England & Wales. *Linguistics & Education* 3, 81–102.

Cancino, H., Rosansky, E. J. and Schumann, J. H. (1974) Second language acquisition: the negative. Paper presented at the 1974 summer meeting of the Linguistic Society of America in Amherst, MA.

Carroll, J. B. (ed.) (1956) *Language, Thought and Reality: Selected Writings of Benjamin Lee Whorf*. Cambridge, MA: MIT Press.

Cheshire, J. (ed.) (1991) *English Around the World: Sociolinguistic Perspectives*. Cambridge and New York: Cambridge University Press.

Christophersen, P. (1992) 'Native models' and foreign learners. *English Today* 31, July, 16–18.

Corder, S. P. (1978) Language-learner language. In J. C. Richards (ed.) *Understanding Second and Foreign Language Learning: Issues and Approaches* (pp. 71–93). Rowley, MA: Newbury House.

Cowan, J. R. and Sarmad, Z. (1976) Reading performance of bilingual children according to type of school and home language. *Language Learning* 26 (2), 353–76.

Cummins, J. (1984a) Mother tongue maintenance for minority language children: Some common misconceptions. *Forum 2*. London: ILEA, Languages Inspectorate, Spring.

— (1984b) *Bilingualism and Special Education: Issues in Assessment and Pedagogy*. Clevedon, Avon: Multilingual Matters.

Cummins, J. and Swain, M. (1986) *Bilingualism in Education*. London: Longman.

Donaldson, M. (1978) *Children's Minds*. London: Fontana.

Downing, J. (1973) *Comparative Reading: Cross National Studies of Behaviour and Processes in Reading and Writing*. New York: Macmillan.

Edelsky, C. (1981) From 'Jimosalcsco' to '7 Narangas se calleron y el arbol-est-triste en lagrymas': Writing development in a bilingual program. In B. Cronnell (ed.) *The Writing Needs of Linguistically Different Students*. Proceedings of a research/practice conference held at SWRL Educational Research and Development, Los Alamitos, California, June.

— (1991) *With Literacy and Justice for All: Rethinking the Social in Language and Education*. London and Philadelphia: Falmer Press.

Edwards, V. (1983) *Languages in Multicultural Classrooms*. London: Batsford Academic and Education.

Ervin, S. and Osgood, C. (1954) Second language learning and bilingualism. *Journal of Abnormal and Social Psychology* 49 (suppl.), 139–46.

Goodman, K. S. (1969) Dialect barriers to reading comprehension. In J. C. Baratz and R. W. Shuy (eds) *Teaching Black Children to Read*. Washington DC: Centre for Applied Linguistics.

Grosjean, F. (1982) *Life with Two Languages: An Introduction to Bilingualism.* Cambridge, MA: Harvard University Press.

Gumperz, J. (1982) *Discourse Strategies.* London: Cambridge University Press.

Hornby, P. A. (ed.) (1977) *Bilingualism: Psychological, Social and Educational Implications.* New York: Academic Press.

Hymes, D. H. (1967) Models of the interaction of language and social setting. *Journal of Social Issues* 23 (2), 8–28.

Ianco-Worrall, A. D. (1972) Bilingualism and cognitive development. *Child Development* 43, 1390–1400.

Kachru, B. B. (1986) *The Alchemy of English: The Spread, Functions and Models of Non-native Englishes.* Oxford and New York: Pergamon Institute of English.

Kaufmann, M. (1968) Will instruction in reading Spanish affect ability in reading English? *Journal of Reading* 11, April, 521–527.

Kingston, M. H. (1981) *The Warrior Woman.* London: Picador.

Kolers, P. (1968) Bilingualism and information processing. *Scientific American* 218 (3), 78–86.

Lado, R. (1957) *Linguistics Across Cultures.* Ann Arbor, MI: University of Michigan Press.

Levine, J. (1993) Learning English as an additional language in multilingual classrooms. In H. Daniels (ed.) *Charting the Agenda: Educational Activity After Vygotsky.* London: Routledge.

Linguistic Minorities Project (1983) *Linguistic Minorities in England.* Report for the Department of Education and Science, Linguistic Minorities Project, University of London Institute of Education.

Martin-Jones, M. and Romaine, S. (1986) Semilingualism: A half-baked theory of communicative competence. *Applied Linguistics* 7 (1), 26–38.

Miller, J. (1983) *Many Voices: Bilingualism, Culture and Education.* London: Routledge and Kegan Paul.

Modiano, N. (1968) National or mother language in beginning reading: A comparative study. *Research in the Teaching of English* 2, Spring, 32–43.

MOTET (1981) *Mother Tongue and English Teaching for Young Asian Children in Bradford.* Report to the Department of Education and Science. *Digest, Vols. I & II.* Bradford University.

Peal, E. and Lambert, W. (1962) The relation of bilingualism to intelligence. *Psychological Monographs* 76 (27), whole number 547.

Phillipson, R. (1992) *Linguistic Imperialism.* Oxford: Oxford University Press.

Poplack, S. (1980) Sometimes, I'll start a sentence in Spanish y termino en espanol (sic). *Linguistics* 18, 581–618.

Price, E. and Dodson, C. J. (1978) *Bilingual Education in Wales 5–11.* London: Evans Methuen and Schools Council.

Rampton, M. B. H. (1990) Displacing the 'native speaker': Expertise, affiliation and inheritance. *ELT Journal* 44 (2).

Ravem, R. (1974) The development of wh-questions in first and second language learners. In J. Richards (ed.) *Error Analysis: Perspectives on Second Language Acquisition.* London: Longman.

Sankoff, G. (1971) Language use in multilingual societies: Some alternative approaches. In J. B. Pride and J. Holmes (eds) (1972) *Sociolinguistics.* Harmondsworth: Penguin Books.

Saunders, G. (1983) *Bilingual Children: Guidance for the Family.* Clevedon, Avon: Multilingual Matters.

Skutnabb-Kangas, T. (1984) *Bilingualism or Not: The Education of Minorities.* Clevedon and Philadelphia: Multilingual Matters.

Skutnabb-Kangas, T. and Cummins, J. (eds) (1988) *Minority Education: From Shame to Struggle*. Clevedon and Philadelphia: Multilingual Matters.

Swain, M. and Cummins, J. (1979) Bilingualism, cognitive functioning and education. *Language Teaching and Linguistics Abstracts* 12 (1), 4–8. London: Cambridge University Press.

Swain, M. and Lapkin, S. (1982) *Evaluating Bilingual Education: A Canadian Case Study*. Clevedon, Avon: Multilingual Matters.

Vygotsky, S. (1962) *Thought and Language*. Cambridge, MA: MIT Press.

Wiles, S. (1985) Language and learning in multiethnic classrooms: Strategies for supporting bilingual students. In G. Wells and J. Nicholls (eds) *Language and Learning: An Interactional Perspective*. London: Falmer.

Williams, P. (ed.) (1984) *Special Education in Minority Communities*. Milton Keynes: Open University Press.

Wright, J. (1982) *Bilingualism in Education*. London: Issues in Race and Education.

7 Neo-Vygotskian Theory and Classroom Education

NEIL MERCER

Introduction

There is a long tradition of psychological research on learning and in recent years there has been a great deal of sociolinguistic and educational research on communication in the classroom. What has still to emerge is a robust theory of teaching and learning as social practice. This paper is about an emergent theory which could possibly fill this gap. In its current form, in which it has already made a significant impact on psychological research into cognitive development, it exists under a number of different names. Smith (1989) refers to it as 'socio-cognitive-developmental theory' (SCD), to Newman, Griffin & Cole (1989) and Moll (1990) it is the 'sociohistorical' approach, while Crook (1991) calls it 'cultural psychology'. I prefer to call it 'neo-Vygotskian theory', so as to reflect L. S. Vygotsky's posthumous influence on current developments while also making it clear that no theoretical fundamentalism is necessarily involved. I have two main aims for this article, and there is a certain degree of tension between them. On the one hand, I want to explain why I think neo-Vygotskian theory has great potential for anyone interested in the process of teaching and learning in the classroom; but on the other hand, I also want to make clear why I believe that there is not yet an adequate neo-Vygotskian theory of classroom education, and to suggest that certain issues need to be addressed directly if such a theory is to be constructed. I will therefore describe what I think are the central features and concepts of the neo-Vygotskian approach, and then go on to consider its strengths and also some of the weaknesses which will need to be dealt with if it is to fulfil its potential.

Essential Features

The essence of the neo-Vygotskian approach is to treat human learning and cognitive development as a process which is culturally-based, not just culturally influenced; as a process which is social rather than individual; and as a communicative process, whereby knowledge is shared and understandings are constructed in culturally-formed settings. It does not, in principle, oppose the idea of innate elements in cognitive development; but it does suggest that cognitive development is *saturated* by culture. Cognitive development is a consequence, in part, of culturally contextualized events, so that Crook (1991) suggests that from this perspective the 'unit of psychological analysis becomes activity in a <u>context</u> — and the study of cognitive change, therefore, must dwell on the settings in which understandings are acquired . . .'

The Origins and Influence of Neo-Vygotskian Theory

Some possible reasons for the growing influence of neo-Vygotskian theory: a psychological and educational research can be summarized as follows.

Anyone who has studied psychology or education since about 1960 will have seen references to Vygotsky's work. So why should it now be exerting its strongest influence, some sixty years after his death? One reason, of course, is that it was suppressed for many years in the Soviet Union, and published only in fragments elsewhere. It was only really during the 1980s that the true scope and significance of his work became apparent outside Russia. It then became clear that Vygotsky's incomplete endeavours (he died in 1934 before he was 40) offered a perspective on human development and learning which was radically different from dominant Western psychological theories. And with the eventual publication in Western Europe and America of much more of Vygotsky's work and scholarly interpretations of it (e.g. Wertsch, 1985a), there came the realization that Vygotsky's theory had not been conceived in isolation, but within a Soviet community of intellectual endeavour that included other cognitive researchers like Luria (see e.g. Leont'ev & Luria, 1968) and literary theorists like Bakhtin (e.g. 1981). Vygotsky wanted to to re-design psychology as part of a unified science of human thought, language, culture and society. This has encouraged the hope amongst some psychologists and educational researchers today that a neo-Vygotskian theoretical perspective, one which would incorporate elements of Vygotsky's work but drawing also on post-Vygotskian research, could help build new theoretical links between different disciplines which are concerned with language use and teaching and learning in social context. What is more, this unification might be more easily achieved today than in Vygotsky's time because some lines of psychological, sociolinguistic and anthropological research have grown closer together in method and focus over the years. For example, as Wertsch, 1990 and Mercer, 1990 suggest, some recent sociolinguistic research on classroom discourse and learning (e.g. Edwards & Westgate, 1987) can be shown to have theoretical affinities with psychological research (e.g. Edwards & Mercer, 1987) and with that strand of anthropological research which treats literacy as social practice

(Heath, 1983; Street, 1984). Two common, axiomatic themes in all such research are that meaningful discourse is necessarily context-dependent, and that knowledge is normally acquired and applied in specific cultural contexts. In fact, some recent work on the development of writing practices (Sheeran & Barnes, 1991; Czerniewska, 1992; Maybin & Mercer, 1990) has now forged such links.

The late 1970s and early 1980s also saw a growing dissatisfaction with psychological theories of learning, cognitive development and intellectual achievement which focus on individual attributes and marginalise cultural and communicative factors. Behaviourism was an early target for such dissatisfaction, as also was psychometric research in the Burt-style nativist tradition. Vygotsky's work provided a valuable source of ideas for an alternative, social perspective to be constructed from those critiques. More recently, the neo-Vygotskian perspective has been used to criticize a new individualistic approach to cognitive development, the 'cognitive science' which is now so influential in the USA (e.g. Simon, 1981: Resnick, 1987: see Newman, Griffin & Cole, 1989 for such critical views). But Vygotskian theory has most typically been contrasted with Piagetian, with Vygotsky being seen as 'social' where Piaget is 'individualistic', and 'historical' or 'cultural' where Piaget is 'biological'. The issue here is not just a different model of cognitive development, but also a different model of classroom education. As Walkerdine (1984) and Edwards & Mercer (1987) among others pointed out, Piaget's developmental theory was transformed by some 'progressive' educationalists into an educational ideology of individualized, activity-based, discovery learning. Piaget has, of course, been staunchly defended (e.g. Smith, 1989) and it is certainly true that critics have focused on the *emphases*, rather than the *scope*, of his theory. As Smith points out that, if you look closely enough, you will find Piaget making numerous references to collaboration, culture and communication. But, as Smith also admits, Piaget gave these factors little attention in his own empirical research.

The third main reason for the ascendancy of neo-Vygotskian theory concerns the relationship between theory and research methodology. During the 1970s and 80s a disillusionment with experimental methods spread amongst researchers into cognitive development. Margaret Donaldson's work, in particular, (e.g. Donaldson, 1978) had fed the suspicion that psychological laboratories were veritable assembly lines for the production of experimental artefacts. Naturalistic, observational methods became rather more popular (especially amongst those researchers with educational interests). Much research into cognitive development was based on Piagetian theory, and that theory seemed firmly tied to an experimental paradigm. In contrast, Vygotsky's work, with its emphases on social, cultural and linguistic factors, seemed to offer a theory better suited to a

naturalistic methodology, and so to the investigation of cognitive development and learning in context.

Talk and Learning

Unlike Piaget, Vygotsky gave a lot of attention to talk as a medium for
sharing knowledge and potentially, transforming understanding. The influence of Vygotsky in recent years has been to revitalise psychological interest
into the relationship between language and thought. One neo-Vygotskian
line of enquiry which has grown strongly from this is research into early language acquisition and cognitive development (see e.g. Bruner & Haste
1987; Wells & Nicholls, 1985; Wood, 1988). A second is the study of collaborative learning (e.g. Forman & Cazden, 1985; Baker-Sennett, Matusov
& Rogoff, 1992). A third, and the one on which I will concentrate here, is the
study of the relationship between teachers and learners.

Vygotsky's own research (ended by his own untimely death at the age of
37) did not include any detailed analysis of classroom discourse. This is one
reason why his theory is not, in itself, one of classroom education. But
Vygotsky argues very persuasively that (a) human thought is shaped by
human language and (b) 'the very essence of cultural development is in the
collision between mature cultural forms of behaviour with the primitive
forms that characterize the child's behaviour' (Vygotsky, 1981: 151). His
work therefore provides an initial theoretical justification for examining
teacher–pupil discourse, and it is also a valuable source of ideas for guiding
observations and shaping analyses of that discourse. For research on learning in classroom contexts, one of the most attractive and significant features
of the emergent neo-Vygotskian theory is that it can deal with two obvious
and central features of classroom life — *talk*, and *teachers*.

Talk as a Social Mode of Thinking

A neo-Vygotskian perspective does not entail the researcher treating
children's talk as some kind of transparent 'window on the mind'. Talk is not
simply 'thinking out loud'. Instead it encourages the view that to talk, to
communicate with others through speech, is to *engage in a social mode
of thinking*. Through talking — and listening — information gets shared,
explanations are offered, ideas may change, alternative perspectives
become available. Educational researchers from other disciplines, notably
sociologists and linguists, have shown a lot of interest in classroom talk as a
medium through which teachers attempt to control children's behaviour,
and through which roles and identities are defined and maintained. They

have shown less interest in it as a medium for sharing knowledge, and one through which adults influence the representations of reality, the interpretations of experience, which children eventually adopt. This is what seems to me to be the crucial area of interest for psychologists. Individuals don't bootstrap themselves into culture, least of all in school. An educationally-relevant account of cognitive development and the acquisition of knowledge needs not just a theory of *learning*, but one of *teaching-and-learning*.

Neo-Vygotskian Conceptualizations of Teaching-and-Learning

The essential psychological assymetry of the teaching and learning relationship may be said to be represented in three neo-Vygotskian concepts: *scaffolding*, the *zone of proximal development (ZPD)* and *appropriation*. I will now go on to discuss each of these in turn, in terms of their value for the analysis of teaching and learning in schools.

1. Scaffolding

The emergence of the concept of 'scaffolding' in educational research can be traced back to its use by Wood, Bruner & Ross's (1976) work on parental tutoring in the early (i.e. pre-school) years. Bruner writes that 'it refers to the steps taken to *reduce the degrees of freedom* in carrying out some task so that the child can concentrate on the difficult skill she is in the process of acquiring' (Bruner, 1978: 19; my italics). It represents the kind and quality of cognitive support which an adult can provide for a child's learning — a form of 'vicarious consciousness' (as Bruner also put it) which anticipates the child's own internalization of mental function. As such, it clearly relates to the concept of the zone of proximal development, and offers something which psychology otherwise lacks — an effective conceptual metaphor for the quality of teacher intervention in learning. Teachers seem to find the concept very appealing, perhaps because it resonates with their own intuitive conceptions of what it means to intervene successfully in children's learning. However, in its application to learning in school (as compared with pre-school learning at home), it has often been used loosely and given a variety of covert interpretations. Bruner's own application of it to the relationship between teacher and pupil (Bruner, 1985: 29) is achieved simply by drawing an analogy between the discourse of parental tutoring and that of classroom teaching: he offers no illustrative examples of its application in the analysis of classroom interactions. Very different emotional and interactional conditions apply in the home and school. The essential problem is to decide what, in the classroom, counts as 'scaffolding' and what is merely 'help'. Is 'scaffolding' a description of a particular kind of teacher behaviour (whatever its outcome for the pupil), or a label that can be applied to any kind of teacher intervention which is followed by learning success for a pupil? In trying to confront these issues, Maybin, Mercer & Stierer (1992) offered the following educationally-relevant formulation of the concept:

['Scaffolding'] is not just any assistance which helps a learner accomplish a task. It is help *which will enable a learner to accomplish a task which they would not have been quite able to manage on their own*, and it is help *which is intended to bring the learner closer to a state of competence which will enable them eventually to complete such a task on their own*. Our use of the word 'task' here is not meant to imply that 'scaffolding' is only applicable if pupils are doing a certain kind of well-defined problem-solving activity: but we do wish to retain the idea (covered in Bruner's original usage) that 'scaffolding' is help given in the pursuit of a specific learning activity, one which has finite goals . . . Whether this distinction (between 'scaffolding' and other forms of 'help') is easy to apply in practice is an open question. To know whether or not some help counts as 'scaffolding', we would need to have at the very least *some evidence of a teacher wishing to enable a child to develop a specific skill, grasp a particular concept or achieve a particular level of understanding*. A more stringent criterion would be to require *some evidence of a learner successfully accomplishing the task with the teacher's help*. An even more stringent interpretation would be to require *some evidence of a learner having achieved some greater level of independent competence as a result of the scaffolding experience* (that is, demonstrating their increased competence or improved level of understanding in dealing independently with some subsequent problem). (p. 188)

The prime justification for employing the concept of 'scaffolding' in an analysis of the process of teaching-and-learning must be that it helps distinguish some kinds of teaching-and-learning from others. The above formulation seems to me to be sufficiently elaborated to allow educational researchers to discuss and explain differences in the quality of intellectual support which teachers provide for learners, while sufficiently stringent to exclude some kinds of 'help' which teachers provide. I can illustrate what I mean here by reference to a piece of teaching and learning, Sequence 1 below. It is taken from Mercer & Fisher (1992), which is a publication of the SLANT (Spoken Language and New Technology) research project on talk in computer-based classroom activities. In Sequence 1, the activity was part of a larger scheme of work on traditional fairy tales, within which the teacher wanted the children (aged 6 and 7) to develop an understanding of the structure of such stories and how characters in them are typically (and stereotypically) represented. She also wanted the children to develop their understanding of a real audience for such stories, as represented by the young children in the nursery class of the school. The actual computer-based task which she chose to help pursue these aims was for the children to design and use an 'overlay' for the keyboard which would transform it into a 'concept keyboard' which the nursery children could use to select a limited set of words to make sentences and so create their own fairy stories. From our discussions with the teacher, we know that she intended this computer-based activity also to fulfil the aim of developing the computing skills of her pupils.

Eight pupils in the class were working on this task in pairs, and the teacher supported their activity by going round to each pair in turn. With each pair, she would observe the current state of their progress, draw attention to certain features and use them to raise issues related to the successful completion of the activity. With all four pairs, her interventions dealt with the following task-specific issues:

(1) the relationship of the design of the overlay to the computer keys which it was intended to cover;

(2) the need to design an overlay which would generate appropriate sequences of words (so that 'beginning words' were in the left-hand column, with suitable following words in the next column, and so on);

(3) the need to select words which were appropriate for the younger children in terms of difficulty and interest.

Sequence 1 is an example of one such of her interventions, with two girls, Carol and Lesley.

Sequence 1: Designing a concept keyboard

In the sequence, simultaneous speech is shown by brackets ([) and unintelligible speech is marked (. . .). An omitted section of discourse is shown by [. . .]. Additional contextual information is in italics. **T** is the teacher. The speech has been punctuated to make it easier to read.

T: (Standing behind the pair of pupils) So what are you going to put in this one? (points to a blank square on their overlay)
Carol: [(. . .) (*mutters*)
Lesley: [(. . .) (*mutters*)
T: Come on, think about it
Lesley: A Dragon?
T: A dragon. Right. Have you got some words to describe a dragon?
Carol: [No
Lesley: [No
T: (*Reading from their overlay and pointing to the words as she does so*) 'There is a little amazing dragon'. They could say that, couldn't they?

Carol: [Yes
Lesley: [Yes
(*Carol and Lesley continue working for a short while, with the teacher making occasional comments*)
T: Now let's pretend it's working on the computer. You press a sentence and read it out for me Lesley.
Lesley: (*pointing to the overlay as she reads*) 'Here . . . is . . . a . . . wonderful . . .'
T: Wait a minute
Lesley: 'Princess . . .'
T: (*turning to Carol*) Right, now you do one. You read your sentence.
Carol: (*pointing to overlay*) 'Here . . . is . . . a little . . . princess'.
T: Good. What do you need at the end of the sentence, so that the children learn about
[how
Lesley: [Full stop
T: Full stop. We really should have allowed some space for a full stop. I wonder if we could arrange . . . When you actually draw the finished one up we'll include a full stop. You couldn't actually do it. We'll put it there. (*She writes in a full stop on the overlay*) so that when you, can you remember to put one in? So what are the children going to learn? That a sentence starts with a . . ?
Lesley: Capital letter
T: And finishes with?
Lesley: A full stop.
T: And it's showing them (*She moves her hand across the overlay from left to right*) What else is it showing them about sentences? That you start? On the?
Lesley: On the left.
T: And go across the page (*She again passes her hand from left to right across the page*).

Sequence 1 includes some good examples of the kinds of discourse strategies commonly used by teachers in their interactions with children (Edwards & Mercer, 1987). Selecting particular themes, the teacher elicits responses from the pupils which draw them along a particular line of reasoning on those themes (a line of reasoning consonant with her own goals for the activity). Moreover she cues some of those responses heavily through the form of her questions (e.g. 'That a sentence starts with a . . ?'). In pursuing this line of reasoning, she has to elaborate the requirements of the activity, and in fact goes on to *redefine* those requirements (in relation to the inclusion of a 'full stop' on the overlay). She also defines the learning experience as one which is shared by her and the children through her use of 'we' and 'let's'. We can see here how a teacher uses talk, gesture and the shared experience of the piece of work in progress to draw the children's attention to salient points — the things she wishes them to do, and the things she wishes them to learn. The nature of her intervention is to remind pupils of some specific requirements of the task in hand, and so guide their activity along a path which is in accord with her pre-defined curriculum goals for this activity. We know that she saw this activity as a demanding one for the children (they had only spent one session using a manufactured keyboard overlay before beginning to design their own), and she was anxious that they all did manage to produce workable models. Her teaching style in all the interventions we observed in this activity can be interpreted as attempts to reduce the 'degrees of freedom' of the activity so as to ensure that its demands did not exceed the capabilities of the children and that the possible directions and outcomes of their efforts were constrained to accord with the specific goals she had set. In fact, we know that Lesley and Carol did produce a satisfactory overlay, and went on to teach the nursery children how to use it.

In Sequence 1 we see an adult effectively performing the role of teacher without employing a traditional, didactic 'chalk and talk' pedagogy or using only the kind of non-directive learning support strategies associated with 'discovery learning' and extreme 'progressive' approaches to primary education. What we see there is also clearly not apprenticeship learning of the 'sitting with Nellie' kind, rarely encountered in school but common in craft training, where a novice is expected to acquire skills and understanding simply through observation and working in parallel with an expert. Using Maybin, Mercer & Stierer's (1992) criteria, Sequence 1 could be said to illustrate 'scaffolded' learning if we are satisfied that (a) Carol and Lesley could not have succeeded without the teacher's interventions; (b) the teacher is aiming for some new level of independent competence on the children's part; and (c) the teacher has the acquisition of some specific skill or concept in mind. From the evidence available, I am satisfied that these conditions are met. The most stringent criteria in the formulation can even be addressed, because there is also evidence of the children successfully completing the task in hand and (though the evidence is not very 'hard') of their success in going on to deal independently with a subsequent related problem (i.e. teaching the nursery children to use the keyboard).

With some educational activities, it might well be argued that such educational tools or 'props' as worksheets or computer software provide an element of 'scaffolding' for the pupils' learning. Certainly, some kinds of software, like adventure games and problem-solving programs, provide *structure* and *guidance* for activity, and such programs also often provide *feedback* to children on their actions (features that are all usually emphasised in the teachers' manuals which accompany most educational software). However, because any educational software that I have observed in use offers, at best, a very limited set of 'feedback' responses to children's input, and because such responses seem never to match the problems actually encountered by children in the classroom, I do not feel that the use of the term 'scaffolding' is appropriate. Moreover, I have observed that (a) pupils often get into difficulties in spite of information or guidance offered by a program; and (b) it is precisely at such times that a teacher's supportive intervention is sought and received.

It is probably in making a direct conceptual link between two very different aspects of teacher's involvement with pupils' learning that the concept of 'scaffolding' offers most to educational research — the pursuit of curriculum-related goals for learning and the use of specific discourse strategies when intervening in childrens' learning. Elsewhere I have used the concept to describe in detail how teachers attempt to support children's problem-solving without taking over complete responsibility for it. It focuses attention on how, and how well, a teacher can actively support children's learning without relying on didactic instruction. For psychological research, the neo-Vygotskian model of learning processes represents a radical shift of theoretical perspective, away from the notion of learners as isolated individuals who succeed or fail by their own resources, towards a view of learning as a situated, culturally-contextualized activity. The concept of 'scaffolding' represents one crucial aspect of such activity, whereby learners' success or failure is often dependent on the quality of the direct or indirect contribution made by others (whether teacher, experimenter, or collaborating peer). However, in defining such support in terms of classroom talk, we must beware of the risk of reducing our conception of what counts as 'scaffolding' to that of *strategic response* rather than the *planning and design* of activity. The ways that cognitive support for an activity may be set up in advance by a teacher in the way a task is defined both in practical terms (e.g. how 'basic' is the equipment, how 'friendly' is any computer software?), organized (e.g. which children should work together, how labour should be divided), related to other learning experiences (e.g. to other work on a particular topic, or to children's broader interests outside school) and how the task is introduced and explained by the teacher to the children. It does not seem sensible to define all such planning outside the realm of 'scaffolding', as it may well be that some of the more profound aspects of pedagogical decision-making (e.g. what curriculum goals are actually to be pursued through a task, and how these goals may be adapted to the needs of particular children) are made at that stage.

2. The Zone of Proximal Development

The Zone of Proximal Development (ZPD) is 'the distance between the actual developmental level as determined by independent problem solving and the level of potential development as determined through problem solving under adult guidance or in collaboration with more able peers'

(Vygotsky, 1978: 86). But although the term and its conventional definition sound complex and abstract, the concept embodies two key features of human learning and development. The first is that *learning with assistance or instruction is a normal, common and important feature of human mental development*. The second is that *the limits of a person's learning or problem-solving ability can be expanded by providing the right kind of cognitive support*.

Within the neo-Vygotskian framework, learning and problem-solving are seen as essentially and inevitably context-bound processes, with the implication that the level of understanding or the success of problem-solving achieved by individuals in specific settings is recognized to be, in part at least, a function of those settings as dynamic contexts for cognitive activity (Crook, 1991). Thus what appear to be variations in the ability of a child to solve 'the same' problem across different experimental settings (for example, as described by Donaldson, 1978) might best be explained in terms of variations between the implicit contextual frameworks surrounding those tasks. As Newman, Griffin & Cole (1989) argue, a great deal of psychological research is flawed because researchers have naively accepted that experimental tasks can be defined independently of the intersubjective contexts in which they are performed.

For research which claims direct educational relevance, then, an implication of the above discussion might be that we should examine the processes of learning and instruction as manifest in particular *events*, and in the relationship between teachers and learners in those events. This suggests that the concept of the ZPD is thus inextricably tied to particular contexts in a much more profound way than has been clearly articulated elsewhere, as its very existence is determined by the intersubjectivity of understanding of 'teacher' and 'learner'.

References to the ZPD are becoming increasingly common in developmental and educational research, but there is a great danger that the term is used as little more than a fashionable alternative to Piagetian terminology or the concept of IQ for describing individual differences in attainment or potential. Such lip-service misses the essence of the concept, and avoids its radical implications for how the process of teaching and learning is theoretically 'modelled'. Two such implications can be summarized as follows:

(1) The limits of the ZPD for any particular child on any particular task will be established in the course of an activity, and one key factor in establishing those limits will be the quality of the supporting interventions of a teacher. That is, the ZPD is not an attribute of a child (in the sense that, say, IQ is considered to be) but rather the attribute of an *event*. It is the product of a particular, situated, pedagogical relationship. Through observing and assisting a child through a particular activity, a

teacher may gain valuable insights into how, and how far, that child may be encouraged to progress. But children do not take their ZPDs with them when they leave a classroom, and new tasks with new teachers may generate quite different 'zones' for the same group of children.

(2) Some influential perspectives on education and learning would suggest that if a problem solving activity or learning task is well-designed, then pupils should be able to pursue it independently and teacher interventions should be minimal. (Examples might be the hierarchical 'mastery learning' programmes (Resnick, Wang & Kaplan, 1973) or, more recently, those approaches to computer-based learning which extol 'student control' over learning pace and learning strategy (Papert, 1980: Laurillard, 1987). However, the neo-Vygotskian perspective does not necessarily support that view. Instead, the necessity of some kinds of teacher support in an activity may be regarded as a virtue, because it is only when 'scaffolding' of some kind is required that we can infer that a child is working in a ZPD. As Vygotsky himself put it, 'Instruction is only good when it proceeds ahead of development. Then it awakens and rouses to life an entire set of functions which are in the stage of maturing, which lie in the zone of proximal development'. (1934: 222, cited in Wertsch, 1985b: 71). We can therefore conclude that a task which is designed so that children are able to accomplish it without any assistance whatsoever is unlikely to stretch their intellectual capabilities!

The concept of the Zone of Proximal Development also embodies a view of the developing child or learner as someone whose learning achievements are, at least in part, situationally determined. That is, actual and potential levels of achievement are never just a reflection of an individual's cognitive potential and learning strategies, but are always also a measure of the strength of the cultural framework which supports that learning. For the psychology of learning and cognitive development, this concept challenges views of problem-solving ability or 'cognitive level' as something abstract and non-task specific. It invites experimental researchers to consider how the learning tasks they set constrain or extend the cognitive potential of their subjects. For educational psychologists and teachers, it encourages an approach to the monitoring of individual children's progress which focuses on future possibilities rather than past achievements ('formative', rather than 'summative' assessment, in the current terminology of the National Curriculum for England and Wales). In practice, children's development might be gauged as they progress through a series of related activities, carried out in the continuity of shared classroom experience, in terms of how far children are able to advance with teacher support. For groups of children working together at the computer, observed relative rates of progress might provide teachers not only with useful information about the learning experience of individuals, but also provide some information about the effectiveness of any particular group as a collaborative learning unit.

However, as mentioned earlier, one of the main problems in employing the concept of the ZPD in classroom-based research (and in most aspects of teaching, outside the formal assessment of individual pupils) is its focus on individual progress. While Vygotsky's own discussions of the concept (e.g. Vygotsky, 1978) may not be predicated on an exclusive relationship between a teacher and an individual child, almost all empirical research into the ZPD has involved experiments in which children are given very specific kinds of prompts by experimenters, and in which the aim is to compare the demonstrated capability of individuals with some other 'decontextualized' measure of intellectual development (like IQ: for example, Brown & Ferrara, 1985. See Wertsch, 1985b, chapter 3 for a review of such research). Generalizations from such research to classroom life are impossible. My own view is that the ZPD is, in fact, less adaptable than 'scaffolding' to the realities of classroom education. Teachers normally have to plan and operate at the level of the class or group, and the idea of a group of learners with a shared ZPD seems to me to stretch the concept too far! Perhaps classroom researchers and teachers simply need a different, though related, concept that deals with the *synergy* of a learning group. This would conceptualize the ways that the organizing and interventional activities of a teacher are related to the creation of a learning culture in the classroom, and hence to the cognitive advancement of the members of a group or class as a whole. In empirical research, this could help shift the focus from the progress of individual children working on individualized learning tasks towards how a class or group of pupils and their teacher function together as a 'community of enquiry' (as Prentice, 1991, puts it) as they progress through a series of curriculum-related activities. In practical educational terms, we might then be able to identify the strengths and weaknesses of that joint learning process, and suggest directions in which the community could most fruitfully be expected and encouraged to advance.

3. Appropriation

The culturally-based quality of most learning is represented in the concept of *appropriation*, introduced by Vygotsky's colleague Leont'ev (1981) but recently taken up and developed by Newman, Griffin & Cole (1989). According to Newman Griffin & Cole (*op cit.*), it was proposed by Leont'ev as a sociocultural alternative to Piaget's biological metaphor of 'assimilation'. In saying that children 'appropriate' understanding through cultural contact, the point is being made that '. . . the objects in a child's world have a social history and functions that are not discovered through the child's unaided explorations' (Newman *et al.*, *op cit.*, p. 62). This is more than a complicated way of saying that children don't need to re-invent the wheel.

At the simplest level, it is arguing that because humans are essentially cultural beings, even children's initial encounters with objects may be cultural experiences, and so their initial understandings may be culturally-defined. In this sense (the one usually applied in early childhood research), appropriation is concerned with what meanings children may take from encounters with objects in cultural context. In relation to schooling, the most interesting application of the concept will not necessarily concern a learner's relationship with meaningful objects, but rather with concepts and ideas. And the crucial field of investigation will be educational discourse, as it is only through that discourse (spoken or written) that concepts are shared and differing interpretations of them can be revealed and resolved (See Mercer, 1992, for a more detailed discussion of the concepts of 'culture', 'context' and 'appropriation' in relation to classroom research). For the study of educational discourse, 'appropriation' provides a useful theoretical link with the work of one of Vygotsky's contemporaries, the literary theorist Bakhtin. He introduced the concept of 'voice' as a way of representing the intellectual presence of more than one person in the authorship of a text (spoken or written). In the recent development of what might be called 'neo-Bakhtinian' research, this concept has been used in discussing children's social and linguistic enculturation. For example, Maybin (1993) shows how children appropriate the ideas and opinions of parents, teachers and others of influence by 'ventriloquating' the voices of these others in their conversations.

Although the concept of appropriation would seem to have its most obvious application in explaining how learners benefit from the previous learning of their teachers, the concept is particularly valuable for the study of classroom discourse because it deals with the *reciprocity* of teaching and learning. That is, the process is not simply one of learners appropriating ideas from their teachers, but is more complex because, in order to teach, teachers may need to appropriate ideas from learners. Thus Newman, Griffin & Cole (1989) use 'appropriation' to explain the pedagogic function of a particular kind of discourse event whereby one person takes up another person's remark and offers it back, modified, into the discourse. They show how teachers do this with children's utterances and actions, thereby offering children a re-contextualized version of their own activities which implicitly carries with it new cultural meanings. Edwards & Mercer (this volume) observed similar things going on in British primary school classrooms. Teachers often *paraphrase* what children say, so as to present it back to them in a form which is considered by the teacher to be more compatible with the current stream of educational discourse. They also *reconstructively recap* what has been done by the children in class, so as to represent events in ways which fit their pedagogic framework. The relationship between the concept of appropriation and these kind of discourse strategies used by teachers is well illustrated in the following sequence of classroom talk (taken from

Mercer, 1991), which I recorded in a primary classroom in 1990. In the sequence the teacher is talking with a group of six children aged 9 who were reading together a picture book called *I'll Take You to Mrs Cole* by Nigel Gray (1985). The teacher told me that this group included children who had severe problems with reading, and with 'making sense of books'. Some of them were also very withdrawn, and usually silent, in larger class settings (including Terry, the boy who talks most in the transcribed sequence). At the point the sequence begins, they are talking about an illustration in the book in which the hero (a boy) seems to appear more than once. There has been some disagreement amongst the children about quite who these two figures are meant to represent.

Sequence 2: 'Perhaps'

In this sequence, simultaneous speech is shown by brackets ([) and long pauses (over 2 seconds) by slashes (/ /). Emphatic speech is in bold type; unintelligible speech is marked (. . .). An omitted section of discourse is shown by [. . .]. Additional contextual information is in italics. The teacher is **T**, and unidentified speakers (children) are marked **P1** and **P2**.

T: Which one's the boy in the story then?
P1:   That [one
P2:   [That one
T: Why do you say that?
P1:   'cause he's got spiky hair and he's wearing long trousers
T: Sarah disagrees. Why not?
Sarah: It can't be the boy because he's not got spiky hair.
          (*Some of the children begin talking at once*)
Terry: (*loudly*) No, he's thinking again, he's not gone to
          Mrs [Cole yet
T: [Hold on, remember, one at a time please / / Sorry?
Terry: He's thinking again, that's why he's got 'perhaps perhaps she kept'
          (. . .)
T: Ah
Terry: He's thinking what it's like.
T: He's thinking what it's like. So is he actually in this picture (*points to
          one of the scenes shown*)
Terry: No
Sarah: No
T: What part of him is in the picture?
Terry: His mind
Sarah: Yeh, his mind's in the picture
T: How can a mind get into a picture?
Sarah: I'm a / / Thinking about it
Terry: Yeh

[. . .]
T: Let's go back. It's interesting isn't it.? First of all, let's reflect on this
a minute. First of all, some people thought, somebody thought that
he was in there . . .
P1:   yeh
P2:   yeh
T: . . . and then Terry disagreed with that, or Sarah, is it? / / And then
we said, what part of him is in there, and you said his mind, right? So
this (*points to the picture*) is his mind still, is it? And Terry picked up
a clue from the writing that made him think of the mind. What word
was it Terry that gave you that idea about it being in his mind?
Terry: Well, in the writing / /
T: [Yeh
Terry: [bit. 'Perhaps', it said 'perhaps she kept them locked up in dark / /
dungeon'
T: So 'perhaps', 'perhaps'. Was that the key word for you?
Terry: Yeh
T: 'Perhaps'. It goes on to say 'perhaps', doesn't it? (*Reads from page*)
'Perhaps she fed them' / / It's still all in his mind, is it?
Sarah: Yeh

(from Mercer, 1991: A8–A9)

In this sequence, the teacher appropriates an issue which has been raised
by the children themselves. He asks for their views of the problem, which
not only tells him what they think but also helps the group share ideas. He
notices that Terry may have got an idea from the text which would resolve
the issue. After helping the children clarify their ideas, he recaps the discussion and so tries to provide a firm context based on shared experience within
which Terry can offer his 'clue'. Through being appropriated by the teacher
Terry's discovery is made explicit and legitimised, and what he has found
becomes part of the shared understanding, the 'common knowledge', of the
group. By strategically appropriating children's words and actions in such
ways, teachers may help children relate their thoughts and actions to the
broader parameters of educational knowledge.

Summary and Conclusions

I have argued that educational research needs concepts to describe teaching-and-learning as a culturally-based, interactive process, and my strong
support for neo-Vygotskian theory reflects the fact that I have not found
such useful concepts within other theoretical frames. But having put the case
for the neo-Vygotskian framework as a suitable basis for a theory of classroom education, I readily accept that in its current state of development

it does not yet represent such a theory. The main reason is that — with the possible exception of 'scaffolding' — its principal concepts have still to be precisely formulated for classroom research. Most of the emipirical research on which neo-Vygotskian theory is based deals only with the supportive intervention of adults in the learning of *individual* children (i.e. through experimental learning tasks, or observations of parents and young children at home). Indeed, it seems ironic that, while the model of learning and development which these concepts offer educational research is 'socio-cultural' rather than 'individualistic', the development of the concepts themselves has not taken account of the social and cultural realities of classrooms, in which one adult is responsible for the learning of many children, and in which (in British primary schools, at least) children commonly work in pairs or groups. My response to these issues has been to treat them as a stimulus for further theoretical development and classroom-based investigation and I hope that my efforts encourage others to do likewise. At the very least, I hope that I have shown how the three main neo-Vygotskian concepts — scaffolding, the zone of proximal development and appropriation — can, even in their present state of development, provide useful insights into the process of teaching and learning in classrooms. Any educationally relevant theory of learning should enable us to describe, 'model' and evaluate this process: and it seems to me that, for all its current limitations, the neo-Vygotskian framework offers the best theoretical basis for doing do.

Note

This is an updated and extended version of 'Accounting for what goes on in class-rooms: What have neo-Vygotskians got to offer?', which appeared in the *British Psychological Society Education Section Review,* Vol. 15, No. 2, in 1991. It now incorporates research from SLANT (Spoken Language and New Technology), which was a joint research project of the Open University and the University of East Anglia, funded 1990–92 by the Economic and Social Research Council.

References

Baker-Sennett, J., Matusov, E. and Rogoff, B. (1992) Sociocultural processes of planning in children's playcrafting. In P. Light and G. Butterworth (eds) *Context and Cognition.* Hemel Hempstead: Harvester-Wheatsheaf.
Bakhtin, M. (1981) *The Dialogic Imagination.* Houston: University of Texas Press.
Brown, A. L. and Ferrera, R. (1985) Diagnosing zones of proximal development. In Werstch (1985a, *op cit.*).
Bruner, J. (1978) The role of dialogue in language acquisition. In A. Sinclair, R. Jarvella and W. J. M. Levelt (eds) *The Child's Conception of Language.* New York: Springer-Verlag.
— (1985) Vygotsky: A historical and conceptual perspective. In J. Wertsch (*op cit.*).
Bruner, J. and Haste, H. (eds) (1987) *Making Sense: The Child's Construction of the World.* London: Methuen.
Crook, C. (1991) Computers in the zone of proximal development: Implications for evaluation. *Computers in Education* 17, 1, 81–91.

Czerniewska, P. (1992) *Learning About Writing: The Early Years*. Oxford: Blackwell.

Donaldson, M. (1978) *Children's Minds*. London: Fontana.

Edwards, A. D. and Westgate, D. P. G. (1987) *Investigating Classroom Talk*. London: Falmer Press.

Edwards, D. (1990) Discourse and the development of understanding in the classroom. In O. Boyd-Barrett and E. Scanlon (eds) *Computers and Learning*. Wokingham: Addison-Wesley.

Edwards, D. and Mercer, N. (1987) *Common Knowledge: The Development of Understanding in the Classroom*. London: Methuen.

Forman, E. and Cazden, C. (1985) Exploring Vygotskian perspectives in education: the cognitive value of peer interaction. In J. V. Wertsch (ed.) (*op cit.*).

Gray, N. (1985) *I'll Take You To Mrs Cole*. London: Anderson Press.

Heath, S. B. (1983) *Ways With Words*. Cambridge: Cambridge University Press.

Laurillard, D. (1987) Computers and the emancipation of students: Giving control to the learner. *Instructional Science* 16, 3–18.

Leont'ev, A. N. (1981) *Problems of the Development of Mind*. Moscow: Progress Publishers.

Leont'ev, A. N. and Luria, A. R. (1968) The psychological ideas of L. S. Vygotskii. In B. B. Wolman (ed.) *The Historical Roots of Contemporary Psychology*. New York: Harper and Row.

Maybin, J. and Mercer, N. (1992) 'Scaffolding' literacies: Supporting readers in YTS and primary school. In *The Proceedings of the Conference 'Literacy for the 21st Century'*, Brighton Polytechnic, July 1990.

Maybin, J., Mercer, N. and Stierer, B. (1992) 'Scaffolding' learning in the classroom. In K. Norman, (ed.) *Thinking Voices: The Work of the National Curriculum Project*. London: Hodder and Stoughton for the National Curriculum Council.

Maybin, J. (1993) Children's voices: Talk, knowledge and identity. In D. Graddol, J. Maybin and B. Stierer (eds) *Researching Language and Literacy in Social Context*. Clevedon: Multilingual Matters.

Mercer, N. (1990) Context, continuity and communication in learning. In F. Potter (ed.) *Reading. Learning and Media Education*. London: Blackwell.

— (1991) Learning through talk. In *Talk and Learning 5–16: An In-service Pack on Oracy for Teachers*. Milton Keynes: Open University.

— (1992) Culture, context and the construction of knowledge in the classroom. In P. Light and G. Butterworth (eds) *Context and Cognition*. Hemel Hempstead: Harvester-Wheatsheaf.

Mercer, N. and Fisher, E. (1992) How do teachers help children to learn? An analysis of teachers' interventions in computer-based tasks. *Learning and Instruction* Vol. 2, No. 4.

Moll, L. (1990) (ed.) *Vygotsky and Education: Instructional Implications and Applications of Sociohistorical Psychology*. Cambridge: Cambridge University Press.

Newman, D., Griffin, P. and Cole, M. (1989) *The Construction Zone*. Cambridge: Cambridge University Press.

Papert, S. (1980) *Mindstorms: Children, Computers and Powerful Ideas*. Brighton: Harvester Press.

Prentice, M. (1991) A community of enquiry. In *Talk and Learning 5–16: An In-service Pack on Oracy for Teachers*. Milton Keynes: Open University.

Resnick, L. B., Wang, M. C. and Kaplan, J. (1973) Task analysis in curriculum design: A hierarchically sequenced introductory mathematics curriculum. *Journal for Applied Behaviour Analysis* 6, 679–710.

Resnick, L. B. (1987) *Education and Learning to Think*. Washington, DC: National Academy Press.

Sheeran, N. and Barnes, D. (1991) *School Writing: Discovering the Ground Rules*. Milton Keynes: Open University Press.

Simon, H. A. (1981) *The Sciences of the Artificial*. Cambridge, MA: MIT Press.

Smith, L. (1989) Changing perspectives in developmental psychology. In C. Desforges (ed.) *Early Childhood Education* (British Journal of Educational Psychology Monograph Series: No. 4). Edinburgh: Scottish Academic Press.

Street, B. (1984) *Literacy in Theory and Practice*. Cambridge: Cambridge University Press.

Vygotsky, L. S. (1978) *Mind in Society*. London: Harvard University Press.

— (1981) The genesis of higher mental functions. In J. Wertsch (ed.) *The Concept of Activity in Soviet Psychology*. Amonk, NY: Sharpe.

Walkerdine, V. (1984) Developmental psychology and the child-centred pedagogy: The insertion of Piaget into early education. In J. Henriques, W. Hollway, C. Urwin, C. Venn and V. Walkerdine (eds) *Changing the Subject*. London: Methuen.

Wells, G. and Nicholls, J. (eds) (1985) *Language and Learning: An Interactional Perspective*. Brighton: Falmer Press.

Wertsch, J. V. (ed.) (1985a) *Culture, Communication and Cognition: Vygotskian Perspectives*. Cambridge: Cambridge University Press.

— (1985b) *Vygotsky and the Social Formation of Mind*. Cambridge, MA: Harvard University Press.

— (1990) In Moll (*op cit*).

Wood, D. Bruner, J. and Ross, G. (1976) The role of tutoring in problem-solving. *Journal of Child Psychology and Child Psychiatry* 17, 89–100.

Wood, J. (1988) *How Children Think and Learn*. Oxford: Basil Blackwell.

8 Sponsored Reading Failure

MARTIN TURNER

Introduction

There is now clear evidence that hundreds of thousands of British schoolchildren, south of a line from the Mersey to the Wash, are subject to a sharply downward trend in reading attainment at seven or eight. The nature and extent of that evidence will be dealt with fully later in context. The downturn in reading standards is unprecedented in peacetime in modern educational history — and only in this century have reading standards been monitored. If for hundreds of years those who learned to read at all did so by letters at their mother's knee, then they may need to do so still.

The evidence of progressive decline in reading attainment at eleven is not to be confused with the trend in infant reading in the 1980s. Where it exists, such a trend at eleven is stark: the percentage of children obtaining low scores on the London Reading Test in ILEA primary schools rose uninterruptedly from 24.3% in 1983 to 28.8% in 1988 (ILEA, 1989).

If the new evidence means anything, it must be that a far greater haemorrhage in literacy standards is moving up the system, and is yet to appear at 11 or 16, for these children have been tested at key stage one (7–8 years), and we know from correlational studies that there is a very strong tendency for status at seven to predict status at eleven.

It is important to examine alternative explanations before suggesting even tentative conclusions. Are parents too busy hustling a living? Is there a general breakdown in family values and integrity? Are children watching too much television? Time passes slowly for academic debate but quickly for children. Those politically responsible, and the ever-increasing numbers of concerned parents, will want to attend first to a curriculum trend which is heavily implicated in the debacle: during the 1980s there has been a 'progressive' but, in view of the research into reading, capricious movement in the teaching of reading which has confused and disconcerted infant teachers. This is a hydra-headed beast named:

111

— real books

— storybook method

— emergent reading

— wholistic approach

— osmosis

— apprenticeship approach

The movement stems largely though not exclusively from two North American gurus who, for purposes of glory like to appear severally, but who to weather obloquy might prefer to be lumped together: Frank Smith and Kenneth Goodman. Their 'real books' movement, as I shall call it for convenience, has been associated with failing schoolchildren at class level, school level, local authority level and, thus far, regional level (the south and south-east) in Britain. There are in addition indications that national trends can be expected to follow, though there is no national monitoring of reading at present; and evidence of similar popularization and controversy, with consequent harm to children, is becoming apparent internationally elsewhere in the English-speaking world.

If, as seems possible, the downward trend in infant reading is to be associated with a fashion or movement rather than with general social or environmental conditions, then the failure of so many of our children will not have been accidental or attributable to obscure or uncontrollable causes: it will have been *sponsored*. The political conditions of local government in which such havoc can be perpetrated without accountability, and the timidity of politicians in the face of 'experts', need to be addressed.

The pretensions of this movement will be exposed, and its claims refuted. The uninspiring history of 'debate' into reading teaching methods will be reviewed and clear recommendations for action formulated.

History of an Hysteria

Print seems to be the gateway to civility. The Farsi word *adab* means both literature and politeness. And so it is in the European cultures. For hundreds of years now, societies and conversations have been shaped by ideas which were first written down: the ideas of Hobbes, Hume, Johnson, Locke, Milton, Newton, Rousseau, Smith, Voltaire. Indeed our world of discourse is in some ways like a Regency parterre.

Nevertheless this does not explain why the teaching of reading serves to excite primitive passions on quite the scale that it does. These disputes about reading, whose comical aspect is tempered by their violence, are characterized by two features: their rigidity and their ignorance. Whole decades pass and do little to alter the terms of debate. In a book published in 1965, which students of 'modern methods' will find sobering, Hunter Diack (1965) gives an account of controversies in the teaching of reading which sounds in part as if it were written today; and *at the time of writing* Diack was commenting on how little the debate had altered since 1908.

However, the level of ignorance as regards research into reading is truly appalling. The main focus of debate during the post-war years was the relative merits of 'phonics', which teaches letter sounds and blends, and 'look-and-say', which goes straight for whole-word recognition. Both approaches are easily ridiculed: *Can a pig jig in a wig?* is not regarded by reasonable children as a sensible question; and

> *'Look, look' said Dick.*
> *'See Sally. See funny Sally and Father.'*
> *'See, see,' said Sally.*
> *'Sally is up, up, up.'*

from the *Dick and Jane* series (Gray *et al.*, 1956) exemplifies the linguistic poverty and repetitious character of look-say materials.

However, the principle at stake was essentially decided, in a way consistent with linguistic theory, in 1967. All writing is information storage. As societies become more organized and trade regulated by property laws, so alphabetic scripts — phonetic, consonantal, syllabic — manifest an advantage over ideographic systems, in which ideas are directly represented by symbols. Clearly an alphabetic script, in which a set of 20–60 signs can account for the phonology of a whole language, is more efficient than a script of pictures or rebuses: Chinese requires 2,000–4,000 signs for elementary, and 50,000 for literary use (Gaur, 1987). An alphabetic script is a transcription of speech-sounds into written symbols, used in orthographical sequence. English orthography has been stable for 350 years or so, while dialect and usage have varied considerably both in England and the many portions of the globe (and airspace) where the language has flourished. Consequently the correspondence between written and spoken English is no longer perfect, if it ever was. Nevertheless to teach children to read while concealing from them the principle upon which the written language has been nurtured and lovingly elaborated over thousands of years while learning, in quantities however small, was revered, is mischievous.

In 1967 Jeanne Chall published *Learning to Read: the Great Debate* (Chall, 1967) which reviewed hundreds of method comparison studies and found that children taught by means of programmes which emphasized code showed superiority in reading and spelling, accompanied by no lack of motivation and interest, over children taught by approaches which emphasized meaning.

Since this is a point of some importance and I would not want the reader to suppose it to be my own opinion, let alone to place any credence in such an opinion, let me sample a few authorities. Charles Perfetti (1985) writes: 'There is no getting around the conservative conclusion that code-emphasis programmes do not hurt comprehension and provide at least some help with word recognition . . . as far as the evidence is concerned, the great debate seems over, and Chall's conclusions hold'. Jane Oakhill and Alan Garnham (1988) review additional studies and conclude 'that the evidence in favour of a phonics-based approach is, if anything, stronger than it was . . . early intensive instruction in phonics produces readers who are more proficient at pronouncing words than are those taught by a whole-word approach . . . Although an early phonics emphasis is often criticized as having a detrimental effect on comprehension, there is little evidence to support this claim. Many studies have shown no clear difference in comprehension ability between children taught by whole-word and phonics approaches'. In the 1983 *Introduction to the Updated Edition* of her book, Chall concluded that 'it appears as if the research of the 1970s continues to support beginning reading programmes that are code-oriented as compared to those that are meaning-oriented. Indeed, the research support seems to be even stronger than it was in 1967 . . . The current research also suggests that some advantage may accrue to direct as compared to indirect phonics. It would seem that many of the characteristics of direct phonics, such as teaching letter-sounds directly, separating the letter-sounds from the words, giving practice in blending the sounds, and so forth are more effective than the less direct procedures used in current analytic phonics programmes. These conclusions follow review of numerous further studies and every serious student of the subject will want to go beyond these summary conclusions to the detail in the original.

The main features of the research landscape, then, have been clear for over twenty years; only over minor features are there still interesting arguments. So how is it that no-one has told teacher trainers, curriculum leaders, language advisers and 'English' inspectors?

The ignorance, if that is what it is, is striking. Not only are discussions being prosecuted now much as they were in 1908 (on the publication of Edmund Huey's book on reading), but there is a widespread lack of understanding that these are *empirical* issues, capable of being investigated experimentally.

Such poor relating of theory and evidence to practice could simply demonstrate the poverty of a 'humanities' education when it is on scientific ground. Numbers, and particularly statistics, do demonstrably alarm highly educated adults. And — a more compelling explanation — ideas with a durable emotional appeal enable ideological managers in the state sector to secure and enhance their hold on power.

Keeping Children Guessing

If the robust fun of punch-and-judy (phonics and look-and-say) was not to be curtailed by mere science, who was to say that Smith and Goodman should not have arisen, with 'psycholinguistics', a third player in the reading teaching game?

The Smith/Goodman movement for 'real books' and reading through language experience reaches the classroom, by a series of dilutions and distortions, as a sort of non-teaching of reading. In so far as it can be propositionalized — and its real motive force derives from its ability to flourish in what might, accordingly, be called the Dewey/Plowden classroom melee — it has been well rebutted in academic circles. But the counter-argument, even subject to simplification, does not reach the classroom at all.

In addition to its many names this philosophy is characterized by its negativities: it is against instruction or 'didacticism', against testing, against reading schemes, against phonics, against dyslexia, against the notion of skills, against formal methods, against the notion that a child *ever* fails. It is *for* empathetic sharing of stories, for parental involvement in such story-sharing, for role modelling (children come to view themselves as readers and writers), for books which have an intrinsic interest and literary value rather than an instructional purpose, for language enrichment as a precursor of reading development, for reading as itself a 'natural' development, for according syntactic and contextual cues, such as illustrations, status equal to that of phonic cues (sound-symbol regularities). As a little girl said to me in a classroom recently, after displaying the gaps in her front teeth, 'It's the pictures that tell you what the words say.'

Idealism often leads before long to demoralization. This child-centred and plausible methodology produces strikingly opposite effects: working-class children are disproportionately disavantaged by middle-class romanticism; the casualties wear an unmistakable air of failure, while their parents — what else are they to do? — press in painful turmoil for recognition of dyslexia; and numerous children, demotivated for life not only from books real and unreal but from school altogether, require expensive and very directive remedial education.

Critique

It is true that on the ground, in schools, following experience of the results of wholistic methods and petitions from incensed parents, there is now a general retreat from them.

The cry for balance, which was always the teachers' cry, is now occasionally heard from inspectors and advisers also! It is held that real book approaches do not exclude the teaching of letter sounds or spelling patterns. True enough: but rich. Six years ago this movement was led by hot gospellers livid with intolerant enthusiasm, who promoted their storybook methods with evangelical zeal, producing bigots, converts, heretics and martyrs all over the humdrum classrooms of the nation. (Could this have happened in a Catholic country?) It is a sad and unexplored phenomenon that sheer emotion convinces much like an argument, such is the respect of the apathetic for deep feeling. Indeed the resort to emotion often signals the point at which an argument has run into the sand.

Balance was what was sacrificed. Balance was what the ordinary main grade teacher secretly preserved, once she had finished the course, once the visiting inspector's back was turned. In her cupboard, under her desk were the word lists, the spelling sheets. About the only thing going for British primary schoolchildren in the last decade has been the commonsense of teachers.

But even if these methods are discredited in practice, and we want to pass on to count the cost and assess the damage in terms of an unprecedented slide in reading attainment, even if the serious lessons are political ones (how could it all have happened?), let us pause to test the claims and theories, which are still influential. 'Language' post holders are still arriving in schools and looking for reading schemes to burn or lock away or tip, in black plastic bags, on the rubbish skip. The damage continues.

Here is a sentence misread by a four-year-old from the Oxford Reading Tree's 'Spots' (Hunt, 1989): 'Everyone good better'. She went back, examined the word, and corrected: 'Everyone *got* better.' This use of syntactic cues from sentence and story structures which, in principle, may be very complex is not in doubt. However, it is in practice retrodictive. Sentence meanings are internally modelled, it is agreed if not generally understood, and the text proof-read in a hypothesis-testing, checking manner *after* being read. There is little guesswork involved.

Is reading natural? Do children discover reading for themselves? It is highly unlikely. The 32 children studied by Margaret Clark (1976) who were reading well at school entry, had a mean IQ of 123 (upper 86% of the population), and Professor Clark avoids the obvious implication that her very co-operative and committed parents had themselves taught the children to read. The proposition that children can learn to read inferentially must be regarded as untested, improbable, and limited in principle to the very brightest children.

Is the real books approach *developmental*? We are told that the sequence of skills is not linear, which would make the development highly unusual, and that story book reading is hugely demanding of the class teacher, which runs counter to our experience of the emergence of locomotor and language skills: biological programming in these areas is not in doubt and requires only threshold levels of stimulation.

A recent dignified rebuttal of several manifestations of the 'real books' fad has come from Margaret Donaldson in her booklet, *Sense and Sensibility* (1989). This distinguished child psychologist and researcher urges on us an unfashionable plea for rigorous thinking and intellectual seriousness. Nevertheless something of the scale of the disaster may be sensed by the author's apparent need to 'make a positive case for such teaching (any teaching) in the specific field of literacy'. Worse, Professor Donaldson feels obliged to take seriously and devote time to the claim that 'as one reads one need not attend to the words on the page'!

At school and local authority level, discussion is nasty, brutish and short. Terms such as *wholistic, behaviouristic, modern, structure* and *rote-learning* are shuffled around, cards in a soiled deck. So much talk about today's methods, modern ways, is mesmerizing. In fact it is possible to get people to do almost anything if you can convince them they are carrying forward the banner of progress. However, the higher up the pay scales you look on the curriculum side, the more people you meet who are wedded to an antique Fabian vision of pre-war vintage.

But in fact there is no discussion, no criticism or counter-criticism, no attempt at effective argument. If clear and expert advice, targetted at highly relevant 'quality and standards' committees, together with unequivocal evidence of serious decline, can safely be ignored in Conservative-led councils, then there is only the question of whose education system is it, who is in control, who — in the notorious comment of Humpty Dumpty on 'language' — is to be master? (Carroll, 1871).

The Decline in Reading Attainment at 7–8

Back in the real world a few local education authorities, not the majority and usually Conservative (testing reading is 'right-wing'), have steadily been collecting test data on all their children over the past decade. (Some have been aggregating reading data over much longer periods and making use of computers to analyse the trends.) In all cases but one — so far as I can discover — the results are not made public. Especially is this true where a decline is concerned. Large LEAs in Tory heartlands have been sitting secretly on desperately unfavourable downward trends in reading attainment. The information is withheld from elected members, who have to remember to ask for it — a difficult task. Education officers change the subject when it is mentioned by lowly psychologists concerned for children. Even when bad results are reported to committees of accountable (electable) members, their significance is not made clear and comment is kept to a minimum.

The arguments rehearsed so far are such as to predict a decline in reading attainment if 'real book' or other meaning-emphasis approaches were to enjoy a significant revival. In fact I predicted (in an unpublished paper) such a decline in May 1986 and am in the Tiresias-like position of saying, 'I told you so'. Nevertheless these arguments stand or fall on their merits and evidence of reading failure is not proof. So the data presented in Table 1 should be investigated as of interest in their own right and susceptible of numerous different interpretations, none of them, needless to say, conclusive.

This information has been assembled voluntarily by concerned professionals, following the chance discovery that several large authorities had testing programmes which showed a steady decline through the latter half of the eighties. At a specially convened conference it was agreed that in the public interest the position should be made known. It was felt, in addition, that the identity of the LEAs should be protected: at least these LEAs had attempted to monitor standards and several used the figures to direct remedial teaching help where it was needed. The necessity to put the reading curriculum house in order is not limited to any local authority or region.

Representatives of ten LEAs have concerned themselves actively with this issue. Nine have been able to provide data. In one there is no evidence of decline (this authority appears in Table 1 as area B). In another (Area A) the evidence is limited to a verified increase over five years in the number of poor readers. The effect is strikingly independent of the tests used. The commonest tests in use are the Young Group Reading Test, the MacMillan Group Test, the Neale Test, the Suffolk Test and other instruments developed by the LEAs themselves whose names they bear.

In most cases the LEAs concerned have taken active steps to prevent this data from becoming known; at officer level its publication has been delayed or suppressed; at adviser level the testing of reading has been repeatedly attacked in attempts to discredit it, chiefly on grounds — that testing is objective, gives valid measurements and is precise — which render all defence superfluous; in several LEAs the collection of data has been discouraged or discontinued.

Table 1 Reading tests results: Data from 9 LEAs

Total statutory school-age population:
| 15,000 – 60,000 | | 60,000 – 100,000 | | | 100,000 – 250,000 | | | |

Total primary-age population
| 9,000 – 20,000 | | 20,000 – 50,000 | | | 50,000 – 130,000 | | | |

Size of annual cohort tested
| 1500 – 3000 | | 3,000 – 7,000 | | | 7,000 – 25,000 | | | |

LEA code	A	B	C	D	E	F	G	H	I
No. of Years of testing	6	15	14	6	12	7	4	18	9
No. of Years of decline	5	–	5	5	10	4	4	9	9
Period of decline	1985-9	–	1985-9	1985-9	1979-89	1986-9	1985-8	1980-9	1980-9
No. of Children tested in this period	8,000	–	9,000	18,000	50,000	25,000	30,000	100,000	150,000
Observed decline in population mean (av. p.a)	NA *	None	0.55	0.94	0.40	0.60	0.49	0.68	0.71
Observed % decline > +1.3 SDs (av. p.a.)	NA	NA	NA	None	NA	0.36	NA	NA	NA
Observed increase < −1.3SDS, av. p.a.	1.2	None	0.66	1.34	0.34 ʸ	0.78	1.41	0.58	0.54
Increase in % < −1.3 SD during 1985-9	5.9	–	2.64	5.36	1.36	3.12	4.56	2.3	2.18
Decline in population means 1985-9	NA	None	2.75	4.7	2.0	3.0	2.45	3.4	3.55

Notes

NA Not available
*   A decline in population mean of 0.8 points per annum can be inferred from the observed increase in the proportion of pupils below 1.3 standard deviations
ʸ   Inferred from population mean.

Comments

Such a striking downturn in reading scores has not been encountered before in peacetime in public education in Britain. The results show a similar pattern in several, not all, areas. It could be that a new national survey would find no such downward course in measured reading attainment because local effects might disappear in national ones. However, this is unlikely, because of the magnitude of the observed trends.

What observations may be made of this data?

It should be noted, first, that, except for the notes at the foot of the table, no inference or statistical 'adjustments' have been performed except in order to provide a uniform basis of comparison. A distribution is not described sufficiently by its arithmetic mean and standard deviation. It is necessary to observe the frequencies with which scores fall into the various portions of the distribution. Where such observations are lacking they have not been synthesized. However, in order to provide a uniform basis of comparison the mean has been supplemented where possible with the changes in the proportions falling above and below 1.28 standard deviations of the normal curve. In a normal distribution this would describe the top 10% and the bottom 10% of readers.

Secondly, clearest evidence of a consistent downturn in reading levels is apparent in the period since 1985 — a finding which agrees with a curriculum explanation. Consequently the fall in means over this period has been calculated for all authorities as a point of interest.

Thirdly, one authority shows no decline and two others show signs of decline over a much longer period. In one case — authority E — there is similar evidence available for reading ability at eleven, and this also shows a downward inclination. Here a possible curricular explanation would be in terms of trends antithetical to 'structured' teaching; of these the 'real books' phenomenon is just one special accentuated case. (The authority in question reports, bizarrely, that the phonically prescriptive spelling program for the BBC computer, *Starspell*, is banned, as are all computer applications which are structured, not 'content-free'!) Nevertheless for trends of this size and consistency a preferred explanation would be in terms of demographic change, for instance shifts of population. Different such demographic explanations would have to be found for authorities E and H which also show longer-term decline. Two data sets are available for authority I, one for 1982–8 and the other for 1980–9. I have used the second, which show steeper decline, on the grounds that a longer timescale gives fuller information.

What of authorities which show no downturn (area B) or which report no strong 'real books' movement? Area B is geographically isolated and curriculum trends arrive late. However, of Area A it is said that only one school notably espouses 'real books' and 'their results are all right'. In Area G there are said to be marked 'real books' tendencies only in a few, urban schools. In another authority (not represented in the table) whose results have reached me in summary form, there are stable or improving results; here, it is said, 'real books have only just arrived'.

So how is one to interpret the movement in reading standards? What explanations are possible? My own preference in the matter is theoretical: simply from knowledge of the research into reading one can predict, from an analysis of the 'real books' claims and practices, that their implementation will result in children learning to fail instead of learning to read.

But surely such a widespread curriculum trend would be expected to show by now some sort of effect? The results from authority D are revealing in this respect. Here the children concurrently sat Tameside tests of number (skills and concepts) which show no downward or any other trend. At a stroke the demographic variables, the socio-economic effects, the rise in single-parent families, the mortgage interest rate, the low morale of schools' staff, the long teachers' strike over this period, the interaction with the curriculum of hyperactivity and low attention span in children at school entry — all disappear. The curriculum itself is effectively implicated. Any environmental factors would disproportionately have affected the number attainment. After all, number tasks require manipulation of symbols and even demand a fair level of reading skills — most number texts and tests contain many words on the page. If any factors other than reading curriculum were at work, surely they would have depressed number test scores first.

With reading as such implicated, however, it is still possible to argue that changes in reading behaviour are relevant. Here the favoured explanation is in terms of the quantity of television that children are watching now. I accept that reading experience promotes reading skill, and that television probably usurps reading for many children. What evidence, however, other than the acquisition in large numbers of video recorders during the decade, is there of a change in viewing habits sufficiently sharp to explain the drop in reading levels in the short-term?

In authority H the results have prompted an analysis of verbal intelligence profiles (on the Young Non-Readers Intelligence Test) and shown that there is little difference in the mean IQ between the successful and the unsuccessful readers. I have done the same analysis at school level with children on average eighteen months retarded in reading age at junior transfer. The language ability (on the British Picture Vocabulary Test) of these children was average: in terms of standard scores 67% fell in the range 86–112.

This group of thirteen demoralized children was at percentile 46.8 for language ability but 9.7 for reading ability.

Caution prompts only the conclusion that several authorities, with affected primary populations (the *means* have declined) reaching towards half a million, show a particularly painful downturn in the latter half of the eighties, and that subsets of evidence imply that the children themselves give little evidence of intellectual defect and in one area are able to achieve in everything except reading. Fuller pronouncement must wait upon a systematic survey of all LEAs who survey reading regularly on consistent measures (and who will co-operate). This is now being attempted. The results will eliminate the bias that could arise in a self-selected sample.

The data reported on here have come to light as a result of quite casual enquiries. I do not claim more than a *prima facie* case for the general argument. As yet there may be a suspect, even a smoking gun, but no culprit. The children do not comprise a sample — they are unselected and unstratified. However, nobody really seems to believe that elsewhere are another half million children, news of whose steadily elevating reading skills has been modestly suppressed. Moreover the size of the cohorts reported in Table 1 is about 6% of the British primary population — twenty-five times the size required for a scientific survey. Thus they can hardly fail to be representative.

The argument, then, must be moved on by turning it around. If the *absence* of a reading curriculum whose efficacy is attested by twenty years of research is likely to compromise the progress of very many school children, then the *presence* of a dynamic reading curriculum should bear on the same point by showing the positive benefits of even a little of the right kind of method.

The effect of a focus on reading in a school galvanized by unwelcome publicity is shown by the case of a south London infant school, too often named to deserve further exposure. After a number of parents had presented a petition protesting against a 'real books' curriculum which had left 35% of top infants (7 year olds) two years retarded in reading ability, a new head and her staff concentrated on reading with the help of several reading schemes, *Letterland,* and 'the learning of phonics and a core sight vocabulary'. The results, two years after the caravan of the national press corps had moved on, show that only 4% of children tested on the Suffolk Reading Test fall into the bottom quartile into which 25% of children nationally, and locally, fall.

A similar consideration encourages us to look at the rapidity with which disaffected, behaviourally disordered, often non-attending, sometimes dyslexia-labelled secondary pupils aged 11–13 can be taught to read using

Distar — Direct Instruction (Corrective Reading). These children have experienced six years of progressive, Plowden-type primary education in outer London without learning how to read. In the school year 1988–9 forty pupils received this structured, phonically-based reading programme (which uses highly unnatural and contrived texts to minimize psycholinguistic guessing!) at Sylvan High School in Upper Norwood. The children aged 11–13 began with a mean reading age of 7.75 years and achieved an improvement to 9.25 years (Turner, 1990a). To examine the pronounced early effect of the reading programme we evaluated the progress of 25 children in just the first term of the following school year: on average they made sixteen months of gain in reading age in four months of schooling! (Turner, 1990b).

If even children at secondary school, in other words, whose attitudes to learning have become hardened, can make rapid progress with a system which feature by feature contradicts everything in the accepted progressive philosophy of Frank Smith and Kenneth Goodman, then on what grounds may we continue to adhere to dogmatic ideas which deny children that most basic of their educational rights — the right to learn to read?

The Future

The lines of defence used by paladins of the progressive establishment may readily be observed:

— suppress the data; (this is managed constantly with impressive success)

— discredit the tests; (yet the downturn is completely impervious to the choice of test and shows up on all instruments, old or new)

— discredit all tests; testing is a bad thing, it is unfair to all children, especially when it shows up failure!

— break the statistical series; (note the current move to stop contributing British achievement data for purposes of international comparisons).

Even if all these lines of defence fail, then there is still the National Curriculum, that covered waggon which has fallen into safe hands! Gain control of the curriculum (done). Gain control of the assessment process (likely).

In the case of reading in particular (to ignore in this context the grade inflation at GCSE, the etiolation of history, the disappearance of separate sciences and the sequestration of English literary classics), incoherent mediocrity has enshrined itself in attainment target 2 of 'English' in the National Curriculum. In the 'statements of attainment' at 'level 2' (the average, it is suggested, for seven year olds), the advanced skill of alphabet use with dictionaries is set alongside 'listen and respond to stories, poems and other material read aloud' (attainment target 1 is 'speaking and listening'); 'read accurately and understand straightforward signs, labels and notices' co-exists with 'read a range of material with some independence, fluency, accuracy and understanding' (spot the difference?); and 'bring to their writing and discussion about stories some understanding of the ways stories are structured' at level 3 is from attainment target 2 (reading), not 3 (writing) or 1 (listening and speaking).

The word *story* or *stories* occurs nine times in statements of attainment for the first three levels; the word *letter* once. Evidently the whole thing was put together by people who can read (and who no longer remember learning or needing to learn) and for whom the only professional skill required in the teaching of reading is similarly the ability to read.

It should be apparent by now that an entire control-centre of public education, that for reading, subsumed under 'language', subsumed under 'English', has fallen prey to a *corps de ballet* of managers, impresarios, dispensers of favour: an unelected, unaccountable, uneducated, upwardly mobile cadre of ideologues of a quite Jacobin flavour. Why is there no response to reasoned appeal? None can be expected from people preoccupied with the epic of promotion. Fashion is the raw material of careers. There is, if anything, a secret dialogue between left and right. Something irrevocably silly has happened in the educational world when wives of aspiring Labour prime ministers announce to the media that they are very left wing about teaching reading! What, on a commonsense view, could possibly be political about teaching young children to read?

More to the point, a large, publicly owned system has become unaccountable and unresponsive to its clientele — children and parents. Parents are still astonishingly weak partners in the educational process. The private sector exists and flourishes as a direct result of the hopes and aspirations of parents (many of them teachers): 'pressure' in this case is for regular homework, annual written reports and firm evidence of results.

Children in state schools are not guinea-pigs for an irrelevant sociological agenda of race, sex, class, ever-multiplying affronts to the spiritual unity of mankind, the small change of contemporary intellectual ferment (if ferment is not putting it too strongly) in this age of unprecedented intellectual poverty. Nor for a propaganda blitz on Aids, homosexuality, abortion, divorce, physical and sexual abuse — the gory adult menu.

Learning the Political Lessons

It may be shocking and disappointing that such a simple mistake should have taken hold so widely and disadvantaged unnecessarily thousands of children; but such an outcome is not at all surprising. That literacy skills are code-based and different from natural language is an obvious truth which no-one with a training in science could possibly have mistaken.

In a sense, though, there is a quite simple market solution to this predicament: *reading* needs first to be set free from *language* and then language from English (which is only a single example, after all, of a language). This false subsumption, now vertically enforced, is at the root of the misunderstanding and some deregulation would dissolve it quickly enough. Let schools and districts compete, using their own perceptions of what methods will best produce results, and the edifice of illusion (*prelest,* in Eastern Orthodox theology) will collapse.

The 'real books' movement is a typical supplier fad; it would have been unthinkable, and therefore impossible, in the independent sector. Throughout this decade a monopoly (monotony?) of advice has issued from LEA professional centres, those centres of ideological control. Schools have not had alternative sources of in-service education in reading to call upon, nor their own funds to pay for what they might choose.

Inspections offer instructive instances of failing schools receiving glowing inspection reports and successful, popular schools receiving harsh criticisms of their language policies. There is a need for schools to be able to escape from the ideological control of the inspectorates and call upon independent research groups to tell them what policies or organisational features are effective, what direction their standards are moving in, and how better to meet the requirements of parents and the local community. In an educational free market demand would make formal inspections unnecessary.

And what of our own National Curriculum, introduced to lever standards upwards?

It has become clear that the National Curriculum is now diverted to the longer-term purpose, already in train, of reducing the intellectual content of subject areas across the board. This ambitious enterprise began with the desire to reduce the traditional focus upon the most academically able and enfranchise the 60% who leave full-time education as soon as they possibly can — at 16. (In Britain 45% of pupils leave school without even an O-level or its equivalent (*The Economist*, 1990).)

How or why good intentions go astray, or produce lamentable unintended consequences, is beyond the scope of this essay. However, it may be thought surprising that central political control of the curriculum should ever have been considered a good thing.

Solutions

Why should there not be a plurality of curricula and syllabi, competing, as examination boards do, in a free market in which the prize is excellence? Competition between schools of thought, textbooks, courses of differing kinds, alternative conceptions of what history should consist in or how to teach reading, would bring about contrasts between successful and unsuccessful runners (the term *curriculum* itself embodies the Roman conception of a race).

The National Curriculum's present mandatory status should be rescinded; the National Curriculum should instead have advisory, exemplary status. Districts and regions should be encouraged to produce their own, better curriculum documents. Where local curriculum documents have been produced the results command the commitment of those who have participated in the (usually wide) consultations.

But let there be, by contrast, a clear national framework for assessment. At 16 we need to know outcomes: how well pupils have performed in subject areas at a GCSE revised to former O-level standards. Before this schools and parents (and taxpayers) need benchmarks and objective, independent testing at 7 and 11 in 'toolkit' areas only: writing (to include reading) and number skills.

Let agreement be sought (non-governmentally) that if you really want children to learn to read, you do have to teach them. That this is the case with mathematics is not disputed, least of all by mathematicians.

Let national monitoring of reading standards, including the use of NS6 and other tests with known histories, be resumed through an independent research agency.

There is always the possibility that with so much terrain already irradiated by the *ignes fatui* and marsh-lights of zany optimism, a beacon of hope would go unnoticed. 'Superstition sets the whole world in flames'; wrote Voltaire, 'philosophy quenches them' (1964). And critical thinking, experimental method, rational enquiry and logical argument are an excellent basis for the rest of children's careers as pupils and can be taught, and learned, young.

Afterword

Sponsored Reading Failure was written in four days in an empty flat in Taunton. I had corresponded with, but not met, its subsequent publisher. The analysis was my own, an ediface reared in isolation. At the time child-centred orthodoxy seemed unshakable, the English Order immutable as the laws of the Medes and Persians.

In June 1990 a group of educational psychologists, convened by myself, met privately to address disturbing trends in local authority reading test data; we rashly communicated to a reputable journalist working on a background feature for *The Times Education Supplement* who had already published data similar to ours. The news story that developed contended for months on equal terms with Saddam Hussein for front page space.

The number of LEAs with a confirmed downward trend in measured reading attainment at seven has since risen inexorably to 37; one, Cheshire, has been able to report full data showing no such trend; only 51 LEAs ever performed such systematic testing. The loss of progress represents about seven months for the average child in five years. My thesis that the concurrence of reading failure with the Whole Language movement was unlikely to be a coincidence has since been widely, if hypocritically, accepted.

The political construction of different approaches to the initial teaching of reading is eye-opening. It appears that there is, at bottom, a religious dispute about values, with two opposing sides still fighting the English Civil War, and those sceptical about religion likely to be credulous about all else.

Martin Turner, 15th May 1993.

References

Carroll, L. (1871) *Through the Looking Glass*. London: Duckworth.
Chall, J. S. (1983) *Learning to Read: The Great Debate* (2nd edition). New York: McGraw-Hill.
Clark, M. (1976) *Young Fluent Readers*. London: Heinemann.
Diack, H. (1965) *In Spite of the Alphabet*. London: Chatto & Windus.
Donaldson, M. (1989) Sense and sensibility: Some thoughts on the teaching of literacy. University of Reading School of Education, Reading and Language Centre (mimeo).
Economist, The (1990) 10.3.90.
Gaur, A. (1987) *A History of Writing*. London: British Library.
Gray, W. S. *et al.* (1956) *Fun with Dick and Jane*. Exeter: Wheaton.
Huey, E. (1908) *The Psychology and Pedagogy of Reading*. Cambridge, MA: MIT Press.
Hunt, R. (1989) *Spots!* (Oxford Reading Tree). Oxford: Oxford University Press.
Inner London Education Authority (ILEA) (1989) Report on the London Reading Test. London: ILEA Research Statistics Branch (mimeo).
Oakhill, J. and Garner, A. (1988) *Becoming a Skilled Reader*. Oxford: Blackwell.
Perfetti, C. (1985) *Reading Ability*. New York: Oxford University Press.
Turner, M. (1990a) Positive responses. *The Times Educational Supplement* 19.1.90.
— (1990b) Letter to the Editor. *The Times Educational Supplement* 27.4.90.
Voltaire, F. M. A. (1764) *Dictionnaire Philosophique*. Quoted in *The Oxford Dictionary of Quotations*.

9 Simply Doing Their Job? The Politics of Reading Standards and 'Real Books'

BARRY STIERER

> Yet the New Literacy finds that even the limited case it makes on its own behalf is dismissed, not because its claims are unfounded, but for failing to use the measures currently governing education. The predominant discourse of quantitative studies and standardized measures makes it difficult for New Literacy programs to gain a national hearing . . . By dominating the form, as well as the substance, of educational discourse, this reading tradition, in effect, suppresses the spread of new programs seeking to overstep the governing cartel in reading of researchers, professional associations and publishers . . .
>
> John Willinsky, *The New Literacy*, p. 164

> At school and local authority level, discussion [of different methods for teaching reading] is nasty, brutish and short . . . So much talk about today's methods, modern ways, is mesmerizing. In fact it is possible to get people to do almost anything if you can convince them they are carrying forward the banner of progress . . .
>
> But in fact there is no discussion, no criticism or counter-criticism, no attempt at effective argument. If clear and expert advice, targetted at highly relevant 'quality' and 'standards' committees, together with unequivocal evidence of serious decline, can safely be ignored in Conservative-led councils, then there is only the question of whose education system is it, who is in control . . . ?
>
> Martin Turner, *Sponsored Reading Failure*, p. 15

These two conflicting observations, each alleging that the world of early reading has been commandeered, through various forms of ideological influence, by the opposing factional interest group, provide the starting point for this article. The last few months have seen sustained media interest in the subject of early reading, fuelled by reports of declining reading standards among seven-year-olds. Teachers adhering to certain philosophies and using certain practices have been identified as culprits. Teacher-trainers, LEA advisers and inspectors, and so-called reading 'gurus' have been savagely criticised. Indeed in some quarters this has been an opportunity to question the very political and cultural basis of state education. The purpose of this article is two-fold: to analyse this episode in order to gain a more critical understanding of it, and to propose an agenda for research and evaluation which might enable a more informed and rational debate.

'Progressivism' Under Attack

On 29 June 1990, the *Times Educational Supplement* carried a front-page story reporting a claim made by nine unnamed educational psychologists that reading standards among seven-year-olds had declined dramatically in their LEAs. The story was picked up by all the national newspapers and by many television and radio news programmes, leading to emotive accusations of unstructured and uninformed teaching in schools, inflexible 'bandwagoning' amongst teacher-trainers and LEA inspectors and advisers, and lax control by politicians and policy-makers. The press (and by no means exclusively the tabloids) had a field day: 'Children's reading ability plummets' (*Guardian*, 29.6.90); 'MacGregor to investigate reading crisis' (*Daily Telegraph*, 30.6.90); 'Scandal of our young illiterates' (*Daily Mail*, 30.6.90); and 'More dunces' (*Daily Mirror*, 29.6.90).

This was an extraordinary episode in the history of educational opinion-formation, since within a matter of days these unsubstantiated allegations by unnamed individuals had assumed the status of self-evident fact. The press referred to 'objective data', 'rigorous investigation by experts' and so on, when in fact no evidence had been made available. The political climate of opinion was clearly receptive to alarmist reports.

This episode was followed in the early autumn by the publication of *Sponsored Reading Failure: An Object Lesson* by Martin Turner, Senior Educational Psychologist in the London Borough of Croydon and one of the nine who had been behind the earlier furore. In fact, Turner's pamphlet is an attempt to publish, analyse and explain the 'findings' which had been anonymously promulgated in the June. It is therefore the nearest thing we have to a presentation of the evidence purporting to document a decline in standards and an explanation of the alleged link between this apparent decline and the so-called 'real books' approach. The pamphlet deserves to be taken seriously — not as a research report, but as an expression of a particular ideological position, as well as for the disproportionate impact it has had on public opinion.

The 'Evidence'

Turner's main points are these:

- Educational psychologists in nine LEAs pooled their reading test data for seven-year-olds going back in some cases ten years or more.

- The mean reading score in eight of the nine LEAs had declined in the period 1985–89, on average by 3.12 points of standard score.

- Again in these eight LEAs, the proportion of pupils with reading scores in the lowest band increased by about 50%.

- Changes in teaching and curriculum appear to Turner to be the most compelling explanation for the decline — in particular, the (allegedly) widespread take-up of the 'real books' approach.

Two points are worth noting here. First, of the nine LEAs taking part, one did not show a decline. The validity of this result is dismissed by Turner on the grounds that the LEA in question uses an unorthodox approach to annual comparison (it readjusts its norms each year). It has been excluded from the analysis. So, although it was widely reported that nine LEAs were involved in the survey, only the eight which found a decline were included in the analysis.

Second, the figure of 347,000 children involved in the survey, which was widely quoted in the press (Turner himself refers to 'affected populations reaching towards half a million' children), is based on the numbers of children for whom test data are available going back 10 years, for all nine LEAs. In fact the number of children tested each year by the eight LEAs involved in the analysis would probably have been less than 30,000. Turner does not in fact specify the size of the annual cohorts tested.

The claim by Turner is therefore based upon a fairly small number of children chosen only from those authorities which showed a decline. Most people reading the press reports at the time would be forgiven for concluding that the claim was based upon a large and representative sample, but this may merely have been the result of press misrepresentation.

Assumptions

For Turner to move from these sketchy data, to a claim that reading standards have declined, requires acceptance of a number of crucial assumptions, none of which he makes explicit. The first assumption is that *a decline in scores on conventional reading tests is synonymous with a decline in reading standards.* Nowhere in the pamphlet is the validity of the tests used in the survey scrutinised. In fact, all of the tests mentioned by Turner are outdated and have been widely discredited, since they only provide a crude measure of children's ability to decipher decontextualised print, or to comprehend unseen text which is read for no real purpose (see, for example, Levy & Goldstein, 1984; Barrs & Laycock, 1989; Cato & Whetton, 1991). Even the government's Assessment of Performance Unit has acknowledged that tests of this kind produce unreliable results. Nevertheless, press treatment of the claims consistently referred to 'objective data' and 'scientific findings'.

A second assumption is that *using a wide range of available reading tests prevents the weaknesses of a single test from distorting the data*. The decline was, according to Turner, observable across a range of tests: the Young, the Edinburgh, the Neale, the Macmillan, the Suffolk and tests developed in-house by some of the (unnamed) authorities. He writes: 'The effect is strikingly independent of the tests used' (p. 20). In fact, at an overarching level of analysis they are all the same, since they are all based on the same conceptions of reading and the same principles of psychometrics.

A third assumption is that *the methods used by the psychologists to analyse their data followed established canons of scientific rigour*. In fact, many of the psychologists' procedures are suspect, if not actually improper. In order for the psychologists to compare scores from different LEAs, they had to aggregate scores from widely differing scales (e.g. reading ages, reading quotients, error counts, etc.). They converted scores from all of them to a standard currency, using a form of statistical manipulation, as if all the tests were technically comparable, which they are not. They also excluded inconvenient cases from the analysis, as described above, which violated principles of statistical analysis to which the psychologists themselves would normally subscribe. Indeed Professor Asher Cashdan, writing in *Education* on 28 September 1990, observed that Turner's analysis 'would not have been allowed to appear in its present form in any publication of standing', and that we should treat it with great caution since it 'has not gone through the normal process of peer examination such as would be the case if it were a journal article'.

A final assumption is that *educational psychologists have no particular educational axe to grind*. Melanie Phillips, writing about this case in the *Guardian* on 6 July 1990, exemplifies this attitude when she praises 'the experts [the educational psychologists] who are *simply doing their job* in providing the information' (my emphasis). 'The psychologists', she writes, 'owe no allegiance to educational theories but simply observe children in the classroom and record their findings in a scientific manner'. In fact, educational psychologists, like any other professional grouping, subscribe to a set of values and perspectives which reflect the history of their discipline and their positioning within the education system. Most educational psychologists have strong views about the way in which children should be taught to read, how reading should be assessed, and how poor readers should be helped. Any analysis by them is bound to be guided by their assumptions and preconceptions. Curriculum and pedagogy are highly contested areas, and no-one can legitimately claim impartiality.

Hence, although Turner's allegations were popularly accepted as unambiguous evidence which demonstrated that standards had declined, they are simply too selective and open to too many interpretations to be taken as proof one way or the other. In a democratic society we all have a right to know how effective schools are in helping children to become literate, but we shan't know this until new kinds of research and evaluation are carried out, linked to new thinking about suitable methods and valid evidence, as I shall discuss at the end of this article.

Declining Standards and 'Real Books'

Having demonstrated to his own satisfaction that reading standards among seven-year-olds showed a marked and alarming decline in the 1980s, Turner then considers possible explanations for this worrying trend. He rejects a whole range of possible causes: demographic changes; socio-economic factors; the effects of the 1984–86 pay dispute; the rise in single-parent families; the mortgage interest rate; low teacher morale and high staff turnover; hyperactivity and distractability of children at school entry; lessening of parental involvement in pre-school activity; the influence of television. These kinds of factors, he claims, would have taken their toll indiscriminately across the range of children's learning, whereas the only evidence of significant decline is in the area of reading. The only explanation which remains credible, he claims, centres upon the allegedly widespread take-up of 'real books' philosophies and practices through the 1980s.

The section of Turner's pamphlet dealing with possible causes of his alleged decline is pure polemic: he produces no evidence whatever which would enable us to evaluate the validity of his assertions. In particular, he provides no evidence to substantiate his claim that 'real books' approaches were widely taken up in the LEAs featuring in his analysis. In fact, he fails even to offer an unambiguous definition of the 'real books' approach which would enable us to identify those classrooms guided by such principles. To Turner, 'real books' is synonymous with 'no teaching'.

An alternative interpretation of Turner's evidence is that it demonstrates the rapidly accelerating obsolescence of standardised reading tests, since models of teaching and learning no longer reflect the psychometric conceptions of reading built into the tests. It's plausible to assume that children taught to read in traditional ways perform well on traditional tests. We may discover that children who are introduced to print through their experience of language and literacy, rather than through the teaching of deciphering skills, out-perform other children on a whole range of literacy competences, provided the assessment procedures used are sufficiently sensitive, but that they do not acquire the specific narrow skill of 'sounding out' individual decontextualised words until later in childhood.

Motives

It is possible to consider two theories to account for the decision by Turner and his colleagues to publish their 'findings' and to release them to the press prior to publication. On the one hand, we could consider that they were honestly surprised and genuinely concerned at their unexpected discovery, and simply felt a responsibility to share their findings with the educational community. Martin Turner invites us to view him and his colleagues in this light:

> The data reported on here have come to light as a result of quite casual enquiries. I do not claim more than a *prima facie* case for the general argument. As yet there may be a suspect, even a smoking gun, but no culprit (pp. 24–5).

He implies that they did not wish to induce a moral panic over standards, or to trigger an emotive series of press attacks on particular approaches to early reading in schools, but merely to 'draw attention' and 'call for investigation'.

On the other hand, there is evidence to suggest rather more calculating motives. Many of the press reports in the summer used identical or very similar phraseology in their reports (e.g. 'the sharpest decline in reading standards in more than 40 years', 'secret data', 'bound to fuel concern over methods', 'trend discovered by accident at an informal meeting' etc.), suggesting that press correspondents were carefully briefed or that the press-release went far beyond the psychologists' evidence. In his own pamphlet, Turner makes no effort to disguise his own conviction that the decline has been caused by the moral and professional pressure which LEA advisers and inspectors have brought to bear upon otherwise reasonable classroom teachers to abandon their 'tried and tested' and 'commonsense' methods in favour of 'real books'.

Educational psychologists have in recent months displayed growing professional anxiety over what they perceive as their increasing marginalisation. In particular, they have witnessed a gradual erosion of their previously unchallenged expertise in the province of reading. A large proportion of them are disturbed by, among other things:

- the way in which reading was formulated in the report of the national curriculum English working group (DES, 1989), which reflected an essentially psycholinguistic view ('Reading is much more than the decoding of black marks upon a page: it is a quest for meaning and one which requires the reader to be an active participant . . . meaning should always be in the foreground' [para 16.2]);

- the approach to assessing reading adopted by the consortia developing SATs for 7-year-olds, which is essentially a diagnostic one and not a conventional test of reading ability;

- the growing shift away from traditional approaches to meeting special educational needs (holistic as opposed to skills-based);

- changing models of learning, e.g. social constructivist models replacing behaviourist and cognitive psychological models;

- the uncertain funding base for educational psychological services as LEAs devolve increasing proportions of their budgets to schools;

- the signs that headteachers might be prepared to 'make do' with national curriculum assessment results, however crude, rather than 'buy in' the assessment services of educational psychologists.

In this light, it is not fanciful to speculate that the psychologists who released this explosive information on the public will have had a number of implicit messages they wished to communicate. They may, for example, have wished us to conclude that SATs will not deliver diagnoses of individual children's reading competence, and that only educational psychologists can do this. Moreover, there is the implicit message that if it weren't for the testing done by educational psychologists, if it weren't for their conscientiousness in pooling their data for the purposes of comparison, and if it weren't for their courage in making their 'findings' available, *we would never have known about this alarming trend.* Certainly SATs and other forms of national curriculum assessment will not be able to deliver data on reading standards over time. Educational psychologists therefore have a demonstrably valuable role to play.

Turner and his colleagues must have known that their report would be accepted on trust by the media. They must have known that it wouldn't matter whether their evidence was valid, or whether their speculations about possible causes were responsible and informed. This was, I suspect, a well-orchestrated media campaign, carefully timed and planned. The psychologists have capitalised on the scientific mystique which surrounds their profession, and the high esteem in which they are generally held (as Melanie Phillips's *Guardian* article revealed), to create an atmosphere which would quickly restore them to what they consider to be their rightful place within the education system.

It must also be appreciated that Martin Turner, in his pamphlet, goes well beyond the 'standards and methods' debate, and attempts to articulate a more overarching ideological position which employs the familiar discourse of 'New Right' polemic. In particular, he claims that the allegedly widespread take-up of 'real books' is the result of a strangle-hold which has been achieved on all aspects of the teaching of reading by 'paladins of the educational establishment' (i.e. LEA advisers and inspectors, teacher-trainers), and that 'real books' reflects an attempt by this group to promulgate a wider political programme of left-wing causes. His proposed solution is to dismantle the institutions of state education in order to free schools from the shackles of LEA control: if 'real books' had to compete in an educational free market with other approaches its irrelevance to the concerns of parents would soon become apparent, since schools offering a 'real books' approach would quickly go to the wall. These portions of his pamphlet demonstrate that Turner's attack on 'real books' is ultimately a platform from which to argue a New Right educational manifesto.

In a telling remark, Turner bemoans the 'politicisation' of the teaching of reading:

> Something irrevocably silly has happened in the educational world when wives of aspiring Labour prime ministers announce to the media that they are very left wing about teaching reading! What, on a commonsense view, could possibly be political about teaching young children to read? (p. 27)

In this reference to Glenys Kinnock, Turner reveals his 'paradigm blindness'. He appears to be unaware of the fact that *all* approaches to the development and use of literacy will reflect cultural values. Whilst Turner's own caricature of the 'real books' movement is simplistic and ill-informed, it is nevertheless true that 'progressive' methods are 'biased' in that they stem from a pluralist intellectual root. Turner's perspective is *equally* ideological, but because it conforms to dominant values in education and society it appears to him to be politically neutral. Turner repeatedly underscores the need for structure and discipline in education, the importance of deferring to 'scientists' (psychologists) on matters of children's learning, the necessity of separating reading from other language experiences, and the vital assimilating function of schooling. His numerous references to the 'classics' of British philosophy and literature reflect his privileging of enduring elitist traditions. These views help us to draw a map of his ideological terrain. Turner would have been more intellectually honest had he declared his own ideological colours and argued his corner accordingly. Instead, he claims ideological neutrality in an area of the school curriculum as hotly contested as literacy, and accuses his opponents of dragging politics into the argument.

Towards a Reading Research Agenda for the 1990s

The mainstream professional response to Turner's position has been to ignore its wider professional and ideological underpinnings, and to treat the debate as an unnecessarily polarised comparison of two techniques for teaching reading. 'Moderates' quoted in the press refuted Turner by reporting that most teachers use a combination of methods, and that the world of reading is not as fraught a battleground as Turner would have us believe.

This response appears in one sense to be appealing, since it promises to introduce commonsense into the argument and reconcile the growing polarisation. However, in its claim to impartiality, this response falls into the same trap that Martin Turner does: it is blind to its own ideological underpinnings. As Carole Edelsky (1990) writes, 'There can be no eclecticism at the level of deep underlying beliefs' (p. 7). So, this kind of response seems to me to be a spurious attempt to reconcile fundamentally irreconcilable philosophical positions, under the guise of impartiality, by reducing the debate to one of techniques and by accepting implicitly all of the assumptions about teaching, learning and schooling underpinning Turner's stance. It leaves unanswered the really crucial questions about literacy, which stand at the frontiers of practice, crying out to be investigated.

Another problem inherent in responding to Turner relates to the dilemma summarised by John Willinsky in the quote at the beginning of this article: the traditional psychometric methodologies which might be used to compare competing approaches to early reading are artefacts of the dominant perspective rejected by New Literacy adherents. In short, in its rejection of quantitative measures of reading, and quantitative procedures for evaluation and comparison, progressives leave themselves open to this kind of attack.

There are therefore several related questions which urgently need to be addressed:

(1) Are studies which compare traditional methods with progressive methods worth supporting? The Leicestershire Literacy Initiative Evaluation Project and the ILEA Hackney Literacy Study were modest beginnings at such comparison, but they did not begin to explore the deeper questions raised by competing notions of literacy, such as the effect of different approaches on disadvantaged and lower-ability children and the relationship between effectiveness and teachers' personal styles. Is further research and evaluation in these areas worthy of support, or would it simply perpetuate the sense of inquisition felt by progressives?

(2) Is the issue of standards in reading across large populations of children a legitimate concern? If so, what kinds of evidence would progressives accept?

(3) Are qualitative methods of recording and assessment such as the *Primary Language Record* (Barrs *et al.*, 1988), which are embedded in

the processes of teaching and learning, suitable for larger scale assessment purposes, such as monitoring standards over time, allocating resources, facilitating transfer, identification of children for special help etc.? If so, what kinds of work need to be done in order to promote this extension of the use of qualitative methods into previously unexplored areas? If *not,* are conventional quantitative methods being implicitly condoned for these purposes?

(4) Are progressives prepared to define the essential features of a 'real books' methodology in suffient detail to enable it to be distinguished from traditional approaches for the purposes of comparative research and evaluation?

(5) Might one unanticipated result of 'New Literacy' programmes be that children will tend to develop the ability to decipher unseen decontextualised print at a later age than children introduced to reading through the acquisition of decoding skills? Would this matter?

I suggest here a few fruitful areas for research and evaluation, which might arise from the process of answering the above questions, or might alternatively help to answer them:

- Small-scale descriptive studies of the *Primary Language Record* in use, including use of the two five-point 'reading scales'.

- Small-scale descriptive studies of teacher assessment and moderation in the area of children's reading.

- Analyses of *PLR*-type teacher–pupil conferences and teacher–parent conferences.

- Small-scale descriptive studies of any existing attempts to use the PLR for assessment purposes such as monitoring, transfer, resources allocation, referral, etc.

- Analyses of the attitudes of parents in relation to issues such as national standards in reading, competing methodologies for teaching reading, etc.

At the moment, prophets of doom such as Martin Turner occupy the high ground, monopolise the most compelling discourse, enjoy the patronage of the powerful and influential, and have successfully created a climate of opinion which will enable the likely backlash to appear sensible, moderate, fitting. We are likely to observe this backlash in areas such as: revisions to national curriculum programmes of study and statements of attainment; the revised specification of standard assessment tasks for key stages 1 and 2; protectiveness towards schools psychological services by local authority education committees when devising LMS formulae; the winding down of specialist language services; escalation of LEA-wide testing programmes for reading; and further central control over the content of teacher-training courses.

This kind of backlash cannot be prevented head-on. It can only be challenged indirectly through new kinds of research and evaluation which aim to produce new kinds of evidence. There is an urgent need for imaginative thinking which can lead to the development of reading assessment procedures capable of discriminating more dynamically between individual readers than does the national assessment scale but which employ texts, tasks and social structures reflecting non-psychometric principles. The other is the need for a concerted effort to strengthen the credibility of teacher assessment through supportive in-service work and collaborative moderation exercises. The two 'reading scales' developed as part of the *Primary Language Record*, which set a range of descriptive criteria against a five-point scale, represent a promising start on both these fronts. Systematic research into, and evaluation of, the uses of these scales and others like them would go some considerable way towards obviating the need to use psychometric procedures for assessing children's reading to serve larger scale assessment purposes. Such work might gradually enable progressives to regain the high ground and to find a discourse which can win hearts and minds both in high places and at the school gates. In the meantime, we can expect the polarisation of paradigms for the assessment of reading to continue.

References

Barrs, M., Ellis, S., Hester, H. and Thomas, A. (1988) *The Primary Language Record: Handbook for Teachers*. London: Centre for Language in Primary Education.

Barrs, M. and Laycock, L. (1989) *Testing Reading*. London: Centre for Language in Primary Education.

Bird, M. and Norton, N. (1988) *The Hackney Literacy Study*. London: ILEA Research and Statistics Branch.

Bridge, M. (1988) *Learning to Read: Literacy Initiative Evaluation Project — 1986–87*. Leicester: Leicestershire Literacy Support Service.

Cashdan, A. (1990) The great unproven failure. *Education*, 28.9.90.

Cato, V. and Whetton, C. (1991) *An Enquiry into LEA Evidence on Standards of Reading of Seven-year-old Children*. London: Department of Education and Science (with NFER).

Department of Education and Science (1989) *English for Ages 5 to 16*. London: DES.

Edelsky, C. (1990) Whose agenda is this anyway? A response to McKenna, Robinson and Miller. Educational Researcher 19, 8, 7–11.

Levy, P. and Goldstein, H. (eds) (1984) *Tests in Education*. London: Academic Press.

Phillips, M. (1990) Commentary. In *The Guardian*, 6.7.90.

Turner, M. (1990) *Sponsored Reading Failure: An Object Lesson*. Warlingham, Surrey: IPSET Education Unit.

Willinsky, J. (1990) *The New Literacy: Redefining Reading and Writing in the Schools*. London: Routledge.

10 Talking in Class: Four Rationales for the Rise of Oracy in the UK

MAGGIE MacLURE

Which of the Possible Oracies . . .

Many people, myself included, think 'oracy' is a good thing. It seems to appeal to a loose grouping of educators and social scientists who — whatever their disciplinary allegiances, and this is partly my topic in this chapter — approve the general idea of letting students talk in class, and helping them get better at it. But are we all talking about the same oracy? I am not the first to ask that question: Douglas Barnes, speaking to the launch conference of the National Oracy Project in 1988, felt it was timely to ask 'Which of the possible oracies . . . are we promoting?' (reported in Horner, 1988). And others have recently been asking the same question. There seems to be a feeling, then, that some of the possible oracies are less desirable than others — though what counts as desirable depends of course on where you stand. This chapter represents a further attempt to name the possible oracies that are in circulation. My aim is not to arbitrate amongst competing definitions — though I certainly have my own preferences — but to ask how we might characterise these different versions; what interests (and whose interests) are served by each; what the implications might be of choosing one version rather than another; and indeed whether it is possible to choose one 'pure' strain and discard the others.

My starting point is to look at the various rationales that have been put forward for including oracy in the curriculum. What is oracy *for*, for those who practise and/or promote it? What kind of claims — educational, disciplinary or ideological — do people make on its behalf? I want to suggest that oracy has made itself promiscuously available to a number of rather different enterprises — including economic recovery, cultural transformation, personal emancipation and cognitive enhancement. It has been endorsed (though not always under the name of 'oracy') by sociologists, linguists, educationalists and industrialists. Trying to disentangle these various

139

influences and allegiances, it is possible, I think, to discern at least four rationales for oracy, which I shall label *personal growth, cultural transformation, the improvement of learning* and *functional competence* respectively.

Like all taxonomies of social phenomena this one is an oversimplification: I am not suggesting that the four categories are discrete and complete. On the contrary, there is a pervasive tendency for one rationale to shade off into another, and even to borrow the coloration and rhetoric of its opposite. So there is a constant traffic between the four rationales, and between the discourses that they represent; indeed this is what makes them of more than taxonomic interest. But as broad orientations, the four rationales are useful as starting points for 'interrogating' the notion of oracy, especially if we take a historical look at their emergence in educational discourse over the past twenty-five years or so.

Oracy for Personal Growth

In its earliest guise, oracy was associated with developments in English education in the mid 1960s, when a group of academics and teachers of a broadly liberal-humanist persuasion argued that the main aim of English teaching should be to encourage children's 'personal growth'. The personal growth model (see especially Dixon, 1969) was based on the conviction that language is central to the development of the individual on all fronts: creative, imaginative, expressive, social, intellectual. Children's 'own' language was to be valued. They were to be encouraged to express their thoughts and give shape to their experiences in writing and speech; to refine their feelings and sensibilities through imaginative engagement with literature and drama. Language was the main instrument in the 'humanizing of the species', in Andrew Wilkinson's words (1965: 40), and the individual's main resource in the struggle for self expression, self knowledge and self improvement. In subjecting our experience to language, John Dixon claimed, we 'bring order and composure to our inner selves' (1969: 13).

Spoken language was an essential part of this liberal-humanist project, and people began to argue for a much more central role for speaking and listening in the classroom, especially the English classroom. Andrew Wilkinson's case for including oracy in the curriculum is worth quoting at some length, as it represents a particularly clear statement of the personal growth rationale.

> The development of the personality is inextricably bound up with the development of language. Language is the basic and essential instrument in the humanizing of the species; without it thought above very primitive levels is impossible. Language and man are in continual

interaction; change the man in some way and you change the language he [sic]¹ uses; change the language he uses and you change the man. On the one hand the process of growth through education and experience causes him to reach out for new language in which to understand and communicate. On the other hand this language contains new thought and shades of thought, new feelings and shades of feeling, which help to determine such growth. His ability to direct rather than to be directed by experience, his ability to establish human relationships, are intimately related to his capacity for language; the frustrations of the inarticulate go deep. And it must be borne in mind that 'language' in this context is overwhelmingly the *spoken* language . . . Without oracy human fulfilment is impossible; speech and personality are one. (1965: 40; reproduced in Wilkinson *et al.*, 1990: 7; original emphasis)

This new English was democratic and egalitarian in intent: diversity and difference were to be valued, and teachers were charged with preparing children for their adult roles as responsible, active citizens. It is not surprising then that the kinds of talk that Wilkinson, Dixon and others had in mind included the demotic or informal genres found in everyday talk — discussion, anecdote, story, folk-tale, as well as the more formal ones such as debate, recitation and monologue. This was an innovation: previously, spoken language had been allowed into the classroom only in its best clothes — in what Roger Hewitt (1989a) has called the 'augustan' tradition. The new model celebrated informal speech genres, and the languages, dialects and speech cadences of children's home communities and cultures. But as Hewitt has pointed out, the concern with cultural diversity was essentially romantic rather than critical or political — a matter of cherishing the local and picturesque, rather than directly confronting the status quo.

In any case, the 'celebration' of children's home language and environment by educationalists was seldom whole-hearted. Wilkinson, for instance, while passionately asserting the validity of non-standard accents, nevertheless designated working class homes sites of 'language deprivation' because of the fragmentation of family life brought about by shift work, 'school and canteen feeding', and too much television (1965: 46). This negative stereotyping of the language of working class families, fuelled subsequently by (misinterpretations of) Basil Bernstein's (1971) work on restricted and elaborated codes and by Joan Tough's functional theories of class-based language deficit (e.g. 1977), is still heard in many quarters today.

Despite the appeal to communal and societal values, the personal growth model of oracy was essentially an individualist one. The main concern was the development of the 'whole person' (see Wilkinson, 1965: 40), whose social responsibilities were to be developed in much the same way as their other sensibilities — moral, ethical, intellectual and creative. Social justice and social order would be regulated and administered through the rational and co-ordinated actions of such fully developed individuals. The rationale for oracy was enlightenment rather than social transformation therefore, and teachers were the guardians of that enlightenment, even if this meant altruistically giving up the centre stage so that pupils could do more of the talking, and being more attuned to pupils' 'own' meanings and point of view. This distinguishes the personal growth rationale for oracy from the next to be discussed below, where spoken language becomes a site of struggle *within* the classroom, and teachers' monopoly of language is read, more sinisterly, as a reflection of the inequalities of power that exist in the outside world.

In terms of its intellectual influences, the personal growth model of oracy was the product of a vanguard of English school teachers and English subject specialists in the teacher training colleges and university education departments, many of whom were founder members, or early members, of the National Association for the Teaching of English.[2] But there were influences too from contemporary developments in linguistics and sociolinguistics. Notions of register and style were borrowed from the British functional linguists, notably Michael Halliday; and the studies of non-standard dialects by sociolinguists such as Labov and Trudgill were used to endorse the position of cultural pluralism in language practices. Sociological ideas had very little impact, with the notable exception of Bernstein's code theory, as noted above. This version of 'oracy' was firmly embedded therefore in the professional culture of teaching. It could hardly be called a grass roots movement, since its disciples were innovators from the colleges and the academy, but in distinction to the other rationales it developed out of the subject-teaching concerns of practitioners, and those who wrote about it wrote from their grounded knowledge of those concerns.

I have spoken of the personal growth rationale as if its time had passed; but in fact it is very much alive in the nineties. Many teachers — particularly primary teachers and secondary teachers of English — would recognise at least some of their own values in it, and its traces can be found in contemporary books and policy documents, as we shall see below. What is distinctive, I think, is that it now has to jostle for space alongside other rationales and ideologies — although I may be guilty of retrospectively tidying up history by imagining a time when a notion of 'oracy' was more purely or singularly held.

Oracy for Cultural Transformation

During the 1970s pupils' talk came in for attention from a rather different perspective — one which was much more strongly influenced by sociological ideas, and by new developments (at that time) in discourse and interaction analysis. People started, for a number of reasons, to look closely at class-rooms, and consequently, at the talk that took place within their walls. Here, though, the immediate interest was as much in teachers' talk as in pupils' — indeed teachers came to bear the brunt of a critique of classroom talk which found them guilty of wielding unjustifiable power over children, and of acting as unwitting perpetrators of social inequities. Oracy — though it was never known by this name — became a weapon in the struggle to redress social ills and transform society.

One strand of this work belonged within the approach that came to be known as the 'New Sociology of Education' — a radical critique of the role of schooling in the production of the social order. This work was strongly influenced on the one hand by Althusser's neo-Marxist theory of the relation between education (and other 'ideological state apparatuses') and the economic superstructure; and on the other by 'qualitative' disciplines such as symbolic interactionism and ethnography. Social reproduction theorists such as Bowles & Gintis (1976) and Bourdieu (1977) argued that the primary function of schooling was to reproduce in successive generations of pupils the social relations, skills and forms of consciousness necessary for the con-tinued operation of capitalism. Schools were as much about turning out a stratified and acquiescent workforce and reproducing the class system as they were about education, according to these theories, and teachers were the primary agents. Teacher–pupil interaction came to be seen as a key arena for enacting these processes, through the asymmetrical power relationship between the teacher and her pupils. Studies of classroom talk, even when not directly influenced by neo-Marxist and Althusserian ideas, repeatedly came up with the same sorts of observations: of teachers talking most of the time; deciding what should be talked about; exercising strict con-trol over turn-taking; asking 'closed' or 'pseudo' questions with pre-decided answers, and dispensing (or withholding) approbation to pupils who ven-tured a response. And conversely, of pupils continuously obliged to guess what was in the teacher's mind, wait their turn, know their place, and be con-tent to be passive receivers of pre-digested knowledge (see for example Edwards & Furlong, 1978; French & MacLure, 1979; Mehan, 1979).

A classroom study by Martyn Hammersley from the mid 70s gives a good idea of the climate of the time. In an analysis of the 'cultural resources' needed by a class of secondary pupils to answer a question from their teacher, Hammersley found that 'being able to produce "the answer" to the teacher's question requires knowledge of the conventions governing a parti-cular kind of teaching and the ability to "read the signs" in the teacher's structuring of the lesson' (1977: 82). The pupils were obliged to pick up whatever clues they could, in other words, in the attempt to come up with the answer the teacher was looking for. Hammersley's closing remarks spell

out the kinds of linkages that analysts were making at the time between the
minutiae of teachers' and pupils' talk and (much) larger social structures.
They incidentally highlight the period flavour of this kind of analysis for contemporary readers — or this reader at least:

> The methods the pupils must use if they are to answer the teacher's
> question sustain his claim to legitimately control classroom events
> [. . .]. The socio-cultural forces operating on this teacher and on
> others in similar social structural locations need to be explored. It is
> in this complex of forces that the explanation will lie, though
> whether these forces can simply be traced back to the nature of
> capitalism or industrialism remains to be seen (1977: 83–4).

Work in this vein amounted to a pathology of classroom talk. Far from
seeing teachers as the guardians and guarantors of pupils' enlightenment
through talk, it cast them as their oppressors — denying them the chance of
an active role as speakers, learners and social agents, and thereby dampen-
ing down the possibility of resistance and social change in the next generation of workers. Control over talk would need to be relinquished by (or
maybe wrested from) teachers, and the rules of the game changed to accommodate challenge, dissent and cultural difference on the part of pupils. It
was nothing personal however — teachers were not doing it deliberately.
Indeed they were taken to be ignorant of their reproductive role — buffeted
by 'socio-cultural forces', in Hammersley's words; 'cultural dopes', to use
Garfinkel's (1967) term. I exaggerate the tone and the polemic intransigence
of this kind of work, of course — which is especially unfair of me since my
own work at that time was very much of that coloration. But in any event
there was a definite sense abroad that classroom talk was centrally implicated in the inculcation of class-based orthodoxies, and that creating new
conditions for children's talk was an emancipatory, if not a revolutionary
task. Bernstein's code theory was turned on its head for instance, and
schools were found to be responsible for imposing a middle class 'restricted
code' upon the diversity of children's indigenous language practices (see for
example Edwards & Furlong, 1978).

Classroom talk was also identified as a site for the reproduction of
inequalities related to race and ethnicity (and later, and to a lesser extent,
gender). Shirley Brice Heath (1983) found the rules of talk in a Carolina
primary school subtly attuned to the language experiences of children from
the white middle class community, and blind to the different linguistic patterns and perspectives of the children from the white, and especially the
black, working class communities. Cultural difference got translated into
school failure, as a result of the black children's seeming 'incompetence' at
routine activities such as story time. Again, although the perspective dif-
fered from the work discussed above, it was schools that were found to be
derelict in their duty to meet the linguistic needs of all children.

As already noted, the main interest guiding this particular approach to classroom talk was sociological: issues of class, culture, race and, especially, power were in the foreground. But in pursuing this sociological interest, a range of other, related disciplines were important — especially ethnography, with its origins in anthropology, and a number of relatively new approaches to the analysis of discourse, originating both in linguistics and in an esoteric branch of sociology known as ethnomethodology. These disciplines brought a new kind of focus, and a new kind of purchase upon classroom talk — firstly, because they asserted the importance of understanding schools and classrooms as *cultures* — with meanings and values for the participants that remained to be discovered. Secondly, they forced a much closer attention than before to the *specifics* of classroom talk. People were looking much more closely at what pupils and teachers actually said, and how they interpreted one anothers' meanings and intentions, than had typically been the case before. So this strand of work — paradoxically perhaps, in view of its lofty social programme — significantly enhanced the empirical basis of our knowledge of what classroom talk looked like at the time. However there has been relatively little cross-over of ideas between this and other approaches to children's talk, because of its particular intellectual lineage and, especially, its extended sociological critique of schooling. The work discussed here was not primarily addressed to teachers as professionals or subject specialists, with a view to advising them on ways of improving their practice. Consequently, although interesting studies are still being carried out (see for example Edwards & Westgate, 1987) it has never entered the professional discourse of teachers to any great extent.

Nor has it entered the 'official' discourse of oracy, as enshrined in the sacred texts that codify the National Curriculum for English. The personal growth rationale for oracy is about changing individuals. Here the aspiration was, through talk, to change *society* (though the details of that programme were never spelled out). Of the four rationales discussed in this chapter, this one has, overall, failed to thrive. At best, pupils are encouraged to be armchair connoisseurs or spectators of language difference — exercising a limited sociolinguistic awareness of, for example, 'some of the factors that influence people's attitudes to the way other people speak'.[3] They are not invited to contemplate any need for change. It seems a pity that this radical edge has been lost amongst the advocates for oracy, and not only for the loss of whatever potential it embodied for social change and social justice. One of the strengths of the work referred to here was its insistence on classroom talk as a product of the *relationship* between teacher and pupil (or between pupil and pupil, though this received much less attention), and the need to understand classroom talk as embedded in a particular kind of sociocultural milieu, with its own particular constraints, rules of engagement, and symbolic systems. This understanding is scarcely represented in official pronouncements about speaking and listening. Classroom discourse has become invisible, or at least transparent: it is assumed that we can simply look 'through' it to get at the oral competence of each individual child. This has some serious implications for pedagogy and for the classroom assessment programme which is being implemented in schools.

Oracy for Learning

This rationale for oracy, still very much in currency, asserts the centrality of talk in the learning process. Children learn best, the argument goes, when they are actively involved in exploring ideas and creating meanings through talk with other people. This perspective has been strongly influenced by research which began to emerge in the 1970s into the development of language and thinking in pre-school children. Psychologists and linguists such as Jerome Bruner (e.g. 1975) and Gordon Wells (e.g. 1978) showed that children are encouraged from a very early age to become active communicators, and argued that it is this prolonged involvement in making sense of the world through talk that is central to the huge learning gains that they make in the first five years of their lives. Parents and other carers have a crucial role to play in supporting their children's development, according to this model: their job is to provide a secure yet stimulating conversational environment that encourages children to extend their knowledge and their communicative resources. Wells for instance claimed that parents were particularly good at 'fine tuning' their own responses to their children's communicative needs, giving just enough support in the way of clarification, explanation and contextual clues to help them to express the meanings that they were grasping towards. Bruner called this kind of supportive interaction 'scaffolding' — a term which has now entered the educational vocabulary.

It is easy, at least with hindsight, to see the relevance of these ideas to post-five education: if talk was central to pre-school learning, why should this cease to be the case once children started school? Teachers too could act as facilitators and 'scaffolders' of children's learning, gradually effecting the 'handover' process, as Bruner (1983) called it — the progressive transfer of power, knowledge and autonomy from one side of the adult–child partnership to the other. Chang & Wells (1988) referred to the process, using one of the emancipatory metaphors of the 80s, as 'empowerment' through talk. Vygotsky's ideas have also become very popular in relation to talk and learning in the classroom (see for example chapters in Rogoff & Wertsch, 1984). Although Vygotsky's work has been around for a long time, certain aspects of it have become much more widely discussed recently — in particular, the so-called 'zone of proximal development'. The term (chattily abbreviated to the 'zoped' by Griffin & Cole, 1984) refers, loosely, to the discursive space within which speakers operate, where a novice or less expert participant can extend their abilities with the help of a more expert partner.

There is obviously an overlap in these various notions; indeed they seem at times to be used almost interchangeably in educational writing to indicate a general notion of the teacher as a facilitator or 'talk partner'[4] who supports without seizing overall control of the interaction.[5] The teacher's role in this view of oracy is a benevolent, indeed an indispensable one. But Derek Edwards and Neil Mercer warn against adopting too idealised a position on the nature of the teacher–child relationship, while agreeing with the general proposition that cognitive development is anchored in social interaction, and that teachers initiate children into the system of 'common knowledge' which comprises educational discourse. They remind readers that Vygotsky's theory is essentially about the mediation of culture, and describe the induction of children into new realms of educational knowledge as *cognitive socialization* — an inescapably ideological matter.

> Teachers have the task of 'scaffolding' children's first steps towards and into [the educational] culture, of supervising their entry into the universe of educational discourse. [. . .] One of the main purposes of education is thus to develop a common knowledge. This is a problematical process, not only because the creation of successful discourse is in itself problematical [. . .], but also because education is necessarily ideological and predicated upon social relations in which power and control figure largely. The extent to which educational knowledge is made 'common' through classroom discourse is one measure of the effectiveness of the educational process. The importance of a teacher–child asymmetry of power also makes problematical one of the major goals of education — the eventual 'handover' of control over knowledge and learning from the teacher to the child . . . (Edwards & Mercer, 1987: 161)

The recourse to power, control and ideology here recalls the cultural transformation analysis of classroom talk.

One way of trying to overcome that problematical 'asymmetry' of interactional power is through peer group talk — a pedagogical strategy which has become increasingly popular amongst teachers interested in exploring the potential for learning through talk.[6] The value of peer group talk as a medium for learning has been argued for many years, on the grounds that (in optimal conditions) it allows children to take joint and individual responsibility for creating meanings without deferring to a more expert adult, encourages socially valued skills such as collaboration and mutual support, frees them to explore ideas and formulate new knowledge in an open-ended situation, and encourages intellectual competences such as problem-solving and decision making (see for instance Barnes & Todd, 1977; Phillips, 1988). Pedagogies for peer group talk have been a major focus for the National Oracy Project, which ended in 1993. Many of the teachers and co-ordinators involved in the project devoted their time to developing new techniques and tasks for stimulating and organising learning through small group talk. By the time the project ended some of those techniques — 'jigsawing', 'pairs to fours', 'envoys' — had become standard practice, and entered the professional discourse, across all of the participating LEAs (see Johnson, 1992: 49).

The commitment to learning through peer group talk undoubtedly owes something to the general ethos of progressivism which has been part of the ideology of primary teaching since the Plowden Report of 1967, and to similar values embodied in the innovative curriculum development projects of the 60s and 70s, such as Nuffield Science and the Schools Council Humanities Curriculum project. Broadly progressive notions such as child-centredness, active learning, 'learning by discovery' and the teacher as facilitator or counsellor are quite compatible with the arguments for learning through small group talk. It is perhaps more surprising, at least on the face of it, that those arguments have latterly been embraced also by the 'New Vocationalism', as embodied, for instance, in the pedagogies advocated in the Technical and Vocational Educational Initiative (TVEI). Groupwork, teamwork, collaborative learning, problem-solving and joint decision-making are now considered essential competences for the modern workforce. This vocationalist emphasis within the talk-for-learning rationale links it, however, to the final rationale for oracy that I want to discuss.

Oracy for Functional Competence

In contrast to the learning rationale, this one is utilitarian: it is concerned with oracy as a repertoire of language skills or competences. Oracy is about 'equipping' children to cope with the many communicative demands that they will face in adult life — especially those of the workplace. The second Cox Report, for instance, which formed the basis for the National Curriculum in English, emphasises 'the importance of talking and listening both in obtaining employment and performing well in it', and refers to a survey of Marks & Spencer which stressed the need for employees to be able to cope with 'a variety of complex situations' (DES, 1989: 15.5–6). The report, in common with other policy documents, mentions other important social functions for oracy — such as being able to complain effectively as consumers, or to fulfil democratic obligations successfully as 'potential jurors or witnesses, voters or representatives of political or interest groups' (1989: 15.7). But we could be forgiven for thinking that the work ethic has a particular place in the priorities of the policy makers. In the National Curri-culum (hereafter NC) Attainment Target for Speaking and Listening, the examples accompanying the statements of attainment at the upper levels (7–10) invoke a population of young middle managers, ad-persons and market researchers — flourishing slides, OHPs, databases and diagrams as they attend committee meetings, design campaigns, give presentations, con-duct surveys, give reports and interview people for mini-companies (DES, 1990: 5–6).[7]

However, despite this noticeable tilt towards the world of work in the examples that accompany the NC statements of attainment, the statements themselves are couched in a distinctively neutral functional language. The overall aim of the Speaking and Listening attainment target is expressed as 'The development of pupils' understanding of the spoken word and the capacity to express themselves effectively in a variety of speaking and listen-ing activities, matching style and response to audience and purpose' (DES, 1990: 3). As I have argued elsewhere (e.g. MacLure, 1988), this functional model of talk has become the 'official' version of oracy, and stands in a direct line of descent from the assessment model developed by the Assessment of Performance Unit (APU) in the early 1980s. Borrowing loosely from Halliday's functional theory of language, the model defines competence according to certain key concepts: specifically, as the ability to communicate *effectively* and *appropriately*, for a range of different *purposes*, to different *audiences*, in a variety of *situations*.

The statements of attainment, which specify what pupils should be able to do, are couched accordingly in an impersonal language of communicative purposes or functions, such as conveying information or expressing a point of view. To take just a few examples:

— convey accurately a simple message (Level 3b);

— give a well-organised and sustained account of an event, a personal experience or an activity (Level 5a);

— use language to convey information and ideas effectively in a variety of complex situations involving a range of audiences and in language which is matched to audience and purpose (Level 8b).[8]

We can get a glimpse of this neutral language in action in the following commentary, taken from a booklet of sample assessments illustrating the application of the NC assessment system:

Thomas' account is coherent, sustained, detailed and reasonably accu-rate. His grasp of sequencing and his concentration on the task indicate that this is a strong level 2 performance but he will need to show greater awareness of his audience in order to meet the appropriate statements at level 3 (SEAC, 1992: 11).

Children would, not so long ago, have been assessed for their 'fluency', 'liveliness' 'cheerfulness' or 'clarity' — with all the scope for subjectivity, personality assassination, moralizing real and ethnocentric bias that such judgements often entail, as Roger Hewitt points out (1989b: 5–6). And indeed, as Hewitt goes on to note, those kinds of preconceptions may continue to colour assessors' 'unofficial' judgements these days. But the official model as laid out in Attainment Target 1 betrays only a kind of grey-suited indifference to culture, class, passion, ethics or values. Children are judged, like Thomas above, in terms of their grasp of sequencing and their audience awareness. The model recognises sociolinguistic and stituational variation, but in contrast to the cultural transformation model, that recognition leads to recommendations for cultural *versatility*; it does not connect at any point with a prospect of struggle, change or irresolvable cultural differences. The aim of oracy is to turn out versatile people who can 'adjust' their talk to meet the exigencies of each and every situation appropriately — including those which 'require' people to use Standard English.

The functional competence model of oracy strips spoken language of its cultural and symbolic features. Roger Hewitt suggests that this is an inherent tendency of functionalism, and one which acts in the interests of the prevailing economic regime, while seeming, by its very cultural 'indifference', to accommodate a wide range of political interests. Drawing on Sahlins' critique of Malinowski, and by extension the sociolinguistic functionalism of Halliday, he points to:

> the absence within functionalism of any notion of culture other than as background and resource, and any concept of the human subject beyond the role of executor of functions. There is no sense of culture as symbolically ordered in its own right or constitutive to any degree. It is not surprising, therefore, that even under a Thatcher government [in 1989] the notoriously liberal tones of sociolinguistic discourse could smooth the way for an essentially de-cultured concept of English, and an oracy which places considerable, indeed almost evangelical stress on the transactional and pragmatic needs of our future citizens in the economic order they are to inhabit (1989a: 6).

In another article Hewitt suggests that this indicates a trend towards 'supra-cultural communication', as a result of the globalisation of economies and cultures. In the interests of universal transactions, supra-cultural communication becomes, 'like certain foods in the supermarket, "the produce of more than one culture" and, conversely, the product of none' (1989b: 11). Hewitt is not the only person to note a trend towards the elimination of context and culture from oracy. Douglas Barnes, voicing the same sorts of concern which led him to raise the question of 'possible oracies' with which this chapter opened, warns against classroom exercises which construe oracy as a set of decontextualised skills, and which merely make 'meretricious gestures towards the real world' (1988: 52).

Conclusion: Which are the Probable Oracies?

It is difficult to say, however, whether the functional rationale for oracy will ultimately prevail over all the others — or even whether this is a sensible question to ask. Practice on the ground may be at variance with official policy, as a result of the inertia of institutions, the tenacity of teachers, or the domestication of reform. But in any case, the official policy documents are not all that consistent in themselves. Hewitt detected an 'enchanting dance' in the second Cox report between cognitive and social arguments for oracy; but, he says, it was always the cognitive rationale that got caught in the spotlight when it came to fixing the targets and programmes (1989b: 8). So the contest between the two rationales was textually rigged. The same might be said of the review of the NC arrangements for English which was published by NCC in the summer of 1992.[9] In its preamble and asides the review seems to endorse every rationale for oracy (except the cultural transformation one). It strongly supports the importance of talk for learning; and in one rather feverish paragraph, it manages to cram both the functional and the personal growth arguments: 'English teaching must, above all else, be about fostering the child's ability to use language purposefully and creatively. It must encourage the powers of the imagination and promote spiritual, moral and cultural understanding' (NCC, 1992b: 9–10). But in spite of this keys-to-the-kingdom flourish, the main substantive recommendation relating to oracy is a muscular injunction to 'strengthen' the regulations by requiring 'mastery of Standard English' from all pupils right from the start, rather than from level 7 onwards (1992b: 1 & 11). So again, we might say that while there is more than one voice discernible in the text, one of them is shouting much louder than the others.

Even so, I am not convinced that such attempts at textual hegemony are — or ever could be — entirely successful. As Bakhtin (e.g. 1981) insists, texts — spoken or written — are always peopled with many 'voices', since the words out of which they are constructed contain the sediment of other, prior meanings and values, from other contexts. There is always a tension, according to Bakhtin, between the homogenising tendencies of the 'authoritative' discourse, and the dispersion of meaning that is constantly threatened by the proliferation of unruly and diverse other voices. So we could read the NCC review as an attempt to patch up some of the holes in the authoritative discourse — but an attempt that cannot ever be totally successful. The same can be said of the statutory orders themselves. Even though the functional model has reached perhaps its purest expression here, there are entertaining little anomalies — small ruptures and disjunctions in the smooth and dispassionate discourse of purpose and audience, hinting at other voices and disorderly meanings. Take, for instance, the example accompanying the statement of attainment concerning group discussion at level 7:

> Introduce a new, relevant idea to a group discussion about the planning of a visit, or the making of a database; *show respect for the contributions of others*. [my emphasis]

Where does 'respect' come from? Surely this is pushing a functional model a little beyond its scope . . . But here it is again, in the non-statutory guidance for English, at Key Stage 1:

> [Children] develop an ability to adjust their talk to suit the audience and purpose, *to respect others* and to take turns [my emphasis (NCC, 1990a)].

These are blanket moral, or at any rate cultural precepts, inserted — literally — into the neutral propositions of the functional framework. The execution of linguistic functions is to be done civilly and courteously — in line with the precepts of a liberal democracy. But at the same time there are whispers of a more exacting discourse of 'clarity', 'accuracy', 'precision', 'order' and 'reason'. The programmes of study state for instance that '*All* activities [my emphasis] should [. . .] help to develop in pupils' speaking and listening their grasp of sequence, cause and effect, reasoning, sense of consistency, clarity of argument, appreciation of relevance and irrelevance, powers of prediction and recall' (DES, 1990: 23). This harks back to what Hewitt called the 'augustan' model of oracy, with its emphasis on logical rigour and the exercise of reason. And we could note that it is not strictly compatible with the principle of situational/functional variation at the core of the model. There are some 'purposes' for which precision, accuracy and the application of causal reasoning are not always particularly 'appropriate', and which would probably startle the 'audience' — for instance, many of the narrative genres. And some would argue that even 'discussion' and 'argument' — those most seemingly 'rational' of genres — are far less bound to the canons of causal reasoning, consistency and precision of outcome than we often imagine (see for example Phillips, 1988). The language of precision is itself situationally bound therefore; it is 'appropriate' for some activities — station announcing, air-traffic controlling, reporting an accident, taking part in a debate — and not for others.

So, in short, there are tensions, inconsistencies and a plurality of voices in the official documents relating to oracy. In fact, I suspect the discourse of situational/functional variation is inherently unstable and unsettling for policy makers who are also deeply convinced of the superiority of the linguistic and literary habits of a white middle class. The functional competence model may suit the economistic rhetoric of neo-conservatism, with its demands for an articulate, versatile and itinerant workforce, equipped to work collabora- tively in 'small flexible teams' and move from one job to another in the post- industrial landscape. But it is a threat to the traditional conservativism which sees dissent as dangerous and the middle classes as the custodians of culture and the guarantors of social order. There is an ever-present danger, for the traditionalist tendency, that language 'difference' will be construed by some as cultural disadvantage or social injustice, and that people might stop being simply spectators of a colourful sociolinguistic pageant, and start trying to change things.

This is not to say that we can expect the current policy statements to col- lapse under the weight of their own internal contradictions — though they have certainly become a target for critique and review by policy makers at the time of writing this chapter. Nor would any changes necessarily be for the better: most of the current policy reviews have a 'traditionalist' slant which is deeply disconcerting to many teachers and educationalists. But at least the current models are less determined and buttoned down than they might at first appear.

The most important place to look for instances of contemporary thinking and practice in oracy, however, is in the schools themselves. What kind of models — tacit and overt — are teachers and children operating? How do these relate to the 'official' models in the policy documents? Are we seeing, for instance, the emergence of a strange new oral genre, born out of the criteria for group discussion in the GCSE exams, and nurtured by the National Curriculum attainment targets? Roger Hewitt's research identifies a kind of group discussion which he calls 'synthetic tableau' — notable for its politeness, carefully organised turn-taking, and tendency towards 'con- sensual, uncontroversial, "respectable" and socially well-underwritten points of view' (1981: 9). This mirrors Douglas Barnes' concern, mentioned earlier, that classroom talk was becoming divorced from the 'real world'. There is a need, then, to document current practice in oracy, and to ask whether classroom talk has begun to change under the spotlight of official recognition.

Notes

1. In common with most other work of the period (i.e. the 1960s), there is an untroubled assumption that the masculine forms will suffice to indicate, generi- cally, the other half of the human race as well. Rather than pepper the text with 'sics' in order to distance myself from this practice, I merely point it out here, and will pass over subsequent occurrences without comment.
2. Despite calls for oracy to be taught 'across the curriculum' — calls which have intensified over the intervening years — it was seen as primarily a job for the

English specialist, as Andrew Wilkinson insisted, in a slightly bizarre analogy: 'Inevitably however the English teacher will be held to have the greatest share of [the] responsibility; and rightly so — just in the same way we are all accountable for the moral health of the community, but it is the parson who is the sin specialist' (1965: 64).

3. From the Statement of Attainment at Level 10 in Attainment Target 1: Speaking and Listening (*English in the National Curriculum (No. 2)*, DES, 1990).

4. This term has become popular in publications by those involved in the National Oracy Project: see below.

5. Edwards and Mercer (1987) provide a useful critical interpretation of such terms as scaffolding and the zone of proximal development.

6. The popularity of group work appears to be losing popularity, however, with policy-makers. A report commissioned by Secretary of State, and carried out by three academics who were swiftly dubbed the 'three wise men' by their opponents, recommended greater attention to whole class teaching (Alexander *et al.*, 1992). Calls by policy-makers for a return to 'traditional' methods of classroom organisation were intensifying at the time of writing this chapter.

7. It is no surprise to find examples of this kind of thing in NCCs cross-curricular booklet *English and Industrial Understanding at Key Stages 3 and 4*. Examples of projects involving the community, for instance, include operating a minicompany: 'four boys who had set up a pop group had to present the TVEI Coordinator with a flow sheet . . .' (NCC, 1992a: 14).

8. As I argue elsewhere, the functional basis of the NC framework makes it highly unsuitable as a model of *progression*, expressed as a hierarchy of levels. Based as it is on an inclusive metaphor of competence, as a full repertoire or assemblage of functions across a totality of situations, it does not lend itself to expression as a step-wise accumulation of skill, wisdom or complexity. Hence the resort to a kind of progression-by-adjectives, as in the move from giving a 'detailed oral account' at level 4 to giving a 'well organised and sustained account' at level 5 (see MacLure, 1992: 6).

9. At the time of writing this chapter it was still unclear which, if any, of the review recommendations would be implemented.

References

Alexander, R., Rose, J. and Woodhead, C. (1992) *Curriculum Organisation and Classroom Practice in Primary Schools. A Discussion Paper*. London: DES.

Assessment of Performance Unit (APU) (1984) *Language Performance in Schools. Report of the 1982 Primary Survey*. London: DES.

Bakhtin, M. M. (1981) *The Dialogic Imagination: Four Essays by M. M. Bakhtin*. M. Holquist (ed.). Austin: University of Texas Press.

Barnes, D. (1988) The politics of oracy. In M. MacLure, T. Phillips and A. Wilkinson (eds) *Oracy Matters*. Milton Keynes: Open University Press.

Barnes, D. and Todd, F. (1977) *Communication and Learning in Small Groups*. London: Routledge & Kegan Paul.

Bernstein, B. (1971) *Class, Codes and Control, Vol. 1*. London: Routledge & Kegan Paul.

Bourdieu, P. and Passeron, J. C. (1977) *Reproduction in Education, Society and Culture*. London: Sage.

Bowles, S. and Gintis, H. (1976) *Schooling in Capitalist America*. London: Routledge & Kegan Paul.

Bruner, J. S. (1975) From communication to language: A psychological perspective. *Cognition* 3, 255–87. Reprinted (1979) in V. Lee (ed.) *Language Development*. London: Croom Helm.

— (1983) *Child's Talk*. London: Oxford University Press.

Chang, Gen Lin and Wells, G. (1988) The literate potential of collaborative talk. In M. MacLure, T. Phillips and A. Wilkinson (eds) *Oracy Matters*. Milton Keynes: Open University Press.

Department of Education & Science (DES) (1989) *English for Ages 5 to 16*. Proposals of the Secretary of State for Education and Science and the Secretary of State for Wales. (The Second Cox Report). DES & Welsh Office.

— (1990) *English in the National Curriculum (No. 2)*. DES & Welsh Office. London: HMSO.

Dixon, J. (1969) *Growth Through English* (2nd edition). London: Oxford University Press, for the National Association for the Teaching of English.

Edwards, A. and Furlong, V. J. (1978) *The Language of Teaching*. London: Heinemann.

Edwards, A. and Westgate, D. P. G. (1987) *Investigating Classroom Talk*. Lewes, E. Sussex: Falmer.

Edwards, D. and Mercer, N. (1987) *Common Knowledge*. Milton Keynes: Open University.

French, P. and MacLure, M. (1979) Getting the right answer and getting the answer right. *Research in Education* 22, 1–23.

Garfinkel, H. (1967) *Studies in Ethnomethodology*. Englewood Cliffs, NJ: Prentice-Hall.

Griffin, P. and Cole, M. (1984) Current activity for the future: The zoped. In B. Rogoff and J. V. Wertsch (eds) *Children's Learning in the Zone of Proximal Development*. New York: Jossey-Bass.

Hammersley, M. (1977) School learning: The cultural resource required by pupils to answer a teacher's question. In P. Woods and M. Hammersley (eds) *School Experience*. London: Croom Helm.

Heath, S. B. (1983) *Ways with Words*. Cambridge: Cambridge University Press.

Her Majesty's Inspectorate (HMI) (1984) *English from 5 to 16*. London: HMSO.

Hewitt, R. (1989a) The new oracy: Another critical glance. Paper presented to the BAAL Annual Conference, September 1989.

— (1989b) Oracy, culture and bias: Some preliminary issues concerning ethnicity and oral assessment. Paper presented to the CLIE seminar, 'Some Issues in Oral Assessment', November 1989.

— (1991) GCSE oral communication assessment and inter-ethnic variation. A Report to the Economic and Social Research Council. University of London Institute of Education: Mimeo.

Horner, D. (1988) More questions than answers. *Oracy Issues* 1, Autumn, 1.

Johnson, J. (1992) Pondering the project. *Talk* (The Journal of the National Oracy Project) 5, Autumn, 48–50.

MacLure, M. (1988) Assessing spoken language: Testing times for talk. In N. Mercer (ed.) *Language and Literacy from an Educational Perspective, Vol. 2: In Schools*. Milton Keynes: Open University.

— (1992) How has linguistics contributed to the assessment of speaking and listening? In J. Swann *Assessing Speaking and Listening*. CLIE Working Papers, 13, Spring 1992.

Mehan, H. (1979) *Learning Lessons: Social Organisation in the Classroom*. Cambridge, MA: Harvard University Press.

National Curriculum Council (NCC) (1990a) *English Non-Statutory Guidance*. York: NCC.
— (1990b) *Core Skills 16–19. A Response to the Secretary of State*. York: NCC.
— (1992a) *English and Economic and Industrial Understanding at Key Stages 3 and 4*. York: NCC.
— (1992b) *National Curriculum English: The Case for Revising the Order*. Advice to the Secretary of State. York: NCC.
Phillips, T. (1988) On a related matter: Why 'successful' small group talk depends upon not keeping to the point. In M. MacLure, T. Phillips and A. Wilkinson (eds) *Oracy Matters*. Milton Keynes: Open University Press.
Plowden Report (1967) *Children and their Primary Schools*. London: Central Advisory Council for Education.
Rogoff, B. and Wertsch, J. V. (eds) (1984) *Children's Learning in the Zone of Proximal Development*. New York: Jossey-Bass.
Secondary Examinations and Assessment Council (SEAC) (1992) *Pupils' Work Assessed: English. Key Stage 1*. London: SEAC.
— (1984) *GCSE: The National Criteria for English*. London: SEAC.
Tough, J. (1977) *The Development of Meaning*. London: Allen & Unwin.
Wells, G. (1978) Talking with children: The complementary roles of parents and teachers. *English in Education* 12, 2, 15–38.
Wertsch, J. V. (1985) *Culture, Communication and Cognition: Vygotskian Perspectives*. Cambridge: Cambridge University Press.
Wilkinson, A. (1965) *Spoken English*. Educational Review Occasional Publications, No. 2. University of Birmingham.
Wilkinson, A., Davies, A. and Berrill, D. (1990) *Spoken English Illuminated*. Milton Keynes: Open University Press.

11 Distinctive Features of Pupil–Pupil Classroom Talk and Their Relationship to Learning: How Discursive Exploration Might Be Encouraged

EUNICE FISHER

Introduction

A good deal is already known about the distinguishing features of teacher–pupil discourse. Teachers ask a lot of questions; they often *initiate* discourse topics and they attempt to control the content of classwork by a variety of discourse strategies such as *feedback* (Sinclair & Coulthard, 1975) and through *elicits, reformulations, reconstructions* and selected emphasis through *repetition* (Edwards & Mercer, 1987). We also know from this and other research that the pupil's role in these discourse processes is often one of mere respondent, where the skill of the exercise tends to be more related to 'finding out what the teacher wants to hear' than to any pursuit of understanding. This is not to say that pupils *never* take the leading or even an equal role in talking with their teachers, but merely to emphasize that the necessarily asymmetric relationship between them means that, when seeking out or formulating new ideas, there is a tendency for pupils (and perhaps teachers too) to see the teacher's ideas as the ones which should be accepted. Indeed, it may be that it is only through pretence (e.g. asking questions to which they know the answer) or through absenting themselves from the discourse entirely, that teachers can reduce the influence of their own greater knowledge of most topics which are discussed in school. As a result, some teachers seek to promote pupil–pupil discourse, though they do so through a wide variety of strategies with great diversity of results.

In this paper some examples of pupil–pupil (p–p) discourse will be examined in which peer groups develop their ideas, and these are contrasted with teacher–pupil (t–p) discourse as well as with some p–p discourse which fails to develop the pupils' ideas. The aim in so doing is to identify the differences in the three types of discourse and describe some of the factors which may have contributed to those differences. The implications of these discourse features for learning will also be discussed.

The classroom discourse on which this paper draws was recorded during the research of the SLANT (Spoken Language and New Technology) Project. This two-year ESRC-funded project investigated the potential of computers as a medium for promoting *exploratory* talk (Phillips, 1990) in the primary classroom, by gathering video data of small groups of children working at computers, as part of their normal classroom work. Data was collected from 10 schools (15 teachers) based in Buckinghamshire, Cambridgeshire, Norfolk and Northamptonshire.

Although the examples given are drawn from a computer setting, much of what goes on and the discourse strategies used are applicable to group work and paired activities in other contexts. However, there are some aspects which are computer-specific, and the effects of these are also discussed. Our interest in exploratory talk arises from earlier work by Phillips (*op. cit.*), in which he suggests that talk which features argument and exploration through hypothesis and challenge may be more valuable for learning than talk which features consensus and so leads to early closure of discussion. The features of exploratory and other classroom talk will be discussed in more detail below.

Background

Classroom talk has recently become a focus of interest in educational research not only amongst those whose prime interest is in language use and development but also amongst those who recognize its importance as a vehicle for teaching and learning. This interest, stimulated by the work of the National Oracy Project (SCDC, 1987–93), has been reflected in the prominence given to oral language in National Curriculum for English for England and Wales and in N. Ireland (DES, 1990a, 1990b).

Vygotsky emphasized the important function of language in learning; he proposed that learning occurs *first* in a social or *interpsychological* context, prior to its becoming internalized or individualized within an *intrapsychological category* (Vygotsky, 1978: 57). He was also critical of instruction which concentrated on developmental stages which had already been achieved, and emphasized the importance of focusing on instruction which 'proceeds ahead of development'. He labelled this new frontier the '*Zone of Proximal Development*' *(ZPD)*, and argued that learning would most readily be achieved in the ZPD with the help of another (more experienced) person (Vygotsky, 1956). Consequently the learning which takes place between individuals forms the basis for later development.

Following the socio-cultural perspective developed by Vygotsky, subsequent research has stressed the context-specific nature of learning (Cole, 1985; Crook, 1987; Edwards, 1991). It has also been shown that children may be able to accomplish activities within familiar or supportive contexts which they cannot do in unfamiliar or unsupported situations (Donaldson, 1978; Mercer & Fisher, 1992). What is more, even when children seem to have learned what their teachers have taught them, there are often large and fundamental differences between their understanding of particular concepts and that of their teachers (Driver *et al.*, 1985). The situationally-specific nature of their learning, and the narrowness of their previous knowledge both conspire to lead children to conclusions which focus on particular rather than general and more fundamental aspects of the activity. It is only in attempting to reformulate and express their ideas that they may come to realize the inadequacy of them. For these reasons, activities which encourage a true sharing of ideas amongst essential equal partners are likely to be a fruitful way of encouraging children to test out their assumptions and develop their thinking, and pupil–pupil discourse offers a potentially rich setting for pupils, teachers and researchers to look more closely at pupils' learning.

Research into classroom discourse has generally been undertaken with a view to explicating what teachers do when they teach (Edwards & Mercer, Sinclair & Coulthard (both *op. cit.*); Maybin *et al.*, 1992; Mercer & Fisher *(op. cit)*. Many researchers have also examined what children do when they learn, though this has often been done by contrasting pre-tests with outcomes rather than by examining the *processes* of learning, and has also often been carried out in experimental rather than classroom situations. (For example, see Light & Glachan 1985; Webb, Ender & Lewis, 1986).

Classroom discourse research also suggests that many teachers control the content and direction of the discourse by asking questions and by reformulating the answers which the pupils give. Mercer & Fisher *(op. cit.)* suggest that, in successful teaching episodes, these discourse strategies are carefully employed so as to offer pupils appropriate help at crucial points *without* discouraging the pupils from seeking their own solutions to problems. This help or *scaffolding* (Wood, Bruner & Ross, 1976) must be sensitive to what the individual pupils are doing, and the teacher must know of the particular difficulties that pupils are facing with their task if she is to offer help which supports but which does not override the pupils' efforts to solve their problems. Help which is too much or too soon can easily discourage pupils from making efforts for themselves, whilst help which comes too late can lead to frustration and loss of interest. Support of this kind cannot therefore be available to all pupils all of the time, and given the practical realities of large school classes, may only very occasionally be available.

Whilst teacher–pupil discourse (including teacher-led discourse in which the teacher sets up lessons for the whole class) is clearly appropriate for new or difficult situations, many teachers are aware of its limitations and so encourage some p–p discussions (particularly at primary level) in those contexts in which they judge pupils able to work without direct teacher support. Many teachers claim to organise their classrooms so that children *work in groups* though as Galton *et al.* reported (1980) this claim was not at that time substantiated by the evidence. Whilst children *sat in groups,* they mostly worked on individual pieces of work. More recent research into the nature of the interactions which ensue and their effectiveness in promoting learning has received mixed reports from researchers. As Galton (1992) suggests, this is probably due at least in part to a lack of comparability of measures across studies. It is therefore worth examining how some teachers encourage p–p talk, and the part that their teaching strategies play in promoting (or discouraging) pupils' exploratory talk when that occurs.

Aims of Teachers in Grouping Pupils

Within the SLANT Project we have found that teachers often have explicit aims in grouping their pupils, not all of which are directly related to maximising the short-term outcomes of the topic in hand. These strategies have direct implications for the subsequent discourse, and the criteria by which they are implemented fall under two broad headings:

(1) ability and other cognitive factors

(2) personality and social factors

(1) Teachers use their knowledge of pupils' ability and of their task expertise to group children, though they do not necessarily attempt to group 'like with like'. They may see one child as being able to offer some knowledge to the group which the others don't have, or they may choose children whose abilities they see as complementary. Sometimes teachers will designate a group leader, or a group reader, and sometimes they merely suggest that the children 'help each other' or that one helps the other with particular tasks.

Regardless of how the teacher perceives their abilities, the children will also have their own views on who is 'clever'. No doubt these views often do coincide with the teacher's, but however the children perceive their respective abilities is likely to affect the kind of contribution they make to the task. Consequently, whilst it may sometimes be effective for pupils of differing abilities to work together so that one can help the other with a specific difficulty (as Galton (*op. cit.*) also concluded), it can be counter-productive to put together pupils who see themselves as sharing little common ground. For example, we frequently found that disparate expertise at the keyboard or in reading can lead to one pupil doing the work and the other becoming disenchanted.

In their study of 'The Effects of Group Composition on Group Inter-active Processes and Pupil Understanding', Bennett & Cass (1988) report complex results. Although they found that Mixed groups (2 High attainers and 1 Low or vice versa) on average produced more talk than either Homogenous groups (of either Low or High achievers) and Heterogeneous groups (1 High, 1 Average and 1 Low), they also found that High attaining Homogeneous groups spoke much more than the Low (167 and 34 speech acts, respectively). Their units of analysis of talk types were Instructional — giving and seeking, and Procedural — managing. The former was the largest category of talk and the one that they suggest links group processes to outcomes. Within this category, they found that their Mixed groups gave more explanations, answers, suggestions and judgements (their four sub-categories) and sought responses more often than either of the other two groups. They also found that on average High attainers provided twice as many explanations as others. In fact nearly two thirds of all explanations were provided by these children.

In SLANT we focused not on the quantity of initiations or responses, but on the interactional nature of the talk insofar as utterances open opportunities for explanation, and insofar as those opportunities were then taken up. This slightly different focus, it is suggested, might be expected to yield a different pattern results from those of Bennett & Cass in that where they assessed the quality of explanations or the appropriateness of suggestions, they did so in terms of an *individual's* contribution to the task processes and outcome. This obviously important focus is, nonetheless, different from our own, which attempted to examine the talk as an interactional process, with the group's task outcomes being of more central concern than those of individuals. What is of particular relevance to us from Bennett & Cass's work is that High Attainers, both boys and girls, made more suggestions than either Average or Low attainers (though Low attaining boys made 54, against High boys' 66 and Average boys only 25). In addition, the High attainers had far more accepted, fewer rejected and fewer ignored. These results suggest that the lower ability groups are being less successful in influencing group decisions and, since Mixed groups are talking more, we might expect Low attainers' lack of success to be exacerbated in those groups. Indeed, Bennett & Cass suggest (page 30) that where Mixed groups include two High and one

Low attainer, the Low attainer tended to 'opt out', though they do say that with one High and two Lows performance was much better. This work therefore raises interesting issues for the optimum constitution of groups in relation to ability levels, and draws attention to the need for teachers to be clear of their purpose in using group work.

(2) Personality and social factors such as gender, also affect how groups work together, and may well interact with ability/perceived ability in a complicated way. The effects are also likely to vary with age.

Class teachers in primary schools generally know their pupils well, but in spite of this, there were some examples within SLANT where teachers only appreciated how dominant one pupil was within a group when they subsequently viewed a video of the group working without the teacher. Because the *product* may be satisfactory, and perhaps more speedily produced when one child dominates a group, it may be difficult for teachers to appreciate within the normal classroom activity just how little others in the group have contributed. Asking the children afterwards who did what can also be misleading. In SLANT we have found instances where those who claim to have done most work were mistaken, and some who claimed not to have been allowed to make any decisions or key the computer had in fact dominated the activity!

We have not in our study analysed the data overall for age or gender effects, though we are in the process of detailed analysis of some of the mixed-gender groups (Swann & Watson, in preparation). The work so far has found that the boys made more suggestions which are taken up. This is somewhat at odds with Bennett & Cass (*op. cit.*) who found that girls talked slightly more, made fewer suggestions, but that more of these were accepted despite being inappropriate. However, the small numbers on both studies and the different type of computer tasks could account for these differences. Swann & Watson (above) are analysing work with wordprocessing software whereas Bennett & Cass are using a pre-programmed simulation/game (comparable to that we describe in Extract 4).

Influences on Groups Using Computers

The individual characteristics listed in (1) and (2) above may well be more import in groups working with computers than for those doing other classroom work. Computer work tends to be isolated from other classroom work for several reasons. Drawing on our experience in SLANT, it seems likely that:

(1) The physical location of the computer, even within the classroom, usually separates it to some extent from other activities. The computer must be

within access to a socket; it is usually on a trolley; children at the computer often face away from the rest of the class.

(2) The group around the computer develops a degree of working autonomy since the computer, rather than the teacher, often serves as their source of information (until things go wrong!). Even when the teacher does intervene, it is not always immediately apparent to her what the children have done, and she must then spend time retracing their steps in the program before she can appreciate their problem. As suggested above, the nature of this intervention may be crucial to the pupils' progress.

(3) Finally there is the element of excitement which computers generate. Whether this is due to their comparative novelty or to some intrinsic feature of the computer and the software which children experience is unclear. As with the 'couch potato' syndrome and television, there seems to be a willingness to focus attention on screen displays for surprisingly long periods of time. Even quite young children (5/6 years) will work at the computer for as long as an hour. For some children 'key pressing' and the dynamic changes which appear on screen as a result (at least in games, simulations and similarly pre-programmed animations) produce uncharacteristically high levels of commitment and tension.

These factors can have positive and negative effects on work done. The motivation which computer work engenders offers the potential for concentration and significant learning outcomes. However, the physical distance and dedication of the pupils can discourage teacher intervention even when help is needed. This physical and psychological separation makes crucial, therefore, the way that the teacher sets up the task at the outset, and the ways in which the children interpret her instructions and perceive the activity. Quite minor modifications can lead to very different outcomes (as shown below).

In spite of these peculiarities of computer work, it is suggested that the factors affecting how these groups work together are likely to affect all group work, even if, for the reasons set out above, they are of more influence at the computer than elsewhere. At the very least, the sharing of computers in primary schools provides a context in which p–p discourse rather than t–p discourse may be common.

Pupil–Pupil Talk

In this section, the contextual differences of t–p and p–p discourse will be discussed, and the features of p–p talk will be examined through selected examples.

If we wish to contrast t–p and p–p talk, bearing in mind teachers' strategies which seem to arise from their leadership role, and assuming for the moment an approximate equivalence between pupils, we might expect to find the following aspects of p–p talk, not common in t–p talk:

(1) No one consistent leader or initiator of exchanges

(2) A lack of 'eliciting' and 'reformulating' which characterises teacher talk

(3) Little attempt at summarizing, other than where the activity demands it.

Instead, we might expect to find initiation of new exchanges by any and all members of the group. Questions that arise would be genuine attempts to solve problems rather than a testing of the other partner's knowledge. Discourse strategies which aim at clarifying the position and/or reinforcing the learning are also likely to be rare, owing to their direct relationship to the leadership role. This lack of an unchallengeable leader has other implications for the discourse. It places a *responsibility* on the participants to manage their exchanges if anarchy is to be avoided, so that a new set of classroom discourse rules might be expected to emerge. However, even five year olds are experienced in talking with their peers, and it may be that the strategies which serve them outside will also serve well inside the classroom.

Set out below are examples of p–p discourse. By examining the characteristics of that presented and the contextual setting in which it occurred, it is hoped to identify the features which lead to the exploration and development of ideas through talk, as well as those which may inhibit or prevent discursive exploration.

In the first example, two Year 2 pupils, Milly and Charles, have been asked to write their own version of the Nativity story, using Folio, together with a concept keyboard which their teacher has prepared so as to give them easy access to the more difficult words they may need to spell (for example, 'Bethlehem').

The school which these pupils attend has a population drawn exclusively from the nearby council estate, and a very high proportion of the children come from materially poor backgrounds. The school staff actively pursue a policy aimed at encouraging the resolution of difficulties through negotiation. This class has already done work earlier in the term 'talking about talk' in which they considered the differences between talk for a variety of purposes, for example argument, chatter, screaming, discussing, telling stories. They are very used to group discussion, brainstorming and role play activities.

The teacher has asked them to plan their story before they begin writing it (though they are already at the computer and are free to begin when they wish). She has also suggested that they should see themselves as ordinary people who happen to be in Bethlehem at the time of the nativity.

Transcription conventions

In the following extracts only minimal punctuation has been used. A new line which begins with a capital letter may be interpreted as the start of a new utterance.

The *function* column indicates the purpose that the utterance(s) seem to perform *in this context*. It is not intended to be an exhaustive categorical description, but merely to facilitate our understanding of the interaction taking place.

EXTRACT 1 — *Planning the Nativity Story*

They begin, facing towards each other and sideways on to the computer.

Discourse	Function
C. We could live in Bethlehem	**initiates with suggestion**
M. Yes we'll live in Bethlehem right Then then we're That could be something like if were were playing out the backway And then they came across and some And then you heard some voices saying about it And we'd go out wouldn't we	**accepts and extends**
C. Right then	**accepts**
M. That would mean that we would go out	**extends**
C. The front	**extends/ ? challenges**
M. And see what was happening And then you'd see a person on a donkey And a women next to him wouldn't yer	**extends**
C. Yes	**accepts**

In this extract the children stick fairly closely to their brief and draw on their knowledge of the nativity story, whilst making some effort to incorporate themselves into their version. Their discourse is characterised by an acceptance of what the other says, followed by an extension of their partner's proposition. Although Charles challenges Milly's suggestion that they are:

playing out the backway

by finishing one of her utterances with:

the front

she ignores (accepts?) this suggestion and continues her extension of what has gone before. However, as they go a little further with their planning, they begin to challenge one another. The next sequence follows immediately:

EXTRACT 2 — *At the stable*

M. So they were going to the stable	**extends**
C. No	**challenges**
No pretend they were already in the stable	**counters and offers an alternative suggestion**
M. In the stable	**? tentative acceptance**
C. And we just see this strange star And then we go and see what it is And say 'why are all these people in the stable?'	**extends**
M. Or we could We could just wait and not see the star And then the shepherds could come	**challenges with a counter suggestion**
C. Yeh	**accepts**

In each case the challenge is followed by an alternative suggestion, but one which remains an extension of the discourse that has gone before.

We have here examples of two of the three kinds of talk which have been identified in other SLANT word-processing data (Scrimshaw, 1992); *cumulative text talk, exploratory talk and disputational talk*.

Scrimshaw has described cumulative text talk as that which:

'involves children speaking in turns to create the text to be entered, each speaker accepting without reservation the previous offering'.

In the examples above, the sequence opens with cumulative text talk and there are many other examples of this type of discourse throughout this activity.

Exploratory talk occurs in Extract 2, where the children debate the issue of whether to be outside or inside the stable. Although Charles challenges Milly's suggestion:

No
No pretend they were already in the stable

he only amends rather than rejects it outright and goes on to elaborate, in effect providing a justification for this alteration:

And we just see this strange star
And then we go and see what it is
And say 'Why are all these people in the stable?'

In these examples, both children contribute ideas to the planning, and each seems to listen to the other's offering, even though they do not always agree. Later they run into difficulty with spelling, but they still tackle the problem in a reflective and interactive way. Although Milly seems to be more accurate with her spelling, they both offer insightful comments.

The next example is taken from another pair of children, Hettie and Mark from the same class also writing a nativity story in which they are participants, though they interpret their possible roles quite differently.

EXTRACT 3: *Packing for the journey*

H. OK Let's start	**initiates with instruction**
M. They're packing	**responds with suggestion**
Or do you want to do them on the journey	**questions**
H. No	**challenges**
I'll be Mary	**makes new suggestion**
You be Joseph	**instruction**
M. No	**challenges with explanation**
You were Mary last time though	
H. Well I can still be Mary	**challenges with counter explantion**
M. Mary's saying (pause)	**ignores H's explanation**
Alright I'm Joseph and you're Mary	**then accepts**

This rather negative beginning, in which almost every turn represents a challenge to the one above and in which there is little evidence of either partner attempting to build on the other's ideas, is an example of *disputational* talk. On this occasion, it sets the tone for a session which failed in that neither the teacher nor children were satisfied with the process or outcome, and which finished in frustration. These children have shown at other times that they are capable of productive investigative discourse, but in this example they failed to resolve their power struggle (and the girl failed to 'give way'!) so that the whole session is affected. However, it may be that their attempt to role-play the principal characters was the origin of their problems in that Hettie, at least, seems to feel she should be *individually* responsible for Mary's lines, so making a *shared responsibility* difficult. There are several confusions in their discourse which appear to arise from this source.

Teachers, pupils and their influence on discourse

From the above it seems that p–p talk contains very different features from the t–p talk, described above. Most notably, it lacks the teacher strategies described by Edwards & Mercer (*op. cit.*) though it does contain genuine questions or requests for information. As has been suggested the teacher's responsibility in the classroom and the necessarily asymmetric relationship between teacher and pupils might be expected to affect t–p discourse in specific ways, not apparent in discourse between 'equals'. However, there are also wide ranging differences within p–p talk, even in the same classroom or with similar activities. Some of these are likely to be the result of individual pupil differences and some may be due to the type of software being used (Fisher, 1993). Although discourse strategies such as those often used by teachers are less frequent in p–p talk, teacher *influence* is nonetheless still very strong. In the next examples we will examine the discourse of a group of 11-year-old children in a class where the teacher, disappointed by her pupils' poor discourse skills, attempted to raise their awareness of appropriate strategies by means of explicit teaching and practice in discursive activities, using a pack for teachers, Developing Oral Skills (Brookes, Latham & Rex, 1986).

After some weeks of preparation, including talking about talk and about group responsibility, Peter, Adrian and Diana are working with a simulation game, *The Vikings*. (The whole class has been studying the Vikings as part of their history project.) This program is designed to encourage the users to adopt the role of Viking raiders, and requires them to make a variety of interdependent choices in conducting their raids. In the extract below, the children have already selected the equipment they wish to take on their journey and have chosen their route. They now have to organise a camp, and select from the following in order of importance:

  A   Find food
  B   Find grazing
  C   Set up defences
  D   Provide shelter
  E   Hide the boats
  F   Find slaves

EXTRACT 4: *Organising a Viking Camp*

D. Place in order of importance	**initiates with instruction read aloud from the screen**
P. Set up defences I choose 'set up defences' Then there's a place to hide behind	**suggests and then explains**
D. Wait Why do you want	**challenges** **seeks explanation**
A. Because then we're safe	**responds with explanation**
P. Because we're safe aren't we	**. . .**
D. Yes but suppose someone spots our boat Oh no	**renews challenge**
P. OK what about defences Say we get attacked and can't hide the boats Then what would happen	**challenges by counter explanation and question**
D. What do we do if we run out of food	**counter challenge**
P. I'd say we put 'Find slaves' last (he has earlier suggested this is an important one)	**suggests**
D. We can't find the slaves until we've raided sort of thing	**extends with explanation**
P. Yeh I'd say D first, then E, then B and C A and F Which do you reckon we should go for then	**accepts** **suggests** **questions/seeking consensus**
D. I think we should do D first ['Cos [[(turning to Adrian) [Do you agree with that	**accepts** **attempts** **explanation** **questions/seeks consensus**
A. Yes	**accepts**

P.	But say we get attacked while hiding the boats	**challenges with alt. suggestion**
D.	It shouldn't take that long to hide the boats though would it	**counters with explanation**
P.	Well there's four of them	**counters with alternative**
	They're quite big	**explanation**
	OK	
	Press D then	**instructs based on own initial suggestions**

(Adrian presses and they go on to discuss the rest of the sequence)

As in Extracts 1–2 above, these children use exploratory talk by making a series of suggestions with explanations.

For example, in answer to Diana's renewed challenge about the risks of not hiding the boats first, Peter counters her with:

> OK what about defences
> Say we get attacked and can't hide the boats
> Then what would happen

This sophisticated countering is ultimately successful, though once again it is the girl who gives way — however, this is by no means always the case in this session. Although the group becomes increasingly excited as the session progresses, they never become aggressively confrontational.

They also use *cumulative talk* (rather than *cumulative text* talk, since here they are not composing) in which they pick up and add to previous statements, apparently accepting without challenge. Adrian, in extract 4, picks up Peter's suggestion of the need to hide by answering Diana's challenge with:

> Because then we're safe

and this is followed by a repetition from Peter. However, rather than being a means of drawing attention to key points, as are teachers' repetitions, these pupils' repetitions seem to serve a group cohesion function. They occur in much of our data and are most commonly used by the group member who contributes least to the decision making. In this group, repetitions are most often made by Adrian. Although he is probably as vocal as the others and also does most of the keyboard work, he is the weakest contributor in terms of ideas which are taken up. He has, in fact, been identified in the school as a 'problem' because of his aggressive behaviour, and his work is below average within the class. The teacher considered his inclusion in this group was a risk (especially in front of the camera), yet he remained involved with the task and the group throughout the session, and seems to have found a positive and satisfying way of taking part. The teacher had emphasized to the children the notion of *group responsibility* for failures as well as successes, and suggested to the pupils that abstaining from decision making did not absolve the abstainer from responsibility for failure. The children seemed to have taken this notion to heart, as is apparent from their discourse strategies — for example Diana's frequent use of 'Why?' and Peter's use of 'What do you think?' both serve to encourage other members of the group to reflect on the decision-making process. This awareness of the group responsibility was also evident in their responses to a short question-naire which was administered to the whole class by their teacher after the activity, in which there were several responses stipulating that responsibility lay with the whole group.

As with our earlier examples (Extracts 1–2), the discursive strategies that these pupils use are ones which have been explicitly encouraged by the teacher during the previous few weeks and also were restated by her at the beginning of this session. It is of note that those sessions within these two classes which did not 'work as well' were set up (because of clashes between school timetables and research visits) in a more 'ad hoc' fashion, with the teacher commenting at the time on the constraints which she felt. It is suggested, therefore, that outcomes may relate very directly to the prior work done in the class and to the instructions at the beginning of the activity.

Discussion of Findings

In the above it has been shown that p–p discourse differs from t–p dis-course in that it frequently lacks those strategies reported by Edwards & Mercer (*op. cit.*), which teachers use for directing the content of classroom talk. The range of features occurring in p–p discourse varies across and within groups, and seems to be dependent on several contextual factors including the nature of the task (and software), how the teacher 'sets up' the task and the pupils' perception of the task, as well as their skills and previous experience. As we have seen, the range and sequence of these features has implications for the progress of the task, and it seems likely, therefore, that they may also have more far-reaching effects on the pupils' intellectual and social development.

Within cognitive psychology there has been considerable debate as to the relationship of talk to thinking (Cromer, 1979). A less tortuous and perhaps more fruitful approach follows if, instead of attempting to understand how what is said might relate to cognitive representation, we adopt an approach suggested by Middleton & Edwards (1990) and examine how cognition is represented in conversation. This then allows us to examine talk as the best indicator we have (however inadequate) of the speakers' thinking.

Following this approach, we can now consider the potential for learning and understanding of the discourse features described in this paper.

In the above extracts, the talk generally falls under one of three headings:

Disputational talk, which can be characterised as an initiation in various forms (e.g. suggestion, instruction), followed by a challenge (either a direct reflection or a counter suggestion). This results either in a lack of any clear resolution, or a resolution which does not build directly on the previous utterances.

Cumulative talk, in which initiations are accepted either without discussion or with additions or superficial amendments.

Exploratory talk in which the initiation may be challenged and counter-challenged, but with suggestions which are developments of that initiation. Progress then rests on the joint acceptance of one of the suggestions, or of a modification of what has been put forward.

Exploratory talk offers a potential for learning not obvious in the other two types indicated here, and suggests a means by which pupil–pupil groups can extend their knowledge. Because of the strategies they use, the pupils are avoiding early closure to the debate, and it is in exploratory talk, therefore, where we may hope to find evidence of pupils extending their learning within the ZPD. It is usual to consider ZPD learning as that which takes place between individuals where one is more 'expert' than the other and, as Rogoff & Wertsch (1984) suggest, ZPD development:

involves joint consciousness of the participants, where two or more minds are collaborating on solving a problem. A corollary of this notion of intersubjectivity is that the participants do not have the same definition of the talk or of the problem to be solved. Through their interaction, the child's notion of what is to be done goes beyond itself, with the adult's support, and comes to approximate in some degree that of the more expert adult. [. . .] both participants play an important role in using the zone of proximal development, even in situations that are not directly conceived of as instruction by the participants. (p. 5)

Rogoff and Wertsch are referring to child–adult interaction, but other writers have been concerned with peer learning in groups which are asymmetrical (peer tutoring, for example see Foot, Shute & Morgan, 1990) or symmetrical (peer collaboration, for example see Doise, 1990). What is of interest here is the notion of *both* participants playing an important role to enable learning which 'goes beyond itself'. Illustrated in the extracts above is one mechanism by which ZPD development might occur in a situation in which the participants have equal status and in which *both* are struggling to develop an idea. Their resulting concepts may perhaps still be ill-matched to those of the teacher or other 'expert', but in seeking solutions to their task and in orally formulating those solutions, it is suggested that the participants will at the very least develop their awareness of the major points at issue. They may also, through their joint resolution of the task in hand, move nearer to a workable or teacher-acceptable definition.

It should be remembered that in classroom peer-group learning contexts, pupils do not generally work without the support of a teacher, even though she may not be actively involved in the particular task. As Mercer & Fisher (*op. cit.*) argue, where pupils work effectively to develop new skills, it is likely that the teacher will have defined the task in such a way that it is (in her estimation) at a level which will be within the pupils' ZPD, and she will have provided the 'scaffolding' which will enable them to do things which they otherwise could not. As has also been suggested above, the teacher's role in developing her pupils' discourse strategies may be crucial. In particular we have noted the efficacy of the pupils' commitment to group responsibility. In Vygotsky's terms these pupils in this context have progressed to a shared understanding of the task which will allow them to develop their ideas on an intrapsychological plane through interpsychological functioning (i.e. talk).

Conclusions

P–p talk often lacks the eliciting and reformulating features of t–p talk, but has its own distinctive features, depending on the context in which it occurs and the discursive strategies which the pupils have been encouraged to use. Where the discourse leads to successful exploratory talk, it is characterised by suggestions with challenges and explanations, consensus being sought only after these have taken place. Where talk fails to be exploratory, it may be of a cumulative nature in which ideas are accepted unchallenged and without justification, or continuously disputational leading to a breakdown of communication within the group.

For exploratory discourse strategies to be optimised, they need to be explicitly taught by teachers and exercised within pupil groups in contexts in which a *requirement* for discursive problem solving is apparent to the pupils. This may further lead to an awareness of the need for group responsibility which is itself a support for learning.

Acknowlegements

The SLANT team are grateful to the ESRC for funding this research and to pupils, teachers and heads in the following Buckinghamshire, Cambridgeshire, Norfolk and Northamptonshire schools for their collaboration: Brampton Infants, Cavell First, Chapel Break First, Cloverhill First, Old Stratford Primary, Oakway Junior, Bignold Middle, George White Middle, Greenleys Middle, Watling Way Middle.

References

Bennett, N. and Cass, A. (1989) The effects of group composition on group interactive processes and pupil understanding. *British Education Research Journal* 15 (1), 19–32.

Brooks, G., Latham, J. and Rex, A. (1986) *Developing Oral Skills.* Heinemann Educational Books.

Cole, M. (1985) The zone of proximal development: Where culture and cognition create each other. In J. V. Wertsch (ed.) *Culture, Communication and Cognition* (pp. 146–61). Cambridge University Press.

Cromer, R. (1979) The strength of the weak form of the cognition hypothesis for language acquisition. In V. Lee (ed.) *Language Development.* Croom Helm.

Crook, C. (1987) Computers in the classroom: Defining a social context. In J. Rutkowska and C. Crooks (eds) *Computers, Cognitition and Development* (pp. 35–53). John Wiley.

Department of Education in N. Ireland (1990) *English Programmes of Study and Attainment Targets.*

Department of Education and Science (1990) *English in the National Curriculum.* London: HMSO.

Donaldson, M. (1978) *Children's Minds.* Fontana.

Doise, W. (1990) The development of individual competencies through social interaction. In H. C. Foot, M. J. Morgan and R. H. Shute (eds) *Children Helping Children.* John Wiley.

Driver, R. (1983) *The Pupil as Scientist.* Milton Keynes: Open University Press.

Edwards, D. (1991) Classroom discourse and classroom knowledge. In C. Rogers and P. Kutnick (eds) *Readings in the Social Psychology of the Primary School.* Croom Helm.

Edwards, D. and Mercer, N. (1987) *Common Knowledge.* London: Methuen.

Fisher, E. (1993, in press) Characteristics of children's talk at the computer and its relationship to computer software. *Language and Education* 7, 2.

Foot, H. C., Morgan, M. J. and Shute, R. H. (1990) (eds) *Children Helping Children.* John Wiley.

Galton, M, Simon, B. and Croll, P. (1980) *Inside the Primary Classroom.* London: Routledge and Kegan Paul.

Light, P. and Glachan, M. (1985) Facilitation of individual problem solving through peer interaction. *Education Psychology* 5, 217–25.

Maybin, J., Mercer, N. and Stierer, B. (1992) Scaffolding in the classroom. To appear in K. Norman (ed.) *Thinking Voices: The Work of the National Oracy Project.* Hodder and Stoughton.

Mercer, N. and Fisher, E. (1993) How do teachers help children to learn? An analysis of teachers' interventions in computer-based activities. *Learning and Instruction* 2, 339–55.

Middleton, D. and Edwards, D. (1990) *Collective Remembering.* Sage Publications.

Phillips, T. (1990) Structuring contexts for exploratory talk. *Talking and Listening Scholastic* 59–72.

Rogoff, B. and Wertsch, J. V. (eds) (1984) Children's learning in the zone of proximal development. In series W. Damon (ed.) *New Directions in Child Development* No. 23, March 1984. Jossey-Bass.

School Curriculum Development Committee (1987–93) *National Oracy Project.*

Scrimshaw, P. (1992) *Word Processing, Collaboration and Exploratory Talk: Some Preliminary Results from the Spoken Language and New Technology Project.* Paper presented to the 1992 ECEC Conference, Melbourne, Australia.

Sinclair, J. McH. and Coulthard, R. M. (1975) *Towards and Analysis of Discourse: The English Used by Teachers and Pupils.* London: Oxford University Press.

Swann, J. and Watson, M. (in preparation) *Gender Effects in the SLANT Project.*

Vygotsky, L. S. (1956) *Selected Psychological Investigations.* Moscow: Izdstel'sto Akademii Pedagogicheskikh Nauk SSSR.

— (1978) *Mind in Society: The Development of Higher Psychological Processes.* M. Cole, V. John-Steiner, S. Scribner and E. Souberman (eds). Cambridge: Harvard University Press.

Wood, D., Bruner, J. and Ross, G. (1976) The role of tutoring in problem solving. *Journal of Child Psychology and Psychiatry* 17, 89–100.

Webb, N., Ender, P. and Lewis, S. (1986) Problem solving strategies and group processes in small groups learning computer programming. *American Educational Research Journal* 23, 247–61.

12 What Do We Do About Gender?

JOAN SWANN

Gender Inequalities in Classroom Talk

The last twenty years or so have seen a growing concern about gender differentiated language use in schools and classrooms. Evidence has accumulated of boys' 'dominance' of classroom talk and of girls' relative invisibility and marginalisation. Teachers, it is argued, favour boys by giving them more attention, and by sanctioning behaviour such as calling out that is not acceptable from girls. Boys themselves, in addition to hogging the verbal and physical space, are frequently disparaging towards girls. Female teachers are subject to verbal harrassment — from male pupils and sometimes also from male colleagues. Alongside evidence from schools and classrooms have come studies of gender differences and inequalities in language use in other contexts, and of sexist language that, in various ways, discriminates against women and girls. (I have reviewed this area elsewhere — see Swann, 1992; Brophy, 1985, reviews studies from the 1970s and early '80s. For examples of specific studies of classroom talk, see Bousted, 1989; Fisher, 1991; French & French, 1984; Morse & Handley, 1985; Randall, 1987; Rennie & Parker, 1987; Sadker & Sadker, 1985; Swann & Graddol, 1988; Dart & Clarke, 1988, provide some counter-evidence to the general patterns.)

Specific concerns provoked by such evidence have to be seen in the light of the more general concern, within education, about the part played by schools in maintaining gender inequalities (there is a vast array of published work. For examples see Deem, 1978; Spender, 1982; Spender & Sarah (eds), 1988; Whyte, Deem, Kant & Cruickshank (eds), 1985). The argument has perhaps been most succinctly stated by Sara Delamont in her classic account of *Sex Roles and the School*:

> . . . schools develop and reinforce sex segregations, stereotypes and even discriminations which exaggerate the negative aspects of sex roles in the outside world, when they could be trying to alleviate them.
>
> (Delamont, 1980; revised 1990: 2)

176

There have been concerns that schools contrive to address boys' interests rather than girls'. Overall, girls do well academically but they are channelled into traditional subjects which eventually provide them with limited career opportunities; in school, girls and boys also learn to conform to traditional gender roles — to behave appropriately *as* girls and *as* boys — thus restricting their personal and social lives. Given the pervasiveness of spoken and written language within education it is hardly suprising that attention has focused on the contribution of language to this process of differentiation and discrimination. In his US review of teacher–student talk, for instance, Jere Brophy argues that teachers' 'socialisation' of girls and boys is accomplished 'through subtle yet systematic (but often unconscious) differential treatment of boys and girls — treatment communicating the expectation that certain characteristics and behavior are associated with boys, and that other characteristics and behavior are associated with girls' (1985: 117).

There has been a range of responses to such concerns — from individual teachers, schools and educational policy-makers — and these, too, have a history that runs back well over a decade. Initially the level and type of response depended on the interest and commitment of educationists working in schools and local authorities. With the advent of the Education Reform Act in 1988 the context has been changing — with, for instance, the weakening of local authorities and the centralisation of curriculum planning. Recently also some feminists have begun publicly to question the value of earlier 'anti-sexist' initiatives. It is these developments that I wish to review in this paper. I shall distinguish three sets of responses to gender inequalities in language: the anti-sexist tradition; a liberal response evident in the early stages of development of English in the national curriculum; and what might be termed a 'pro-female' response. Because of the confines of space I shall focus primarily on spoken language.

The Anti-Sexist Tradition

Listen to your tapes and to your friends talking and answer the questions below:

(1) Do boys swear as much as girls?
(2) Are girls as polite as boys?
(3) If they wanted to criticise something would they use the same words?
(4) Do they tell the same jokes?
(5) Do they talk to teachers in the same way?

(6) Are girls cheekier than boys?

(7) What do you think people mean when they say 'Talk like a lady' or 'It's unladylike to talk like that'.

(8) What do they mean when they say 'Boys will be boys'?

(9) What *messages* are we given about
      girl talk?
      boy talk? (Healy, 1981: 102)

> You should have respect for yourself and other girls and women. This means you should not use words which are offensive about women. Women have fought very hard to gain respect in society; you throw this away when you call someone 'slag' or worse. (Extract from an equal opportunities policy in a girls' secondary school, cited Smith, 1986: 11)

Within the UK the first wave of responses to charges of imbalances and inequalities in classroom language took off in the 1970s — though most of the published evidence comes from the 1980s, and it was during this period that the movement to redress gender inequalities gathered momentum. Language became a priority in several 'anti-sexist' policies: for instance, the Inner London Education Authority's guide to *Implementing the ILEA's Anti-sexist Policy* included the following questions on 'Language':

> Has there been discussion or formulation of a school policy on written and spoken language? Is a conscious effort made to use language which promotes a positive self-image of pupils and staff, black and white, female and male? Is gender stereotyped language avoided, e.g. 'strong lads', 'giggly girls'? Are pupils addressed similarly regardless of sex in terms of praise, compliments, reprimands, assessment?

> Do school notices and displays always refer to both sexes and 'people' rather than 'man'? Do all school publications and communications use non-sexist language?

> Do all materials, worksheets and examination questions use non-sexist language? How is this monitored? Have all teachers/departments been asked to review their use of language with regard to sex and gender?

> (ILEA, undated: 8)

The importance of spoken language is also apparent in other sections of the guide — as shown in the following extracts from a section on 'The classroom':

> Have teachers monitored the amount of time and attention they give to girls and boys? [. . .] Do girls and boys sit separately? Are they ever encouraged to work together or in mixed groups? What interaction takes place in this situation? When is single-sex grouping more appropriate? [. . .]

What kinds of behaviour are permitted and encouraged in the classroom? Do some pupils' dominate at the expense of others? [. . .] Is it
made clear that offensively sexist language and behaviour will not go
unchallenged in class in the same way that racism would not be? Are
boys and girls encouraged to discuss and consider their behaviour and
attitudes towards each other in class? [. . .]

In whole class teaching are questions directed equally at both sexes?
[. . .]
                                                        (ILEA, undated: 7)

Here, teachers are expected to monitor their own spoken language and
that of their pupils; to develop strategies to equalise relations between the
sexes (different ways of grouping children, including single-sex groups; in
class discussion, devoting an equal amount of attention to girls and boys);
and to promote discussion of gender issues.

Such strategies are designed to affect several aspects of school and classroom life — the hidden curriculum through which social values are often
transmitted. But gender issues have also made inroads into the formal
curriculum. Textbooks such as Maura Healy's *Your Language* encourage
discussion of 'sexist' language and girls' and boys' talk; a small number of
secondary schools have offered assertiveness training to increase the confidence, particularly, of female students (for an example, see Hordyk, 1986).

While I'm dealing principally with spoken language here, anti-sexist
initiatives have also tackled reading and writing — most notably sexist bias
and stereotyped images in school books and resources.

The project, overall, has been one of social and educational change. Such
change necessarily affects both girls and boys, and many initiatives have
been designed to open up a wider range of opportunities and choices for
both sexes. However, because it is girls who have traditionally been seen as
disadvantaged they have tended to be the focus of attention. ILEA's policy,
although it explicitly addresses the needs of boys and girls, seems implicitly
to be more strongly motivated by concerns about girls ('sexist language' is
normally thought to be detrimental to girls; the 'some pupils' who dominate
classroom talk are usually boys; concerns about teachers' questions have
come about because teachers have tended to ask questions more often of
boys). Introducing change has meant attempting to redress these imbalances
and to change the power relations that obtain between girls and boys — to
empower girls relative to boys.

Changing classroom practice has not been without its problems. Focusing
on girls and the ways they interact may suggest that their interaction styles
are in some way inadequate and in need of support (I return to this point
below). Attempts to promote change will also be constrained by prevailing

sets of beliefs and values: classrooms are not cultural islands. There may be clashes between the values pupils and teachers bring with them into the classroom; and between the values promoted in any one classroom, in other parts of the school, and in out of school contexts. Anna Hordyk, for instance, in her account of assertiveness training in a girls' secondary school, recognises the social and physical constraints on girls' speech and behaviour in other contexts, and concedes that there are occasions when the best course of action for girls is silence.

A Liberal Response to Gender and Language — Cox and the National Curriculum

There are [. . .] considerable differences between the sexes in typical *speech styles*, which carry implications for assessment. For example, boys are more likely than girls from the same social background to:

- speak with a broader regional accent and use more non-standard grammatical forms;

- talk about their interests and experiences with less overt enthusiasm, using a narrower pitch range, less variation in speed and volume, and fewer intensifying words and phrases;

- express beliefs and opinions more confidently;

- give direct instructions rather than negotiate, in group activities;

- use ritual insults, jokes, verbal bantering and aggressive argument;

- interrupt girls rather than boys in conversation.

[. . .]

Whether these characteristic differences are judged positively or negatively will depend on the context and purpose of the task. For example, in some tasks the more direct way of speaking that is more common to boys will be advantageous; in others, the more tentative approach more frequently found in girls will be more appropriate.

(DES/WO, 1989a, paras 11.14 and 11.15)

The National Curriculum English Working Group, chaired by Professor Brian Cox, was set up to advise on a framework for the teaching of English within the national curriculum in England and Wales. It was asked to set attainment targets for pupils of different ages and abilities, and programmes of study for each key stage of compulsory schooling. The supplementary guidance to the working group's terms of reference specifies that the group should 'bear in mind that the curriculum should provide equal opportunities for boys and girls'. The quotation above comes the working group's final report, popularly referred to as the Cox report. It is part of a discussion of 'tasks and assessment' in a chapter on equal opportunities.

If traditional anti-sexist responses have been about educational and social change, the Cox report seems more concerned to promote peaceful co-existence. The report's discussion of equal opportunities pays only limited attention to published work on gender and classroom talk — nor, in dealing with spoken language, does it take into account the range of anti-sexist initiatives that I have mentioned above. (It does mention that, as part of language awareness, pupils should discuss 'matters such as sexist language' and 'styles of interaction in social groups'. The discussion of reading goes a little further, arguing that girls and boys need to read a range of books 'including those which challenge stereotypes of the roles of the sexes and of different cultural groups' (DES/WO, 1989b, para 11.8).)

The characteristics of boys' language identified by Cox are rather a mixed bag: some characteristics relate to specific linguistic features, such as aspects of the sound system ('broader regional accent') and syntax ('non-standard grammatical forms'); others constitute interpretations ('confidence', 'enthusiasm') that are presumably based on complexes of linguistic (and paralinguistic, etc.) features. There are no references to support Cox' list, but judging by its content the list seems to derive from sociolinguistic studies carried out in a range of settings — but not, particularly, educational ones.

Cox clearly has a different starting point from the feminist-inspired work I mentioned above. The working group was concerned with speaking and listening as part of pupils' overall language development — hence, presumably, its interest in language use in non-educational settings. Like much recent work on teaching and assessing language in the school years, it is underpinned by the notion of communicative effectiveness — the ability to use language effectively in a range of contexts — which, itself, derives from sociolinguistic ideas such as communicative competence (see Maclure, 1988, for a discussion of communicative effectiveness). Language development in the school years has tended to be conceived of as children expanding their repertoires to communicate in more complex ways in a wider range of contexts, and this may lie behind Cox' suggestion that girls and boys need to add to their repertoires by adopting characteristics associated with the other sex.

This additive model of language development begs a number of questions. In relation to gender differences one needs to take into account that, in speaking more 'directly' girls may be departing from social conventions: it is not clear that their speech will be responded to in the same way as boys'. The same point would apply to boys adopting characteristics more commonly associated with girls. Different speakers (the point does not relate simply to gender) may use different features of language to achieve a similar communicative effect. However, the main problem with Cox's discussion of gender differences in spoken language is that it totally ignores issues of power: the power differences that exist between females and males as social groups, and that frequently exist between individual female and male speakers. Cox ignores the evidence that boys' ways of speaking are not simply more 'direct' but also allow them to dominate mixed-sex interaction. What is missing from the report is a recognition that, in developing pupils' language, or changing the ways they speak, one is also necessarily changing the ways they relate to others: this is not simply a linguistic issue and nor is it unproblematical.

While the English Working Group at least devoted a chapter to the discussion of equal opportunities issues, by the time their report had become translated into the statutory Order for English in the national curriculum, and associated non-statutory guidance, equal opportunities issues had become almost totally submerged. The non-statutory guidance for English at key stage one, for instance, mentions the importance of equal opportunities for all pupils, but one is hard-pressed to find any specific guidance on this in relation to gender and spoken language. The issue resurfaces only occasionally in bland pronouncements such as the following:

> Children with special needs, the specific needs of bilingual children and the need for equal opportunities for boys and girls should receive consideration. Group composition should always be the result of a conscious decision. A guiding principle should be to ensure that over a period of time children learn to work harmoniously and effectively with a range of other children.
>
> (NCC, 1989: B3)

The appeal to harmony is part of a 'consensus' view of language that underlies both the Cox report and the resulting national curriculum documentation (children are allowed to have opposing points of view but must 'voice disagreement courteously' (DES/WO, 1989b: 13). Similar notions (appeals to collaboration, consensus, peaceful resolution of conflict) have a long history in relation to spoken language in the classroom. They are consistent with the rhetoric of good practice that has informed the work of those concerned, since the 1960s, to establish 'oracy' as an essential part of the curriculum. The oracy movement has stressed the value of collaborative talk, in which children pay attention to one another, encourage one another to speak, and value and support one another's contributions. This has been part of an enlighted, liberal pedagogy, designed to give everyone a chance to be heard, but there are risks in containing dissent: it is perfectly possible for children to collaborate in order to maintain existing (gendered) relations, leaving issues of power and inequality unchallenged.

Pro-Female Responses

While these liberal responses were notable for failing to take account of earlier work on gender inequalities in classroom language, and anti-sexist initiatives designed to counteract them, other responses have come about as a development from, and partly in opposition to anti-sexist initiatives. They are a critique from within — that is, they constitute a feminist critique of earlier feminist-inspired initiatives. I shall take extracts from Gemma Moss' (1989) book *Un/Popular Fictions* as an example of this position. *Un/Popular Fictions* addresses the issue of pupils' use of popular fiction models for their own writing, and teachers' responses to the use of such models. Many of the points Moss makes, however, are relevant to other aspects of language use, and a brief case study of an effective response takes spoken language as a starting point.

Moss takes issue with the determinist position that has underpinned much earlier anti-sexist work, and that, she argues, sees girls in particular as passive victims of sexism (the point is made in relation to 'sexist bias' in written texts, but I think it would apply equally well to concerns about discriminatory practices in spoken language). Moss argues that much anti-sexist work has actually contributed to a view of girls as passive victims:

> By worrying about all the negative pressures on girls and their ability to cope, whilst insisting on the importance of our help, aren't we turning them into the passive, helpless victims we came to save? Meanwhile, the security of boys' identity is not subject to the same sort of scrutiny, the same doubts.
>
> (Moss, 1989: 54–5)

Moss' position is broadly post-structuralist. She argues, in relation to language, that meanings are not fixed but are continually (re-)negotiated and therefore subject to change. Children's adoption of certain language forms does not signal their acceptance of (associated) values:

> If meaning has to be re-established in any one context, I do not consider that the rehearsal of a particular form brings with it for the writer a firm grasp or the outright acceptance of a particular set of values. Writing alone does not shape what we think. We bring what we know to the text and try to push it into shape.
>
> (Moss, 1989: 105)

Teachers' responses should exploit the gaps and contradictions that are inherent in language use. They should also be contingent upon girls' own responses: Moss argues that teachers should support girls in 'what they are already up to', and this need not involve mounting a direct challenge — different strategies will be effective in different contexts.

As an example of this position, Moss describes a lesson she had with a secondary school class who had been asked, for homework, to write an account of the sort of talk that went on in their own (single-sex) friendship groups during registration. They were then to write an account of what they thought members of the other sex talked about under similar circumstances. During class discussion, it was possible to compare girls' and boys' perceptions of their own talk, and their perceptions of talk amongst pupils of the other sex. Initially, the boys were disparaging about 'girls' talk'. The girls attempted to refuse the boys' evaluation of them. A turning point in the discussion came when one girl, Angelique, challenged the boys on the girls' own terms — asserting that the boys didn't have any feelings. Moss supported the girls by treating Angelique's charge seriously and calling upon a boy to answer it. The ensuing discussion exploited a gap in the boys' discourse — their public show of impersonality covered over other, more personal aspects of their lives. It also allowed the girls to 'win back the agenda' by exploring what was absent in the boys' talk.

Moss' work is 'pro-female' in that it is intended to support girls, and in that it rejects a negative evaluation of girls' language. It is part of a more general move, amongst feminists, to understand and value female activities and attributes. There have been criticisms, for instance, of anti-sexist stories for children that turn girl characters into surrogate males, and a 'feminist' argument has been put forward that books should portray positively, and from a female perspective, traditionally female concerns (see, for instance, Sue Adler's (1992) discussion of feminism in children's books). Feminist studies of spoken language have also sought to rediscover and revalue traditionally female speech genres, along with the supportive speaking styles that are associated with female speakers and that are felt to characterise, particularly, talk in all-female groups (see Jennifer Coates' (1988) study of 'gossip').

Perceptions of female speech (and of female language use more generally) have often been negative, and a focus on more positive aspects no doubt forms a useful corrective. There is a need to avoid the risk, however, of perpetuating stereotypes of a unified female speaking style. There is also an abiding tension between the wish to revalue speaking styles that are associated with female speakers and the recognition that it is precisely these styles that, in mixed-sex groups, have enabled some male speakers to dominate the interaction.

To return to the forms of positive action suggested by Moss: the value of Moss' approach is that it points up the need for a differentiated response to gender inequalities, recognising that the strategies that girls themselves employ (and are able to employ) will be sensitive to particular contexts. Her suggestion that teachers should support girls in what they are already up to, however, may lead to a reactive approach in which teachers simply leave girls where they are, rather than making available to them alternative strategies for resistance. In an earlier part of her book (pp. 71ff) Moss makes it clear that Angelique, the girl whose intervention marked a turning point in the class discussion of girls' and boys' language, is highly aware of gender issues as well as issues of race and language. It is the concerns of educationists and others working within an anti-sexist tradition which have raised public awareness of gender inequalities, and lent legitimacy to attempts at resistance from girls such as Angelique.

In the event, Moss' approach seems to be more proactive than her phrase might suggest. For instance, although she spends her time during class discussion supporting the girls, she notes that she has 'set the agenda' for discussion (presumably by selecting a topic that would allow a focus on gender issues). It's not possible to analyse in any detail the nature of Moss' support for the girls — given her own aims, she provides only a brief account of the lesson. However, if one considers in a general sense the ways in which one may support other speakers it is clear that this may operate in a partial and subtly directive fashion: even while not laying down their own points of view teachers, or other relatively high status participants in asymmetrical discourse, may select certain speakers (and not others) to contribute; and by their management of the talk they may allow certain topics (and not others) to be elaborated. One difference between an anti-sexist 'fixed position' and a pro-female facilitatory approach may simply be that the latter is more subtle.

Conclusion

I have sketched out briefly three types of educational response to imbalances in girls' and boys' spoken language — responses that, while they are all broadly concerned with equal opportunities, have different starting points and different implications for action: the anti-sexist tradition, which has sought to rectify perceived inequalities between girls and boys; a liberal response, which has seen girls' and boys' language as 'different but equal'; and a pro-female response, designed to revalue girls' language and to support girls on their own terms. Though they come from different traditions and have different motivations, liberal and pro-female responses have in common that they both recognise the value of speaking styles associated with girls. Pro-female responses, as articulated by Moss, also point to the need for a differentiated and context-sensitive approach to gender issues. I have suggested that, while these insights are valuable, there is a danger in feminist responses becoming too muted and reactive. It is partly through language, including the ways girls use language, that inequalities between the sexes are sustained, and that inequalities may be contested. What girls need, however, is not simply support in what they are already up to but also the provision of alternative strategies for resistance.

References

Adler, S. (1992) Aprons and attitudes: Feminism and children's books. In H. Claire, J. Maybin and J. Swann (eds) *Equality Matters*. Clevedon: Multilingual Matters.

Bousted, M. (1989) Who talks? *English in Education* 23, 3, 41–51.

Brophy, J. (1985) Interactions of male and female students with male and female teachers. In L. C. Wilkinson and C. B. Marrett (eds) *Gender Influences in Classroom Interaction*. London: Academic Press.

Coates, J. (1988) Gossip revisited: Language in all-female groups. In J. Coates and D. Cameron (eds) *Women in their Speech Communities*. London: Longman.

Dart, B. C. and Clarke, J. A. (1988) Sexism in schools: A new look. *Educational Review* 40, 1, 41–9.

Deem, R. (1978) *Women and Schooling*. London: Routledge and Kegan Paul.

Delamont, S. (1980, revised 1990) *Sex Roles and the School*. London: Methuen.

Department of Education and Science/Welsh Office (DES/WO) (1989a) *English for Ages 5 to 16* (The Cox Report). London: HMSO.

— (1989b) *Programme of Study for Speaking and Listening: Key Stage 1*. London: HMSO.

Fisher, J. (1991) Unequal voices: Gender and assessment. In Open University (1991) *Talk and Learning 5–16*. Milton Keynes: The Open University.

French, J. and French, P. (1984) Gender imbalance in the primary classroom: An interactional account. *Educational Research* 26, 2, 127–36.

Healy, M. (1981) *Your Language: Three*. London: Macmillan.

Hordyk, A. (1986) Assertion and confidence training with girls. In Inner London Education Authority (ILEA) *Secondary Issues? Some Approaches to Equal Opportunities in Secondary Schools*. London: ILEA.

Inner London Education Authority (ILEA) (undated) *Implementing the ILEA's Anti-sexist Policy*. London: ILEA.

MacLure, M. (1988) Assessing spoken language: Testing times for talk. In N. Mercer (ed.) *Language and Literacy from an Educational Perspective, Vol. II: In Schools*. Milton Keynes: Open University Press.

Morse, L. W. and Handley, H. M. (1985) Listening to adolescents: Gender differences in science classroom interaction. In L. C. Wilkinson and C. B. Marrett (eds) *Gender Influences in Classroom Interaction*. New York: Academic Press.

Moss, G. (1989) *Un/Popular Fictions*. London: Virago.

National Curriculum Council (NCC) (1989) *English Key Stage 1: Non-statutory Guidance*. York: NCC.

Randall, G. (1987) Gender differences in pupil–teacher interaction in workshops and laboratories. In G. Weiner and M. Arnot (eds) *Gender Under Scrutiny: New Inquiries in Education*. London: Hutchinson in association with the Open University.

Rennie, L. J. and Parker, L. H. (1987) Detecting and accounting for gender differences in mixed-sex and single-sex groupings in science lessons. *Educational Review* 39, 1, 65–73.

Sadker, M. and Sadker, D. (1985) Sexism in the schoolroom of the '80s. *Psychology Today* March 1985, 54–7.

Smith, P. (1986) School policy, in Inner London Education Authority (ILEA) *Secondary Issues? Some Approaches to Equal Opportunities in Secondary Schools*. London: ILEA.

Spender, D. (1982) *Invisible Women: The Schooling Scandal*. London: Writers and Readers Publishing Cooperative.

Spender, D. and Sarah, E. (eds) (1988, revised edition) *Learning to Lose: Sexism and Education*. London: Women's Press.

Swann, J. (1992) *Girls, Boys and Language*. Oxford: Blackwell Publishers.

Swann, J. and Graddol, D. (1988) Gender inequalities in classroom talk. *English in Education* 22, 1, 48–65.

Whyte, J., Deem, R., Kant, L. and Cruickshank, M. (eds) (1985) *Girl Friendly Schooling*. London: Methuen.

13 Communication and Control

DEREK EDWARDS and NEIL MERCER

It is our purpose in this chapter to examine how particular sorts of classroom discourse carry classroom knowledge. Our first impression of the lessons was that they were relatively informal, progressive, child-centred sorts of pedagogy of the type advocated by the Plowden Report. It is an unforseen consequence of examining the data more closely that we are in fact largely concerned here with control processes, that is, with ways in which the teacher maintained a tight definition of what became joint versions of events, and joint understandings of curriculum content.

The process of creating joint understandings in the classroom is a problematical one. There appear to be a set of properties and constraints under which the educational process works, which are not always harmonious, and which make the process problematical. These include:

(1) the assumption on the part of teachers that educational failure in individual pupils can be attributed to individual factors, and principally to innate ability;
(2) a philosophy of education which assumes a self-actualising process of inductive and experimental learning through practical activity;
(3) The socialising function of education, in which the teacher exercises a large degree of control over what is done, said and understood;
(4) The separation of formal education from the contexts of everyday, out-of-school experience and learning;
(5) the largely implicit basis of much classroom activity and discourse.

The notions of 'scaffolding' (Bruner) and of the 'zone of proximal development' (Vygotsky) appear to be appropriate to the description of classroom education, but are often compromised by the somewhat inconsistent nature of these listed properties. While teachers engage in a great deal of skilled tuition, prompting and helping children to develop their understanding of curriculum topics, their own conceptions of what they are doing may be at odds with such a process. Success and failure are conceived largely in terms of inherent properties of pupils rather than as outcomes of the communicative process of education itself, and understandings on the part of pupils are seen as essentially inductive insights that the pupils themselves must achieve on the basis of their own experiences. The fact that a particular syllabus has to be taught, or, at least, that a planned set of concepts and activities has to be covered, leads to a sort of 'teacher's dilemma' how to get the pupils to learn for themselves what has been planned for them in advance.

We shall argue that these dilemmas and compromises can have a destructive effect on the effectiveness of education, by spoiling the essential purpose of the Vygotskyan process: that is, the process often remains incomplete, with no final *handover* of knowledge and control to the pupils. The pupils frequently remain embedded in rituals and procedures, having failed to grasp the overall purpose of what they have done, including the general concepts and principles that a particular lesson's activities was designed to inculcate.

In looking for some way of organising our treatment of these communicative processes, we have chosen what appears to be a central theme of classroom talk, the extent of teacher control over both the discourse and, through that, the content of knowledge. The following list of classroom communications is presented as a scale of teacher control of the nature, content and coding of knowledge, with the extent of control increasing as we descend the list. It is not an exhaustive list, and the qualitative nature of its contents precludes any precise notion of hierarchy or order. Nevertheless, it is useful in that it helps us to define the sorts of phenomena that we shall be dealing with, and their role in the establishment of shared understandings. We shall argue that it is essentially through the pervasive phenomena of teacher control over the expression of knowledge that pupils' understandings of things are frequently created as procedural rather than principled — saying and doing what seems to be required, rather than working out a principled understanding of how and why certain actions, expressions and procedures are appropriate or correct.

The following list of features of classroom discourse is cast in terms of the teacher's role in them.

elicitation of pupils' contributions
significant markers, e.g.   special enunciation
                            formulaic phrases
                            ignoring pupils' contributions
joint-knowledge markers, e.g.   simultaneous speech
                                'royal' plurals
                                repeated discourse formats
cued elicitation of pupils' contributions
paraphrastic interpretations of pupils' contributions
reconstructive recaps
implicit and presupposed knowledge

Spontaneous and Elicited Contributions

The *spontaneous contributions* offered by the pupils were by definition those communications least influenced by teacher control. But they were not devoid of it. It was the teacher who had set the agenda, defined the topic of discussion, and established in advance the criteria of relevance and appropriateness of any contributions that the pupils might offer. And the teacher generally remained in control of the ultimate fate of any such contributions — of whether they were acted on, taken up and incorporated into the development of ideas in further classroom discourse, or whether they were discouraged, disapproved or ignored. Most contributions to classroom discourse offered by the pupils were, as other research has abundantly demonstrated (e.g. Galton, Simon & Croll, 1980) made by invitation from the teacher. *Elicited contributions* were those that fell into the familiar and pervasive IRF[1] structure, where pupils' contributions were directly constrained by teachers' questions.

The importance of IRFs in the establishment of joint understanding lies in the way in which they express the complementarity of teacher's and pupil's knowledge. Teachers' questions are of a special sort, in that they do not carry the usual presupposition that the speaker does not know the answer to the question asked. They function as discursive devices through which the teacher is able to keep a continual check on the pupils' understandings, to ensure that various concepts, information or terms of reference are jointly understood, so that subsequent discourse may be predicated on a developing continuity and context of intersubjectivity. IRF structures also function in defining and controlling what that knowledge and understanding will be. They are part of a set of communicative devices whereby the teacher acts as a kind of filter or gateway through which all knowledge must pass in order to be included in the lesson as a valid or useful contribution. This is particularly noticeable in instances of what may be called 'retrospective elicitation', where the teacher invites a pupil's response after it has already been made.

A particularly interesting example of retrospective elicitation occurred where the teacher was eliciting hypotheses about the effect on period of swing of shortening the pendulum's string:

Sharon:	It would be slower.	
T:	What do you reckon/	Sharon?
Jonathan:	Much faster.	
Sharon:	Slower./	Faster.
	I think it would be faster.	

Sharon first offered the hypothesis 'It would be slower'. The teacher then retrospectively defined Sharon's contribution as welcome and proper, by explicitly inviting it. Sharon then vacillated and changed her mind. Two things may have influenced her. First, Jonathan was simultaneously suggesting that the pendulum bob would swing faster. Second, and at least as important, there may have been another ground-rule at work. Rather than making a retrospective invitation, the teacher may have been interpreted by Sharon as repeating the question, as asking the same question after having received an answer. This is generally a signal that the first answer is wrong, and that an alternative answer is expected. What we have here is probably a conflict between two alternative discursive ground-rules. While the teacher sought to make a retrospective elicitation of Sharon's answer, Sharon herself read this as a repeated question and changed her mind.

In the case of less welcome responses, the teacher ignored, or simply failed to encourage or develop, several attempts to introduce ideas that were not part of the planned course of the lesson.

Marking Knowledge as Significant and Joint

Apart from pervasive phenomenon of inviting pupils' contributions, and of occasionally ignoring them, expressed knowledge was sometimes given special prominence by discourse devices such as special enunciation and the use of formulaic phrases. Shifts of intonation served pedagogic functions by highlighting important information, and marking other comments as 'asides', or as having different functions. Apart from the conventional use of devices such as pauses and rising intonation to mark the asking of questions, or of falling intonation to mark the confirmation of answers, shifts particularly in the rate and loudness of speech generally occurred at the boundaries of shifts of pedagogic significance, rather than merely of conversational function.

Sequence 1: Intonation and knowledge

(Note: relevant speech segments italicised.)

Pendulum lesson:

T is establishing that the pupils know how to measure pendulum swings, and can calculate an average period of swing.

T:	OK? So that makes ten seconds. So. how much then is each swing roughly?	*T looks at Antony.*
Antony:	Two seconds.	
T:	Two seconds. Good. OK. We'll write than down.	*T writes '2 seconds'.*
	Everybody understood that bit?	*Spoken quickly.*
	Now then. I wonder if this pendulum	*T reaches for Jonathan's pendulum.*

	would also take the same time.	*T's intonation now slow, deliberate, in marked contrast to preceding speech.*

.
.
.

T:	What did you get darling?	*T looks beyond Lucy to Karen.*
Karen:	Mine says eight and a half.	
T:	Eight point five and a half. What did you get Lucy?	*T writes down '8.5'.*
Lucy:	Er I think/I think mine's eight and a half.	*Lucy showing T the watch.*
T:	No. Yours is/yes it is acutally I haven't got my glasses on. I can't see. *Yes it is. Eight point five the same.* Right. So it looks as if/if we round off the two eight point fives and take into account the ten point twelve/ten point one two/	*T speaking quickly and quietly.* *T writes '8.5'.* *Voice louder and slower.*
Jonathan:	Five into eight goes one/ and/	*Jonathan pauses, pen over paper, frowning.*
T:	Anybody help him?	
Jonathan:	I think it's three isn't it?	*In fact the sum is:*
T:	Three/yeh/	
Jonathan:	Fives into three/is that it? Fives into three go	
Pupil:	Fives into thirty goes six/	
Jonathan:	Fives into thirty goes six. Fives into two goes/ one point six five	*Jonathan mumbles from here.*
T:	*One point six five/* So it's not very far away from two which was David's	*T's speech slow and loud.*

$$5\overline{)8.250}^{\displaystyle 1.65}$$

.
.
.

		T elicits suggestions for the total number of swings from which an average swing will be calculated
T:	An even number/ makes it/ you reckon you can divide by six better than you can divide by five.// *Will it make any difference to the* **accuracy**/ *of what she's doing if she did* a **larger**/ *number of swings?*	*T looking at Antony.* *T laughs, then Sharon does.* *T speaking slowly and clearly, with small pauses as indicated.*

The italicised speech in sequence 1 is that to which the contextual comments about intonation apply. It is speech marked by intonation as having a special significance in relation to the rest of what is said. The choice of slow, deliberate enunciation, or of faster and quieter speech, was clearly determined by the content of what was said, and its pedagogic function. The important curriculum-oriented content was given prominence with careful, clear enunciation, while 'asides' about the teacher's vision, and the check on continuity of understanding, were marked by a drop in volume, and a sudden increase in rate of speech.

Cued Elicitation

The process of cued elicitation was a pervasive one in our data transcripts.

Cued elicitations are IRF types of discourse in which the teacher asks questions while simultaneously providing heavy clues to the information required. This simultaneous provision of information may be achieved merely by the wording of the question, but is often accomplished via some other communicative channel such as intonation, pausing, gestures or physical demonstrations. It may also be done implicitly, by an unspoken appeal to shared knowledge. Sequence 2 is a clear example.

Sequence 2: Cued elicitation: Galileo's pulse

T:	Now he didn't have a watch/ but he had on him something that was a very good timekeeper that he could use to hand straight away/	*T snaps fingers on 'straight away', and looks invitingly at pupils as if posing a question or inviting a response.*
	You've got it. I've got it. What is it?//	*T points on 'You've' and 'I've'.*
	What could we use to count beats? What have you got?//	*T beats hand on table slowly, looks around group of pupils, who smile and shrug.*
	You can feel it here.	*T puts fingers on T's wrist pulse.*
Pupils:	Pulse.	*(In near unison.)*
T:	A pulse. Everybody see if you can find it.	*All copy T, feeling for wrist pulses.*

Cued elicitation is an important process for at least two reasons:

(1) It demonstrates a general point of method and theory — that, if we are going to make proper sense of the process of classroom education, then we need careful records of gesture and activity as well as detailed transcripts of classroom discourse, that these need to be closely integrated, and that we do not make the error of trying to account for educational processes solely in terms of classroom talk and discourse structures.

(2) It is a communicative process of substantial intrinsic interest. Classroom questions and answers have peculiar characteristics: the teacher, who knows the answers, asks most of the questions, asks questions to which she already knows the answers, and, additionally, it appears, may

ask questions while simultaneously doing her best to provide the answers via an alternative channel. We have to seek an understanding of the pedagogic function of this sort of thing.

The best interpretation that we can make of the pedagogic function of cued elicitation is that it embodies an educational process in which the pupils are neither being drawn out of themselves, in the *e-ducare* sense, nor simply being taught directly, in the 'transmission' sense. Rather, they are being inculcated into what becomes for them a shared discourse with the teacher (discourse in the broadest sense, including concepts and terminology as well as dialogue). As such, it falls neatly into the sort of educational process defined by Vygotsky's 'zone of proximal development', in which pupils' knowledge is aided and 'scaffolded' by the teacher's questions, clues and prompts to achieve insights that the pupils by themselves seemed incapable of. It is a device which requires that the pupils actively participate in the creation of shared knowlege, rather than merely sit and listen to the teacher talking. Cued elicitation is also a process which constitutes a solution to what we have called the *teacher's dilemma* — a necessary compromise between two conflicting requirements that the lesson had to achieve. These requirements were that the pupils should (apparently, at least) generate their own understandings of things through their own thought and experience, and that they should come to do and to understand specific activities and concepts planned at the outset — to test three specified hypotheses, to find that only one of the variables was effective, to calculate average times over twenty swings, and to make matrices and draw graphs of the results.

The danger of cued elicitation is that, until it is examined closely, it can give a false impression (presumably to the participants as well as to the observers) of the extent to which pupils understand, and are ultimately responsible for, what they are saying and doing. It can easily mask rather than bridge the gap between teacher and child that is the basis of Vygotsky's developmental process.

Reconstructions, Presuppositions and Paraphrases

Moving down our scaled list of communicative processes, we come next to a set of discursive devices through which the teacher was able to maintain a strict control over the content of common knowledge. Through paraphrasing what the pupils said, and through reconstructing what occurred in the lesson when recapping later, she was able to redefine these things as altogether neater, nicer and closer to the intended lesson plan. Similarly, by presupposing certain things as known or understood, she was able to forestall disagreement, and shape the direction of the discourse and the interpretations put upon experience. Paraphrases were often seemingly small and accidental, as when, in Pendulum lesson 2, Lucy appeared to mis-remember one of the timed scores obtained in lesson 1 when she and Jonathan had varied the weight of the pendulum bob.

Sequence 3: Paraphrasing Lucy

T:	Now what about when you had **one** washer? Can you remember what the time was there Lucy?	*T points to the '1 washer' position on graph.*
Lucy:	Erm/ one point one four.	
T:	One point nine four?	
Lucy:	⎰ Yes.	
T:	⎱ That's right there it is.	*T pointing to where the number is plotted on the graph.*

The teacher also used paraphrasisng more directly as a teaching method, as in sequence 4, when she tried to elicit as much as possible of the explanation from the pupils, and then recast the explanation offered by Antony into a preferred (and, indeed, more precise) form:

Sequence 4: Paraphrasing Antony

Pendulum lesson 2

The teacher is discussing what makes the pendulum continue its swing past the mid-point, against gravity; see sequence 1.

T:	OK, so it's gravity that pulls it down. What causes it to go up again at the other side?	*T swings one of the pendulums.*
Antony:	The string/ it forces up the string/ going down	
T:	It gets up speed going down.	

.
.
.

And it's the/ energy the force that it builds up that takes it up the other side.

These reconstructive paraphrases demonstrate another function of the 'feedback' stage of IRF sequences; they provide an opportunity for the teacher not only to confirm what the pupils say, but to recast it in a more acceptable form, more explicit perhaps, or simply couched in a preferred terminology. The most extensive reconstructions occurred during the second of the pendulum lessons, when the teacher was recapping (via the familiar sorts of IRF elicitations) on the material covered in lesson 1. Both teacher and pupils took advantage of the opportunity to reconstruct a more acceptable version of events.

Information can be *introduced* into a conversation through its role as an implicit context for what is explicity stated. The implicit part of a message can be recovered from the situational context and from what is explicitly said, and this again is a normal feature of everyday discourse. If someone asks us in the street for directions to the nearest post office, we would have reasonable grounds for assuming that they want to go there, do not know the way, and so on. The use of presuppositional implication in educational contexts has a pedagogic function over and above its uses in many other contexts (though much persuasive rhetoric, propaganda, advertising and so on, clearly works in a similar fashion); it serves to introduce certain items of knowledge and assumption as things to be accepted without question, as understood but not on the agenda for discussion or disagreement, and, in a more general sense, is therefore available to the teacher as an instrument of control over what is known and understood.

A particular instance of implicit teaching occurred when the teacher introduced preferred terminology, scientific jargon such as 'mass' and 'momentum'. Sometimes these terms would be introduced through what we may call 'direct teaching', where the teacher explicitly introduced the words, defined them and encouraged the pupils to use them. At other times new terms of reference were introduced by elicitation, or cued elicitation, as was the case with the terms 'momentum' and 'acceleration' in lesson 2 ('Does anyone know the word for it when you get up speed/ as in a car when you press the pedal?'). Sequence 5 shows how various terms were introduced simply by the teacher's using them in an understood context, as an alternative, implicity preferred vocabulary.

Sequence 5: Acquiring a shared vocabulary: Teacher's usage

(Video camera concentrating on T's actions; pupils sometimes unidentified.)

T:	Yes, Let's have a closer look at this one.	*T takes off the pendant she is wearing and puts it on the table.*
	Right. Now then. What does the pendulum have to have to be a pendulum?	
Boy:	String.	
T:	A string/ yes. In this case it's a/	*T holds pendant chain up.*
Pupils:	Chain.	
T:	Chain/	
	So it has to be suspended doesn't it?	*T raises and suspends pendant by its chain.*
Boy:	A weight.	
T:	It has to have a weight doesn't it/ a mass at the end which this one has. OK?/ Right/ let's have a closer look at	

mine. Is it a pendulum// now? *T lays pendant flat on table, looks at Lucy.*

Lucy: No. *Rising intonation (signalling 'is this the answer you want?').*

T: You agreed Jon? *Jonathan nods.*
Lucy: Mm.
T: Not./ What does it have to do then to be a pendulum?
Boy: Be straight.
T: It has to be straight. *T straightens the pendant's chain, still flat on table.*

Is it a pendulum now? *Pupils shake heads.*
Pupils: No.
Girl: Hanging.
T: It's got to hang. *T lifts pendant and holds chain stretched out between her two hands.*

Girl: Hang straight.
Boy: Hang straight down { from one finger.
T: { Why isn't it a pendulum now?
Same boy: { 'Cause it won't swing. *Boy quiet, almost mumbles.*
T: { You've said it's got to have a weight on the end/ You've said that it has to have string to be suspended and it **has**.// Why isn't it a pendulum then?
Karen: It has to hang straight down.
T: It has to hang straight down Karen/ there it is/ so that's right isn't it? So it has to/ *T holds pendant string in the finger and thumb of one hand, suspended now in a straight vertical line with the pendant at the bottom.*

hang from a fixed point./ *T points to fingers holding chain with free hand.*

It has to be suspended/ from a string or a chain or whatever/ and it has to have a mass at the end. Right/ *Runs hand down chain.*

While the pupils have used everyday terms such as 'weight' and 'hang straight down from one finger', the teacher herself not only has used these terms, but has also introduced the more technical jargon 'mass', 'suspended' and 'from a fixed point'. Having established the various component attributes of a pendulum, the teacher then recaps these with the pupils.

Sequence 6: Acquiring a shared vocabulary: Pupils' usage

T: Now what did we say that they had to have Jonathan? A pendulum? *Jonathan is next to his pendulum.*
Jonathan: A weight at the bottom.
T: Yes and yours **has**/ OK? And yours is a washer.

Jonathan:	Mm.
T:	Right. David what else does a pendulum have to have?
David:	A mass.
T:	Jonathan's mentioned that.
David:	A string.
T:	A string or a chain or some means of suspending the mass/ of hanging it down.
	Whoops/

Pendulum topples and is caught by Sharon and Antony; all laugh.

T:	Right/ and Antony what was the third thing it had to have?
Antony:	Suspended.
T:	Right./ From?
Antony:	A fixed point.

The pupils have quickly grasped the new terminology introduced by the teacher, and have begun to use it themselves. It is not clear that they immediately understood what it all meant. David's suggestion 'a mass' is ambiguous between his not understanding that 'mass' means something equivalent here to 'weight', and his sense that the teacher simply prefers the term 'mass', which makes it worth mentioning. Despite the absense of direct teaching — the teacher has not explicityly taught these terms, nor required or overtly encouraged the pupils to adopt them — they have become common terms of reference to signal common understand. Simply by using the terms in a context in which they could be understood, in this case as alternatives for everyday words used by the pupils, the teacher has managed to induct the pupils into a shared scientific discourse, a shared frame of reference and conceptions. Indeed, this is probably the best description we could offer of the nature of this sort of teaching and learning: it is all about the induction of children into the academic world of knowledge and discourse inhabited by the teacher. It is a process of cognitive socialisation through discourse, a process akin at least as much to general behavioural and ideological socialisation as to the cognitive psychological notions of mental growth or development.

Classroom Discourse and Classroom Knowledge

One general finding that surprised us was the extent of control exercised by the teacher, even in lessons that were characterised by the more progressive sorts of teaching. In the pendulum lessons, for example, the pupils worked in small groups, subdivided into pairs of pupils working jointly on each pendulum, discovering through their own activities the principles that govern the motion of pendulums. At first sight, the teacher's role appeared to be essentially facilitative, shaping the general direction of the lesson, but largely relying on the pupils themselves to invent hypotheses, procedures and criteria for testing, performing the experiments themselves and making their own observations and measurements. On closer examination, the extent of teacher control became clearer. As we have demonstrated in this chapter, the freedom of pupils to introduce their own ideas was largely illusory; the teacher retained a strict control over what was said and done, what decisions were reached, and what interpretations were put upon experience.

We are, of course, wary of generalising from a small sample of classroom discourse to an analysis of the general state of British primary education. That is not our purpose, and this is the reason why we have not coded and counted the various types of phenomena we have identified. Such a procedure would lend itself to the sorts of statistical comparisons between different classrooms and schools that our research was not designed to achieve. Rather, we have chosen to subject small samples of classroom discourse and activity to close qualitative analysis, in the hope of discovering in that discourse clues to how knowledge is actually built and shared between teacher and pupils.

Nevertheless, the discovery of an overwhelming sense of control by the teacher, in setting the agenda, determining in advance of the lesson what the knowledge outcomes should be, and, in general, expressing the authoritative social role of teacher in terms of epistemic as well as behavioural control, is a discovery that others too have made. Some, such as Edwards & Furlong (1978), base their analysis on classroom discourse as we have done. Others use more specific and quantified linguistic indices. Feldman & Wertsch (1976), for example, measured the frequency with which American teachers used a set of auxiliary verbs that express degrees of uncertainty (may, might, could, etc.). They found a greater use of them in the staffroom than in the classroom; classroom talk was judged to be authoritative, certain of its facts, and 'closed' in comparison to the more open, hypothetical and uncertain talk between teachers.

Our findings suggest these main conclusions about the educational processes we have observed:

(1) *Experiential learning and teacher control.* Despite the fact that the lessons were organised in terms of practical actions and small-group joint activity between the pupils, the sort of learning that took place was not essentially a matter of experiential learning and communication between pupils. The role of the teacher was crucial throughout, both in shaping the general pattern and content of the lesson, and in producing the fine-grained definition of what was done, said and understood. The pupils were in no sense left to create their own understandings and interpretations.

(2) *Ritual and principle*. While maintaining a tight control over activity and discourse, the teacher nevertheless overtly espoused and attempted to act upon the educational principle of pupil-centred experiential learning, and the importance of pupils' engagement in practical activity and discovery. This led to the pupils' grasp of certain important concepts being essentially 'ritual', a matter of what to do or say, rather than 'principled', i.e. based on conceptual understanding. Particular sorts of classroom discourse that appeared to underlie the creation of such procedural knowledge included a heavy reliance on 'cued elicitation', together with an overriding concern to conduct the lessons in terms of getting through the set of planned activities, rather than, say, making sure that a planned set of concepts was understood by everyone. The sheer extent of teacher control over activity, discourse and interpretation was also likely to have contributed to the fact that pupils' understanding of the lessons often became a matter of knowing what was done (or, at least, the official reconstructed version of this), and what one was required to say.

(3) *Language and the socialisation of cognition*. We have concentrated on the 'content' of knowledge and discourse, on what was said and done, the words used, the concepts at issue, the actions performed. Others have looked largely at the 'form' of classroom discourse, either its sociolinguistic structures (e.g. Sinclair & Coulthard, 1975; Mehan, 1979), or its relations to formal properties of thought, such as logical reasoning abilities (Walkerdine, 1984). The overriding impression from our studies is that classroom discourse functions to establish joint understandings between teacher and pupils, shared frames of reference and conception, in which the basic process (including the problematical features of that process) is one of introducing pupils into the conceptual world of the teacher and, through him or her, of the educational community. To the extent that the process of education can be observed taking place in the situated discourse of classrooms, it is on our evidence essentially a process of cognitive socialisation through language.

The relation of power and control to the creation of joint understandings is both problematical and of great importance. According to Habermas (1970: 143), 'pure intersubjectivity' is achieved only under conditions of 'complete symmetry in the distribution of assertion and disputation, revelation and hiding, prescription and following, among the partners of communication'. But education is inherently concerned with introducing children and adults into a pre-existing culture of thought and language. However active a part pupils are allowed to play in their learning, we cannot assume that they can simply reinvent that culture through their own activity and experience. It is necessarily a social and communicative process, and one which has an inherent part of it an asymmetry of roles between teacher and learner. Pre-school cultural learning, and especially the learning of a first language, has been described by Lock (1979) as a process of 'guided reinvention'. In schools the power asymmetry is more marked; schooling is compulsory, separated from life at home, more formal, and with a more arbitrary syllabus. Many children go unwillingly to school. Teachers are often perceived primarily as sources of punishment (Hood, McDermott & Cole, 1980). If the educational process is not to be completely compromised by the asymmetry of teacher and learner, then we need to develop an understanding of the process which recognises and encourages that asymmetry in a manner that fosters rather than hinders learning.

Part of the problem for pupils is that much of the process remains mysterious to them. In however friendly and informal a manner, they are frequently asked to do things, learn things, understand things, for no apparent reason other than that it is what the teacher wants them to do. The goals and purposes of the lesson are not revealed. Indeed, neither often are the concepts that the lesson may have been designed to 'cover'. In the ethos of pupil-centred inductive learning, it is not acceptable to tell the pupils what they were supposed to discover for themselves, even after they have completed the various activities involved.

The major components of the teacher–pupil learning process as we have presented it are present in Vygotsky's conception of it. The asymmetry of teacher and learner is essential to the 'zone of proximal development', and so also is the notion of control. Children do not simply acquire knowledge and vocabulary. They acquire at the same time the capacity for self-regulation. Just as verbal thought originates as social discourse, so self-regulated behaviour begins with the regulation of one's behaviour by other people. The successful process involves a gradual handover of control from teacher to learner, as the learner becomes able to do alone what could previously be done only with help. In formal education, this part of the process is seldom realised. For most pupils, education remains a mystery beyond their control, rather than a resource of knowledge and skill with which they can freely operate. The contrast between formal schooling and first-language learning is stark, as Bruner (1985) and others have pointed out. Here, for example, formal education is contrasted with learning to play peekaboo:

> the mother initially enacts the entire script herself and then the child takes an increasingly active role, eventually speaking all the parts initially spoken by the mother. The contrast between such learning environments and the classroom is striking. In school lessons, teachers give directions and children nonverbally carry them out; teachers ask questions and children answer them, frequently with only a word or a phrase. Most importantly, these roles are not reversed . . . Children

never give directions to teachers, and questions addressed to teachers are rare except for asking permission. (Forman & Cazden, 1985: 344)

A successful educational process is one which transfers competence to the learner. It is almost as if formal education, for most pupils, is designed to prevent that from happening.

Note

1. 'The basic "I-R-F" exchange structure — an *initiation* by a teacher, which elicits a *response* from a pupil, followed by an evaluative comment or *feedback* from the teacher — is, once seen, impossible to ignore in any observed classroom talk' (Edwards & Mercer, 1987: 9). See also Sinclair & Coulthard (1975).

References

Bruner, J. S. (1985) Vygotsky: A historical and conceptual perspective. In J. V. Wertsch (ed.) *Culture, Communication and Cognition: Vygotskian Perspective*. Cambridge: Cambridge University Press.
— (1986) *Actual Minds, Possible Worlds*. Cambridge, MA: Harvard University Press.
Edwards, A. D. and Furlong, V. J. (1978) *The Language of Teaching*. London: Heinemann.
Feldman, C. and Wertsch, J. V. (1976) Context dependent properties of teachers' speech. *Youth and Society* 8, 227–58.
Forman, E. A. and Cazden, C. B. (1985) Exploring Vygotskian perspectives in education: The cognitive value of peer interaction. In J. V. Wersch (ed.) *Culture, Communication and Cognition: Vygotskian Perspectives*. Cambridge: Cambridge University Press.
Galton, M., Simon, B. and Croll, P. (1980) *Inside the Primary Classroom* (the ORACLE project). London: Routledge and Kegan Paul.
Habermas, J. (1970) Toward a theory of communicative competence. In H. P. Dreitzel (ed.) *Recent Sociology*. New York: Macmillan.
Hood, L., McDermott, R. and Cole, M. (1980) 'Let's try to make it a good day' — some not so simple ways. *Discourse Processes* 3, 155–68.
Lock, A. J. (1979) *The Guided Reinvention of Language*. London: Academic Press.
Mehan, H. (1979) *Learning Lessons: Social Organization in the Classroom*. Cambridge, MA: Harvard University Press.
Plowden Report (1967) *Children and their Primary Schools*. London: Central Advisory Council for Education.
Sinclair, J. McH. and Coulthard, R. M. (1975) *Towards an Analysis of Discourse: The English used by Teachers and Pupils*. London: Oxford University Press.
Vygotsky, L. S. (1978) *Mind in Society: The Development of Higher Psychological Processes*. London: Harvard University Press.
Walkerdine, V. (1984) Developmental psychology and the child-centred pedagogy: The insertion of Piaget into early education. In J. Henriques, W. Hollway, C. Urwin, C. Venn and V. Walkerdine (eds) *Changing the Subject*. London: Methuen.

14 The Value of 'Time Off Task': Young Children's Spontaneous Talk and Deliberate Text

ANNE HAAS DYSON

The ability to construct, display and analyze hypothetical themes and imaginative scenarios is a hallmark of intelligent behavior in our culture. We are builders of 'possible worlds', worlds of actors, objects, and actions that exist through words alone (Bruner, 1986). When children go beyond themselves to share experiences, ideas, and opinions, they engage in much of their most intellectually demanding work (Vygotsky, 1978). Given tasks worth talking about and the right to talk, children's interactions can contribute substantially to intellectual development in general and literacy growth in particular. Those interactions can provide both social support and social energy — the capacity for action fuelled by human desire for social communication and individual expression.

In the following pages, I take readers into an urban primary-grade classroom that is filled with children talking. Drawing upon data collected over a two-year period in this classroom, I present an analysis of children's spontaneous talk while writing stories, revealing the children at their intellectual best — their reflections formulated through talk and, at times, deliberately shaped in worlds of written words. Specifically, the following questions are addressed:

— What purposes did the children's talk serve?
— What intellectual tasks did the children spontaneously and collaboratively accomplish?
— In what ways did independent child writing behaviors reflect previous interactions with peers?

Certainly, talking can cause difficulties for children; there are children who are socially isolated or whose interest in social linking overpowers their interest in work. Given the potential value of talk, however, the solution to these difficulties may well lie in working with — and not against — the social energy that talk reflects. This article provides descriptive evidence of that value.

The children and their classroom

To illustrate how children's social talk gives rise to intellectual accomplishment, I turn to observations made in an urban magnet school on the West Coast. The social and ethnic diversity of the school population reflected that of the city: the children were of White, Asian, Black, Hispanic, Middle Eastern, and mixed ethnicities. The school's seventy-nine primary-grade (kindergarten through third) children were separated into three 'home classrooms': a kindergarten, a first/second grade, and a second/third grade. Margaret, a White woman in her sixties, taught the kindergarten. Beginning in January, the primary-grade children moved among the three teachers' classrooms during the school day. From that point on, Margaret taught all of the children language arts.

Margaret's language arts program included an emphasis on the use of journals (books composed of construction paper and alternating blank and lined paper). From January through May, as the children drew and wrote daily in their journals, Margaret circulated and talked to them about their story ideas and the mechanics of production, and, in the kindergarten, acted as scribe for the children's dictations. Whereas in one study of an urban primary classroom the children were described as uncommunicative during pencil-and-paper writing activities (Dickinson, 1986), Margaret's classes were characterized by the pervasiveness and tolerance of talk. Margaret did not view the children's chatting as 'on-task' behavior; that is, as benefitting their writing growth. But she did consider it a natural byproduct of children's interest in each other and in 'expressing themselves'. While she consistently told loud children to 'stop talking and get to work', she neither encouraged nor scolded the children who spoke unless she felt a child was bothering someone else. Each day, Margaret allowed time for children to share two or three entries from their completed journals with the class.

I observed the language arts period in Margaret's kindergarten and first/ second grade classes an average of twice per week from January through May 1985 and February through May 1986.[1] During 1986, I was aided by two research assistants, Carol Heller and Mary Gardner; we each observed twice weekly in the first/second and the second/third grade classes. We were participant observers who adopted the role of reactive adult, rather than that of directive teacher (Corsaro, 1985). Moreover, we gathered holistic, descriptive data: audiotapes of the children's talk, their drawn and written products, and handwritten observations of their behavior.

Although data were gathered on all children, eight students — four kindergarteners and four first graders — were chosen as case studies during the Spring of 1985 (see Table 1). Although all of these children were judged by Margaret and the observers to fall within the range of 'normal', both academically and emotionally, they exhibited different artistic and social styles. To illustrate: for some children, 'drawing' was more 'talking' — an opportunity to dramatize an elaborate adventure orally and perhaps to involve peers in their drama. For others, 'drawing' was a methodical manipulation of strokes and colors, leading to a product to display for others. Further, the children spoke different varieties of English and spoke of strikingly different home neighborhoods.

Table 1 Age, gender and ethnicity of focal children

	Age[a]	Gender	Ethnicity
First graders			
Maggie	5, 0	Female	Anglo
Regina	6, 0	Female	Black
Jesse	5, 6	Male	Anglo
Reuben	5, 10	Male	Hispanic
Second graders			
Sonia	6, 2	Female	Hispanic
Mitzi[b]	6, 3	Female	Anglo
Jake	6, 5	Male	Mixed (Black/Anglo)
Manuel	7, 3	Male	Mixed (Hispanic/Anglo)

[a] Age as of January 1, 1985 (given in years, months)
[b] During the observations from February through May 1986, Mitzi was not in the same classroom as the other seven children

Herein, I focus on the intellectual tasks the children accomplished through their interactions. These tasks were not consciously pursued, but *unintentionally* encountered as the children responded socially, and often playfully, to each other's strengths and shortcomings — that is, as they went 'off task.'[2] The question I address is: Within the literacy environment of this classroom, in what ways did spontaneous child interactions foreshadow more deliberate and individual accomplishments?

The nature and purposes of child talk during 'world-making'

In my initial analysis of the first-year kindergarten data, I developed categories to describe how the children used talk, pictures, and written text to create and to enter into imaginary worlds (Dyson, 1986). One set of categories applied to the ways in which the children used language to represent real and imaginary situations, or 'worlds', to monitor and direct the behavior of themselves and others, to seek information, to express their feelings and attitudes, and to manage social relationships. Because of my interest in how children construct imaginary worlds, I focused particularly on the distinguishing features of the messages behind the children's representational talk. Differences were noted in the *relevance* of the talk to the ongoing journal activity, some talk being *task involved,* other talk being *non-task involved.* Only talk that was directly relevant to the child's own ongoing journal entry was considered task involved.

During the analysis of the first grade data, the inadequacy of the coding system became obvious. The simplistic distinction between task-involved and non-task-involved talk was discarded in favor of two additional categories for coding relevance. This modification was needed, first, because the children frequently entered into the task of a peer, commenting on the peer's actions or even entering into a peer's imaginary world. That is, their talk was *other's task involved,* the first new coding category. This talk could also be coded for degree of symbolic involvement and for the type of time frame governing that talk. For example, a child could stretch a peer's world forward in time or elaborate on a point in time.

Further, the children's comments on others' work often led to talk that was *task related,* the second new coding category. This task was outside the boundaries of the particular imaginary worlds the children were creating but clearly related to those worlds. For example, a picture of one child's mother as a teenager led to a discussion about teenage mothers. As the project continued and case studies were written describing how the children's behavior changed over time, I realized that the roots of many of the children's achievements as independent writers — as constructors of imaginary text worlds — were made visible by these new coding categories, that is, by studying carefully the rich and noisy talk of the peer group. Indeed, as will be illustrated, some talk that seemed clearly non-task involved, such as talk about the children's feelings toward each other, could later be seen, in a broad sense, as task related, for the children's lives together were often transformed into the imaginary world.

Entering and stretching the boundaries of another's world

During journal time, certain children accompanied their drawing or writing with representational dramatic or narrative talk, thereby making their imaginary worlds accessible to peers. Peers could serve as an interested audience for another's world, or they could cross the boundaries into that imaginary world and suggest new meaning elements that more directly extended and refined its time and space boundaries. This stretching of boundaries is illustrated in the following excerpt from the first grade year of Jake's case study:

Example 1

Jake has been drawing and talking. Manuel first questions and then enters into Jake's world.

Jake: I'm gonna make a mechanical man.
Manuel: A mechanical man? You mean a robot man?
Jake: Yeah. I'm gonna make a robot man. You got it, Manuel.
                   . . .
                   Here's a bomb head. [*The 'mechanical/robot' man's head has two lines extending from it.*] It's gonna explode. It hasn't even exploded yet. When it does . . .
Manuel: I hope it explodes in the next century.
Johnny: It's not going to be for real.
Manuel: Well, in the future it is.
Jake: Yeah, in the future it is.
Manuel: I just don't like the whole journal to blast.
Jake: Huh?

Manuel's comment initially makes no sense, until he explains that he is treating Jake's imaginary and pictorial world in a literal way.

Manuel: I think this picture might blast because his mechanical man has a bomb head.
                   . . .
Jake: Here comes the bomb explosion! There is the fire, a little smoke. [*Jake is making quick back-and-forth motions with his marker.*]

Although Jake's talk suggests that the explosion is beginning, his subsequent remarks postpone that explosion, thus keeping the time frame of his imaginary world consistent with earlier talk.

Jake: It's gonna explode in the next few days.
Sonia: What?
Manuel: I hope it happens on the weekend and then I won't be around. [*Manuel again takes a playful but literal stance toward Jake's world, and this time Jake plays along.*)
Jake: Not for long this school will be around.
                   . . .
Sonia: You're crazy.

In the second grade, the observed children more explicitly manipulated the boundaries between the imaginary and the real worlds. Their texts did not reflect consistent boundaries — time and space markers vacillated, as did first- and third-person stances. Nonetheless, the children's talk reflected an awareness of these boundaries and of the logic of action unfolding within them. Moreover, these boundaries were often made 'concrete' by the presence of peers.

In the following example, we see Jake and Manuel one year later. Jake has been writing an adventure story in which Manuel, as a literary character, meets Buck Rogers. Jake tells Manuel to be careful because if he doesn't do what Buck Rogers says, he will get blown to pieces when Manuel and Buck take on the bad guys. This time Jake, rather than Manuel, extends the plot's consequences into the everyday world. He warns Manuel's brother that he may never see Manuel again. With Manuel's assistance, however, Jake qualifies that extension, highlighting the boundaries of the imaginary world.

Example 2

Jake: Uh, Manuel, you get to see Buck Rogers!
Manuel: What?
Jake: Buck Rogers.
Manuel: Oh. Oh. *You mean in your story.* [*emphasis added*]
Jake: Yeah. Buck Rogers, twenty-first century person . . . [*to Marcos, Manuel's brother*] You wouldn't see your brother again, ever again Marcos. *You would never see him in a story again.* [*emphasis added*]
Marcos: I wouldn't?
Jake: In my stories, uh uh. Cause that would be the last. Eepoof! Nothing.
Manuel: Oh God. Oh, well, it's been fun having adventures with you. Um, but I'm gonna get blown to pieces.
                . . .
Jake: You might get your butt saved by Buck Rogers. You want your butt saved by Buck Rogers?
Manuel: What I want is my body saved. I don't wanna die. I don't wanna . . .
                . . .
Jake: You want your whole body saved by Buck Rogers?

*In Jake's story, Buck does teach Manuel how to take on the bad guys —
Manuel is saved, his existence in the text world secured.*

Providing the intentional characters of imaginary worlds

As suggested in the examples above, not only did the children enter into and help construct the actions of each other's imaginary worlds, their social relationships could provide the stuff of the less tangible aspects of those worlds — the feelings, thoughts, and motives of characters.

In the first grade, children's talk about friends as well as any written references to friends were typically straightforward 'I like [name]' statements. Consider, for example, the following excerpt from the first grade year of Mitzi's case. In this example, too, note that apparently non-task-involved talk appears task related when Mitzi begins writing her new journal entry and, then, task involved when she draws an accompanying picture.

Example 3

As she completes a journal entry about a girl who lived under a rainbow, Mitzi talks with her peer Sonia about her upcoming birthday/slumber party.

Sonia: Where am I going to sleep?
Mitzi: Me and Bessie are gonna sleep up on the top [*of Mitzi's bunk bed*].
Sonia: Oh. Who's gonna sleep on the bottom? Your brother. Where am I gonna sleep, Mitz?

Mitzi immediately begins writing a new journal entry; this entry includes the names of all the children invited to her party:

> I like Sally. And I like Sonia too. And I like Elizabeth and I like Sarah. The End

Sonia does not dismiss the significance of this text.

Sonia: Mitzi, you love me. [*very pleased*]
Mitzi: I said *like*, not *I love*. [*firmly*]

And Mitzi begins to draw a picture of her friends, each bearing a present.

In the second grade, the children's talk about relationships with friends revealed greater complexity. Friends were understood to have feelings and motives that one could not always comprehend. Mitzi, for example, explained to her friend Jenni, 'I didn't know that. I didn't know that *you* knew that I knew that I — I knew.' This greater thoughtfulness about characters was evident in the construction of the children's stories as well. Consider the following example.

Example 4

Mitzi has begun writing:

> Me and My Dream
> I had a dream and My dream was a Big Nightmare and This is My Nightmare. Once there was a boy

Mitzi stops and erases boy. *She turns to Jenni . . .*

Mitzi: Now this is going to be a true dream.

          . . .

This is a nightmare I once had and the girl was you.

Jenni: Yeah?

Mitzi: And you really hated me.

Jenni: No wonder it's a nightmare.

The ideas contained in Mitzi's talk with Jenni appear in Mitzi's story, which is about the bad deed done to her by a girl whose 'name was Jenni' and who 'hated me but I do not know why.' Thus the children's talk supported the unfolding of action, feeling, and motive within the boundaries of Mitzi's imaginary world.

Analyzing and critiquing possible worlds

The children not only helped each other extend and elaborate their worlds, they also critiqued those worlds. As time passed, they became increasingly sensitive to the logic of texts, rather than simply the logic of drawings ('An orange house?'). Such critiquing of texts depended upon the nature of the social relationships among peers. For example, a focus on logic was dependent upon, first, the displaying of the text; such displays occurred through re-reading the text for oneself (but loud enough to be heard by one's neighbors) or through spontaneous sharing. Second, a focus on logic was dependent upon the children's willingness to challenge the logic of each other's efforts, an action much more likely to be directed toward a peer than toward a teacher.

When children critiqued a story they referred to its internal consistency, or more frequently, the consistency of objects or characters in the story with the way the world worked. Consequently, the children often were forced to wrestle with the distinction between the real and the story worlds. The requirements of truth are different in a story from what they are in real life. What is 'not real'? How real does 'not real' have to be? These were the problems the children confronted as they moved between the story and 'real life' worlds, as illustrated in the following excerpt from Jake's case study.

Example 5

A small group of first grade boys is sitting around a table working on their journals. Jake has finished his drawing and is ready to begin writing. He has his whole story planned and, in his 'reading' voice, he narrates the intended text:

Jake: One day I saw a tiger jet going over the desert, and it bombed — it bombed the, the, desert, and the desert made a volcano and the volcano erupted and the, all of the people that lived on the um desert were DEAD from the volcano.

His classmate Hawkeye objects to this text, given the nature of Jake's drawing (a jet flying over the desert).

Hawkeye: That can't happen! Volcanoes are made out of rock, not sand! Plus the lava on the volcano comes from the center of the earth. That doesn't come from that. You have to draw a hole all the way down to the center of the earth. That'd make a volcano out of sand, if you'd do that.

Jake: Uh huh. Look. You bomb something and you pull it out.

Peter: Uh huh.

Hawkeye: Yeah, but you can't make a volcano out of sand.

Peter: Right.

Jake: Oh yes you can.

Hawkeye: Yeah, but not the lava.

Jake: It can go all the way to the earth.

Hawkeye: You can't make a volcano out of sand.

Peter: Yeah, but not the lava. The lava's way down in the center of the earth. You can't get there. It's too hot.

Hawkeye: I know.

Manuel: Well, anyway, it's a pretend story. In real life, it may be true.

Anticipating audience reaction

In previous examples, the children spontaneously reacted as an audience to each others' efforts. The first explicit child references showing awareness of other's reactions occurred in talk related to drawing, as did the first exercise in critique. In the first grade, none of the case study children made explicit reference to an audience's ability to understand their journals.

In the second grade, all of the case study children paid explicit attention to how their texts would influence others' opinions of them; for example, Jake's peers told him that his 'invention' of 'bubble car' stories would make him famous. The following interaction between Manuel and Josh shows the children's concern about how comprehensible their texts would be to their peers.

Example 6

Manuel has been writing a long story about a snowman who comes to life before the eyes of a young man. Manuel is writing the story from the point of view of the man. At one point, the snowman disappears from the man's view, saying 'I must go into the house' [emphasis added]. The picture shows that the snowman actually has gone behind the house to look at the thermometer on the side of the house. Josh has wandered over to where Manuel is working and reads the text on Manuel's page:

The snowman said I must go into this house. I didn't know what to think. The snowman went in back of the house.

Josh stumbles over 'went in back'.

Josh: Went inside, went inside?

Manuel: No he didn't go inside. He went right by, there on the other side of the house. See, they're on this side of the house [*turns to previous picture showing front of house*]. Then they went in the back [*turns to current picture*]. This is the back of the house.

The next day, Manuel worries aloud about this page to the adult observer.

Manuel: I think this page is a little bit hard, how he went into the house.

Manuel seems to inidicate that it is 'hard' for his readers.

Manuel: Went into the house, I mean, went *by* the house.

. . .

I think people can tell just by the picture that um [*laughs*] — but I hope they can cause I don't know how I'm gonna write it so that this is . . . [*Manuel points to the pictured back of the house — the front was shown on the preceding picture*].

I have given examples of the children collaboratively building worlds of words that included both dynamic action and characters. I have shown the children analyzing the soundness of those possible worlds and manipulating the boundaries between the imaginary worlds and the shared real world. Finally, I have presented examples of the children worrying about how peers would view the worlds and themselves. Yet presentation of selected excerpts does not illustrate how individual children evolved as careful constructors of written texts. Thus two brief case-study summaries follow, based on the two-year data collection period. The cases, of Jake and Mitzi respectively, refer to previous examples and present additional ones in order to illustrate how the children's growth as writers reflected their experiences as peers.[3]

Case Study Summary of Jake

During Jake's first grade year, his narratives evolved during drawing, as he talked about the actions of adventurous men and powerful vehicles, especially jets. His peers' laughter and comments led to more elaborate plots, as in Example 1.

Although Jake told dynamic narratives while drawing, his written stories simply described his pictures. While writing, Jake struggled with words — figuring out some for himself, asking peers and available adults for theirs. In the time-consuming encoding process, Jake leaned on his completed picture for support: 'I copy offa the picture.' During the event in which he narrated the adventures of the 'robot man' and the 'flying earthling' (Example 1), he wrote:

> Once upon a time there were two men. One was flying up in the clouds.
> The other man was staying on the ground.

Perhaps because of this focus on encoding, Jake did not talk about his *written* text with friends — nor did he comment on others' texts. During the third month of observation, however, Jake's peers began to critique his written texts. As he would reread his story, often to find his place after a struggle with encoding, a peer might comment on the sense of his story or on his use of grammar (for example, Hawkeye objected to 'There is a three designs', insisting that Jake change his text to 'There is three designs'). Thus, Jake's peers directed his attention to the language and logic of his evolving text, rather than simply to the spelling of his words; Example 5, which presented peer talk about Jake's proposed 'volcano in the desert' text, serves as an illustration.

In the following example, Jake's first-person stance in his clearly unreal story led to Mitzi's objection: first-person stories — 'I stories' — should be true.

Example 7

Jake has written 'I saw a jet. It shot the sun.'

Mitzi: You're lying. You're lying. This isn't a true story.
Jake: After all, I did see a jet once. I saw a 100 jets once, 'cause I have —
              I got a jet collection.

Through their spontaneous comments, Jake's friends appeared unintentionally to help him gain distance from his dramatized worlds. They demonstrated that texts could be talked about as objects that must sound right — just as pictures must look right — and whose truth, value, and logic can be evaluated.

In his second grade year, Jake continued to dramatize stories during drawing, but he was more critical about the development of his plots — more concerned that his imaginative worlds be sensible. Moreover, as Jake's struggle with encoding eased, narrative and dramatic interaction with peers began to accompany his writing and, eventually, to appear within texts. His stories broke free of the static time frame of a picture and attempted to capture the dynamic movement of a movie.

Jake's focus on the development of his written stories was supported by his friend Manuel. In Example 2, Manuel provided Jake with a fictional character with whom a fictional Jake could interact. In addition, Manuel appeared to help Jake clarify the distinction between real, dramatized, and text worlds. For example, Jake and Manuel once had a playful argument in which Jake threatened to 'blow up' Manuel in his story; Manuel countered by threatening to turn Jake into a snowman in his own text, which was about a magical snowman.

Example 8

Manuel: In my story you're going to meet a magician who's going to turn *you* into a snowman.
Jake: Well, actually, guess wha . . .
Manuel: And melt you in the sun.

Jake seems to back down.

Jake: Actually, um, I . . . I'm, I . . . we're gonna, I'm writing about um us flying the fastest jet in the world.

   . . .

   None of us — both of us are — isn't gonna get blown to pieces because it's the fastest jet — it can outrun any bullet.
Manuel: Oh wow! I like that.
Jake: And it's as bullet-proof as it can get.

But later:

Jake: Manuel, you're still gonna get blown to pieces.
Manuel: And a magician is still looking at you, and you're gonna turn into a snowman, and be melted in the sun.
Jake: That's fine with me, but I still can be water and splash you.

In the course of this event, Manuel not only made explicit Jake's fictional world; he also called attention to Jake's prospective audience. Immediately before Jake writes about Manuel's headquarters being blown up. Jake comments.

Jake: Watch out Manuel! [*writes* blow up]

Manuel at this point does something that Jake has not yet explicitly done — anticipate audience reaction.

Manuel: Just at the very end when they're just so happy, it's almost — they're just so happy and they read the entire story and they loved it, I get blown up.
Jake: Yeah
Manuel: And they cry and cry and cry and cry — it's so dramatic.

Later, Jake reads his story to Manuel:

Once there was a boy that is named Manuel. Manuel is going to fly the fastest jet and I am going to fly the jet too. But Manuel's headquarters is going to blow up But I am OK. But I don't know about Manuel but I am going to find Manuel. But when I find him I like him. But I think

I see him. He is in the jet. Manuel are you OK? Yes I am OK, you are being attacked. I will shoot the bad guys out of the universe. OK yes shoot them now. The end.

By the end of the second grade, Jake was able to move through present time without including himself or a peer and without ongoing dramatization. The actors, actions, and objects of his later stories had originated in the talk accompanying earlier periods of drawing or writing. Now, however, the plot unfolded primarily within the narrative world of a text, rather than in the static world of a picture or the dialogue-carried world of dramatic play. In the last event observed in his second grade year, Jake, rather than entering into his symbolic world as an actor (as in Example 8), remained outside the boundaries of that world. He was a distant narrator, carefully controlling all his actors and their actions.

Example 9

Jake has just written:

Once there was a men there from planet X and they are controlling the world.

He then remarks:

Jake: Uh, I got to think of a counter. I got to think of something that's from, that's in the world. Uh, let's see.

Then Jake thinks of a 'counter' and continues writing:

But the Russians had a bubble car and the bubble car is going to America.

Although Jake neither talked with Jesse nor played with Manuel as he constructed this story, echoes of those earlier conversations shaped his interactions with and critique of the text.

Case Study Summary of Mitzi

During the two years of the project, Mitzi, like Jake, became an increasingly skillful creator of written worlds, producing more elaborate and logical texts, as well as showing greater concern for her audience. For Mitzi, too, friends figured in the story of her development.

During journal time in the first grade, Mitzi seemed to focus primarily on producing an entry as efficiently as possible, yet one that included her feelings about people. She usually drew pictures of little girls against a background. While drawing, she often talked with her friends, but that talk was not directly involved in her ongoing work. She talked about her family, the friends she liked (Bessie or Sonia), and the people she hated (her brother). Generally her written texts were labels for her pictures and revealed her feelings (or 'yours') about the depicted figures. As the following example illustrates, her texts were repetitive.

Example 10

> Once there was a girl. She might like You. She liveds under a Rainbow. I Like You. The End.

For Mitzi, producing written texts was no doubt made easier through the repetitive use of 'I like', but her products were not simply texts of convenience. Rather, as illustrated in Example 3, relationships provided the central theme of her talk with friends. Mitzi's texts seemed to grow from her social relationships with children and family members who were important to her, and not from any specific story suggested by her drawing.

Mitzi also was sensitive to others' behavior toward her. Tears and hurt looks followed perceived injustices, as when a friend failed to sit next to her when the opportunity was clearly there. Similarly, Mitzi demonstrated sensitivity when peers responded to her work. As in Jake's case, Mitzi's peers helped her become aware of the logic or lack of logic of her text and the reaction of her audience.

Mitzi herself voiced opinions, as a member of the audience, about the work of others. She was constantly concerned about whether or not journal entries were 'true' as in Example 10, where she accused Jake of 'lying' in his story.

In the second grade, Mitzi, like Jake, began to involve friends and family more directly as characters in her written texts. Similarly, she started to include herself as the character 'I', and thus was able to use the narrative form dynamically to play out her relationships with others.

Her peer relationships now appeared more complex, and she displayed greater reflectiveness about that complexity, about her motives and feelings and those of others. The following excerpt demonstrates Mitzi's heightened ability to consider the perspectives of others.

Example 11

The children sitting by Mitzi are complaining that Alexander and Rachel have told Ruth, the retiring reading teacher, about a surprise gift the children had planned for Ruth, a book they have been faithfully working on every day. Apparently, Alexander was the first to reveal the children's secret.

Ian: Rachel knew that Alexander told, so she told her, Ruth, and
             she already knew that Ruth knew.
Mitzi: Mm mmm. But she knew that they were gonna get Ruth to not
             know that — she knew that they were gonna get her to not know
             that, the real surprise.
             . . .
Ian: I hate Alexander for what he did.
Mitzi: I hate Rachel for doing it, cause she did it too.

Like her talk, Mitzi's stories showed this increased awareness about
human relationships. In the following imaginative story, for example, secrets
and potential betrayal played a strong role. This text, entitled 'How My Life
Was', featured Mitzi and a twin sister (in real life, her friend Jenni had a twin
brother) who seemed to be intent on repeating Rachel's earlier misdeed.

Example 15

> I said to my sister one day that I was going to run away. My sister
> screamed, Oh no. My mother and father ran down the stairs. What
> happened they said My sister was beginning to say that I was going to
> run away when I ran across the room and covered her mouth. The End.

Above this 'twin sister' story was written 'not true'. Thus the text not only
illustrates Mitzi's continued concern with relationships, but also her concern
about 'truth'. Note that the story does not begin with a variation of 'once
upon a time.' Recall also that in the first grade, Mitzi had objected strongly
to Jake's imaginative personal narratives as 'lies' (Example 7). When Mitzi
herself began writing both fictional and nonfictional first person narratives,
she had difficulty starting them — writing, for example, 'Once there was a
girl. The girl that was named Mitzi.' She primarily distinguished between
'true' and 'not true' stories by labeling them as such. The twin story suggests
that by the end of the second year, Mitzi was more flexible about openings;
she no longer felt compelled to begin true personal narratives with 'Once
upon a time.'

Like Jake's stories, Mitzi's texts did not escape the critical attention of
others. In the following example, friends Yahmya and Jenni offer their opinions while Mitzi revises her planned and actual story. Her peer talk is
focused on the text that she is forming instead of on her family and friends.
Mitzi here seems particularly anxious for peer support, perhaps because she
is writing a significantly different text. She does not rely on her picture or on
repetitive patterns for her text, nor does she depend on personal — or
imagined personal — experience. Like Jake, Mitzi, writing her last text of
the year, is no longer in the thick of things but the distant creator of a logical,
yet fanciful world.

Example 13

Mitzi's friends have been writing about cats, and, on this day, Mitzi wants to write about cats too. Days earlier, she wrote the title for this entry (Mitzi comes up with titles separately from planning stories), so she knows that the story has to have something to do with 'The Surprise Party'.

Mitzi: Jenni, what can I write about? Um, I'm thinking about cats. It's gonna be a surprise party about cats. What should I write about? You're good, you're good at that. You're good at this [writing about cats]. Jenni. Jenni, you're good at that! [*pause*] I know! A bird that'll go and kill a cat!

Yahmya does find this surprising.

Yahmya: A vulture?
Mitzi: No! they're my made-up cats. Once I made up some cats. And there were some birds. Birds! And they eat 'em too.
Yahmya: They eat *cats?*
Mitzi: Mm mmm.

When Mitzi finally begins writing, however, she writes about cats that eat birds. Perhaps Yahmya's critique of the reverse situation has made her reconsider.

> The Surprise Party
> Once there was a bunch of cats. Then all of a sudden there came a flock of birds. This was a big surprise to the cats. At once they started to kill them.

After writing her piece, Mitzi begins drawing a tree and soon realizes that she needs 'dead birds down here' under her tree. Jenni has another idea.

Jenni: You can put some flying away up here.

Mitzi pauses and then has yet another thought.

Mitzi: No, I know what I'm going to do.

Mitzi then adds 'and eat them' to the last of line of her text, eliminating the need for dead birds. She draws one bird; it's crying as it hovers near the tree.

Mitzi had progressed from 'I like you' journal entries made amid social talk to written worlds in which characters were liked and hated, surprised and saddened, betrayed and befriended. Her journey to dynamic literary worlds was mediated, like Jake's, by lively talk with supportive, if critical, peers.

Peers: Classroom Possibilities and Realities

The descriptions of Mitzi, Jake, and their peers have demonstrated that children's independent mental worlds are nurtured by their cooperative social lives. In light of the data, we may now consider the questions advanced earlier.

What purposes did the children's talk serve?

As the children worked individually on their journals, their talk served to create and critique imaginary worlds. However, their representations, directions, questions, and opinions applied not only to their own worlds, but to others' as well. Journal time was a social occasion during which children engaged in *joint* activity — constructed worlds together — and interacted about their separate activities — analyzed the adequacy of each other's efforts and served as an interested and perhaps even appreciative audience.

What intellectual tasks did the children collaboratively accomplish?

Through their interactions with each other, the children collaboratively and spontaneously accomplished tasks that often are considered 'over their heads'. Together, the children extended story boundaries, critiqued the logic of texts, and considered the response of others to individual efforts. In fact, their peer relationships typically provided the psychological substance of their stories — the children could fictionalize themselves and their friends, and thereby create comfortable characters with familiar motivations and feelings.

How did independent child achievement reflect previous collaborative achievements?

The most elaborate verbal stories and the most flexible manipulation of narrative time and space occurred, not in the text themselves, but in the children's talk. Even children like Manuel, who did not offer others entry into his stories, commented upon and playfully entered those of others. The children's use of one another as characters brought their interactive stories into written texts, as did the use of dialogue. Further, the children pointed out to each other the limits of both their written and their orally created texts. As the research on older school children indicates (Bartlett, 1981), the first observed critiques of story logic were of others' work. But just as elaborate, interactive oral stories foreshadowed interactive written ones, interactive critiques foreshadowed children's explicit references both to their own story's logic and to audience response.

Consistent with the Vygotskian perspective of this report, individual reflections were linked to spontaneous social accomplishments. However, unlike most reports of children's literacy learning from this perspective, the social interactions highlighted were those among peers, not those between teacher and child, and were more spontaneous than the deliberately structured teacher–child talk occurring in writing conferences (Sowers, 1985).

The intention here is not to minimize the teacher's role, but to suggest that children's achievements may not be linked solely to teacher–child interactions. Children's academic accomplishments can be influenced by their relationships with each other, as well as with the teacher.

In this study, Margaret, the teacher, did much more than talk to the children about their efforts. She legitimized the children's interest in each other; they were free to tease, challenge, question and giggle over each other's work. The children were thus free to leave their own tasks momentarily and enter another's. In this way, the social life of the children energized rather than interfered with the academic curriculum. At the same time, Margaret held the children accountable for their work and helped instill pride in themselves as artists and as authors.

Limitations and Extensions

This article has focused on only one group of peers. Children may not always be as supportive of each other as they were in this particular group. Further, certain children's interest in social linking may overpower their interest in academic tasks, while other children may be unable to find a comfortable niche in the peer group (Garnica, 1981).

Yet, the very power of children's social lives to contribute to and alternately detract from school learning suggests a need for comparative studies of peer group life. Such studies should give more than cursory attention to academic learning and should consider as well the intertwining of peer social life with the official school world. What forces, both inside and outside the classroom, promote collegiality that is at once social and academic?

Reports of successful literacy programs with older students suggest that important factors include teacher awareness of students' social concerns, encouragement of talk about those concerns, and curricula that are permeable enough to allow student concerns to connect with academic learning. Indeed, teachers who have successfully worked with adolescent and adult students have written about their efforts to help students find both personal and social meaning in academic learning (Elsasser & Irvine, 1985; Hardcastle, 1985; Heath, 1983). Through talk and writing about common experiences, students become a group, collectively engage in reflection, and, one may hope, gain greater control of their individual lives. In Margaret's classroom, no such effort was made to tap students' social concerns, but those matters were present. From lost puppy dogs to teenage mothers, from new bikes to nuclear war, children's out-of-classroom concerns appeared through in-classroom concerns about connecting with each other as experienced, competent, and special people.

The existence and nature of the peer group seem particularly important for those concerned with literacy development. Writing is an interactive or 'involvement-focused' skill (Tannen, 1985). That is, writers must reconcile the meaning of their emerging text with the demands of their own evolving goals and of their potential audience. In fact, professional writers of fiction often describe their writing processes as interactive, as a collaboration — and often a struggle — with the characters, who have their own visions (Tomlinson, 1986). An interactive skill should be supported by interactive experiences, in which a real, rather than a hypothetical, audience makes its demand known (compare Heath & Branscombe, 1985). Students should find the concepts of logically ordered plot, realistic development, authentic image, and the like, more sensible if they are articulations of spontaneous experiences within interactive communities, which indeed gave rise to such concepts in the first place (Britton, 1985). In fact, the 'characters' professional writers speak of may be linked to real people, real players who joined in on the writer's own dramas.

Talk about academic tasks is often contrasted with social talk: individuals achieve because of the time they spend 'on task'. My observations suggest that the 'academic' and the 'social' are not so simply — or so profitably — separated. The social laughing, teasing, correcting, and chatting that accompany children's academic work are byproducts of the need to link with others and be recognized by them. But they can also be catalysts for intellectual growth.

Acknowledgements

Support for this work was provided in part by a seed grant from the Spencer Foundation, distributed by the School of Education, University of California, Berkeley, and by the Office of Educational Research and Improvement/Department of Education (OERI/ED), through the Center for the Study of Writing. However, the opinions expressed herein do not necessarily reflect the position or policy of the OERI/ED, and its official endorsement should not be inferred.

I thank Mary Gardner and Carol Heller, my research assistants. I thank also the children's teacher, who provides her children with ample opportunity and support for writing — and thus provides me with ample opportunity to learn about learning to write.

Notes

1. A teacher strike necessitated a February, rather than a January, starting date.
2. For an elaboration of 'unintentional helping', see Dyson (in press, b).
3. For more detailed summaries based on the first year of data collection only, see Dyson (in press, a).

References

Bartlett, E. J. (1981) *Learning to Write: Some Cognitive and Linguistic Components.* Washington, DC: Center for Applied Linguistics.

Britton, J. (1985) Research currents: Second thoughts on learning. *Languages Arts* 62, 72–7.

Bruner, J. S. (1986) *Actual Minds, Possible Worlds.* Cambridge: Harvard University Press.

Corsaro, W. (1985) *Friendship and Peer Culture in the Early Years.* Norwood, NJ: Ablex.

Dickinson, D. (1986) Cooperation, collaboration, and a computer: Integrating a computer into a first-second grade writing program. *Research in the Teaching of English* 20, 357–78.

Dyson, A. H. (1986) Transitions and tensions: Interrelationships between the drawing, talking, and dictating of young children. *Research in the Teaching of English* 20, 379–409.

— (in press, a). Individual differences in beginning composing: An orchestral vision of learning to write. *Written Communication* 4.

— (in press, b). Unintentional helping in the primary grades: Writing in the children's world. In B. A. Rafoth and D. L. Rubin (eds) *The Social Construction of Written Communication.* Norwood, NJ: Ablex.

Elsasser, N. and Irvine, P. (1985). English and Creole: The dialectics of choice in a college writing program. *Harvard Educational Review* 55, 399–415.

Garnica, O. (1981) Social dominance and classroom interaction: The omega child in the classroom. In J. Green and C. Wallat (eds) *Ethnography and Language in Educational Settings.* Norwood, NJ: Ablex.

Hardcastle, J. (1985) Classrooms as sites for cultural making. *English in Education* 19 (3), 8–22.

Heath, S. B. (1983). *Ways With Words: Language, Life, and Work in Communities and Classrooms.* New York: Cambridge University Press.

Heath, S. B. and Branscombe, A. (1985). 'Intelligent writing' in an audience community: Teacher, students, and researcher. In S. W. Freedman (ed.) *The Acquisition of Written Language: Revision and Response* (pp. 3–32). Norwood, NJ: Ablex.

Sowers, S. (1985) Learning to write in a workshop: A study in grades one through four. In M. F. Whiteman (ed.) *Advances in Writing Research: Children's Early Writing Development*, Vol. 1. Norwood, NJ: Ablex.

Tannen, D. (1985). Relative focus on involvement in oral and written discourse. In D. R. Olson, N. Torrance and A. Hildyard (eds) *Literacy, Language and Learning: The Nature and Consequences of Reading and Writing.* New York: Cambridge University Press.

Tomlinson, B. (1986) Characters and coauthors: Segmenting the self, intergrating the composing process. *Written Communcations* 3, 421–48.

Vygotsky, L. S. (1962) *Thought and Language.* Cambridge: MIT Press.

— (1978) *Mind in Society.* Cambridge: Harvard University Press.

15 Talk and Assessment

HARRY TORRANCE

Introduction

The increased involvement of talk in assessment in schools is part of a broader shift in emphasis in the school curriculum over recent years; a shift which has derived from debates over the content of the curriculum, over how assessment might be conducted more validly and reliably, and over the way in which children learn (and thus the way in which teaching and assessment ought to contribute to the process of learning).

With regard to the content of the curriculum, both socio-economic and educational arguments have been advanced to further the development of a more relevant and practically-oriented curriculum, particularly at secondary level, and schools are now urged to devote more time and resources to the development of a whole range of new skills, capacities and understanding such as problem-solving, gathering and analysing data, effective communication, and the application (as well as the recall) of knowledge.

Throughout the United Kingdom, debates over changing the curriculum — changing the educational objectives which schools are to pursue — have overlapped with and in significant respects fed into discussion about improving the validity of assessment, particularly formal examinations. In brief the argument here has been that for more complex and open-ended educational tasks to be assessed validly, those assessments must take place over an extended period of time in the 'natural' setting of the classroom or laboratory, rather than in the artificial setting of the examination hall. Moreover, including teacher assessment of course work, oral work and so forth, in formal grade-awarding procedures, can be said in principle to improve the reliability of final grades since it increases the sample of work on which such grades can be based.

Paralleling such debates has been a growing understanding of the interactive nature of learning, of the role that diagnostic assessment might play in promoting learning, and of the role that talk can play in helping children to explore and understand the educational activities in which they are asked to engage. This understanding has been fed by a variety of fairly disparate psychological and linguistic theories and can in no sense be seen as a single or coherent body of work (some of the strands are explored in Torrance, 1989). Yet taken overall it is clear that theorists, policy-makers and teachers alike are beginning to work with a much broader conception of the process and purpose of assessment, with particular attention being given to the provision of 'formative feedback' to pupils and the development of dialogue with pupils about their strengths and weaknesses. Improving the *process* of assessment and its impact on learning, has come to be perceived as important as improving the overall pattern and product of assessment (i.e. the objectives tested and marks or grades awarded) and their impact on the curriculum.

What all this has meant in practice of course, at school level, is a substantial increase in teacher involvement in the formal assessment and grading of pupils: teachers being in the best position to observe pupil achievement in a variety of activities over an extended period of time. The relationship of this expansion to the increasing focus on talk in assessment is complex and sometimes confusing however, and teachers can be faced with a bewildering and often contradictory array of 'oral assessment' practices. Talk has now come to occupy a significant role in both the content and process of curriculum and in turn it is recognised as an appropriate medium in which to test for knowledge and understanding; as an appropriate vehicle in which pupils' capacities to organize and articulate ideas can be assessed; and is perceived as crucial to the interface between assessment and learning. (Note that although 'talking' and 'listening' are discussed separately in Scottish proposals (e.g. SED, 1990), I am using 'talk' here to include both aspects of spoken language use.) Teasing out the similarities and differences between these roles and functions is going to be extremely important when trying to analyse the various purposes of assessment based on talk and how it might be organized and accomplished in schools. In particular we need to be clear about whether talk is being treated *as a medium of assessment* or whether it is *the quality of the talk itself* which is being assessed. In this article, I will distinguish between these two kinds of talk, calling the first 'oral assessment' and the second 'the assessment of oral communication'. The distinction between these two cannot be hard and fast and (as I discuss below) assessments made in school are concerned with both. But confusion amongst teachers and children about whether assessment criteria are primarily concerned with (a) subject knowledge and understanding as demonstrated through talk or (b) the ability to speak and listen effectively in a variety of contexts is liable to cause problems (some examples and discussions of this kind of confusion can be found in Maybin, 1988; Mercer, Edwards & Maybin, 1988).

Oral Assessment

For some years now talk has indeed been treated as a medium of assessment in a variety of subjects. Sometimes such assessment virtually parallels the conduct of written examinations, with pupils being asked specific questions (in science for example) and having to give short, succinct answers in a one-to-one interview situation with the examiner (often, but not always, their subject teacher). Sometimes oral assessment is conducted more flexibly, for example when pupils might be asked to elaborate on and explain more fully the written product of a local history or geography project (which in itself may have used interviews as a way of gathering data). Such assessment is claimed to be testing subject-based knowledge and understanding. It is justified in terms of improving the quality of the assessment (being able to probe for real understanding rather than memorised response); and in terms of giving those pupils who cannot write particularly well a chance to demonstrate what they know.

Designers of formal oral assessment techniques have increasingly recognised that what is being assessed in such situations is communication in a particular context (and a pretty unreal one at that). Words alone do not flow in a single direction but are uttered for and take account of the listener, who in turn seeks to render them meaningful through both thought and action (interpreting pauses, seeking clarification, etc.). So, for example, to test understanding in science or history more thoroughly and validly one ought to set up a much more 'realistic' reporting situation than a stilted one-to-one question and answer session.

Thus even in oral assessment of a subject like science, the communication of knowledge and understanding is increasingly being considered as well as the assessment of knowledge and understanding *per se*. However, this could pose problems for pupils who still interpret the purpose of the exercise in traditional terms: demonstrating all they know about a topic to the teacher rather than reporting coherently and succinctly to a particular audience. Likewise test designers and teachers have to decide what audience it is appropriate to specify for assessment activities: other pupils, other teachers, invited guests, in small or large groups; or perhaps some selection from these at different points in time (to sample communication under different circumstances)?

Assessing Oral Communication (Speaking and Listening)

A report produced by the Oxford Delegacy Local Examinations Board prior to the introduction of GCSE identified reading aloud combined with a one-to-one interview as the way 'spoken English' was still being largely assessed at that time (King, 1985). The implicit model being operated was that of 'social accomplishment' rather than communicative competence and the assessment procedure was almost wholly divorced from teaching (where it took place at all — the assessment of spoken English being overwhelming confined to CSE).

A good deal has changed in the intervening years as interest in the National Oracy Project and developments in GCSE demonstrate, yet changes in assessment practices have still not kept pace with changes in the curriculum and with teachers' ambitions to encourage small group work and to involve pupils in their own assessment. The basic issue for designers of assessment procedures is that of reconciling the traditional examination imperative of standardising the assessment situation (to make comparisons possible) with the need to assess student's abilities in real (and hence variable) contexts for communication. In particular there is the problem of making individual assessments of contributions to collaborative activities. However, this issue is compounded in the case of English because of the sheer variety of contexts which not only can but should arise in the course of attempting to develop pupils' communicative abilities. Thus pupils can talk to teachers or to other pupils, individually or in small and large groups; such talk might be technical or emotive and persuasive; it might be extemporary or be part of a debate or less formally organized discussion; and so on. Likewise to come to an understanding of the nature of talk and communicative effectiveness, pupils need to reflect on the effectiveness of their talk: that is assessing themselves and others, and coming to an appreciation of the fact that the criteria which they employ will change over time and across circumstances. Thus assessment as individual and collective reflection has a central place in the process of developing speaking and listening, though to what extent this can be included within, or indeed facilitated by, formal schemes for assessing talk is a moot point and one to which we will return below.

Talking and Learning

Encompassing the whole of this consideration of the purpose and practice of assessment of and through talk is the relationship of language to learning. Assessment procedures not only measure learning outcomes, they impact on learning processes. As children rehearse, interpret and articulate their developing understanding of a topic in collaboration with a sympathetic listener (peers as well as teachers), they may identify more clearly, and reflect upon, their strengths and weaknesses and what they might do about them. With this kind of diagnostic approach to assessment, the key issue becomes that of exploring pupils' understandings and helping them develop further rather than using 'oral assessment' as simply one more method of generating decontextualised assessment data.

Developments in Assessment at National Level

Most of the ideas and practices outlined above are present in varying degrees in current national developments such as GCSE and the assessment procedures envisaged by the Task Group on Assessment and Testing (TGAT) for the National Curriculum. Yet clearly some of the ideas have been taken on board much more fully than others. Thus GCSE seeks to ascertain what pupils 'know, understand and can do' (DES, 1985: 2) and justifies teacher involvement in assessment first and foremost in terms of the validity of the examination since teachers can test 'aspects of attainment which may not be easily or adequately tested by (final) papers' (SEC, 1985: 2). The TGAT report argues in similar vein:

> We recommend that the national system should employ tests for which a wide range of modes of presentation, operation and response should be used so that each may be valid in relation to the attainment targets assessed.
>
> (TGAT, 1987: para. 50)

Of course the Task Group also recommended a central role for routine teacher assessment ('teacher ratings') and argued at length about the diagnostic function of assessment. Yet its interpretation of the diagnostic process tends towards the static and mechanistic, with assessment providing:

> Some information which will help in the diagnosis of strengths and weaknesses . . . [and] indicators of learning problems which require further investigation.
>
> (TGAT, 1987: para. 27)

There is no recognition here of the value of dialogue with pupils about these strengths and weaknesses or indeed of encouraging pupils to identify strengths and weaknesses for themselves rather than await the results of tests. Furthermore the role of teacher ratings, not particularly well develop or articulated within the report in any case, has been steadily eroded over the intervening period with the subsequent 'advice' from the School Examinations and Assessment Council (SEAC) to the Secretary of State for Education being that:

> The SAT (Standard Assessment Task) assessment is thus 'preferred' to TA (Teacher Assessment) where it is available.
>
> (SEAC, 1989: para. 23)

What we seem to have here then, with both GCSE and the National Curriculum assessment arrangements, is an acknowledgement that teachers are best placed strategically to carry out the technical role of administering assessments devised by external agencies (e.g. SATs), but cannot be entirely trusted to generate and utilise their own routine assessment processes which can contribute to both pupil learning and more public accounts of achievement.

The implications of this for some of the issues pertaining to oral assessment outlined earlier are potentially very severe, and derive once again from the necessity of nationally administered tests, Standard Assessment Tasks, to be just that — standardised — and thus inevitably highly circumscribed in the way they can attend to the subtleties and complexities of communication-in-real-contexts. It remains to be seen what SATs at key stage 3 will look like but the possibility of teachers having to administer tedious and potentially invalid standard oral report formats, debate formats, and so forth, is all too real.

An alternative still exists in the form of the Record of Achievement (RoA) developments which have been taking place over recent years although it does seem as though these will be almost wholly ignored by the National Curriculum assessment arrangements, with RoAs being little more than a device for reporting levels reached on attainment targets. Nevertheless RoAs do offer the possibility of combining the articulation of clear goals for pupils — making curricular aims and objectives more apparent — with responsive dialogue between teachers and pupils about how these goals might be accomplished and what other achievements pupils consider significant for themselves (Broadfoot et al., 1988; Torrance, 1990). Dialogue between teacher and pupil with regard to a Record of Achievement also provides a real, meaningful context for communication since what is at stake is the pupil's developing sense of self, their interests and aspirations, their strengths and weaknesses, and how these are perceived by others. Certainly RoAs can provide a vehicle within subject boundaries for the identification and exploration of pupils' understanding in science, maths, the humanities, and so on, and in English in particular for the generation of multiple perspectives on language use and its assessment.

The extract below (Figure 1) from a formative Record of Achievement used in one English Department offers an example of what can be put into practice, but it also demonstrates that the culture of secondary schooling is still very oriented towards writing, even when listening and talking are the focus of concern. Great care would obviously have to be taken to ensure that such an approach to pupil self-assessment and communication with the teacher did not solidify into a routine activity devoid of dialogue and any real consequence for the development of pupils' abilities.

ENGLISH DEPARTMENT

NAME ....   CLASS ....   TEACHER ....

....   DATE ....

Section One – LISTENING AND UNDERSTANDING

Try to write a statement assessing how well you can follow your lessons and the type of difficulties you still face. You should try to include these points:

a. The aspects of English you find most straightforward and those which still cause you difficulty.
b. The steps you take when you cannot follow an exercise or explanation.
c. Your ability to concentrate. Mention, too, what makes you lose your concentration.
d. Your attitude towards the contributions made by your classmates. Do you listen carefully to what they have to say? Are you becoming a better listener?
e. Your view of how mature your class is as a group in its readiness to listen to all points of view and the contributions made by every pupil.

Section Two – ORAL ENGLISH

In a similar way, please assess your progress in spoken English since the last profile. Consider the following points when preparing your statement:

a. The situations you most enjoy speaking in (groups, pairs, solo talks, using tape recorders, etc.) Explain why you have certain preferences.
b. Situations you dislike. Give the reason.
c. Your self-confidence (or lack of it) as a speaker.
d. Your ability to use language appropriately and effectively (e.g. the care you put into the vocabulary you use; your ability to adapt your speech to particular circumstances).
e. The improvement you have seen over this year.
f. The improvements you feel must still be made.

Figure 1 Assessment sheet

School-Based Development of Policy and Practice

It is too early to say how the assessment of the National Curriculum will impact upon the lower years of secondary school and eventually on GCSE. On the positive side much new thinking on oracy and communications has been incorporated into the various National Curriculum Working Group reports. The English Working group in particular resisted attempts by the government to devalue the importance of speaking and listening, and the National Curriculum Council has successfully maintained this emphasis. On the negative side including the formal assessment of speaking and listening in SATs may well confound and run counter to the very logic underpinning the expansion of such work in schools. With regard to English in particular the working group argued that 'the bulk of assessment in speaking and listening should be conducted locally (DES, 1989c: para. 15.42) but this could still mean teachers merely administering SATs. (Interestingly, and perhaps significantly, the same phrase appears in the earlier 5–11 document with the word 'internally' used instead of 'locally' (DES/WO, 1988b: para. 8.31)).

Whatever the eventual form and content of SATs, however, there are some important issues which any developing programme of oral assessment needs to acknowledge and which teachers can and indeed should begin to confront, particularly when wishing to argue the case for the validity and reliability of internal teacher ratings. Ultimately the crucial point for school-based assessment in general, oral assessment in particular (when so much of the evidence must be ephemeral) is that of teacher attitude and confidence to make assessments in situ rather than set up artificial situations. This can only come from providing opportunities for professional discussion and development.

References

Broadfoot, P. *et al.* (1988) *Pilot Records of Achievement in Schools Evaluation: Final Report.* London: HMSO.

DES (1985) *General Certificate of Secondary Education. The National Criteria. General Criteria.* London: HMSO.

— (1988) *English for Ages 5–11.* London: DES.

— (1989) *English for Ages 5–16.* London: DES.

King, D. (1985) *The Assessment of Spoken English.* Oxford: Oxford Delegacy.

Maybin, J. (1988) A critical review of the DES Assessment of Performance Unit's oracy surveys. *English in Education* 22, 1, 3–18.

Mercer, N., Edwards, D., and Maybin, J. (1988) Putting context into oracy. In M. MacLure, T. Phillips and A. Wilkinson *Oracy Matters.* Milton Keynes: Open University Press.

School Examinations and Assessment Council (SEAC) (1989) National Curriculum Assessment Arrangements: Advice to the Secretary of State for Education, 24 July 1989. London: Department of Education and Science (DES Press Release 240/89).

SEC (1985) *Coursework Assessment in GCSE.* London: Secondary Examinations Council.

SED (1990) *English Language 5–14: Working Paper 2.* Edinburgh: Scottish Education Department.

Task Group on Assessment and Testing (TGAT) (1987) *National Curriculum: A Report.* London: DES.

Torrance, H. (1989) Theory, practice, and politics in the development of assessment. *Cambridge Journal of Education* 19, 2, 183–91.
— (1990) Records of achievement and formative assessment: Some complexities of practice. In R. Stake (ed.) *Effects of Changes in Assessment Policy*. JAI Press.

16 Social Processes in Education: A Reply to Sawyer and Watson (and others)

J. R. MARTIN, FRANCES CHRISTIE and JOAN ROTHERY

Towards a Genre-Based Approach

Genre-based approaches to writing development are the result of a longstanding research initiative within the field of educational linguistics by teachers, teacher/linguists and linguists who have attempted to translate the linguistic theory of M. A. K. Halliday and his colleagues into teaching practice. This research initiative comprises two main phases. The first began in London in 1964, funded by the Nuffield Foundation and later the Schools Council, and directed by Halliday. It brought together a group of academic scholars and experienced school teachers to look into the teaching of English from the standpoint of modern developments in linguistics. The best known publications of this phase focused on the early school years (Mackay *et al.*, *Breakthrough to Literacy*, 1970) and secondary school (Doughty *et al.*, *Language in Use*, 1970); these were later followed by middle school materials (Forsyth & Wood, *Language and Communication,* 1980). The second phase began in late 1975 when Halliday arrived in Sydney to take up the founding Chair of Linguistics at the University of Sydney. At Sydney he quickly built up what was to become one of the largest Applied Linguistics programmes in the world. Over the last few years, teams of linguists, teacher/linguists and teachers have explored the implications of systemic perspectives on language, register and genre for classroom teaching.

What is Genre?

In essence genre theory is a theory of language use. The genre theory underlying the so-called 'genre-based' approaches to writing development was developed by Hasan (1978), Kress (1982), Martin (1985) and others as an extension of earlier work on register by systemic linguists including Halliday, Gregory, Ure and Ellis. Genre theory differs from register theory in the amount of emphasis it places on social purposes as a determining variable in language use.

Martin defines genre as a staged, goal oriented social process. Most members of a given culture would participate in some dozens of these. Australian examples include jokes, letters to the editor, job applications, lab reports, sermons, medical examinations, appointment making, service encounters, anecdotes, weather reports, interviews and so on. Genres are referred to as *social processes* because members of a culture interact with each other to achieve them; as *goal oriented* because they have evolved to get things done; and as *staged* because it usually takes more than one step for participants to achieve their goals.

Like all semiotic systems, genres have evolved in such a way that they introduce a kind of *stability* into a culture at the same time as being *flexible* enough to participate in social change. In this respect they are like language itself. Linguistics has always concerned itself with both aspects of semiosis — stability and change. Building models of language which show more clearly how the two interact will have to be one of the major achievements of linguists of the 21st century. As with language, so with genre. In one sense genres are 'fixed'. A story is different from an essay and at the level of genre the differences are relatively easy to bring to consciousness. Orientation/ Complication/Resolution is not Introduction/Body/Conclusion, as most teachers and students know. The structures are different because they do different jobs. At the same time, genres obviously change. The evolution of narrative in our culture is perhaps the best studied example of this process. Keri Hulme and the Gawain poet for example write different types of story; but neither came out of the blue. Both made small significant changes to the genres with which they worked, helping them evolve to make new meanings to serve a culture at a particular point in time.

Perhaps the single most important fact to keep in mind about genres as far as education is concerned is that genres are *evolved* systems. This is to say that no individual, let alone linguists, sat down and designed the genres we use. Rather, they arose as the members of our culture negotiated meaning to get on with the living of life.

What exactly does it mean to say that genres are evolved systems, and that genres are functional? To explore this further let us consider two small texts from the Year 8 History textbook *Before Yesterday* that is use in some Australian junior secondary schools. The first is a short biography of Joan of Arc.

Text 1: Joan of Arc

But an **uprising** *of French rebels lead to a dramatic* **change***. The French claimant to the throne, Charles VII, was a mean cringing man unable to inspire his troops who were constantly defeated until the French held only one important city, Orleans. Then occurred one of the most famous* **events** *in French history. A poor peasant girl, Joan of Arc, became convinced she heard the voices of saints urging her to save her country. Leaving her native village in Lorraine, she made her way through enemy territory to Charles. She convinced the king that she had a divine* **mission***. In 1429 Joan, then about eighteen years old, was given* **command** *of some 4000 or 5000 men and marched to the relief of Orleans. Wearing armour and riding a white horse she so inspired her soldiers that they defeated the English. In July 1429, she stood beside Charles as he was crowned King of France in the Cathedral at Rheims. Next year Joan was taken prisoner by the Burgundians, allies of the English, who sold her to the English. The English arranged for her* **trial** *at Rouen by a group of Norman clergymen and she was condemned to* **death** *as a heretic. Charles VII made no attempt to save the girl who had secured him his throne. In 1431 Joan of Arc was burned at the stake at Rouen.*

Some twenty-five years later the Pope reversed the **decision** *of the Rouen courts and declared that Joan was no heretic. In 1920 the Roman Catholic Church made her a saint.*

Despite the **death** *of Joan of Arc, the* **faith** *and* **confidence** *she had given the French persisted. The English lost town after town. When the Hundred Years War finally ended in 1453 the English retained only Calais.*
(Nominalisations in bold face.)

It takes very little in the way of technical linguistic analysis to see that text 1 is a kind of story. It focuses on a short but critical chapter of Joan of Arc's life — the part that made her famous. The text is composed mainly of actions, the people involved in them, and the relevant settings in place and time. These actions are sequenced in time.

Text 2 on the other hand is a very different kind of text. Rather than telling a story it analyses the cultural repercussions of the crusades. Generically speaking it is a type of exposition, not narrative.

Text 2: Results of the crusades

Despite the apparent **failure** *of the crusades, these wars had deep economic, social, intellectual and religious* **influences***. One of the most important was the* **revival** *of trade. Many Italian and French towns started to trade with Christian kingdoms in the Syria-Palestine region. Merchants made great profits selling provisions to the crusaders. Soon trade was also conducted with the Moslems and with the Greeks of the Byzantine Empire.*

The **status** *of women seems to have risen as a result of the* **responsibilities** *they undertook while their husbands were absent fighting the crusades. New fashions appeared in the West. Long flowing robes and full beards, in* **imitation** *of Moslem fashions, became popular. Rice, lemons, apricots and shallots were added to the foodstuffs of Europe. Previously honey had been the only sweetening substance known in the West, but now sugar was introduced and* **demand** *became so great that it was grown in southern Europe. Plum trees were introduced from Damascus. Women now had glass mirrors in place of polished metal discs.*

The crusades helped revive the political **influence** *of the kings. Many kings got rid of troublesome nobles during the crusades. The kings of France and England used the crusades as an excuse to introduce a direct tax in 1188. Royal funds thus expanded. The first three crusades also built up the political* **power** *of the church. After the Third Crusade, however, the kings began to act more and more independently of the church.*

Amongst the intellectual **changes** *one of the most important was the* **growth** *of a spirit of* **tolerance***. The early crusaders hated the Moslems. Later, as they got to know their enemies better a degree of* **understanding** *and even of* **sympathy** *developed. Richard I and Saladin respected each other and future generations came to regard them both as figures of* **chivalry** *and* **valor***.* (Nominalisations in bold face).

This text is a kind of argument, outlining four outcomes of the crusades. These it reviews under five headings, which are explicitly foregrounded in the textbook: the revival of trade; the status of women; new fashions; the political influence of the kings; a spirit of tolerance. Four of these (excluding the status of women) are developed in paragraphs that exemplify the heading. Most of the people mentioned appear as generic classes, not individuals (*Saladin* and *Richard I* are the exceptions to *merchants, crusaders, Moslems, Greeks, Byzantines, women*, etc.). And the text makes much more use of abstract nominalisations than text 1: *failure, influences, revival, status, responsibilities, imitation, demand, power, influence, changes, growth, tolerance, understanding, sympathy, chivalry, valor* (see Eggins, Wignell & Martin, 1986 for further discussion).

It is clear then from even such informal analyses as these that texts 1 and 2 differ. They differ in terms of their overall structure; they differ in terms of the language used to code each tag; and these differences are systematic and recurrent across a very large range of history texts. Most significantly these differences are directly related to the different functions of the two texts. Historians used texts like 1 to record the past and texts like 2 to interpret it. Text 1 functions as a kind of evidence, text 2 as analysis. History has evolved in such a way in our culture that both types of text are necessary for historians to get on with their work.

Looked at in these terms it is quite apparent that genres are not arbitrary conventions imprisoning the members of a culture. Quite the opposite. Genres represent the most efficient ways cultures have at a given point in time of going about their business. It is in this sense that genres are functional. And because they are functional, they evolve. In this way genres, like all meaning systems, introduce stability and flexibility into a culture at one and the same time.

Needless to say, genre theory depends on a careful linguistic analysis of the textual features of genres. Any generic categories proposed for texts like 1 and 2 above need to be substantiated by looking in detail at these and a large range of agnate texts.

The work of Christie (1984, 1985, 1986) has shown that the most important factor controlling what children write is not their stage of development, but rather the way in which the teacher sets up the writing context. Research by Martin and Rothery confirms this point. What is needed then is a model that shows systematically how text is related to context. This is the kind of model that teachers require and could use. Hypotheses about language function and writing development which make no direct or reliable connection with what children actually write are an impediment, not an aid to good teaching practice.

Genre and Field

The theory of social context being developed by Kress (1985), Martin (see Martin, Wignell, Eggins & Rothery, to appear), Rothery (1985a) and Christie (1986), though not Hasan, makes a clear distinction between genre and field. This is because social processes like biography and argument can be used to address a number of different activities (or 'topics'). In *Before Yesterday* for example, we find biographies of Joan of Arc, Michelangelo, Leonardo da Vinci and others; and we find arguments about the results of the crusades, outcomes of the rise of towns, the reasons for the revival of classical studies in Italy and so on. Similarly, closely related activities can be explored through different genres: one could have analysed why Joan of Arc had the effect she did, though the text itself treats her simply as a narrative heroine.

It is very important to recognize that genres make meaning; they are not simply a set of formal structures into which meanings are poured. What happened for example in Joan of Arc's life is one kind of meaning; the way we present it — as part of a story or part of an essay — is another. Technically then both field and genre contribute meaning to a text.

This is admittedly not the common sense view in our culture. Our culture prefers to dualise meaning and form, separating what we think and feel from the language we use to express ourselves. It thus feels comfortable thinking about genres as arbitrary sets of conventions we employ when we want to pass our ideas on to others. Genre-based approaches to writing development take a very different view of meaning and form to this. They argue that language *makes* meaning and that dualising meaning and form is fundamentally misleading.

The common sense duality of meaning and form is not a harmless one. In education in particular it is pernicious and has proved a major stumbling block for progressive initiatives. The whole movement toward child-centred education has foundered on the idea that children can understand and undertake history, geography and other subject areas 'in their own words'. That this is a necessary starting point, no one would deny, especially not those interested in genre-based approaches to writing development. But that children should be stranded there, writing stories for example as their only genre in infant and primary school, is impossible to accept. It cuts them off absolutely from any real understanding of what the humanities, social sciences and sciences are on about and denies them the tools these disciplines have developed to understand the world.

These tools are fundamentally linguistic ones — the genres and varieties of abstract and technical language associated with each discipline. Education cannot make access to these tools a viable goal unless it deconstructs the language involved and the ways in which such language can be taught. Ignorance of genre and language, and the dichotomy of meaning and form which sanctions this ignorance, are a major stumbling block to empowering a wider range of children than currently succeed.

Genre and Mode

Another critical variable in the model of context under discussion here is that of mode. This variable is set up in principle to take into account differences between writing and speaking, but goes beyond simple recognition of the channels themselves to consider the different types of meaning that are *typically* associated with each. There is a sense for example in which the Joan of Arc text discussed above was more like spoken language than the discussion of the results of the crusades, although both were written. This is because the second text was more *abstract* than the first; text 2 was somehow further removed from the events it describes than was text 1. How does language achieve this?

In English, one of the most important resources for creating this effect is nominalisation (Martin, 1984a, 1986; Halliday, 1985a, 1985b). And the distancing effect noted in text 2 is in large part achieved by realising what are semantically processes as nouns — as if they were in fact things:

PROCESS	VERBAL FORM	NOMINAL FORM	
'fail'	*fail*	*failure*	(In text 2)
'influence'	*influence*	*influences*	
'revive'	*revive*	*revival*	
'imitate'	*imitate*	*imitation*	
'grow'	*grow*	*growth*	
'change'	*change*	*changes*	
'tolerate'	*tolerate*	*tolerance*	
'understand'	*understand*	*understanding*	

Nominalisation is also an important resource for organising text. As noted above in the discussion of text 2, the argument was organised around five 'headings': *the revival of trade, the status of women, new fashions, the political influence of the kings* and *a spirit of tolerance.* Each of these headings is an abstraction, four of which are developed in paragraphs exemplifying the general statement. So unless young writers learn to shift between spoken and written styles of meaning where appropriate, not only will they sound like children when they write, but they will never master a range of genres depending on abstraction as a basic principle of organisation. All secondary school subjects make use of one or more genres that depend on abstraction in just this way (cf. Eggins, Wignell & Martin, 1986).

Why is writing typically more abstract than speech? Why has written English evolved in this way? From a psychological point of view the critical factor is consciousness. Written text is an object in a way spoken text can never be, and can be worked through and worked over in such a way as to scramble the natural iconic relation (i.e. processes as verbs, qualities as adjectives, logical relations as conjunctions, people and things as nouns, etc.) between meaning and wording made use of in speech.

From a social perspective the answer is again a functional one. Writing is used to store and consolidate information and interpretations, which need to be organised. Abstraction is a powerful resource for achieving this. In addition nominalised text codes an alternative and complementary view of reality to speaking (Halliday, 1985b). It treats the world as if it were a thing — to be classified and partitioned, with the relationships between the bits and pieces at the heart of the interpretation. Speaking tends on the other hand to explore the world as process — a place of dynamism, evolution and change.

Obviously then both spoken and written genres have their place in learning. Sawyer & Watson (1987) ask: 'Why is writing essentially any more a matter of *conscious learning of structures* than is speech?' Part of the answer is that children cannot be expected to understand in their own spoken words what generations of scholars have interpreted in writing. Because of the difference in modes, the understandings could never be the same. This raises the question of how to teach children the more conscious reflective written modes.

Learning Written Genres

Teaching, like writing, is a social process. Genre theory is just as applicable to the ways in which teachers go about teaching writing as it is to what children write. It is simply a question of whether we wish to look at spoken or written classroom genres. Christie (1984, 1985) refers in general to the genres teachers use to teach as curriculum genres. One of the most popular of these at present as far as teaching writing in infant and primary schools is concerned is that proposed by process writing, with its familiar staging: Pre-Writing/Drafting/Conferencing/Publishing.

Genre-based approaches to writing development have been particularly concerned with curriculum genres, both from the point of view of assessing current methodologies as well as from the perspective of developing new genres which will teach writing more effectively to a wider range of children. In order to develop more effective genres it has been assumed that two critical factors must be addressed. First, ways must be found of introducing strategies familiar to children from their experience of learning to talk into their experience of learning to write. A place must in other words be found for interaction and guidance in the context of shared experience. Second, ways must be found to take into account the fact that written language is different from spoken language and that anything even vaguely approximating the kind of immersion experienced when learning to talk is out of the question. Writing is just too slow — exponentially so.

One of Rothery's early suggestions for a genre-based approach to teaching writing is outlined below. Stages 3 and 4 are oriented to developing shared experience as a basis for writing. Interaction is explicitly built into stages 3 and 6. And guidance is a feature of every stage.

(1) *Introducing a genre* — modelling a genre *implicitly* through reading to or by the class; for example reading *Little Red Riding Hood.*

(2) *Focusing on a genre* — modelling a genre *explicitly* by naming its stages; e.g. identifying the stages Orientation, Complication and Resolution in *Little Red Riding Hood.*

(3) *Jointly negotiating a genre* — teacher and class jointly composing the genre under focus; the teacher *guides* the composition of the text through questions and comments that provide *scaffolding* for the stages of the genre; e.g. in a narrative the following question might point towards a Resolution stage: 'How will x escape from the witch? Does she have to do it alone, or will someone help her?'

(4) *Researching* — selecting material for reading; notemaking and summarizing; assembling information before writing (normally these skills cannot be assumed).

(5) *Drafting* — a first attempt at individually constructing the genre under focus.

(6) *Consultation* — teacher–pupil *consultation,* involving direct reference to the *meanings* of the writer's text; e.g. questions that help the writer to resolve the Complication stage of a narrative; young writers tend to find Complications easy, but resolving their characters' problems is hard; consultation involves getting into the text, not standing aside from it.

(7) *Publishing* — writing a final draft that may be published for the class library, thus providing another input of genre models, and of course enjoyable reading.

The purpose of introducing this particular curriculum genre is not to provide a recipe for teaching practice. It has in fact been superseded by a more general model better integrating both reading and writing perspectives. Nevertheless it does serve to illustrate certain key ways in which interaction and guidance in the context of shared experience can be built into a writing program.

Stages 3 and 6 require special consideration. Stage 3 is based on work by Brian Gray (see Gray, 1980, 1985) on concentrated language encounters. The basic idea is for teachers and students to jointly construct a model of the genre in focus. An excerpt from one such negotiation is reproduced below.

Text 3

(The Year 2 teacher and students have decided on the following opening — the general Classification in Report structure: *There are lots of different kinds of ships. At the Maritime Museum we saw model ships.* Joan Rothery is in the class and contributing to the negotiation.)

T: *Tell me what you know about the ships. Or what we saw.*
C: *What do you mean?*
T: *Well, how can we go on now? Let's read what we've got.* (Teacher and class read first two sentences.)
C: *Do you mean Complication?*

T: *No, it hasn't got a Complication. That's the tricky part in this. This is not a Narrative. This is a Report. We have to say exactly what we saw and exactly what we know about what we saw.* (Teacher reads: At the Maritime Museum we saw model ships.) *Perhaps we could have what sorts of model ships.*

J: *I didn't see them. I'd like to know exactly what kinds of ships. Were they sailing ships?*

T: *That's what we need to do, isn't it? Remember who we're writing for.*

J: *I didn't go. You have to tell me about the ships you saw.*

T: *Remember we're writing a Report for Mr Campbell to put in his book about excursions. If someone picks it up they're like Mrs Rothery. They won't know what's there. But they'll want to say, 'Wow! That's great. Let's go there.' What can we say?*

C: *We saw the Endeavour.*

T: *Right. We saw the Endeavour. What about the Endeavour? What can you tell me about the Endeavour? What kind of ship is it, Jack?*

C: *It's an olden days ship.*

T: (scribing) *It is an olden days ship. What else do we know about it?*

C: *Captain Cook sailed around the world on it.*

T: *This is a great Report.* (Teacher scribes) *What else do we know about the Endeavour, Gordon?*

C: *He sailed to Australia. He discovered Australia in it.*

C: *It was a pirate ship.*

C: *No, it's not. He wasn't a pirate.*

T: *No, he wasn't a pirate.*

(Negotiated text to this point: *There are lots of different kinds of ships. At the Maritime Museum we saw model ships. We saw the Endeavour. It is an olden days ship. Captain Cook sailed around the world in it. He discovered Australia in it.*)

Negotiations such as these are an extremely effective method of modelling genres for children. The text is based on shared experience, with the children assuming the responsibility of developing the field. The teacher's role is that of guiding them into the appropriate genre (in this case taking care to steer them away from recount and into report). This type of interaction makes it possible for teachers to provide scaffolding for writing in a way that is parallel to learning spoken genres. The responsibility for developing a successful text is assumed jointly, as when learning to talk.

Interaction alone, without guidance, is not an effective teaching strategy. Gray (1986) cites the following negotiated text in which photos of the children making toast were used to scaffold the field, but generic guidance is obviously lacking.

Text 4

All the things are on the table. We will use them to make toast. There is honey, vegemite, peanut butter, bread, margarine, jam, a knife, a plate and a toaster. We are ready to make toast. Kevin is getting two slices of bread out of the packet. Then he puts the bread in the toaster. The bread goes down automatically with a spring. The element starts to get hot and red. Kevin puts his hand over the toaster to feel how hot the toaster was. The control switch makes the bread brown. Kevin watches the bread inside the toaster cooking. It is still white. The toast came popping out. Jean is getting the toast out of the toaster. The bread has gone brown. Jean had to be careful because of the electricity and also because the toaster was hot.

This kind of writing is not functional in our culture. Generically speaking it is neither recount (i.e. what we did), nor procedure (i.e. how to do something). And the mode is wrong: parts of the text read like a running commentary on the photos scaffolding the field. But running commentaries are spoken, not written down. Even this is inconsistent, as can be demonstrated by examining the variety of tenses used: *are* (present); *will use* (future); *is getting* (present in present); *came* (past); *has gone* (past in present). Moreover running commentary makes use of (present in present) tense for actions. But actions in 4 are usually the 'timeless' (present) characteristic of reports: *puts, goes, starts, makes* (not *is putting, is going, is starting*, etc.). This is not just a case of mixing up tenses. Tenses, like the rest of grammar, are functional. They are designed to mean. Rather the inconsistency of tense selection is symptomatic of the lack of generic focus given by the teacher to the negotiation. The teacher had no clear social purpose in mind.

Unfocused conferencing is just as ineffective. In the following example from Graves (1983: 114–5) the teacher explores the writer's thoughts and feelings about his field, but does not directly help the young writer shape the structure of his narrative. It may even be of course that narrative is not the appropriate genre for exploring the benefits of football training in the first place. In what sense, one wonders, will the teacher's interaction help his student avoid 'just writing and wandering around?'

Text 5

(Graves style conference showing what he calls 'the process of working on the main idea'.)

Mr Sitka: *What is this paper about, Anton?*
Anton: *Well, I'm not sure. At first I thought it was going to be about when we won the game in overtime with the penalty kick. But when I got going on how our team had won because we were in such good shape for overtime. You see, the other team hardly move at the*

> *end. Took me way back to our earlier practices when I hated the coach so much. Gosh, I don't know what it's about.*

Mr Sitka: *Where are you now in the draft?*

Anton: *Oh, I've just got the part down about when we won in overtime.*

Mr Sitka: *So, you've just got started then. Well, it's probably too early to tell what it's about. What did you figure to do with the next draft, then?*

Anton: *I don't know. I don't want to just write and wander around. I've written about when we've won but it just sort of has me stuck at that point.*

Mr Sitka: *Tell me about that coach of yours.*

Anton: *God, how I hated him! I almost quit three or four times maybe. I thought he couldn't stand me. He'd yell, catch every little thing I did wrong. We'd run and run until we couldn't stand up. Have some passing drills. Then he'd run us some more. He'd just stand there yellin' and puffin' on his cigar. Course he was right. When we won the championship, I think it went right back to those early practices.*

Mr Sitka: *The way you tell it sounds as though you have quite a live beginning to your story. Try just writing about early practices, then see what your piece is about.*

Texts such as 4 and 5 demonstrate the kinds of problems that arise when teachers and students do not share knowledge about language and genre. Guidance becomes at best indirect, and may well be absent completely. Only bright motivated middle class children are sure to read between the lines and learn to write, apparently effortlessly, without being taught.

What about differences between speaking and writing? Why won't it work simply to surround children with print? A glance back at texts like 3 illustrates the nature of the problem. The text is highly interactive; but at the same time, and in fact because of this, it is mainly talk. It does not immerse the learner in writing. The alternative of course is to get the children reading; but this eliminates the interaction and guidance, and possibly the shared experience as well. For these reasons, learning to write can never be the same kind of process as learning to talk. Somehow, shortcuts must be found to get over the difference in mode.

The most obvious of these is to make use of the fact that when children arrive at school they can all use language to learn. This language can be used to acquire knowledge about writing — specifically knowledge about genres and their staging; and about the language used to realise each stage. Rothery (1985) has demonstrated that such knowledge can be introduced to children in infant school, and that once introduced it paves the way for more effective negotiations and consultations as well as providing children with their own individual scaffolding that can be deployed as needed to produce successful texts.

Knowledge about generic structure was used explicitly in text 3 above, and in countless other exchanges in Barbara Ryan's Year 2 class. Knowledge about grammar was also introduced and successfully deployed in order to orient children to the kinds of nominal group appropriate in reports. None of the children felt uncomfortable with knowledge of this kind. For them, learning about language is as natural as learning about any other aspect of their world. They had not yet learned that in our culture knowledge about language is taboo.

It needs to be stressed at this point nonetheless that knowledge about genre and language was introduced in the context of the children's writing, that as far as genre was concerned it was oriented to the structure of whole texts, and that the grammar used was a semantically oriented functional one (based on Halliday, 1985a). It also needs to be stressed that in the past no one has seriously studied the effectiveness of teaching this kind of knowledge about language in this way (John Carr is currently pursuing post-graduate research in this area; see Kolln, 1981, for a thorough critique of the research that is supposed to have demonstrated that teaching grammar does not improve children's writing — Kolln concludes that most of the research is methodologically suspect, and more importantly that when grammar was taught in conjunction with writing, instead of as a separate subject, some studies showed that writing did improve). The real question that needs to be put is: How could one deal effectively with texts like 4 without knowledge of this kind?

Freedom

What is freedom? Is a progressive process writing classroom really free? Does allowing children to choose their own topics, biting one's tongue in conferences and encouraging ownership, actually encourage the development of children's writing abilities? Will genres, if taught, imprison children? Why can't genre theorists just leave children alone and let them get on with learning in their own words? Questions such as these, often couched in deeply ideological metaphors, are a recurring feature in the discourse of those alarmed by the emergence once again of explicit discussion of language and context in educational debates.

Consider then a process writing classroom, in the Northern Territory, with a large population of Aboriginal children. The children are encouraged to choose their own topics. At the end of the year one collects the writing, and analyses it for field. It turns out that all the children have written about one or another of four themes:

(1) visiting friends and relatives;

(2) going hunting for bush tucker;

(3) sporting events;

(4) movies or TV shows they have seen.

Then one examines the texts from the point of view of genre. Here the analysis is simpler still. Every one of the texts is a recount — a simple sequential retelling of events.

One repeats the study year by year, following the children through infants' and primary school. The results are the same (see Gray, 1986, for discussion of the reality corresponding to the scenario posited here). What kind of freedom is this?

Looked at from the point of view of social theories of language development, the results are hardly surprising. Because from the point of view of these theories it is social context, not individual choice, that has the greatest influence on what people say or write. The children concerned have a limited range of personal experiences to draw on, and they make use of these. Their teachers have not guided them into a variety of written genres, and so they fall back on an oral genre that deals effectively with this personal experience. What else could they possibly be expected to do? And are urban Sydney children really different? Will genres in their writing simply spring spontaneously from within?

It is more than obvious that they do not. Martin and Rothery's study of a Sydney western suburbs process writing school showed that city children behave very similarly to the Aboriginal children described above. Their teachers do not create choices for them, so they do not have choices to take up. Offering choice in classrooms such as these is not enabling. It is *pseudo-choice*. Writers cannot take up options they do not have.

The alternative, put simply, is to teach — to create options. But because it has turned its back on language, progressive education is in a very poor position to take up this challenge. It lacks the tools to analyse and construct the curriculum genres that could be used; and it lacks the tools to monitor children's speaking and writing to see if development is taking place. The fact that Sawyer and Watson include no text at all in their critique is symptomatic; and they are in good company — if it were not for the occasional consideration of children's texts from the point of view of handwriting and spelling most process writing publications would not contain any examples of children's writing either, let alone analysed texts (e.g. Walshe, 1981; Turbill, 1982; Graves, 1983, 1984; Walshe, 1986; Cambourne & Turbill, 1987). Similarly Dixon (1987) considers only a single text, and that is one provided by Christie.

Twenty years ago, this was perhaps forgivable. Many of the tools required simply did not exist. But since that time various schools of linguistics, especially systemic theory, have developed socially based theories of language and language learning that are directly applicable in classrooms. The problem now is not with linguistics but with education. Most educators are either unable or unwilling to look seriously at language. They take it for granted in a way which has made and will continue to make it impossible for them to achieve their goals.

Genre theory puts language back into the picture. This is not 'Back to Basics'. But it is the key to providing progressive educators with somewhere to go.

References

Cambourne, B. and Turbill, J. (1987) *Coping with Chaos*. Sydney: Primary English Teachers Association.

Christie, F. (1984) Young children's writing development: The relationship of written genres to curriculum genres. In B. Bartlett and J. Carr (eds) *1984 Language in Education Conference: A Report of Proceedings* (pp. 41–69). Brisbane: Brisbane CAE, Mt Gravatt Campus.

— (1985a) Curriculum genres: Towards a description of the construction of knowledge in schools. Paper given at the Working Conference on Interaction of Spoken and Written Language in Educational Settings, held at the University of New England, November.

— (1985b) Curriculum genre and schematic structures of classroom discourse. In R. Hasan (ed.) *Discourse on Discourse: Workshop Report from the Macquarie Workshop on Discourse Analysis* (Occasional Papers, 7) (pp. 38–42). Applied Linguistics Association of Australia.

— (1986) The construction of knowledge in the junior primary school. Paper presented at the Language in Education Conference on Language and Socialisation: Home and School. Macquarie University, November.

Dixon, J. (1987) The question of genres. In I. Reid (ed.) *The Place of Genre in Learning: Current Debates*. Geelong: Centre for Studies in Literary Education, Deakin University.

Doughty, P., Pearce, J. and Thornton, G. (1971) *Language in Use*. London: Edward Arnold.

Eggins, S., Wignell, P. and Martin, J. R. (1986) The discourse of history: Distancing the recoverable past. Working Papers in Linguistics, No. 5. Dept of Linguistics, University of Sydney.

Forsyth, I. and Wood, K. (1980) *Language and Communication* (3 Vols). London: Longman.

Graves, D. (1983) *Writing: Teachers and Children at Work*. London: Heinemann.

— (1984) *A Researcher Learns to Write: Selected Articles and Monographs*. London: Heinemann.

Gray, B. (1980) Concentrated language encounters as a component of functional language/literacy teaching. In T. and M. McCausland (eds) *Proceedings of the Conference on Child Language Development: Theory into Practice*. Launceston: Teacher's Centre.

— (1985) Helping children to become language learners in the classroom. In M. Christie (ed.) *Aboriginal Perspectives on Experience and Learning: The Role of Language in Aboriginal Education* (pp. 87–104). Geelong: Deakin University Press.

— (1986) Aboriginal literacy: Some implications of genre for literacy development. In C. Painer and J. R. Martin (eds) *Writing to Mean: Teaching Genres Across the Curriculum* (Occasional Papers, 9) (pp. 188–209). Applied Linguistics Association of Australia.

Halliday, M. A. K. (1975) *Learning How to Mean*. London: Edward Arnold.

— (1985a) *An Introduction to Functional Grammar*. London: Edward Arnold.

— (1985b) *Spoken and Written Language*. Geelong: Deakin University Press.

Hasan, R. (1978) Text in the systemic functional model. In W. Dressler (ed.) *Current Trends in Textlinguistics*. Hamburg: Helmut Buske.

Kolln, M. (1981) Closing the books on alchemy. *College Composition and Communication* 32.5, 139–151.

Kress, G. (1982) *Learning to Write*. London: Routledge and Kegan Paul.

— (1985) *Linguistic Processes in Sociocultural Practice*. Geelong: Deakin University Press.

Mackay, D., Thompson, B. and Schaub, P. (1970) *Breakthrough to Literacy*. London: Longman.

Martin, J. R. (1984a) Types of writing in infants' and primary school. In L. Unsworth (ed.) *Reading, Writing, Spelling: Proceedings of the Fifth Macarthur Reading/Language Symposium* (pp. 34–55). Sydney: Macarthur Institute of Higher Education.

— (1985) Process and text: Two aspects of semiosis. In J. Benson and W. Greaves (eds) *Systemic Perspectives on Discourse: Selected Theoretical Papers from the 9th International Systemic Workshop* (Advances in Discourse Process, 15) (pp. 248–74). Norwood, NJ: Ablex.

— (1986) Prewriting: Oral models for written text. In R. Walshe, P. March and D. Jensen (eds) *Writing and Learning in Australia* (pp. 138–42). Melbourne: Dellasta Books.

Martin, J. R., Wignell, P., Eggins, S., Rothery, J. (to appear) Secret English: Discourse technology in a junior secondary school. In L. Gerot and T. van Leeuwen (eds) *Language and Socialisation: Home and School*. Sydney: School of English and Linguistics, Macquarie University.

Rothery, J. (1985a) Writing to learn and learning to write. In J. R. Martin *Factual Writing: Exploring and Challenging Social Reality* (pp. 71–82). Geelong: Deakin University Press.

— (1985b) Teaching genre in the primary school: A genre-based approach to the development of writing abilities. Working Papers in Linguistics, No. 4. Dept of Linguistics, University of Sydney.

Sawyer, W. and Watson, K. (1987) Questions of genre. In I. Reid (ed.) *The Place of Genre in Learning: Current Debates*. Geelong: Centre for Studies in Literary Education, Deakin University.

Turbill, J. (1982) *No Better Way to Teach Writing*. Sydney: Primary English Teaching Association.

Walshe, R. D. (ed.) (1981) *Donald Graves in Australia*. Sydney: Primary English Teaching Associaton.

Walshe, R. D., March, P. and Jensen, D. (eds) (1986) *Writing and Learning in Australia*. Melbourne: Dellasta Books.

17 Genre Theory: What's it All About?

MYRA BARRS

A writer in the American magazine *English Journal* once began an article entitled *How the British Teach Writing* with one brief sentence; 'They don't'. He went on to say that he had been on sabbatical leave for a year in England and that his children had attended the local primary and secondary schools during that time. He was as amazed by the fact that, throughout that year, they received no direct instruction in writing as he was by the amount of writing they actually did, and by its quality. No one, apparently, was teaching them writing, and yet they were learning to write.

For a long time teachers in England didn't teach writing, in the sense that it has generally been taught in the USA, though they did teach spelling and punctuation and a few grammatical points. They did other things. What they chiefly did was to invite children to write and discuss their writing with them. They often put a lot of thought into the nature of the invitation to write, into the way they responded to the writing, and into the most effective ways of helping children to develop and correct their work, but they didn't systematically induct children into ways of structuring written text. American teachers, whose practice in this respect comes out of a very different tradition, were meanwhile instructing children in how to begin every paragraph with a topic sentence, how to write a three-paragraph theme and so on. But in recent years American developments in writing, and particularly the work of Donald Graves and his associates, have influenced practice in the UK, and have focused attention on aspects of the writing process, such as revision. Now, from Australia, we are beginning to learn about genre theory, and about the way Australian linguists are advocating that writing should be taught.

'Genre' is not a term that trips off the tongue, but it is a useful label for different kinds of writing that have different functions in written discourse and in society. Though genre theories generally derive themselves from the work of Michael Halliday in Australia, they began to be diffused in the UK in the form of Gunther Kress's book *Learning to Write* (1982). In this book Kress made the case for thinking about the large scale textual structures in writing: 'linguistic structures beyond the sentence'. He argued that children learning to write have to learn to use these large scale structures, as well as being able to control the smaller units in texts.

In many ways what Kress had to say in this book was exciting, because he was focusing attention on these larger textual structures, rather than on the smaller units of language which have sometimes dominated discussion of children's developing literacy. He was also pointing out the relationship between a particular genre and the smaller elements in text: if you are writing a report of an investigation, for instance, the genre you are writing in will affect everything from the vocabulary you use to the layout of the text on the page. We are only just beginning to realise the full importance of these larger-scale textual structures, and to appreciate how far both readers and writers draw on them.

But all the same, genre theory does present some problems and for the last few years there has been a running debate in Australia on the application of this theory to the classroom. There is now a growing school of genre linguists based at Deakin University publishing a lengthening list of papers on all forms and aspects of genre. (The definition of genre has gradually been widened to mean 'a purposeful staged cultural activity' and 'texts' to include all forms of language use.) Some of these linguists are publishing materials for teachers to use in in-service courses; their ideas have begun to influence linguists and educationalists in this country, and are reflected in both the Cox Report and the LINC Project. For this reason it seems important for primary teachers with an interest in writing to pay them some attention.

Essentially genre theorists argue that schools fail children by not teaching them to write in 'powerful' genres; the impersonal genres of factual and expository prose. They consider that far too much emphasis is placed on personal narrative writing and story, genres which children are unlikely to use in their adult lives. Working-class children and minority groups, they think, are particularly in need of access to these socially important genres.

Writers such as Frances Christie and Joan Rothery argue that genres like this cannot be picked up by osmosis, they need to be explicitly taught. They want teachers to be more informed about the linguistics of texts so that they can teach factual genres more effectively. Their in-service writings aim to provide teachers with the skills to analyse children's writing using Hallidayan linguistics, and to look at development in terms of these linguistic categories.

The Australian genre theorists are not the only people who have suggested that story writing is overvalued, particularly in primary schools. Even in 1967 the Plowden Report was quite scathing about the amount of routine story writing that the committee found was going on in schools, and tried to shift the emphasis towards more personal writing and different kinds of writing. In America, Thomas Newkirk, in his book *More than Stories* (1989) has looked at the kinds of writing that young children spontaneously engage in and has found a tremendous range of types of texts in the writing of pre-school children. Janet White, of the APU, has suggested that there is a widespread presumption in the UK that argumentative writing is difficult for children, and that this has unnecessarily limited children's experience of writing to persuade and to argue a case.

The view of learning and teaching that emerges from the work of many of the linguists concerned with genre is worrying. The children's texts quoted in their books and papers are often viewed as failed adult texts, rather than transitional forms of writing. For instance, Gunther Kress quotes the following text twice in *Learning to Write:*

> The mices enemy are cats and owls, the mices eat all kinds of thingk. Mices are little animals, people set traps to catch mouse, mouse liv in holes in the skirting board. Baby mouse dons have their eis opne, baby mouses can't see and they do not have fer. Some people are scered of mouses.

Of this text Kress remarks that 'The text is not a story in the conventional sense, so the child cannot use the familiar genre of narrative. The topic is not developed in the more mature sense; that is there is no clear indication of a particular ordering of a conceptual kind, neither sequence nor any internal logic.' Later he concludes that 'these sentences hardly form a text at all'. The reader receives the impression that he can find nothing positive to say about this writing. Yet it seems clear that this text is a list, a list of all the things that the seven-year-old writer knows about mice. As a list it makes sense, and reflects the writer's idea of what it is he is being asked to do (write what you know about mice). It might be seen as a step towards more mature forms of factual writing, rather than a failed attempt.

Joan Rothery (1984) reveals a similar inability to decentre when commenting on a text by a six-year-old girl. The text reads as follows:

> I sor a bike a in the shop.
> My dad woot by me the bike.
> After school sar a big box in my bed room.
> A bike.

Rothery remarks:

> The last part of this text, 'A bike' requires some comment. This is much more like spoken than written text. It is the exclamation a child might make on seeing the present. In written language we need to expand this to 'It was a bike!'.

The only possible response to this is 'Who says?' This six-year-old writer seems likely to have made quite a conscious choice of words in ending her story. The words 'A bike', are given a line to themselves, the capital letter, and full stop are firmly marked in the copy of the text that Rothery prints. The writer may well have intended the words to stand as they are, brief and dramatic.

In another article, Martin, Christie & Rothery (1987) comment on the following text, which is a piece of shared writing based on a set of photos:

> All the things are on the table. We will use them to make toast. There is honey, vegemite, peanut butter, bread, margarine, jam, a knife, a plate and a toaster. We are ready to make toast. Kevin is getting two slices of bread out of the packet. Then he puts the bread in the toaster. The bread goes down automatically with a spring. The element starts to get hot and red. Kevin puts his hand over the toaster to feel how hot the toaster was. The control switch makes the bread brown. Kevin watched the bread inside the toaster cooking. It is still white. The toast came popping out. Jean is getting the toast out of the toaster. The bread has gone brown. Jean has to be careful because of the electricity and also because the toaster was hot.

The three linguists comment.

> This kind of writing is not functional in our culture. Generically speaking it is neither recount (i.e. what we did) nor procedure (i.e. how to do something). And the mode is wrong: parts of the text read like a running commentary on the photos scaffolding the field. But running commentaries are spoken, not written down.

They are particularly concerned about the mixture of tenses in the writing:

> The inconsistency of tense selection is symptomatic of the lack of generic focus given by the teacher to the negotiation. The teacher had no clear social purpose in mind.

This sort of incomprehension is hard to understand. The text, despite some inconsistencies of tense, seems quite clear: it is a commentary on the photographs. *Without* the photographs the text obviously doesn't function so well, but we can presume that it is meant to be accompanied by them. (A careful reading of the text makes fairly clear how many photographs there probably were.) To pronounce that 'running commentaries are spoken not written' is to reveal a lamentable lack of knowledge of many popular genres such as action comics, photo magazines, and so on, where pictures are often accompanied by just this sort of text.

Most of the Australian genre school really do think that most children need to be directly and explicitly taught the features of different genres. They argue that children come to school with very different linguistic/generic backgrounds (Kress, 1987) and that only 'bright motivated middle class children' can acquire sufficient knowledge of genres apparently without effort (Martin, Christie & Rothery, 1987). They see some genres as being associated with social power, and want all children to have access to them because of this. Kress puts it this way:

> In my view there are genres; they, and access to them, are unevenly distributed in society, along the lines of social structuring. Some genres — and the possibility of their use — convey more power than other genres. As a minimal goal I would wish every writer to have access to all powerful genres. That is not the position in our society now. (1987)

There is some naïvete in this. Genres in themselves are not powerful; it is indeed the 'possibility of their use' that counts most. It's not only knowing how to write that matters in this world, but being in a position to ensure that your writing reaches an audience, and then is noticed and read. We could all learn how to write certain powerful genres — such as high-level memos — but this wouldn't increase our access to power by one jot.

Kress's statement is disturbing too because it demonstrates how apparently democratic arguments about access can be used to justify authoritarian practices in teaching. In this country we have increasingly seen equal opportunities arguments used by both left and right to justify moves towards what the Cox Report repeatedly called, in a phrase that has recurred in several recent inspectorial and ministerial pronouncements, 'direct and explicit teaching'. But it is hard to see how children are to be either informed or empowered by teaching approaches which are as insensitive to children's attempts, and as relentlessly didactic, as those implied in many of the writings of the genre school.

The subtext of much writing about genre is a contempt for modern approaches to language education, and actually an incomprehension of such approaches. Progressive education has failed, according to these linguists, because it has ignored the formal discipline of linguistics which would enable teachers to analyse children's development as language users more closely, identify the gaps in their knowledge, and fill these gaps with explicit teaching:

> Because it has turned its back on language, progressive education is in a very poor position to take up this challenge . . . It lacks the tools to analyse and construct the curriculum genres that could be used; and it lacks the tools to monitor children's speaking and writing to see if development is taking place . . . Genre theory puts language back in

the pictures . . . It is the key to providing progressive educators with
somewhere to go. (Martin, Christie & Rothery, 1987)

Like the writers of editorials in *The Sun,* or *The Guardian,* these writers
view child-centred education as *laissez-faire,* and progressive teaching as
abandoning children to their own devices.

There is arrogance in this, and some ignorance. The members of the
genre club often write about children's developing literacy, but their papers
and articles reveal little knowledge of this subject. A whole literature that
has grown up in recent years on early literacy, and the relationships between
learning to write and learning to read, is never referred to in their biblio-
graphies; references to reading are conspicuously absent. This apparent lack
of awareness of a mass of material — including the work of Gordon Wells
and Yetta Goodman, and all of the research referred to in, for example,
Awakening to Literacy — means that it is hard to take their work seriously
as a contribution to discussion in this area. There are three key points relating to learning to write which genre theorists seem not to take into account.

(1) A major development in the past twenty or thirty years has been the realisation that learning to read and write has a great deal in common with learning to talk. Children begin to acquire literacy in very much the same way that
they acquire spoken language, because they are members of a society where
written language is omnipresent. All children when they come to school are,
in Gordon Wells' phrase, 'partially literate'. To state this is not, of course,
to state that children acquire literacy 'naturally', or quite on their own,
or that they need no support, feedback, information, or teaching; much
ongoing discussion in this field has to do with the nature of this support, and
of effective intervention. But the basic parallel that is to be drawn between
language development and literacy development now seems inescapable.
Genre linguists, however, are unhappy with this parallel and insist that
learning speech and learning writing are quite different:

> 'Why is writing essentially any more a matter of conscious learning of
> structures than is speech?' Part of the answer is that children cannot be
> expected to understand in their own spoken words what generations of
> scholars have interpreted in writing. Because of the differences in
> modes, the understandings could never be the same. (*Ibid.*)

There is a strong tendency in genre theory to emphasise the differences
between spoken and written language rather than the continuities.

It seems essential to recognise that the statement that children begin to
acquire literacy before school is true of all children, not only well motivated
middle-class children, though children from literate homes obviously do
have more experience of written language. The implication we should draw
from this is not, however, that working-class children or children from less

literate homes, need more 'direct and explicit' teaching and fewer opportunities for self-expression — but this is the conclusion that the genre
linguists arrive at. Gunther Kress writes:

> I worry that overly strong emphasis on individual creativity quite over-
> looks the fact that children come to school with very different linguistic/
> generic preparation from home. To a child from the literate middle-
> class home the teacher's exhortation to express her/himself is no threat
> — she or he will implement the generic forms acquired at home. A
> child from the inner-city slums of Sydney cannot respond in the same
> way. (1987)

This is a concern that needs to be taken seriously, but it should not lead
us to lower our expectations of children from 'inner-city slums', or imagine
that they learn differently or need an entirely different kind of education.
What matters is that the experience of children should be recognised, built
on, and extended in school. Many inner-city primary schools succeed in this,
but we still need to think harder about the ways in which the access of all children to what Margaret Meek has taught us to call 'full literacy', and not any
watered down or minimal substitute, can be assured. We shall not achieve
this by defining learning differently, or advocating different educational
programmes, for children from different social classes.

(2) A second key parallel that needs to be drawn is that between learning to
write and learning to read. Learning to write is one side of a two-sided process. Children learn a great deal about writing from their reading (and vice
versa). Margaret Meek (once more) has demonstrated over and over again
the role of the text in the process of learning to read, and has shown that
many of the 'untaught lessons' which help children see what the reader has
to do are learnt from books, through reading, or through being read to. In
just the same way, children learn a great deal about writing from the texts
they hear or read, and they use this knowledge in their own writing. When
a six-year-old girl writes:

> The circus was coming and the animals had babies. But one animal did
> not have a baby. She looked high and low for a baby to suit her. But no,
> she could not find one.

it is clear that she is using the language of books that she has learnt from
reading or from being read to.

Gunther Kress recognises that this kind of learning exists, but does not
seem to value it:

> . . . children pick up the requirements of the different genres by
> osmosis, as it were. They do, of course, have models, but these are pre-
> sented as models of something else. For instance, the stories which

children read are often presented as reading exercises, or else the texts
for dictation are presented as relevant to dictation alone . . . The children absorb together with whatever other purposes there may be, the
forms and rules of the genre in which the content is presented to them.
(1982)

This reveals some odd ideas about contemporary practice (reading
exercises, dictation) but is an account which does at least recognise that
something is going on when writers read. The tone, however, indicates
that Kress feels this way of learning to be a hit and miss affair. The text
continues:

Sometimes the teacher's instruction is sufficiently detailed and directed to
lead to the constructing of a text which embodies the demands of a
genre.

Nobody learns 'by osmosis' though much language learning is inductive in
character, and learning in this area is sometimes so invisible that we fall into
the error of seeing it as an almost organic process. But learning is a more
active and constructive process than this. Recently, the rediscovery of
Vygotsky, the work of Jerome Bruner, and developments in cognitive and
constructivist psychology in the USA have begun to provide us with an
adequate account of the complexity of human learning. It is interesting to
see how important in the creation of that account, has been the evidence
derived from studies of children learning spoken and written language.
What is striking in any even partially adequate description of acts of this
level of complexity — such as Michael Halliday's highly documented description of learning to talk in *Learning How to Mean* (1975) — is the interactive nature of the learning and of the role of human relationships in it, and
the immense amount of work that both adult and child do in the course of the
learning process. Members of the 'genre school' may know a great deal
about language, but seem to know little about learning, and this handicaps
them when they come to advise teachers about what they should be doing.

(3) Finally, the question of how children do learn written genres needs to be
complicated a little. It seems likely that, as the genre theorists maintain,
most children are less confident at managing factual and impersonal genres
than they are in writing personal or fictional narratives. One major reason
for this must be that they generally have less experience of such genres, both
as readers and as writers. The question of how children can be given more
experience of these important genres might be one we could confront before
getting involved in plans for the 'direct and explicit' teaching of genres.

Moreover, under some circumstances, children do seem to be able to
write in the kinds of genres that genre theorists regard as socially important.
It is observable, for instance, that children writing in role, either as part of

a drama or in what might be termed 'drama on paper', can take on voices
that they never usually use, and write as politicians, scientists, or news
reporters. In the following example, a nine-year-old boy is writing in role as
a scientist reporting on a new planet, in a piece of science fiction which
strikes a deliberately detached and impersonal note:

> The planet from space looks quite hospitable. But that is caused by its
> thick cloud layer. But when you have penetrated the cloud layer it is a
> pleasant planet, 38 degrees Centigrade, one degree over the normal
> body temperature. The planet is green for about 2/4, 1/4 is H2O9 C2
> which is wasoter. Luckily it is safe for people to drink. But the remain-
> ing 1/4 is red this is caused by a disease called ce-mon-frceh-he-mhars-
> ca-clone-fon-nash-agon. The symptoms are: the patient's brain is
> taken over, a plant starts to grow out of the patient's head.
>
> They have to be terminated.

The following piece is not strictly 'writing inrole', but it clearly shows the
nine-year-old girl author assuming an adult voice, the voice of an expert in
this field. Her favourite television series was *Life on Earth,* and after seeing
the series three times she read the book. In this piece of writing the characteristic tones of David Attenborough can clearly be heard, and the young
writer, who is thoroughly acquainted with his style, is obviously trying on his
voice in this piece:

> We have not found enough proof on just how the first living thing
> started; it may always remain a mystery to us. This is just one of many
> explanations. Some time after the earth cooled, and its crust formed,
> after mountains had been raised and eroded over and over again, after
> salt seas had formed in a barren landscape of deserts and hills and vol-
> canoes, some of the elements and simple compounds on and near the
> earth's surface combined to form more complicated compounds. A
> few of these compounds had the ability of taking material from their
> own body and making it the same thing as them. That is by simply
> breaking in two they were able to reproduce themselves.

It may be easier for these young writers to use certain kinds of impersonal
language and formal structures when they are writing in another persona
than it is when they are writing in their own. In drama and dramatic play children frequently reveal that their linguistic range is wider than that which
they normally use. In role they draw on hidden resources. They can assume
adult voices, and show how much they have learned about different registers
from listening and from reading.

Finally, any study of the way children learn to take on particular forms of
language needs above all to examine not only their competence at using formal structures, but also the meanings that they are making. The genres that

Kress and the genre linguists want children to learn are associated with particular ways of thinking. Children's texts differ from adult texts not merely because children have not been inducted into the use of particular linguistic forms, but because their texts express a certain level of conceptual development. We need to attend to children's 'spontaneous concepts' in order to see how we can best support and extend their thinking, and we shall find out more about their understanding if they are encouraged to write in their own voices. This was the theory behind the language across the curriculum movement, which argued for a broader range of language use in school, and against the dominance of impersonal and abstract forms of writing in the secondary curriculum.

Genre is a fascinating subject because it makes us look at the 'big shapes' in text and begin to think about how children learn these high level structures, which affect so many other aspects of text. We are beginning to think more systematically now about the role that these big shapes play in learning written language. Given the importance of genre as an idea, it is disappointing that it is not being developed and used more positively and interestingly by the genre linguists. Like many others in language education, their first response to finding out something important about the way that language works has been to codify their findings, develop rules of use, and advocate the teaching of these rules. If, however, we can broaden out the 'genre debate' and look at genre in a more exploratory and constructive way, we shall be able to consider how genre fits into children's learning of written language, how children's use of written genres develops, what the influences on this development are, and what this developing use of genres reveals about the relationship between language and learning.

References

Bruner, J. (1990) *Acts of Meaning*. Cambridge, MA: Harvard University Press.

DES (1988) English for ages 5 to 11. *The Cox Report*.

Goelman, Hillel, Oberg, Antoinette, A. and Smith, F. (1984) *Awakening to Literacy*. NH: Heinemann Educational.

Halliday, M. A. K. (1975) *Learning How to Mean*. London: E. Arnold.

Kress, G. (1982) *Learning to Write*. London: Routledge & Kegan Paul.

— (1987) Genre in a social theory of language. In I. Reid (ed.) *The Place of Genre in Learning*. Geelong: Deakin University Press.

Martin, J. R., Christie, F. and Rothery, J. (1987) Social processes in education. In I. Reid (ed.) *The Place of Genre in Learning*. Geelong: Deakin University Press.

Newkirk, T. (1989) *More Than Stories: The Range of Children's Writing*. NH: Heinemann Educational.

Rothery, J. (1984) The development of genres — primary to junior secondary school. In *Language Studies: Children's Writing: Study Guide*. Geelong: Deakin University Press.

Vygotsky, L. (1962) *Thought and Language*. Cambridge, MA: MIT Press.

Wells, G. (1987) *The Meaning Makers*. London: Hodder & Stoughton.

White, J. (1989) *Children's Argumentative Writing*. Geelong: Deakin University.

18 Authorizing Disadvantage: Authorship and Creativity in the Language Classroom

PAM GILBERT

Several years ago I planned and directed the production of a short video filmed in a local primary school with a year 2 teacher with whom I had been working over a number of months. I had been impressed with the way in which this teacher organized her writing classroom, and was keen to capture on film some of her strategies and approaches.

When it was writing time, the children were described by their teacher as 'authors', not students; their written work was said to be 'published' when it was typed and put in cardboard covers; they were shown how they might treat their classmates' publications as 'real' literature by giving serious and apparently perceptive consideration to the texts produced; and their teacher acted as an editorial adviser and publicity agent.

The children wrote regularly and chose most of their own topics and writing forms; they read their work aloud to their classmates and their teacher, and were offered comments and advice about how such work might be changed; and the final draft written work — edited by student and teacher for conventional spelling and punctuation, and later typed by a parent — formed one of the main components of the classroom reading materials.

This approach offered a seriousness of purpose ('real' writing, as 'real' writers supposedly write) and some authenticity of response to children's school work — both often regarded as necessary ingredients for a successful writing programme. It meant that children's experiences could be valued and their decision making respected, and it offered the possibility that the work of text construction — the labour of authoring — could become a legitimate focus of study in the writing classroom.

However, in the wider public sphere, authorship has often not been associated with the work of writing, nor with most forms of writing. Consider how few forms of writing are currently associated with an author, for instance, the writing of legal contracts, of advertising copy, of journalist reports, of textbooks, of instruction manuals and leaflets, of the documents of government, banking, commerce and industry. Most of the language encountered in our daily lives is *not* 'authored' language. Instead, authorship has come to be associated with a romantic concept of writing, through its identification with a particular type of reading and writing, a particular form of discourse. The term *romantic* as it is used here derives from its older meaning that developed in the late eighteenth and early nineteenth centuries. It was in particular associated with traditions of writing literature which tended to value freedom of the imagination more than attention to form.

Currently, it is *literary* works — creative, imaginative works — that are traditionally 'authored', and the construction of an artistic text that demands 'authorship'. Of all the many contemporary written forms, it is still only literary discourse which relies so obviously on concepts of authoring and authorship to function. And even this is relatively modern. In the Middle Ages, for example, literary works were not authored, but instead were seen to be part of a collective enterprise, the product of the culture at large. The need to have an author's name attached to a work came with the romantic shift to the individual, the human person. An author's name could then protect the property of a work by indicating if plagiarism had occurred.

Not surprisingly, the introduction of authorship concepts into literacy learning has come since the 1960s, in the wake of a strong classroom commitment to the personal, imaginative and creative nature of language. This focus has been particularly responsible for an interest in children's expressive and imaginative writing, and also, in more recent years, for the switch from basal reading schemes to literature-based early reading programmes. As a result, the aspects of authorship which mesh most closely with popular assumptions in literacy classrooms are not about work, not about texts, and not about construction. Instead they are about imagination, expression, and creation: about personal and creative growth through language.

I now feel less confident than I initially did about the value of terms like *authorship* for literacy classrooms. Far from regarding authorship as a novel and reasonably effective way of encouraging children to write and to read, I am now concerned about the way this term, like many before it, may operate to the disadvantage of many children by perpetuating romantic notions of writing as creative and individual expression, and of reading as personal and original meaning making. I am concerned that concepts like authoring might obscure the fact that school writing is about the acquisition of *specific cultural capital,* to use Pierre Bourdieu's term (1973). The term is a useful one, for it proposes that there are certain kinds of knowledge that are culturally valued and privileged. It is in this sense that knowledge becomes 'capital' which one can use. The cultural capital that concerns me now is knowledge about the ways in which our language system works.

As a result, I would claim that the use of authoring or authorship terms — like the use of the terms 'creative writing' in the 1960s and 'personal response' in the 1970s — may operate to disenfranchise many children from any real understanding of the social, learned nature of writing and reading, and to deny them access to the obvious power of cultural literacy. I would suggest that such terms serve to authorize some children's disadvantage because they construct an image of language learning which is personal, not learned; individual, not social; innate, not environmental.

This may seem an unnecessarily strong criticism to make of pedagogical practices which have offered some useful ideas for classroom strategies in the early years of schooling, and been responsible for a significant interest and concern in children's writing and reading development. But I think a note of warning should be sounded about the authorship fervour. In the rest of this chapter, I shall offer a critical re-examination of the concept of authorship, and in so doing shall:

- consider the way in which the concept has been used in terms of schooling and literacy — particularly in relation to the development of writing ability — and of how it is compatible with a number of other popular assumptions about learning to read and write which have emphasized the 'creative' and 'original' nature of writing, and the 'personal' and 'individual' nature of reading;
- reappraise these popular assumptions about reading and writing, in terms of their inadequacies as a basis for language learning, and in terms of the confusion they have helped to generate in classrooms;
- suggest other approaches to learning to read and learning to write by considering theories about the socially constructed nature of reading and writing practices;
- read some schoolchildren's writing and consider other ways of describing authorship which rely on discussions of textuality rather than creativity.

Authorship and Schooling

The author as creator of texts

An orthodox view of literature — and certainly a prevailing one in school textbooks — is that literature stems from the creative unconscious of the individual author. It is the author who provides the imagination, inspiration and personal vision for the work, who creates and expresses the work. It is also the author who supplies the individuality and originality of a piece of literature, its claim to be treated differently from other works. Significantly, while literary study is concerned with techniques used by authors — narrative structure, characterization devices, symbolism and motifs, points of view and so on — its predominant concern is with an alleged creative vision which guides the use of these techniques, or one which is independent of them. The *craft* of writing is thus bypassed in favour of the *creativity* of writing. As a result, convention and technique — as artificial, contrived, mechanical — are opposed to authorial expression, regarded as individual and spontaneous.

Linked with this 'creative process' is the modern assumption of the unique qualities of the author's vision, of the author's originality and individuality. Such a concept of the literary text as a natural, creative and unified expression from a gifted individual presents literature as a holistic, personal, and spontaneous interpretation of human experience, and thus obscures the process of the *production* of the literary text. The emphasis is not on the nature of the social and ideologically constructed artefact, but on its idiosyncratic interpretation of human experience.

Writing as authoring

This is very much the way in which writing is described in some of the influential school writing textbooks. Consider, for instance, this statement from James Moffett's *Active Voice,* one of the best-known and most widely cited school writing textbooks:

> Educators would do best, I submit, to conceive of writing, first of all, as full-fledged authoring, by which I mean authentic expression of an individual's own ideas, original in the sense that he or she has synthesized them for himself or herself. True authoring occurs naturally to the extent that the writer is composing with raw material, that is, source content not previously abstracted and formulated by others. Teaching aimed this way would emphasize subject matter lying easily at hand within and around the writer — firsthand content like feelings, fantasies, sensations, memories, and reflections, and secondhand content as drawn from interviews, stored information, and the writings of others to the extent that the writer truly abstracts these in his own synthesis. Insisting on maximum authorship should stave off the construing or treating of writing as only some sort of transcription or paraphrasing or verbal tailoring from ready-made cloth. (Moffett, 1981: 89)

Authoring, then, is considered to be the natural and authentic expression of individual subjectivity, and discourses about school writing provide interesting evidence of how such concepts have been constructed. The terms often used to describe authorship — original and creative writing — frequently include adjectives like these: personal, individual, spontaneous, natural, truthful, involved, emotional, real (see Gilbert, 1989, for a fuller discussion of this question). Many teachers will be familiar with such adjectives and comfortable with the dichotomy they establish: writing, assumed to be a natural act, must surely be most successful when it is personal, spontaneous, real, and least successful when it is impersonal, contrived, and artificial.

This emphasis on the natural, the personal, the spontaneous, is often typified in discussions of writing by the use of the metaphor 'personal voice'. Students are advised to find their own voices in writing, teachers are advised to listen to such voices, and a clear personal voice in writing is often regarded as the mark of an effective writer, an effective author. The assumptions on which this metaphor is based are perhaps worth reconsidering.

The metaphor and its associated adjectival terms share a clear commitment to an intensely personalized, individualistic and speech-oriented theory of writing. The view of writing that such concepts support is one which sees writing as 'the guise of speech' (Graves, 1983: 161): as a secondary language system that must always substitute for a missing human 'voice', presence, subject. Writing will thus always seem to be different from speech — and nobody would dispute that that is the case — but different because it has no human being or presence to 'speak'. Speech, because it is delivered by a human voice, is assumed to more natural, personal, individual, spontaneous, truthful, involved, emotional, real . . . Writing, then, in this argument, is at its best when it approximates the features of 'presence' that speech has.

Consider, for instance, how a professional writer and teacher of writing describes the way good writing works:

> The student, in his [sic] writing, is speaking. The student with his own tone of voice rises off the page, perhaps in just a phrase, a sentence, a few words, but enough to reveal his whole attitude, his point of view, his tone of voice. (Murray, 1982: 153)

Or read this recommendation for student writers offered by another well-known and well-published teacher:

> In your natural way of producing words there is a sound, a texture, a rhythm — a voice — which is the main source of power in your writing.

I don't know how it works, but this voice is the force that will make a
reader listen to you, the energy that drives the meaning through his
[*sic*] thick skull. (Elbow, 1973: 6)

Donald Graves calls personal voice in writing 'the imprint of ourselves on
our writing', and suggests that if the voice is missing 'there is no writing, just
words following words'. To take the voice away from writing is, Graves says,
like taking salt from stew, love from sex, or sun from gardening (Graves,
1983: 227). And yet school textbook writers are reticent to discuss how such
an obviously important writing quality might be taught, or even whether it
can be taught. A pattern emerges which claims that learning to write (and to
read) is natural: it is 'predominantly learnt rather than taught', argues Janet
Emig (1983: 140). Elbow says, 'I don't know how it works', and in fact all
that textbooks often advocate is a 'process writing' classroom structure
which assumes that the provision of the right environment will facilitate 'voice'.

If teachers claim that they can recognize personal voice (or 'authentic
authoring', or 'originality', or 'creativity') when they 'hear' it in a text, there
must be identifiable features of the text that have made such recognition
possible. And if that is what teachers want to read in student writing, these
features should be focused on in the classroom. To do otherwise is seriously
to disadvantage many students, both those who have not yet worked out
what particular teachers will 'hear', and those who genuinely believe that if
they write in their own 'voices' they will become successful writers.

A few comments from 16-year-old students perhaps demonstrate this
dilemma most tellingly. Some of these students had worked out what personal voice meant. Others had not.

> *Cathy:* If you're given a question to answer that's your opinion, then I
> feel that no-one can mark you on your own opinion. It's your own feel-
> ings, and nobody can assess anybody I feel on their own feelings.

> *Suzette:* With my reading journal, I got a B. I tried really hard to make
> it more personalized and I rigged the whole thing to make it look really
> personal, whereas all the other ones I'd done, I hadn't, and I'd been
> given really low marks.

> *Susan:* I was pleased when she [the teacher] said she enjoyed reading
> my journal and that I understand personal voice, because that was
> what I was trying to achieve. I was trying to show that I understood it.
> I was happy that she recognized it.

> *Shelley:* I try to work harder . . . try to write the way the teachers want
> me to write — try to figure out what each teacher, what way they like
> you writing to give you the best mark.

While Suzette and Susan claim to have cracked the code, Cathy and
Shelley have not. Cathy seems genuinely confused about how a person (here

the person and the writing are entangled) can be assessed and ranked, while Shelley is convinced that there must be a 'code', a way to write what teachers want — she just doesn't know what it is.

The authorship legacy

The classroom situation these students are grappling with is one that has prevailed for some time. It is a legacy of the language theories authorized by John Dixon's report of the proceedings of the Dartmouth conference held in the United Kingdom in 1966 (Dixon, 1967) — a report which urged 'personal growth' through English and established the Growth Model as the dominant approach to language learning. Subsequent work from James Britton (1970), and his colleagues (Britten *et al.*, 1975; Martin *et al.*, 1976) reinforced such approaches, particularly in terms of the development of writing abilities. More recently, such approaches to writing development have been complemented by a flourishing of personalist and idiosyncratic approaches to reading. Take, for instance, this explanation of the reading of works of art offered by Louise Rosenblatt:

> Every time a reader experiences a work of art, it is in a sense created anew. Fundamentally, the process of understanding a work implies a recreation of it, an attempt to grasp completely the structured sensations and concepts through which the author seeks to convey the quality of his [*sic*] sense of life. (Rosenblatt, 1976: 113)

Reader-response aesthetics, dominated within educational contexts by the work of Louise Rosenblatt and of Wolfgang Iser (1978), have become a dominant approach to secondary school reading, and a host of textbooks advocate the value of the personal, imaginative response to literature (Jackson, 1983; Corcoran & Evans, 1987).

But the difficultly has been that because such approaches to reading and writing cannot account for the social nature of language practices, they create considerable confusion and contradiction in social institutions like schools. A number of different and incompatible discourses mesh at the site of the classroom because schools are about — among other things — selection and sorting, discipline and punishment, knowledge and control. As a result, teachers and students need a socially critical understanding of the way language, particularly written language, works: the way in which it can be used to mystify, to exclude, to distort, to exonerate, or to delude. Such an understanding would seem to provide an infinitely better language base than one which almost implicity endorses a false innocence and neutrality in language, and thus makes dupes of its users.

I shall now consider some of the confusion that language theories can generate in classrooms, by presenting transcripts of several 16-year-old students and their English teacher discussing 'creative writing' (and its variants) set as a school task.

Confusion and Contradiction in Reading/Writing Classrooms

If writing is conceived of as natural — as personal, original creativity rather than social, textual construction — students may have considerable difficulty knowing how they can ever become 'better' writers, and teachers may have considerable difficulty deciding what can or should be taught about writing. Similarly, if reading is predominantly considered as personal discovery — both of an author's intention and of an individual reader's response to that intention — rather than as the application of a learned set of social reading practices, classroom reading is constantly hampered by a confused hunt for 'the personal' in a text, rather than the ideological or the social. The contradictions that result when writing is identified as a natural communication between writer and reader will be emphasized by drawing upon students' and teachers' perceptions of school writing.

Writing 'creatively'

Christine, a student who had repeated her final year and received an average grade for English, was rather disillusioned with English and convinced that there was no way in which she could improve her grades. When she got the results back for an 'imaginative story' she had written for assessment, she claimed that:

> I really dislike writing fantasy essays. It takes a lot of thinking and it's pretty hard to be original and to create characters. You've just got to be a bit wild in the mind to create really interesting characters. I'm terrible at writing fantasy essays. I'm just not creative.

However, another student — one who failed English that year — was far less discerning. When I talked to him before he wrote his 'imaginative essay', he told me that he was sure he would make a better job of this particular task, because in stories 'you can write anything you want':

> The story is better than other forms of writing because you can write what you want to write, type of thing. You're not set by guidelines on what you have to do . . . In a story, you can write it on anything you want, you know, anything you like type of thing.

His mate agreed with him, saying:

A story is sort of your ideas. They're easier to develop than other people's ideas. You're using your own ideas, and you're not trying to react in some way to a certain thing. You're just using your own ideas.

Both these students were obviously convinced that writing a story was a different exercise from other forms of writing, because there were no apparent guidelines: no expectations, no rules. It was personal ('your ideas') and unstructured ('you can write what you want'). Again, a romatic concept of literature dominates in their explanations of narrative construction: stories are created out of individual subjectivity.

However, being a 'creative' individual might well incur a penalty. Another student I talked to was quite confident that she was a creative and original person ('I like art'), but assumed that this prevented her from becoming a critical and rational writer:

Imaginative's my favourite choice of writing. I like art, I like creating. I always create at home. I paint when I feel like it, draw or write poems or anything like that so I suppose that's probably in my line I suppose. It just comes to me more easily than the other forms of writing . . . But when I deal with critical response, I really feel for the characters, so I can't really write down much about them . . . I can't criticize very well. I'm always in two minds about things.

Many of the students interviewed had convinced themselves that the reason for their lack of success in English was that they were not really 'creative' or 'original' people, and certainly the way in which 'creative writing' was treated in the classroom did nothing to alter this assumption. On the surface of things, creativity seemed to have little to do with text construction. Music was played as a stimulus for writing, students were encouraged to draw characters suitable for their stories, and the teacher urged the class to 'dredge up from your minds' descriptions and story ideas. The onus was on the students to 'use your imaginations' — not their textual repertoires — to create stories themselves.

Reading and Writing as Cultural Practice

So far I have argued that the use of concepts like 'authoring' in discourses about school reading and writing serves to perpetuate particular approaches to language development. Such concepts assume — on a simplistic level — that the most desirable form of writing ('authentic authoring') involves the original expression of individuality, whereas the least desirable form of writing ('verbal tailoring') involves the mere imitation of a known language system. I shall now suggest that such a dichotomy is not only inaccurate, but it is also harmful.

Given a fixed language system, the possibilities for generating original pieces of writing are seriously limited, and nowhere is this more obvious than in the close examination of literary texts. In *Literary Theory: An Introduction,* Terry Eagleton questions the linking of authorship to original creativity, and instead argues that literary construction is more akin to Moffett's 'verbal tailoring' concept:

> All literary texts are woven out of other literary texts, not in the conventional sense that they bear the traces of 'influence' but in the more radical sense that every word, phrase or segment is a reworking of the writings which precede or surround the individual work. There is no such thing as literary 'originality', no such thing as the 'first' literary work: all literature is intertextual. (Eagleton, 1983: 138)

His argument is that all texts are intertextual: all rely upon other texts and their placement in terms of other texts for any meanings they might be given. For instance, a child's reworking of the *Little Red Riding Hood* story derives its impact from its textual background — a far from innocent ideological background as Jack Zipes (1983) illustrates very well. Similarly, a child's poem derives its impact from the way in which it joins into and stands beside the vast textuality of lyrics and other verse that surround it.

Indeed this is precisely why writing can be such an enjoyable and satisfying activity for children. Once the vast world of textuality is introduced and explored (and this is clearly a role for the teacher), to write is to play with form, to juxtapose the unusual, to juggle with opposites, to parody, to imitate, to 'blend and clash' as Roland Barthes would say (1977: 146). In other words, writing is about constructing from within an available signifying system — working with the known. And the more texts children know, the more possibilities there are for play and construction.

'Authentic authoring' must rely, to a considerable extent, on imitating a known language system, because if it did not, it would be unreadable: unrecognizable, unidentifiable, unclassifiable. To suggest to teachers and to children that learning to write is not learning how writing has traditionally, generically, conventionally, and playfully functioned, is to do them a major disservice. It is to perpetuate the sort of confused powerlessness that the students in the preceding section of this chapter sometimes suggested.

However, while reading is obviously not always the same, it is misleading to think that reading is individualistic. Ian Hunter claims that while there are many different readings of texts, these readings are not just different

subjective experiences of the text. Instead, he argues that different readings
are 'the result of the application of different rules and practices of reading'
(Hunter, 1982: 86). Reading, then, is like writing: it is a learned cultural
practice and, as such, can be unpicked and examined.

Within an educational context, there are many examples of different
reading practices and of the way in which they may be culturally learned.
One of the best known would be that provided by Britton *et al.*'s study *The
Development of Writing Abilities (11–18)* (1975), which offered an implied
set of practices for producing what is called 'expressive', 'poetic' and 'transactional' writing, and which subsequently spawned an international reading
practice which emulated the rules that Britton's team had formulated. Similarly, Purves (1968) devised a set of practices for recognizing different types
of student response to literature, and again the practices were imitated and
used internationally.

Once reading is acknowledged as a cultural practice, the features of various readings can be examined and critiqued. The features of examiners'
readings, of literary critics' readings, of book judges' readings, of children's
readings, are all important for language teachers, as are, of course, the features of teachers' own different reading practices. The role that reading
plays in any discussion of writing can never be ignored. If the craft of writing
is to become accessible to students, reading — in its strongest sense —
becomes of paramount importance.

Authorship and Creativity in the Classroom

I shall now pose questions about some texts in light of my arguments in
this chapter. The first two pieces of writing come from students in their final
year of secondary school. I have deliberately chosen this level to begin with
because I want to emphasize how, for one of these students, twelve years of
schooling and of writing instruction has been largely unproductive. I shall
then look at two pieces from primary school students: students in the middle
of their compulsory schooling experience.

Authoring in the secondary school

Texts 1 and 2 are extracts from two first pages of a 'magazine' article
students in a year 12 class had been set as one of their school English assessment tasks. This is how the teacher described what they were to do:

> They were given a topic (Are creative writers always abnormal?) and
> they were given a set of information about those people — they were
> given a sheet about Shakespeare or Oscar Wilde etc. so that they did
> not have to research it — they just had to select the information they

wanted to use to back up their argument and we previewed that by a discussion in class about what was abnormal or not . . . After they'd written the first draft we talked about tone and I also read them out some examples from newspapers like the *Australian* that I told them they were trying to aim for, and showed them things. For instance, sophistication of language in the newspaper article — that's what I told them they were trying to aim for. I think they found that pretty difficult. They couldn't imagine that they would write anything like that so I am not sure how successful that was . . .

As it turned out, the magazine article was not very successfully completed, and in a subsequent interview, the teacher offered her reaction to the task:

The only one who did it well was Susan. The others didn't achieve that — well — funny blend between being personal writing and yet impersonal writing, because it's in a newspaper. They equate *personal* with 'I think', not with a style of writing. They don't seem to have that yet. But she did — but then, typical. She's a good English student and does most things well and understood what was wanted.

Both teacher transcripts illustrate some of the points made earlier in this chapter. The teacher was able to recognize a 'style of writing' when she read it, but she lacked the knowledge to deduce from her reading a set of distinguishing features of the style she wished the students to use. As a consequence, she was unable to teach it, and teacher education clearly has much to answer for in this regard. Very few pre- or in-service programmes provide teachers with an understanding of the ways in which language functions in social and cultural practice. At best, secondary English teachers receive some background in university-style literature study, but primary language arts teachers are often given little, if any, specialist language work.

As well, it is obvious from these transcipts that the 'good' English student was able to work out 'what was wanted', to do 'most things well', while less competent children were obviously disadvantaged by the lack of teaching and assistance provided by the teacher for this task. In addition, the teacher and many of the students had quite different perceptions of 'personal', the teacher regarding it as a style of writing, and the students as an indication of personal opinion.

Text 1 is the beginning of the first page of the assignment constructed by Susan, the student who 'did it well'. And text 2 is from the first page of Ken's assignment — a student who did not do well at all.

Initially, the differences in presentation are quite striking and, I would suggest, immediately help to frame the teacher's reading. More importantly, the 'authorship' of both works has influence in an interesting way:

Are creative writers always abnormal?

In many minds exists the notion of a creative writer. It may be the image of a balding poet, a poverous youth, cramped in a dismal attic weaving webs of delight and love. Or perhaps it's the image of an erotic and demonic soul, volatile in temper, unrestrained, wild and bizarre in manner. Whatever your fantasy lies, the perception of a ?writer is that he is inspirational, sensitive or different, thus abnormal.

Yes, we the majority believe creative writers are abnormal. What is abnormally? Is it an exception to the rule, a contrary spirit, the non-conformist, or is it as the dictionary defines something not usual, a deviation from normal? Thus all masterful writers who have won the fruits of success earn themselves distinction and diverge from the essence of the human race. They become celebrities.

Text 1 Extract from English assignment by 'good' student (reduced size).

ARE CREATIVE WRITERS ALWAYS
ABNORMAL

Most Creative writers have been said to have been abnormal but some are normal. These abnormal writers have different ways of putting their works across to the reader of these. Many have been many great writers of the past present who have been abnormal.

Like great number of Poets have shown their abnormality through their own writing + poetry. Some Example of these abnormally made of the Poet were Wilde, Johnson, Coleridge, Byron and to name a few. Article with a poet and playwright at the level of the 19 Century. The actel copyright made

Text 2 Extract from English assignment by less competent student (reduced size).

Susan's name activates particular teacher expectations, as does Ken's. The teacher expects to read Susan's work differently, expects to make meaning, expects to find something of interest. Consider these comments the teacher made to me about Susan's work:

> She immediately had that elevated literary type tone, that being personal, until in the first paragraph she used a word I had to look up in the dictionary to find out what it meant. So that sort of combination made it have an impact.

Not surprisingly, the teacher could not remember a great deal about Ken's assignment when she was interviewed, but she had written on the bottom of his work:

> Ken, you must proof-read *much* more carefully. A magazine article cannot have such basic errors . . .

Even a cursory reading of Ken's assignment will suggest to you that Ken needs to do more than proof-read more effectively, but the teacher felt rather helpless about what else she could suggest and was honest enough to admit this:

> In lots of cases I can say things like 'No — this isn't quite the tone of a newspaper article', but they honestly don't know how to get that tone, and I really don't know how to tell them. And I think that's frustrating . . .

When Susan was interviewed about her work, she explained how she had worked on the magazine article:

> I tried to write really sophisticated, and tried to be really fluent — not stop and start sort of thing. I'm usually stopping and starting. I tried to be more fluent and also to put in lots of big words and things used in the magazines. I got a thesaurus out and sat down and went all the way through it to sort of get words to go with what I was doing.

Susan was able to do more than use 'big words' in her assignment. She demonstrates her awareness of a number of features common to some forms of journalism: the first person plural pronouns, the rhetorical questions, the pairs of juxtaposed sentences. Notice, too, the control she has over sentence introductions and sentence patterns, compared with those in Ken's text. It is interesting to notice that the question mark is missing from Ken's headline, and that his assignment reads like a school essay on abnormality. Ken does not pose a mock internal debate in his assignment. Instead, he has written paragraphs from the notes the teacher gave to the class.

In many ways, the teacher in this classroom tried to set up an exercise for her students which followed most of the prescriptions contemporary writing pedagogy advocates. She framed the purpose and audience of the task, she initiated discussion and some reading beforehand, and she provided the students with information to write about. But she couldn't teach the class the typical generic expectations of this style of writing: she couldn't break down the particular linguistic features of texts that are often recognized as journalistic opinion. Most of the class didn't know how to organize given pieces of information into an acceptable journalistic format, and merely being told the audience and the purpose for this task was no compensation for them. As adults we might well know by whom a legal document is to be read and what its purpose might be, but most of us would still be unable to construct an appropriate legal text — one that would be recognized as conventional and appropriate by the legal profession.

Authoring in the primary school

While it is common to see senior secondary school students trying their hands at a number of different writing forms — in fact that is usually a requirement of any writing curriculum in the secondary school — in the primary school it is unfortunately much more common to see writing classrooms almost totally preoccupied with story writing. However, despite an emphasis on writing narratives in the first years of formal schooling, many children's understanding of the literary devices of written narratives is slight.

Consider, for instance, these two stories (texts 3 and 4) about sea creatures written by 10-year-olds. The first is given to you in its entirety; the second is the first page only of a four-page narrative.

The Sea Creature

In the town of Jughead some people saw a strange sea-creature. One day a child went swimming at the beach. He was in the water and a sea creature attacked the boy and he was gobbled up. The same day a twelve-year-old child saw the sea creature. There were four investigators, Russell, Peter, Keith and myself, Len. The four of us went to see the twelve-year-old boy. He said the sea creature looked like it had red eyes and it was green.

One day I said, 'Let's go to spy on the sea creature.' So we did. We went to the top of the hill. We pitched the tent on the hill. The first night Keith was looking out for the sea creature. When Keith fell asleep, the sea creature popped up and ate him. The next day we found Keith dead.

The next night I had a laser pistol and the sea creature came up and I shot at him but missed. At twelve o'clock that night Peter was on guard but he went to sleep and the sea creature came up to eat him. Russell woke up first and found Peter dead. I saw a hand-print and I checked it with Russell's hand-print. The sea creature came up. I saw it and I raced for the laser pistol. I shot the sea creature but it wasn't a sea creature — IT WAS A MAN!

Text 3 Story by 10-year-old.

Clanie the Seamonster

Clanie was a seamonster that lived in the spooky, misty and scary swamps of Shoogolas.

Clanie had big green eyes and long black eyelashes. Great big spikes on her back made her look terribly, awfully scary. She had a long, long tail with a very sharp point at the end. Clanie was a very shy sort of monster but although she tried not to show it, Clanie could be very angry when somebody interrupted her graceful sleeping. She sleeps like a tyre in the water — she drifts.

One day I was walking on the banks of the Shoogolas swamp when I saw the strangest creature. I described it as 'the strangest thing that ever met my eye'. I froze as I saw it. I don't know what came over me but I started screaming! The animal dashed underwater with a great shock. The water turned green and back to blue again. In two minutes all this had escaped from my mind. I went home that night forgetting all about the sea creature . . .

Text 4 First part of story by 10-year-old.

In this class, both students were identified as 'authors' and both had constructed these stories in the class writing time scheduled daily. The teacher had suggested that the theme of 'sea monster/sea creature' might be a good writing topic, and these students had both chosen to write on that theme. Even when the stories are printed — as they are here — with due regard to conventional spelling, punctuation, and paragraphing, I think there are several differences between them which indicate something of the likely success these students will have in writing classrooms of the future.

While both students construct feasible narratives, text 4 draws more obviously upon literary narrative conventions. Note the title, the first sentence formatted on its own, the concern to provide a verbal picture of the narrative's central character, the use of figurative language. Consider, too, the literary conventions employed in constructing the pattern of events: an important non-human character is introduced, then set aside temporarily; a moment of high significance occurs and is effectively noted; readers gain privileged information and are invited to suspend their disbelief. When *Clanie the Seamonster* is set beside *The Sea Creature,* we can see marked textual differences: differences obviously in length and complexity of the narrative, but also differences in the level of sentence variations and range of vocabulary employed, and differences in mastery and understanding of literary convention. Being able to write an effective short story (an 'original' short story?) has much to do with all these. For those teachers familiar with the short stories that many 10–15-year-olds write, *The Sea Creature* will sound depressingly familiar. Many students never progress beyond a basic competence with subject-verb agreement and spelling and punctuation conventions; they never progress to an understanding of the conventions of literary narratives. And some of this failure to master the conventions of literary 'authorship' must lie in the mistaken belief that writing is not craft but imagination; not construction but creation. Is it creative imagination that will let the writer of *The Sea Creature* do well in secondary school? Or is it an understanding of the recognizable generic conventions that he will be expected to reproduce?

The role of the teacher

Throughout the chapter I have tried to argue for an important role for the teacher in reading/writing classrooms. While the roles of facilitator, organizer and supporter (editor?) may indeed be useful for teachers, they can merely supplement the main role, which is to make written language accessible to students — *all* students. Of course the craft of writing can be taught to students, as those fortunate few who have been taught could well testify. Many adult writers will remember with gratitude the teacher/ lecturer/friend/editor who taught them aspects of how language forms are constructed, and may perhaps wish that many more such people had crossed their paths.

Learning how to write an effective short story or a modern lyric can be compared with learning how to participate in a formal debate, or learning how to chair a meeting. Interestingly enough, it seems easier for teachers to accept that the craft of speech making can be taught than that the craft of writing can. Similarly, one might wonder why the construction of visual art forms — particularly film — is so readily associated with skill and craft. Types of shots, colour, locales, motifs, musical score, actors: the tools of the film director's craft seem readily understood and accepted.

Any semiotic system has rules and conventions — arbitrary and cultural though they are — to which some people have greater access than others. A language is a semiotic system of primary importance, particularly in learning, and any attempt to provide greater equality of access to this system seems to me to be an important part of what literacy learning should be about, and to be an important role for schools. By placing such an emphasis on the personal and idiosyncratic aspects of literacy learning, as often applies in schools today, the social and constructed nature of language tends to be obscured. Concepts like authorship focus on the creation of a text, on the originality of a text, on particular emotional qualities of a text — but not on *how* a text has been made. The making of a text demands that attention be paid both to textual construction and to reading practices: to the social and cultural nature of literacy.

Rather than authorizing disadvantage by focusing onthe mystique of authorship, could we not instead promote critical social literacy by focusing on the cultural construction of reading and writing practices? The way forward lies in shedding much of the unnecessary personal and romantic 1960s discourse while holding firm to its important emphases on children's needs and rights. A fresh look at the basics will start with where children are, and will value the experiences they have. But it will also endeavour to extend them through challenging new learning, and this will necessarily involve introducing them to the broadest possible range of texts, for it is in these that many new forms of experience reside.

Acknowledgments

Thanks to Bill Corcoran, Allan Luke, and Geoff Ward for their advice on earlier drafts of this chapter.

References

Barthes, R. (1977) *Image Music Text* (S. Heath, Trans.). London: Fontana.

Bourdieu, P. (1973) Cultural reproduction and social reproduction. In R. Brown (ed.) *Knowledge, Education, and Cultural Change: Papers in the Sociology of Education.* London: Tavistock Publications.

Britton, J. (1970) *Language and Learning.* Harmondsworth, Middlesex: Penguin.

Britton, J., Burgess, T., Martin, N., McLeod, A. and Rosen, H. (1975) *The Development of Writing Abilities (11–18).* London: Schools Council Publications.

Corcoran, B. and Evans, E. (eds) (1987) *Readers, Texts, Teachers.* Montclair, NJ: Boynton/Cook Publishers Inc.

Dixon, J. (1967) *Growth Through English.* London: Oxford University Press.

Eagleton, T. (1983) *Literary Theory: An Introduction.* Oxford: Basil Blackwell Publishers.

Elbow, P. (1973) *Writing Without Teachers.* London: Oxford University Press.

Emig, J. (1983) *The Web of Meaning.* Monclair, NJ: Boynton/Cook Publishers Inc.

Gilbert, P. (1989) *Writing, Schooling and Deconstruction: From Voice to Text in the Classroom.* London: Routledge & Kegan Paul.

Graves, D. (1983) *Writing: Teachers and Children at Work.* London: Heinemann Educational Books.

Hunter, I. (1982) The concept of context and the problem of reading. *Southern Review* 15 (1), 80–91.

Iser, W. (1978) *The Act of Reading.* London: Routledge & Kegan Paul.

Jackson, D. (1983) *Encounters With Books: Teaching Fiction 11–16.* London: Methuen Educational.

Moffett, J. (1981) *Active Voice.* Montclair, NJ: Boynton/Cook Publishers Inc.

Murray, D. (1982) *Learning by Teaching.* Montclair, NJ: Boynton/Cook Publishers, Inc.

Purves, A. (with Rippere, V.) (1968). *Elements of Writing About a Literary Work: A Study of Response to Literature.* Urbana, IL: National Council of Teachers of English.

Rosenblatt, L. (1976) *Literature as Exploration* (3rd ed.). London: Routledge & Kegan Paul.

Zipes, J. (1983) *The Trials and Tribulations of Little Red Riding Hood: Variations of the Tale in Sociolcultural Context.* London: Heinemann.

19 What Do We Mean by Knowledge About Language?

JOHN RICHMOND

As a phrase, it is like many another in education. People have started to slip it into their conversation with that beguiling confidence which suggests that, of course, they understand perfectly well what they mean by knowledge about language. Knowledge about language. Knowing things about language. Being interested in and informed about language. Seems harmless enough: in fact, it seems like something that every teacher of language or English should have in some measure. There is one worrying thing: the phrase has begun to be written with capital letters (Knowledge about Language) or even abbreviated to KAL. A few people — the sort who are always doing this kind of thing — actually use a new word, kal, to rhyme with pal, in their everyday vocabulary. More seriously still, it is in the National Curriculum. It seems that we shall have to attend to it.

A Bit of History

In tracing the history of the phrase, we need to go back as far as the HMI booklet, *English from 5 to 16,* published in 1984. It proposed that teachers should be promoting children's development as speakers and listeners, readers and writers. It said, fourthly, that teachers should:

> teach pupils about language, so that they achieve a working knowledge of its structures and of the variety of ways in which meaning is made, so that they have a vocabulary for discussing it, so that they can use it with greater awareness, and because it is interesting.

From the perspective of 1990, this proposal, quoted in isolation from the rest of the booklet, interpreted generously, sounds like something we could live with and even in some respects (discussing the variety of ways in which meaning is made, for example) get excited about. Reading the booklet as a whole at the time, however, weighing up what its author might really have in mind as the more important things to teach pupils about language, and putting these thoughts next to worries about other aspects of the booklet (its proposals for age-related objectives for pupils at seven, 11 and 16, its narrow, muddled and often backward-looking collection of statements about what a language or English curriculum should contain), most people came to the conclusion that the booklet was once again proposing something which had been vigorously debated for the previous 20 years and rejected. This is the tempting idea that, in order to help children get better at using an element of language, teachers need to give them a set of rules, definitions and distinctions about that element in advance. We can put the tempting idea in a diagram, clearly marked for what it is:

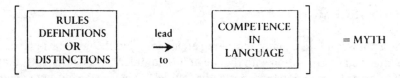

The particular topic of dispute in this part of *English from 5 to 16* and in people's responses to it was, of course, grammar teaching and whether we need to get back to it. Overwhelmingly, those who wrote down their responses to the booklet and sent them in to HMI said: no. When HMI published *English from 5 to 16: the Responses to Curriculum Matters 1* in 1986, they acknowledged the degree of dissent from the original booklet on this and other topics. They suggested that it might be a good idea to have an enquiry, 'with the ultimate object of drawing up recommendations as to what might be taught [about language] to intending teachers, to those in post and to pupils in schools'. (It might have been an even better idea, instead of leaving *English from 5 to 16* and the responses booklet dangling as two contradictory documents for teachers to pay their money and take their choice, to provide a single revised booklet which really did aim to summarise the best recent thinking about what the language and English curriculum should look like. That, after all, was the aim of the series of which *English from 5 to 16* was the first number.)

Good Idea Becomes Committee

The reader may be tiring of this ancient history. We will move on quickly. The good idea about an enquiry became the Kingman Committee, which produced its report in March 1988. On the particular question of grammar teaching, it declared:

> Nor do we see it as part of our task to plead for a return to old-fashioned grammar teaching and learning by rote. We have been impressed by the evidence we have received that this gave an inadequate account of the English language by treating it virtually as a

branch of Latin, and constructing a rigid prescriptive code rather than a dynamic description of language in use. It was also ineffective as a means of developing a command of English in all its manifestations. Equally, at the other extreme, we reject the belief that any notion of correct or incorrect use of language is an affront to personal liberty. We also reject the belief that knowing how to use terminology in which to speak of language is undesirable.

This statement, quoted from chapter 1 of the Kingman Report, was greeted by a large sigh of relief all round, although there was some puzzlement that the Committee had apparently discovered groups of teachers who refused to accept that there was such a thing as an incorrect use of language and never used any terminology in their teaching, and had felt that this tendency was as dangerous as 'old-fashioned grammar teaching and learning by rote'. The report then devotes the whole of chapter 2 to a discussion called 'the importance of knowledge about language'. In fact chapter 2 is not principally about the importance of knowledge about language: it is principally about the importance of language. The chapter says some fine and true things in a general kind of way. For example:

> People need expertise in language to be able to participate effectively in a democracy . . .

> The acquisition of new and difficult concepts, which is integral to education in any subject, is dependent above all on language . . .

> . . . language plays an important role both in exploring and defining responses and feelings and in shaping the kind of people we become.

Not Enough Main Verbs . . . Too Many Pronouns

Chapter 2 is at its weakest, interestingly enough, when it has to commit itself to examples in the section on 'The teaching of language'. We are introduced to a pupil who 'keeps on omitting main verbs from sentences' and told that the pupil would start including main verbs in sentences if he or she were taught the definition and function of a verb. Another pupil, who makes excessive use of pronouns, would be helped to check this habit if similarly taught the definition and function of a pronoun. These are unfortunate examples. I would be glad to meet a pupil who kept on omitting main verbs from sentences. A pupil who had used a verb incorrectly in a sentence would be helped to spot and overcome that difficulty by being asked to read the sentence back and compare the form of the verb as written with the form which he or she, as an experienced user of the language, knows to be correct. The likely cause of the incorrect usage in the first place is that pressure of production of writing has caused a temporary derailment of the trains of grammatical connection between brain and pen. If the writer, guided by the teacher, becomes a critical reader of his or her writing, he or she will solve the problem quickly enough. Similarly, the user of over-frequent pronouns is a type I have not so far met. Much more common is the opposite case: children who, for a while, make repetitive use of nouns in writing because they are not yet confident of the job that pronouns can do in their place. Here again, the advance abstract knowledge of the definition and function of a pronoun will not help. We shall come back to this example later, with some suggestions about what might help. We should just note here, however, the central point that when children compose texts — when they write — they should concentrate on meaning, not on pronouns.

A Language Model

The Kingman Report proposed, in chapter 3, a model of the English language. In detail, there is much to criticise in it on the grounds of obscurity, confusion or omission. It would not be especially interesting to the reader to do that here. In the broadest of terms, the model does, to its credit, say that if we are going to talk about language, we must remember that language is more than just forms. Language *is* to do with forms ('verb' and 'pronoun' are ways of talking about two particular kinds of word doing particular jobs in sentences or other groups of linked words) but it is also to do with the way that speakers and listeners, readers and writers behave towards each other in different contexts; it is also to do with how people acquire and develop a repertoire of competence in language from infancy onwards; it is also to do with the fact that there are variations — of accent and dialect, for example — within any language. We might add that there are variations between languages, important relationships between them, as well as variations within a language. The Kingman Committee was obliged to confine itself to the discussion of English. In fact, the categories it proposes in its model — forms; speaker/listener, reader/writer relationships; acquisition and development; variation — are equally relevant to any language. It would, furthermore, have been good to see multilingualism (a key element, after all, of the language experience of about 70 per cent of the world's population, including many of the children we teach) presented as an integral part of a model of language as a whole.

The dissemination of Kingman's model is, strictly, the purpose for which the government found £15.2 million to be spent by LEAs in England and Wales between 1989 and 1992. Hard on the heels of the Kingman Report, however, has come the National Curriculum for English. It was recognised that any attempt to disseminate a set of ideas about language which failed to notice that teachers' overriding preoccupation at the moment is with the introduction of the National Curriculum would, to put it mildly, have a credibility problem. It is also the case that the Cox Report discusses knowledge about language, in the chapter with that name and also in the chapters on Standard English and on linguistic terminology, and that the Cox Committee has proposed elements of knowledge about language which will be part of the statutory curriculum for English for pupils working at level 5 and above, and has suggested that opportunities for pupils to develop their knowledge about language should be available from the beginning of schooling. So, in addition to the need to discuss teachers' knowledge about language in ways that will seem relevant to teachers amid all their current concerns, we should try to clarify what we mean by pupils' knowledge about language, and see how the two things interact — as of course they must — and what the similarities and differences between them might be. Let us look at some examples of classroom language use to help us do this.

The Development of Implicit Knowledge

First, let us look at the piece of writing by Leanne, aged six, which appears on page 282.

Next, on page 283 there are the first four pages, in reduced size, of a book produced by a class of infants, called *Would you be Scared?* (The teacher has written out the text at the children's instruction.)

The most important kind of knowledge about language is implicit knowledge. Language is such a complex network of meanings and symbols, and the knowledge which users of a language share is so detailed and so vast, that the learning brain, engaged from birth on its enormous task, necessarily operates mainly using the powerful levers of unconscious learning. It could only be that way, for life is not long enough for the conscious acquisition of language to the degree that human beings require and employ it. The gear would be too low, the pace too slow. Much mystery still surrounds the exact mechanisms by which the brain experiences language in the world, and remembers, selects, sorts, extrapolates, generalises; in short, how it draws on experience to develop its own competence, and how experience and competence grow together. The most important job for the adults who care for the child is to help the child's implicit knowledge develop. For teachers, this means providing a classroom environment which supports and affirms the child's achievements, while continually proposing activities calling forth greater powers of articulation and understanding. The essential business of the language and English curriculum is, in fact, to provide opportunities for pupils to compose, communicate and comprehend meanings, their own and other people's, in purposeful contexts. Within these contexts, pupils' competence as users of language develops. Pupils' language competence is their

24th march Tuesday my mummy is
on the 25 of march thats tomoreco
today my mammy is going in too
to hospidil I will Be loney
with out my mammy the
Baby that She is going to
have is going to Be called
Sadie and its going to Be
a girl. We are all atsitde
Me and my mummy
wanted a girl and my
Dally wonted a Boy. My
mummy has got a lucky
dip For me and you have
to pick a number betwen
L and 11 and you get a
paper Bag with a present in
it. And She has Bourt me the
Book oF the little prinsess
so that She can read it to
Me so that I dont get
Bord. When She is Born
I will read here a
Story and it mite go like
this. once down a Dark
oark hole in a Dark
hall there lived a
Bager he was gray
on top Black.....

Leanne
Top Infant

implicit knowledge put to work, as in our two examples. Thousands of examples of implicit knowledge put to work are produced in classrooms every week. The reader will perhaps, however, have noticed some features about the examples presented here which can extend our understanding of implicit knowledge. Leanne offers us a story within a story. At the point when the *she* of her own story changes from a reference to her mummy to a reference to her expected sister (would lessons on pronouns help at this point?) she decides to draw on an event in her own reading, with the proper sense that what has been good for her is likely to be good for Sadie. Of course, simply

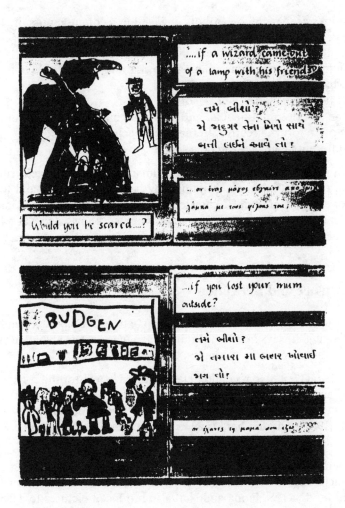

to repeat *Funnybones* word for word would lack ingenuity (or perhaps frighten one so young) so Sadie is to hear of badgers down holes instead of skeletons in cellars. Leanne's pleasure in reading or hearing *Funnybones* is finding a practical application in her writing. The application 'shows', in a way that we find charming. Older writers learn how to cover their tracks.

Would you be Scared? has its origin in a genre of children's book which, starting from a simple but large question (as here) or statement ('If I could have my favourite wish I would . . .', 'I'm happy/unhappy when I . . .'), branches out into many possibilities. The children who produced this book have encountered some of the genre. In producing their own book, they have realised or furthered their understanding that:

- books are 'made' by authors engaged in a common pursuit. There is nothing essential that divides the children from the authors of commercially published and widely distributed books;
- authors borrow ideas from each other and work within conventions which they find effective;
- texts and images need each other;
- the world is multilingual, and many languages have highly developed written forms, greatly different from each other;
- different languages can do a similar job equally well.

In other words, the book, whose primary purpose is to tell truths and explore fantasies in an entertaining way, and which is first and foremost another example of implicit knowledge put to work, causes us to imagine a whole collection of conversations where implicit knowledge was advanced by moments of explicit comparison and reflection.

Competence and Reflection

We can explore further the relationship between competence and reflection, looking at ways in which children's language use is helped forward by reflection, in some more examples.

Fiona and Neil, two reception-class children in a Shropshire school, have already appeared in *Responding to and Assessing Writing,* one of the collections of the work of the National Writing Project (published by Thomas Nelson, 1989). Quoted here is an account of a series of dialogues between them.

> Fiona and Neil were invited by their teacher, Sheila Hughes, to help each other to write, once a week. Fiona wrote herself and Neil dictated to the teacher. Fiona and Neil also produced pictures to accompany the text. Each week they exchanged their writing, read each other's work, and made comments which the teacher wrote underneath. These are some extracts:
>
> **Week 1**
> *Fiona wrote:* 'I like black because I had a toy black dog and I have always wanted a real life black dog.'
> *Neil commented:* 'She could have made it better if she'd put legs on the dog.'
> *Neil wrote:* 'I like yellow wallpaper and I am going to ask my dad if I can have some.'
> *Fiona commented:* 'He should have put "wallpaper" at the end of his story.'

Week 2

Fiona wrote: 'Red makes my Mummy happy. She has a red Renault 5 car and there is a lot of room in the boot.'

Neil commented: 'She should have put spokes on the wheels and two lights front and back.'

Neil wrote: 'This is a red lorry and I like it.'

Fiona commented: 'He should have said where the lorry was going and why he liked it'.

The teacher was, at first, a little discouraged. The children seemed rather negative in their comments and Neil seemed to be concerned only with the drawing. However, they were revealing considerable knowledge about the needs of text and drawings, and they wanted to continue. After six weeks observable changes had occurred.

Week 6

Fiona wrote: 'The bear is trying to get some honey out of a tree. He looks very cuddly but really he is dangerous.'

Neil commented: 'Draw a bigger tree. It is a good story.'

Neil wrote: 'My teddy bear is sitting by a tree thinking about doing something naughty.'

Fiona commented: 'Ears and paws on the bear. I would like to know what naughty things this bear was going to do.'

Flickering into life (stronger so far in Fiona — the more advanced writer — than in Neil) is a critical awareness of a writer's responsibilities and choices. The children are interchanging, productively, the roles of writer and reader. Reflection of this kind on writing, if sustained throughout a writer's development, will significantly help that development; the eye of the reader informing the voice of the writer.

Evacuees on Best Behaviour

One more example of the relationship between doing and reflecting. A group of 60 pupils, with two teachers plus a visitor working together, is considering the wartime evacuation of children as part of a sequence of work on the second world war. The children divide into groups of four. Two take on the role of evacuee 'parents' and two the role of evacuated children. The scene for their improvisation is the railway station in a small Welsh village where 'parents' and children meet for the first time. The groups work on this for 15 minutes, while the teachers move round, listening, helping when asked and noting down observations. Then some of the groups perform their improvisations.

At this point, the teachers ask the children how they felt in role. The children give general answers: 'all right', 'good', 'fine'. Up to now, they have not had any experience of reflecting on their role-play. The teachers want to prompt the children to be more specific in their reflection. The visitor role-plays being a child at home talking with a friend or sibling. The children agree that the teacher's speech style was authentic for that situation. The teacher then mimics the careful, precise speech used by the children in role as evacuees. The children are asked why they spoke in that way. Now they reply: 'for politeness', 'to show that we had good behaviour', 'so that they (the new "parents") would choose and accept us', 'to make a good impression'. The teachers point out to the children how easily they slid from an everyday speech style to more formal language use when they were in role.

As a result of this activity, which depends, it will be noticed, on a crucial and exposed piece of adult intervention in role, children's understanding of an aspect of the way speech varies according to situation is very likely to develop. Both the teachers and I, however, would hesitate to claim that the activity would certainly produce, in any direct sense, children who varied their own speech according to situation more appropriately and skilfully. It might; but even if it did, that was not the main purpose of the activity, which was to enhance the children's understanding of an important aspect of human language behaviour (and to teach persuasively about evacuees).

So, discussing the relationship between competence and reflection, we need first to reverse the equation on page 278, and then to introduce a degree of variation and honest doubt. The nature of the relationship depends on the language activity in which learners are engaged and upon the stage of development which individuals have reached. For example, a pre-school child learning to talk is acquiring and demonstrating large amounts of implicit knowledge, but there would be no point in engaging the child in reflection on the psycholinguistic processes involved. But the same young child, introduced to picture books, will immediately be reflecting on the organisation of words and images there. Meanwhile, older pupils reading poetry are likely to benefit as future readers of poetry if the teacher provides opportunities for reflection on the structure, content and background of the poems being studied, and on the particular characteristsics of poetic language.

Figure 1 on page 287 attempts to visualise the relationship between competence and reflection.

Terminology and Understanding

The reader will notice the phrase 'appropriate use of terminology' on the diagram. There has been much misunderstanding of this issue and false

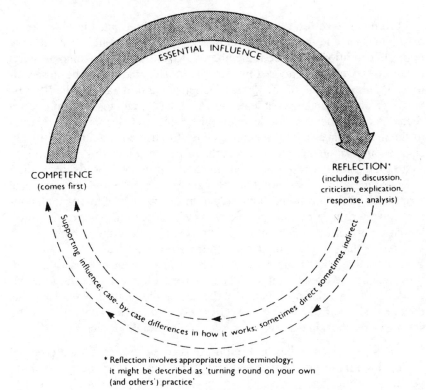

COMPETENCE
(comes first)

REFLECTION*
(including discussion,
criticism, explication,
response, analysis)

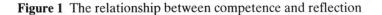

* Reflection involves appropriate use of terminology;
it might be described as 'turning round on your own
(and others') practice'

Figure 1 The relationship between competence and reflection

accusation of teachers on the subject. It has been suggested that teachers are afraid to call a spade a spade (a metaphor a metaphor, speech marks speech marks) because they have some hypersensitivity about pupils' ability to make sense of technical terms or, worse, because they don't know what such things are any more. (Once upon a time they did, of course.) I presume that no reader of this article is afraid, in principle, of the word *word* (a meta-linguistic category which, at an early point in their language development, children have to a come to understand) or *sentence* (though to use the term *sentence* in purposeful discussions with pupils is a very different thing from defining in an abstract way that thing which comes between a capital letter and a full stop) or *story* or *play* or *character* or *chapter* or *rhyme* or *text* or *image.* The central principle that should guide teachers in their decisions as to the use of terminology with pupils is that the introduction of terminology must be based on some prior conceptual understanding of what the termino-logy refers to.

I promised to return to the case of the writer who is in a phase where he or she makes repetitive use of nouns when pronouns could help out (the opposite condition, it will be remembered, to that which Kingman purports to have discovered). I choose this example for closer attention because sentence grammar is one of the areas of language and metalanguage (that is, language about language) in learning which has been most fought over in recent decades; because top-level disagreement over this small (in relation to the major concerns of the language and English curriculum) but highly charged area is the main reason why the project of which this publication is a part exists; and because a provision in the Programme of Study for Writing at Key Stage 1 unrealistically requires teachers to teach pupils 'grammatical terms such as . . . pronoun' (admittedly 'in the context of discussion about their own writing') by the age of seven. We noticed in passing 'Leanne's immature use of *she* which does not acknowledge that a new person is being referred to (hardly an example of 'scattering words such as *she* . . . throughout a text', to quote Kingman). I would challenge anyone to insist that, even if the teacher decided that it would be appropriate to draw Leanne's attention to this usage, the introduction of the term *pronoun* itself would help this confident six-year-old writer. But let us take a somewhat older writer, and see how a teacher, in discussion with the writer, might proceed.

Let us say that teacher and pupil are discussing a draft of a piece of personal writing about the writer's family. There has already been some conversation about the content and organisation of this piece — about what it is telling the reader. The teacher then says: 'You see where you've put *my aunty* all these times here . . . three, four times? Can you think of another word to put instead of some of the later ones, to make it less repetitive?' At this point, the pupil will respond in one of two ways. In the one case, he or she will say: 'I could put in *she*', in which case the teacher knows that the child understands implicitly the function of a pronoun in writing in those places in the text, and suggests that the child should put some in where they would help. The teacher also remarks: 'Words like *she* are pronouns. They stand in for words or phrases (like *my aunty*) which they refer to.' In the other case, the child will not make sense of the teacher's question, because it is pitched conceptually too far in advance of the child's current stage of development as a writer. In that case, the teacher's best professional judgement is a decision *to do nothing*. The child needs more experience of writing and of reading. In the first case the teacher did discover a piece of implicit knowledge which he or she was able to help the child turn into an explicit operation on the text. But even in that case, the teacher made an important distinction between helping the child to see the need to put in *she* (the first priority) and teaching the term *pronoun* (the second priority). The analytical statement about pronouns had a chance of making sense; interestingly, its principal use in the future will be to the child as a talker about texts, as a reader (the texts will, certainly, include some of the child's own writing) rather than directly to the child as a composer of texts, a writer. The learning of terminology from one mode of language often proves most useful to the learner in another mode.

All areas of the language and English curriculum carry terminology, of course; it is not confined to grammar, nor to writing conventions, nor to literary terms. There is no need for teachers to be intimidated by terminology, as long as they are satisfied that it will help pupils to reflect more effectively on language in use. We could set the terms we have used so far within a potentially endless list: *word, sentence, speech mark, metaphor, text, noun, pronoun, genre, paragraph, intonation, accent, alphabet, improvise, role, fiction, database, script, caption, camera angle*; an assortment of terms, some little and some large, all signifying important concepts or referring to potentially valid activities in the language curriculum. The Cox Report sensibly resisted pressure to insist on a roll-call of terms that pupils must have been introduced to during particular Key Stages (with a few exceptions such as the grammatical terms for Writing at Key Stage 1). If we ask ourselves, when in doubt, 'Will this piece of terminology serve meaning?', that will help us in the fine judgements we have to make.

Knowledge About Language and Language Study

The Cox Report recommended: 'Knowledge about language should be an integral part of work in English, not a separate body of knowledge to be added on to the traditional English curriculum' (*English for ages 5 to 16*, 6:2). This means that opportunities for the development of knowledge about language should be found throughout the whole language and English curriculum: speaking and listening, reading, writing, drama, media education and information technology. Such opportunities exist laterally across this range for children of a particular age. They also exist vertically, 'from play activities in pre-school to explicit systematic knowledge in upper secondary education' (ibid., 6:16). In addition to all these opportunities (of which we have already looked at several examples), where children's knowledge about language is being developed, as it were, in the course of other enquiries, the Cox Report said that there ought to be occasions on which children study aspects of language itself, in its own right. Certainly, the requirement in the Programme of Study for Speaking and Listening at Key Stage 2 that pupils should discuss vocabulary specific to local communities, local usages, particular age groups and certain occupations will probably best be met satisfactorily by the teacher devoting a series of lessons to that topic, although the requirement is likely also to be met to an extent in the course of pupils' wider learning. The same would be true of the requirement in the Programme of Study for Reading at Key Stage 4 that 'Pupils should consider not only the extent to which English has changed from the earliest written records, but also ways in which it is changing now.'

Requirements like these are the legal minimum of what might constitute language study: formally, they apply only to pupils working at levels 5 to 10. It would be useful to have some headings for language study, including but not confined to the legal minimum, of potential use throughout all the Key Stages. Suppose we settled on:

- variety in and between languages;
- history of languages;
- language and power in society;
- acquisition and development of language;
- language as a system shared by its users.

Interestingly, our five headings closely resemble Kingman's four headings for teachers' knowledge about language. We have given 'history of languages' a category of its own; 'language and power in society' would take speaker/listener, reader/writer relationships and put them in a broader context, including consideration of mass uses of language; 'language as a system shared by its users' is a bigger and better way of talking about forms. It goes without saying that all these headings overlap, and that their realisation in the curriculum would be through actual examples and experiences of language in use, not through their presentation *as* categories.

Knowledge About Language in the Whole Curriculum

In this article, we have considered pupils' implicit knowledge of language, their reflection on language use (their own and other people's) and the study of language itself. Figure 2 attempts to relate these three things within a whole language curriculum. It is not of course, 'to scale' as an indication of the amounts of time which might be spent on each of its elements; and it should not be forgotten that the development of competence and implicit knowledge remains the fundamental purpose of the language and English curriculum. The area of greatest overlap in the middle of the diagram is not, by that token, the most important thing in the curriculum.

Four notes on the diagram:

(1) The shaded areas in the diagram will often involve use of appropriate linguistic terminology.
(2) The areas of reflective learning will also provide significant opportunities to teachers and pupils for assessing pupils' developing language competence; identifying their achievements and needs.

(3) The Knowledge about Language requirements of Programmes of Study in English all fall within the shaded areas: the areas of reflective learning and the area of language study. The diagram also relates these requirements to the wider elements of the English curriculum as identified in Programmes of Study.

(4) The inclusion of drama, media texts and information technology within speaking and listening, reading and writing is intended to suggest the broadest definition of these language modes. The diagram does not mean to suggest, however, that drama, media texts and information technology can be confined within the modal categories. For example, drama is of course more than speaking and listening (and sometimes, as in mime, something other than speaking and listening).

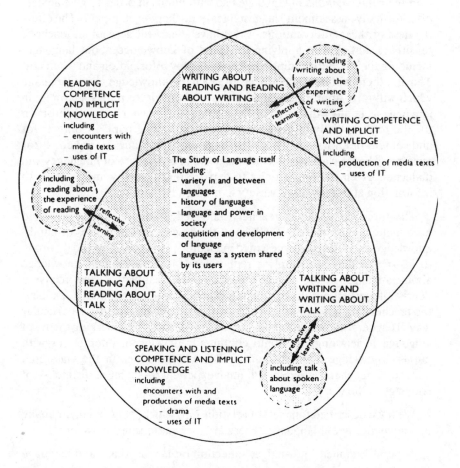

Figure 2 Knowledge about language in the whole curriculum

Pupils and Teachers: The Classroom and the World

Finally, let us try to summarise the relationship between *pupils'* and *teachers'* knowledge about language. Teachers, like pupils, already have much valuable knowledge about language derived from their experience as human beings in the world. There is no hard line dividing teachers' 'human' knowledge from their 'professional' knowledge, any more than it is possible to divide pupils' classroom language development from their experience of language in the world. Moreover, teachers' knowledge cannot simply be communicated in transmissive ways. A large part of the knowledge about language teachers should have will be realised, first, in the creation of *contexts* in which the pupils' implicit knowledge, that is, their competence, is enabled to develop. A second role for teachers' knowledge about language is in their *interventions* in language use with pupils in order to give advice, offer formative assessment, suggest lines of further development. The effectiveness of these interventions, as we have seen, will depend on teachers' sensitivity and skill in applying this kind of knowledge about language, including their understanding of when to deploy information and when not. Thirdly, there will be some aspects of teachers' knowledge about language which will form appropriate and interesting *content* for pupils' learning; in language as in any other area of knowledge, the teacher's own enthusiasm for the topic is likely to generate enthusiasm among pupils. Contexts for and content of knowledge about language may sometimes be linked, as for example when a class which contains users of a diversity of languages and dialects is given the opportunity to explore that diversity and relate it to information about language variety in modern Britain.

The three categories of teachers' knowledge aboutlanguage proposed here make a close match, it will be noticed, with the categories of pupils' knowledge about language presented in Figure 2. However, it would be wrong to insist that they are simply a replica for teachers of pupils' knowledge about language, or are always realised in identical ways. They involve a degree of worked-out understanding which is, at least potentially, explicit; the teacher can, if necessary, explain why he or she has acted in a particular way. Teachers' knowledge about language is, in fact, their working theory of language in learning. It should continually develop in interactions with pupils' knowledge about language. These interactions in the classroom depend on teachers' and pupils' human experience — joint or distinct — of language in the world.

We have described four sets of relationships which, between them, make up knowledge about language. These are the relationships between:

- pupils' implicit knowledge, reflection on language use and language study;

INTERACTIONS BETWEEN PUPILS' AND TEACHERS' KNOWLEDGE
ABOUT LANGUAGE IN THE CLASSROOM DEPEND ON AND DERIVE FROM
THEIR EXPERIENCE (JOINT OR DISTINCT) OF LANGUAGE IN THE WORLD

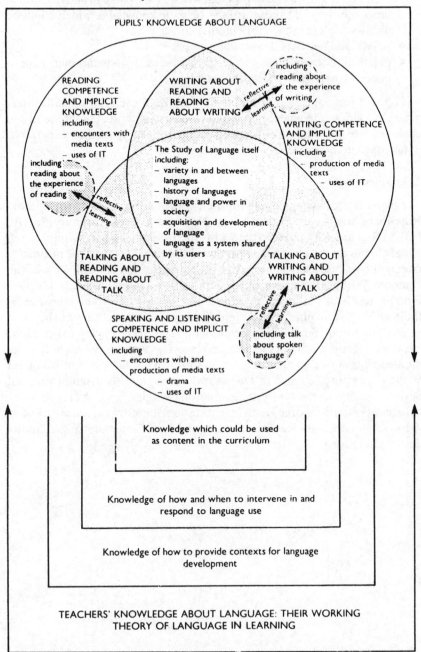

Figure 3 Interaction of pupils' and teachers' knowledge about language in the classroom

- teachers' knowledge of how to provide contexts for language development, their knowledge of how and when to intervene in and respond to
language use, and those aspects of their knowledge which could be
used as content in the curriculum;
- pupils' and teachers' knowledge;
- pupils' and teachers' language use in the classroom and their experience of language in the world outside.

Figure 3 (on page 293) attempts to visualise these relationships interacting in a classroom where pupils and teachers compose, comprehend and
communicate meanings in purposeful contexts, drawing on their experience
of language in the world.

Acknowledgments

I thank the following people for their contributions to this article. Susie
Rosenberg was Leanne's teacher at Newington Green Primary School,
ILEA. Richard Ray provided me with the example of her writing. Sarah
Kingham taught the class which produced *Would you be Scared?* at Bounds
Green Infants' School, Haringey. Ned Ratcliffe was co-ordinator of the
National Writing Project in Shropshire, and encouraged Sheila Hughes,
Fiona's and Neil's teacher, to encourage the children to collaborate on
their writing. Caroline Bishop and Shirley Whitehand taught the class
at Scargill Junior School, Havering, who were role-playing evacuation.
Maureen Harriott, advisory teacher in Havering, was the visitor, and wrote
the description of the work. Figure 2 is principally the work of Margaret
Wallen, advisory teacher in Dorset, who designed its original version.
Several sections of the text and the revision of Figure 2 are the result of my
collaboration with George Keith in writing non-statutory guidance on knowledge about language. Rebecca Bunting and Ron Carter contributed to the
design of Figure 3.

20 Development of Dialectical Processes in Composition

MARLENE SCARDAMALIA and CARL BEREITER

Writers often claim that the process of writing plays an important role in the development of their thought. A collection of testimonies to this effect may be found in a special issue of *Visible Languages* (Vol. 14, no. 4, 1980) devoted to the dynamics of language. In this chapter we want to enquire into the roots of that role and how writing comes to play it. We should make it clear from the beginning that we are not talking about how writing might make one in general a better thinker — through the effects of working with a visual symbol system (Vygotsky, 1978), for instance, or through the mental calisthenics involved. These general effects are probably unresearchable, given the difficulty of separating them from the effects of literacy *per se* and of living in a literate culture. Rather, we are talking about the direct effect of writing. How it is that thoughts and knowledge are enhanced by writing about them? What makes writing our thoughts different from simply mulling them over in the mind or talking about them with people?

The following points embrace most of the direct cognitive benefits we have found attributed to writing:

(1) *The 'emperor's new clothes' phenomenon.* Many ideas that we believe to be clear, well worked out, original, and profound are discovered not to possess these qualities as soon as we try putting the ideas down in coherent prose. Writing, more than conversation, seems to force a critical analysis of our own thoughts.

(2) *Text organicity.* A developing text is sometimes said to take on a life of its own so that the writer does not quite know what it will end up saying and in fact does not have absolute control over the outcome. In this way thought may diverge creatively from its intended channels.

(3) *Revision.* The reshaping of a text through successive drafts produces a corresponding rethinking and evolutionary development of thought.

(4) *Sustained thought.* Writing encourages a more sustained and elaborated thought, partly because of the lack of interruption. Even in solitude,

295

however, writing may be important to keep thought moving ahead. Without it, the mind may perseverate on a single point or go off wool-gathering. An oral equivalent of the treatise is hard to imagine.

While these may be genuine benefits, none of them, we shall argue, is an automatic consequence of engaging in written composition. They are con-comitants of a sophisticated approach to writing that is itself a significant intellectual attainment. When we look at student and novice writers, we are often struck by the opposite of the phenomena noted above:

(1) Writing down ideas does not seem to make their inadequacies apparent to student writers. A recent national evaluation described analytical essays written by school-age students as 'fragmentary, superficial and cryptic' (National Assessment of Educational Progress, 1981: 23).

(2) Text organicity implies that certain unexpected turns in the writer's thought are caused, not by wandering off the point, but rather by the need to preserve the unity of the emerging text, with its stance, structure, layers of meaning, and so on. But student writing is frequently charac-terized by the lack of these qualities (National Assessment of Educa-tional Progress, 1975). In a study by Bereiter, Scardamalia & Cattani (1981), elementary school students showed only the beginnings of aware-ness of internal constraints of text that require certain information to preserve coherence while other information is optional. With specially written paragraphs in which the contrast between essential and optional was striking, they reliably selected the optional sentence for deletion, although they did not offer structural reasons for the choice. But in their own texts they showed only a chance level of selectivity in choosing deletable sentences. That this had to do with a lack of organicity in their texts is indicated by the fact that the one subgroup that did show above-chance selectivity consisted of older children whose texts were judged to be tightly knit and who had received explicit instruction in testing for the effects of deletion on coherence.

(3) The benefits of reshaping through successive drafts are apparently seldom experienced because of the minimal amount of revision students carry out and because of its concentration on small proof-reading types of changes (National Asessment of Educational Progress, 1977; Nold, 1981; Scardamalia & Bereiter, 1983).

(4) Sustained thought in composition presupposes ability to sustain the composing process itself. This appears to be a serious problem in its own right, and the difficulty in sustaining composition appears in turn to depend to a considerable degree on difficulty in generating content. (Bereiter & Scardamalia, 1982). Thought in writing for novice writers seems to be, if anything, prematurely curtailed rather than extended by the writing process (Scardamalia, Bereiter, & Goelman, 1982).

It is indeed worth contemplating the possibility that for most people writing is an impediment rather than an aid to thought. While we have no direct evidence of this, it has been suggested to us continually through comparing what students produce in writing and what they are able to come forth with in interviews and discussions. These oral interchanges reveal substantial pools of knowledge not drawn on in composition. Students appear able to see many possible objections to what they have written, although they do not deal with these objections in their texts (Scardamalia & Bereiter, 1983).

The contribution of writing to thought is quite possibly a contribution enjoyed only by the highly literate few (not even all who could be called skilled writers). In order to discover how the cognitive advantages of writing might be extended to a greater number we need, first, to understand more deeply the process by which these advantages are realized and, second, to understand better the development of these processes in the composing behavior of students. In the present chapter we draw on a number of developmental studies of writing in an effort to make contributions to these two kinds of understanding.

How Writing Influences or Fails to Influence Thought

The process by which conversation promotes the growth of thought is called dialectic. It occurs when conversational partners holding different opinions strive to reach a mutually agreeable position and in the process advance beyond the level of understanding that either partner possessed at the beginning. Is there an analogous process in writing?

The essential role of give and take in conversation has led a number of people to speculate that thought in writing depends upon an internalized dialogue (Gray, 1977; Widdowson, 1983). The writer, according to this view, plays a dual role, alternately taking the part of each partner in a conversational pair. Through such interchange the benefits of a dialectical process might be achieved by the solitary writer.

Although this internal dialogue theory of the composing process has much intuitive appeal, available evidence does not support it. If internal dialogue were a regular and essential part of thoughtful composition, one would expect to see much evidence of it in the thinking-aloud protocols of expert writers. Expert writers do indeed evidence considerable thought about audience reaction when it is appropriate (Flower & Hayes, 1980), but they seem to approach audience-related problems in the same way that they approach other text problems. That is, they approach them through the normal kind of monologue and not through an internal dialogue.

It seems to us that the dialectical character of composition does not arise from any clear-cut dialogue-like process. Rather, it arises from the conflict between requirements of text and requirements of belief. In trying to resolve such conflicts, both the text and the writer's beliefs are subject to change. In the fortunate case, the change is in the nature of a synthesis, the hallmark of dialectic.

We may think of composition as taking place within a problem space (Newell & Simon, 1972). This psychological problem space may be further thought of as divided into two areas, a rhetorical space and a substantive space. Within the substantive space are worked out problems having to do with the writer's beliefs and knowledge. In the rhetorical space are worked out problems related to the composition itself. If one is asked to write an essay on capital punishment, for instance, and one has not thought very much about this topic, a great deal of the problem-solving effort will be concentrated within the substantive space. It will be concerned with working out one's own views on the topic and bringing in relevant knowledge, experience, emotional reactions, relations to other values one holds, and so on. Apart from these substantive problems, however, there is also the problem of producing a successful essay, an essay that accomplishes one's purpose of convincing readers of the validity of one's position or possibility of inducing the reader to share one's doubts and perplexities about the issue.

One way to compose, a way often recommended in composition textbooks, is to keep the two problem spaces separated. First work out the substantive problems, the result being possession of a set of assertions or facts that are to be communicated, then shift to the rhetorical space and devise the means for expressing them. Such a method of composing, if rigidly adhered to, would effectively exclude the dialectical process described above. Writing would not influence thinking in an immediate way. A dialectical process arises, however, when there is interaction between the two problem spaces. This occurs when rhetorical problems are solved through means that involve changes in substance and where substantive changes — that is, alterations in belief or knowledge — are perceived as creating significant problems in the rhetorical space.

This somewhat esoteric formulation of the dialectical process in composition may be brought down to earth with a variety of familiar examples:

(1) Considering why readers might object, misunderstand, or have no interest in what we are trying to say leads us to discover inadequacies in the substance of our message.

(2) Demands of the genre influence content. This is obvious in the example of the research report, where the need to find citations to state purpose and method, to deal with qualifications in the conclusion, and so

forth frequently force substantive changes and developments on us. Less formal genre requirements may also influence content. For instance, the expectation that a business letter will end with some kind of closure may force the writer to think out a next step or a proposed resolution of the issue raised in the letter.

(3) Searching for text elements — transitions, examples, definitions, additional reasons, and so on — often drives the writer back into the substantive problem space to develop content further.

(4) Problems of word choice, initially motivated by the desire to achieve a certain rhetorical effect, often lead the writer to consider alternate shades of intended meaning, thus altering or sharpening the writer's own understanding of what was intended. Abstract thought may be significantly influenced — sometimes for the worse — by the need for purposes of convenient reference, to devise brief labels for complex concepts.

(5) The mere need to achieve sufficient quantity — to say enough about a major point, for instance, to establish its importance in the mind of the reader — may lead the writer to further development and elaboration of ideas. On the other hand, the rhetorically motivated need to delete or rearrange material may force a substantive reconsideration of priorities.

(6) There is a more fundamental way in which rhetorical choices impinge on problems of substance, but it is one that does not lend itself to simple examples. This is through the build-up of internal constraints in text. Explicit statements, definitions, and the like have entailments that accumulate and increasingly constrain the content of subsequent statements. It is through this build up of internal constraints, it would appear, that a text is said to take on a life of its own and to develop in unforeseen directions.

The dialectical process implies a real tension between rhetorical and substantive concerns. If one concern predominates wholly, there will not be sufficient tension to lead to a new synthesis. The writer wholly concerned with rhetorical demands and willing to alter substance in any way to meet them becomes the stereotypic Madison Avenue lost soul, producing carefully calculated vacuities. With student and novice writers, however, the imbalance seems to be in the other direction. Belief tends to predominate, and problems of rhetoric are either not recognized or are solved through ploys that leave the substance unchanged.

In a variety of studies we have questioned students about their writing, listened to them composing aloud, or presented them with special rhetorical problems to wrestle with. From these observations we have gleaned a rather formidable list of ways in which student writers manage *not* to come to grips with rhetorical problems. It should not be thought that all student writers display all of the following attitudes or strategies, nor should it be thought that any of these are deliberately intended to avoid problem confrontation. They undoubtedly have a variety of causes and justifications.

(1) A *take-it-or-leave-it attitude toward audience*. Students can frequently anticipate audience objections, but they do not recognize it as their responsibility to do anything about them. As one student cogently put it, 'Some people won't agree with you no matter what you say.'

(2) *Willingness to put up with recognized weaknesses in structure or content*. In pilot research carried out by Clare Cattani-Brett, subjects had to compose a story based on a picture showing a man up in a tree and a bear on the ground below standing in the remains of a picnic. The typical story, of course, was of a picnic interrupted by a foraging bear. Subjects were then asked to revise their stories to conform to a second picture that was like the first except that in place of the bear was a harmless looking rabbit. The typical strategy was to keep the original story intact, substituting rabbit for bear and adding some explanation such as that the rabbit had rabies or that the person in the tree was allergic to rabbits. On subsequent questioning, subjects would readily admit that the second story was quite feeble and implausible, but until questioned it did not seem to occur to them that they had any choice but to allow it to be feeble. The story's inadequacies, in other words, were accepted as a natural consequence of the nature of the task. One may argue, of course, that this is a reasonable attitude to task toward such a task, as it might be to other school writing tasks that students often do in a perfunctory manner (Britton *et al.*, 1975). Reasonable or not, this 'low road' approach (Bereiter & Scardamalia, 1983) avoids rhetorical problems that could lead to substantive reformulation if taken seriously.

(3) *Poor and vague diagnoses*. Recent studies have shown that while students can frequently detect that something is wrong with a composition, they cannot clearly identify the problem and thus they have difficulty in applying problem-solving strategies to it (Bartlett, 1980; Scardamalia & Bereiter, 1983; Cattani, Scardamalia & Bereiter, 1981).

(4) *Satisfaction with superficial connections*. The search for substantive connection between one idea and another that the writer wants to get to is often a powerful incentive to deeper analysis of content. Novices, however, tend to rely on additive conjunctions (Hildyard & Geva, 1981), juxtaposition (Goldstein & Perfetti, 1979), and superficial linkages that involve little semantic constraint (Paris, Scardamalia & Bereiter, 1982).

(5) *Use of conversational ploys for sidestepping difficulties*. Because of the need to keep up a certain pace in social speech, people develop a variety

of devices for quick solution of rhetorical difficulties. When carried over into written composition these conversational ploys have the effect of neutralizing rather than solving the problems and thus avoiding a dialectical process. A common ploy is to treat a counter-example as an exception without considering its implications. The handy expression for doing this is 'well, anyway'. Another ploy is the 'nod' to opposing viewpoints ('Some people may think . . . but they are wrong') with no further explanation. Perhaps the most common ploy, however, is the topic shift. Whenever a rhetorical difficulty or blind alley is encountered, the topic is shifted. If this is done according to the rules of topic shift in conversation (Schank, 1977) the discourse will remain coherent according to standards of small talk, though generally not according to the standards of prose composition.

(6) *Use of the knowledge telling strategy* (Bereiter & Scardamalia, 1983, in press). This strategy, which we find pervasive in student writing, amounts really to a reporting of thoughts. Rhetorical problems are few and typically confined to low level problems of style.

For the most immature writers it seems that the only rhetorical problem that has an impact on substantive problem solving is the problem of quantity. The effort to fill up the page while staying on topic forces an extended search of the writer's knowledge and beliefs on a topic. This is no doubt helpful to writers in the beginning stages of literacy. Donald Graves (personal communication) has noted, in fact, that essays on the theme 'Everything I know about . . .' constitute a genre that competes in popularity with the personal experience narrative in the writing of primary grade children. For writing to influence thought beyond this rudimentary level, however, it seems necessary for an internal dialectical process to be set in motion, and for this to occur students must somehow be brought into confrontation with and must persist in attempting to solve rhetorical problems of kinds that have substantive implications.

Inducing Thought in Writing

Existing school procedures for improving writing tacitly acknowledge that writing does not spontaneously promote thought. One large class of educational procedures goes by the name of prewriting activities. These activities may be quite various involving discussion, films, readings, drawings or constructions, and the like. Their common function, however, is to provide some sort of stimulus to thought, usually social, so that the student writer need not rely on the composing process itself to provide stimulus to thinking. Other procedures serve to facilitate thinking during the composing process or between drafts of compositions. These include conferencing (Graves, 1978) and peer response (Elbow, 1973). In these cases a definite dialectic process is invoked, but it is a social, conversational one, not an internal dialectical process.

Structured procedures have been developed for working out content in advance of writing — procedures that lead to more extended or analytical thought (Young, Becker & Pike, 1970; Robinson, Ross & White, in press; Jones & Amiran, 1980). Through the use of matrices, tree diagrams, or question sequences, constraints and demands are put upon the student's thinking that are presumably not forced upon it by the looser structure of the composition task. Thus, curiously, instead of relying on composition as a means of promoting thought, other devices are introduced to promote thinking, composition itself becoming a straightforward matter of expression. In terms of our earlier formulation of problem spaces, these devices and prewriting activities promote problem solving and constructive thought within the substantive space rather than promoting an interaction between the two problem spaces.

Consequently, the existing school approaches may be seen as external aids that compensate for the lack of a dialectical process in composition. This does not seem to be their intent, however. Rather, the intent is to educate students to become better writers, and this implies that the external procedures will eventually become internalized, that is, incorporated into the student's thought while composing. Such internalization has not yet been demonstrated. Before we can be optimistic about internalization we need to know how the mental processes involved in prewriting activities correspond to those of expert writers. Practicing writers, we assume, seldom actually fill out matrices, ask themselves fixed series of questions, or do anything else of such a formal nature. The question is, however, whether formal prewriting activities are sufficiently analogous to the mental processes of expert writers that they can serve as a means of internalizing dialectical processes. If not, they may serve as a substitute for dialectical processes, but probably only a partial substitute.

A different type of facilitation has been developed recently, which uses external aids explicitly designed to support a simplified version of the processes used by experts, thus providing a basis for internalization. Procedural facilitation, as it is called (Bereiter & Scardamalia, 1982; Scardamalia & Bereiter, in press), is based on research into the composing process that seeks to identify executive procedures used in composition and their main points of difficulty. The simplification and aids that are introduced to help beginners surmount these identified difficulties are ones that can later be deleted and leave intact the executive procedure that has been set in motion.

These facilitations aim to boost the level of reflective thought or critical thought that goes on in composition, but to do so without stimuli or aids to thought that stand outside the composing process. Rather, the effort has been to introduce procedures that students can incorporate into their composing processes. These facilitations are of both educational and scientific interest. The educational interest lies in investigating ways of improving thought in writing that have promise of eventual internalization into the writer's own strategic repertoire. The scientific interest lies in the light that is thrown on the composing process through interventions that affect it in certain ways and leave it unaffected in others. We shall report one study which deals with aspects of revision.

An Attempt to Boost Problem Recognition in Revision

Revision is a useful point of focus for research on thought in writing because it can be carried out at a range of levels, from a deep level that involves reconsideration of the whole form and content of a composition up to a superficial level that involves only cosmetic changes (Nold, 1981). Students tend toward the latter end of the continuum (National Assessment of Educational Progress, 1975; Bracewell, Bereiter & Scardamalia, 1979). With the help of peer feedback, however, students have shown themselves able to carry out quite substantial revisions and rewritings of text (Graves, 1979). Such dependence on external feedback has made it seem that novices may lack ability to view their own compositions from the reader's standpoint (Barritt & Kroll, 1974). A study by Scardamalia & Bereiter (1983), however, suggests that this is not the source of the problem. When elementary school children were given procedural support and finite lists of possible evaluations, they detected inadequacies in their compositions that agreed very closely with the evaluations by an expert of the same compositions. Students were much less able than the expert, however, to diagnose — that is, to identify the cause or locus of thse inadequacies. Frequently they detected an inadequacy but elected to do nothing about it.

Such failure to confront problems could be due either to (a) lack of motivation, (b) lack of means for dealing with the problem, or (c) not knowing what the problem was. The last factor rests on the distinction between evaluation and diagnosis. This is the difference between 'I feel weak' and 'I have a vitamin deficiency'. Students demonstrated themselves competent at making the former kind of judgment, but the latter, more analytical judgment escaped them. Bartlett (1980) observed a similar phenomenon with respect to pronoun reference. Students could recognize when something was wrong, but they were unable to pin down the difficulty to an unreferenced pronoun, for instance, and consequently they were unable to produce appropriate

Table 1 Thirteen phrases on diagnostic cards used to aid experimental subjects in text analysis

---

Choppy — ideas aren't connected to each other very well.
Hard to tell what the main point is.
Too much space given to an unimportant point.
The writer ignores the obvious point someone would bring up against what they are saying.
Doesn't give the reader reason to take the idea seriously.
Part of the essay doesn't belong with the rest.
Incomplete idea.
Says something that's not believable.
Says the idea in a clumsy way.
The reader will have already thought of this.
Weak reason.
Too few ideas.
Example doesn't help to explain the idea.

---

remedies. For generations, teachers have tried to circumvent this weakness of students in recognizing what the problems are with the composition through the use of the red pencil, pointing out difficulties, suggesting things needing alteration. But what would happen if students, without being told what the problems are in a text, were assisted with a routine to broaden and intensify their effort to define problems? This question was the focus of a study by Cattani, Scardamalia & Bereiter (1981).

This study applied the CDO (COMPARE–DIAGNOSE–OPERATE) model of Scardamalia & Bereiter (1983). The three main components of this model are the ones indicated in its name. The COMPARE phase involves detecting mismatch between the mental representation of the actual composition and of the intended composition. This component was facilitated by having the subject read through the essay to be evaluated, placing down markers wherever some inadequacy was detected. Subjects placed a green marker if they were sure what the problem was and a red marker if they were not. The focus of the study was on the DIAGNOSE component of the process. Experimental subjects were provided with the 13 cards listed in Table 1. Subjects were asked to consider each of these diagnostic cards in turn and to judge whether it applied to the composition and, if so, where — whether to the text as a whole or to a specific part. For practical reasons, the OPER-ATE phase was reduced to having subjects suggest revisions without actually carrying them out.

The study was run individually on 20 students from grade 6 and on 16 from grade 12, each group evenly divided beween experimental and control subjects. The control treatment was the same as that described above, including the placement of markers during the COMPARE phase. But during the DIAGNOSE phase control subjects were simply asked to identify and explain all of the problems they had detected. Each subject diagnosed five essays and suggested revisions for two of them. One of these was an essay previously written by the subject. The other four essays were drawn from a pool of nine grade 6 and 8 essays selected for the number, variety, and representativeness of the inadequacies they contained. Of these four essays, one was the same for all subjects and was presented last. The others were selected randomly and presented in counterbalanced orders, along with the self-written essay, which was placed in either the second or fourth position. Subjects suggested revisions for their own essay and also for the final essay. This final essay furthermore served as a transfer test, in that experimental subjects and control subjects alike performed their diagnoses without benefit of the diagnostic cue cards.

Findings

Each of the essays was diagnosed by a professional editor, who generated for each one a list of diagnostic statements. Two independent raters then evaluated the degree of correspondence between diagnoses made by subjects and each item on the expert's lists. A score of 3 for a given item on the expert's list indicated that the subject had identified that identical problem, whereas a score of 0 indicated that the subject had failed entirely to mention that particular problem diagnosed by the editor. Figure 1 shows quality of diagnosis scores expressed as a percentage of possible points. Thus, 100% would indicate that the subject had identified accurately and thus obtained a score of 3 for each diagnostic statement made by the editor. The combined scores for all four training essays show a significant treatment effect that is common to both grades 6 and 12 ($F_{1,34} = 12.05, p < .05$). Quality of diagnoses on the transfer essay, however, shows an advantage for the experimental group only at grade 12 (F for the treatment effect is 5.59, $p < .05$; F for grade-by-treatment interaction = 7.97, $p < .01$). Thus it appears that students at both grade levels made superior diagnoses when assisted by the diagnostic cards, but only the grade 12 students showed transfer to diagnosis without cards.

Quality of suggested revisions was rated by two independent raters using a 5-point scale, with the top rating indicating a revision that the rater would actually have chosen to make and the lowest rating indicating revision that would be expected to make the composition worse. Subjects suggested revisions for only two of the five essays, it will be recalled, their own essay and the transfer essay. Mean quality of suggested revision scores for these two

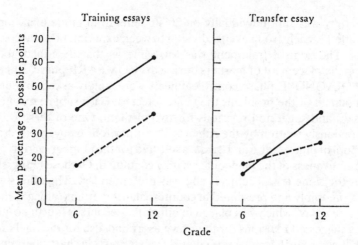

Figure 1 Quality of diagnoses, based on extent to which subjects's diagnoses agreed with those of professional editor. Solid lines = experimental; dashed lines = control.

essays are shown in Figure 2. In suggesting revision for their essays, experimental subjects at grade 6 greatly exceed the controls, whereas at grade 12 there is no difference. On the transfer essay there is a difference favouring the experimental group at both grade levels.

There were indications that the experimental treatment served to direct attention to higher-level text units. Among experimental subjects approximately 79% of diagnoses were directed toward sentence, paragraph, or whole text levels, whereas this was true of only 55% of diagnoses among control subjects. Even the latter percentage seems fairly high, however, in view of findings such as those of the National Assessment of Educational Progress (1977). It is quite possible, therefore, that the process of placing markers in the margin wherever difficulties or inadequacies are detected — a process common to both experimental and control groups — may have been effective in raising attention to a higher level of text features.

This study indicates that students can detect and discover solutions for rhetorical problems, given support in the form of a procedure as well as in the form of cues suggesting possible problem specifications. Performance on the transfer task indicates that by grade 12, at least, there is clearly some internalization of the facilitative procedures, which influences both diagnosis and the selection of problem solutions. The improvement at grade 6 in students' ability to suggest revisions to their own essays suggests that there may even

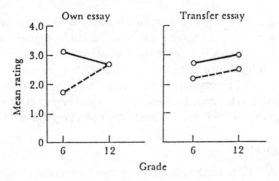

Figure 2 Rated quality of suggested revisions. Solid lines = experimental; dashed lines = control.

have been some internalization at this grade level, even though it was not revealed in an ability to make superior explicit diagnoses without external aids.

Conclusion

From both the testimony of sophisticated writers and what they reveal through thinking-aloud protocols (Flower & Hayes, 1980), we know that writing can be intellectually very demanding, requiring attention to both rhetorical and substantive issues. Our contention in this chapter has been that it is the tension between these two kinds of problems that leads to the deepening of reflective thought through writing. On the other hand, most of the problems of writing can be avoided without disaster. Readers tend to be tolerant and resourceful and can go to great lengths to make up for the inadequacies of the writer. Minimally adequate writing has a low processing demand (Bereiter & Scardamalia, 1984).

When writing is simply a process of assembling knowledge, there is no dialectical process involved, and there is consequently minimal development of knowledge and understanding in the process of composition. The main point of our chapter has accordingly been that the dialectical process in writing that leads to the deepening of reflective thought is not an automatic consequence of experience in writing. It is an achievement. The achievement of dialectical processing in writing, furthermore, would appear to be not only a cause of, but also the result of, reflective thought during composition.

Reflectivity accordingly is both means and goal in learning to become a writer. Nature has ways of solving such chicken-and-egg problems, but in the case of writing it appears that for far too many students, novices, and ordinary people the solution is not achieved and that writing does not serve as a dialectical process for the growth of knowledge and understanding. Our experiments, such as the one reported above, offer some encouragement to the view that nature can be assisted in developing the processes that lead to reflection.

Acknowledgments

We are indebted to the Social Sciences and Humanities Research Council of Canada for making the work presented in this chapter possible. Support for related work has come from the Ontario Institute for Studies in Education and the Alfred P. Sloan Foundation. We wish to thank Rosanne Steinbach in particular, as well as Leslie McIlroy, for data collection and analysis.

References

Barritt, L. S. and Kroll, B. M. (1974) Some implications of cognitive-development psychology for research in composing. In C. R. Cooper and L. Odell (eds) *Research on Composing: Points of Departure*. Urbana, IL: National Council of Teachers of English.

Bartlett, E. (1980) Development of referencing skills in good and poor elementary and junior high school writers. Paper presented at National Institute of Education/FIPSE Joint Conference, Los Alamitos, CA, September 19, 1980.

Bereiter, C. and Scardamalia, M. (1982) From conversation to composition: The role of instruction in a developmental process. In R. Glaser (ed.) *Advances in Instructional Psychology* (Vol. 2). Hillsdale, NJ: Erlbaum.

— (1983) Does learning to write have to be so difficult? In A. Freedman, I. Pringle and J. Yalden (eds) *Learning to Write: First Language, Second Language*. New York: Longman.

— (1984) Information-processing demand of text composition. In H. Mandl, N. L. Stein and T. Trabasso (eds) *Learning and Comprehension of Text*. Hillsdale, NJ: Erlbaum.

— (In press) Cognitive coping strategies and the problem of 'inert knowledge'. In S. S. Chipman, J. W. Segal and R. Glaser (eds) *Thinking and Learning Skills: Current Research and Open Questions* (Vol. 2). Hillsdale, NJ: Erlbaum.

Bereiter, C., Scardamalia, M. and Cattani, C. (1981) Recognition of constraints in children's reading and writing. Paper presented at the annual meeting of the American Educational Research Association, Los Angeles, April 1981.

Bracewell, R. J., Bereiter, C. and Scardamalia, M. (1979) A test of two myths about revision. Paper presented at the annual meeting of the American Educational Research Association, San Francisco.

Britton, J., Burgess, T., Martin, N., McLeod, A. and Rosen, H. (1975) *The Development of Writing Abilities (11–18)*. London: Macmillan Education.

Cattani, C., Scardamalia, M. and Bereiter, C. (1981) Facilitating diagnosis in student writing. Typescript, Ontario Institute for Studies in Education.

Elbow, P. (1973) *Writing Without Teachers*. London: Oxford University Press.

Flower, L. and Hayes, J. R. (1980) The Cognition of discovery: Defining a rhetorical problem. *College Composition and Communication* 31 (2), 21–32.

Goldstein, E. and Perfetti, C. (1979) Psycholinguistic processers in writing: Preliminary studies of memory and text structure. Paper presented at conference of Canadian Council of Teachers of English, Ottawa, May 1979.

Graves, D. H. (1978) *Balance the Basics: Let Them Write*. New York: Ford Foundation.

— (1979) What children show us about revision. *Language Arts* 56 (3), 312–9.

Gray, B. (1977) *The Grammatical Foundations of Rhetoric*. The Hague: Mouton.

Hayes, J. R. and Flower, L. (1980) Identifying the organization of writing processes. In L. W. Gregg and E. R. Steinberg (eds) *Cognitive Process in Writing*. Hillsdale, NJ: Erlbaum.

Hildyard, A. and Geva, E. (1981) Understanding and using conjuctions. Paper presented at the annual meeting of the American Educational Research Association, Los Angeles, April 1981.

Jones, B. F. and Amiran, M. (1980) Applying structure of text and learning strategies research to develop programs of instruction for low achieving students. Paper presented at the National Institute of Education — Learning Research and Development Center Conference on Thinking and Learning Skills, Pittsburgh, October.

National Assessment of Educational Progress (1975) *Writing Mechanics, 1969–1974: A Capsule Description of Changes in Writing Mechanics* (Rep. 05-W-01). Denver.

— (1977) *Write/rewrite: An Assessment of Revision Skills: Selected Results from the Second National Assessment of Writing* (ERIC Document Reproduction Service ED 141 826). Washington, DC: US Government Printing Office.

— (1981) *Reading, Thinking, and Writing: Results from the 1979–80 National Assessment of Reading and Literature* (ERIC Document Reproduction Service ED 209 641). Washington, DC: US Government Printing Office.

Newell, A. and Simon, H. A. (1972) *Human Problem Solving*. Englewood Cliffs, NJ: Prentice-Hall.

Nold, E. W. (1981) Revising. In C. H. Frederiksen and J. F. Dominic (eds). *Writing: The Nature, Development, and Teaching of Written Communication*. Hillsdale, NJ: Erlbaum.

Paris, P., Scardamalia, M. and Bereiter, C. (1982) Synthesis through analysis: Facilitating theme development in children's writing. Paper presented at the annual meeting of the American Educational Research Association.

Robinson, F., Ross, J. and White, F. (in press) *Curriculum Development for Effective Instruction*. Toronto: OISE Press.

Scardamalia, M. and Bereiter, C. (1983) The development of evaluative, diagnostic, and remedial capabilities in children's composing. In M. Martlew (ed.) *The Psychology of Written Language: A Developmental Approach*. London: Wiley.

— (in press) Fostering the development of self-regulation in children's knowledge processing. In S. S. Chipman, J. W. Segal and R. Glaser (eds) *Thinking and Learning Skills: Current Research and Open Questions* (Vol. 2). Hillsdale, NJ: Erbaum.

Scardamalia, M., Bereiter, C. and Goelman, H. (1982) The role of production factors in writing ability. In M. Nystrand (ed.) *What Writers Know: The Language, Process, and Structure of Written Discourse*. New York: Academic Press.

Schank, R. C. (1977) Rules and topics in conversation. *Cognitive Science* 1, 421–41.

Vygotsky, L. S. (1978) *Mind in Society: The Development of Higher Psychological Processes*. Cambridge: Harvard University Press.

Widdowson, H. G. (1983) New starts and different kinds of failure. In A. Freedman, I. Pringle and J. Yalden (eds) *Learning to Write: First Language, Second Language*. New York: Longman.

Young, R. E., Becker, A. L. and Pike, K. E. (1970) *Rhetoric: Discovery and Change*. New York: Harcourt, Brace and World.

Index

abstraction
— and genre 238, 299
— and infant cognitive development 63-4, 72
accent, used by boys 180, 181
accountability
— in education 4, 6, 112, 118, 124
— procedures 27-8
acquisition
— and communicative intent 68-9
— Language Acquisition Device 64, 65-6, 70
— literacy acquisition device 22
— simultaneous 78-9
— spoken language xv, 22-5, 57, 59-60, 64-70
— support for 70-2
— written language xv, 18-19, 22, 253
advisors, and real books approach 114, 116, 135
Althusser, L. 143
Anglo-American Seminar on the Teaching of English 7-8
anti-racism 38
anti-sexism xiv, 38, 177-80, 181, 183, 185
apprenticeship approach to reading 12
appropriation xii, 104-7, 108
Arnold, Matthew 8-9
assertiveness training, for girls 179, 180
assessment
— of bilingualism 85-6
— by teacher 223-4
— developments in 227-9
— diagnostic function 226, 227
— oral xiv 224, 225-8, 230
— of oral communication xiv, 226-7
— of reading 118-22, 123, 126, 130-2, 134, 136-8
— self-assessment 228, 229
— teacher 137-8

Assessment of Performance Unit 130, 149
attainment targets 4, 123-4, 149-50, 152, 180, 227-8
audience
— in attainment targets 149-50, 152, 153
— in media education 35
— for writing xv, 1, 97-8, 211-12, 214, 215-16, 221, 297, 300
Augustine of Hippo, St 64-5
Austin, J. 68
authorship xv-xvi, 258-60
— and author as creator of texts 260-1
— and cultural practice 266-8
— legacy of 264-5
— in primary school 273-5
— and role of teacher 275-6
— in secondary school 268-73
— writing as 261-6
awareness of language
— in education x, xvi, 145, 181, 277-94
— and language acquisition 23
— metalinguistic 87, 89

Bakhtin, M. 93, 105, 151
Bantock, 4
Barnes, Dorothy 9
Barnes, Douglas 8, 9, 139, 150-1, 153
Barrs, Myra xv, 248-57
Barthes, Roland 267
Bartlett, E. 303
behaviourism 65, 94
Ben Zeev, S. 87
Bennett, N. 161-2
Bernstein, Basil 13 n.1, 43 n.2, 141-2, 144
Bickerton, Derek 59, 71
bilingualism 74-89
— advantages 85-8
— balanced 76

310